"Meyrowitz takes a panoramic view of American culture—its politics, its gender relations, its educational standards, its attitudes toward history and literacy, and much more. He's a fine example of an interdisciplinary risk-taker. . . . By daring to stray beyond the safety of a single discipline, he has wrought a fascinating quilt out of scraps most of us hadn't ever thought of stitching together. Television, itself a patchwork of ideas, needs his kind of analysis." *The Christian Science Monitor*

"Loaded with fascinating material . . . Profoundly original."
New England Journal of Medicine

"Written in the spirit of Alexis de Tocqueville's *Democracy in America* and Max Lerner's *America as a Civilization, No Sense of Place* is a cornucopia in the grand style: a breathtaking flurry of crisp insights, homey illustrations, ingenious tropes. . . . [Meyrowitz] gives the reader full value in erudition and liveliness. . . . We owe him a debt for demonstrating how thoroughly media permeate our culture." *Quarterly Journal of Speech*

"There is enough in this book to rightly place Meyrowitz on the same shelf—and plane—as Marshall McLuhan. . . . The applications of the author's basic thesis are nearly universal. . . . His theory explains so much so easily." *The Philadelphia Inquirer*

"One of the most ambitious, refreshing, and provocative attempts to expand our understanding of communications technologies. As one rarely says about such works, it is 'a good read.'" *Technology Review*

"An indisputably impressive work. . . . Within the space of a brief review it isn't possible to do justice to the numerous insights and enlightening illustrations which fill this book. . . . Our understanding of contemporary social life has been measurably advanced." *Best Sellers*

"A masterful study, a fine combination of perceptive analysis and creative synthesis . . . Required reading at all levels." *Choice*

"Nearly every paragraph contains an apt phrase, new angle, example or insight." *Whole Earth Review*

NO SENSE OF PLACE

The Impact of Electronic Media on Social Behavior

Joshua Meyrowitz

OXFORD UNIVERSITY PRESS
New York   Oxford

Oxford University Press
Oxford   New York   Toronto
Delhi   Bombay   Calcutta   Madras   Karachi
Petaling Jaya   Singapore   Hong Kong   Tokyo
Nairobi   Dar es Salaam   Cape Town
Melbourne   Auckland

and associated companies in
Beirut   Berlin   Ibadan   Nicosia

Library of Congress Cataloging in Publication Data

Meyrowitz, Joshua.
No sense of place.

Bibliography: p.
Includes index.
1. Mass media—Social aspects.   2. Communication—
Social aspects.   3. Electronic apparatus and appliances
—Social aspects.   4. Space and time—Social aspects.
5. Personal space.   I. Title.
HM258.M49   1984   302.2′34   84-3950
ISBN 0-19-503474-0
ISBN 0-19-504231-X (pbk.)

Printing (last digit):   9 8 7

Printed in the United States of America

Nothing can be further from the spirit of the new technology than "a place for everything and everything in its place."

Marshall McLuhan

Among all the things of this world, information is the hardest to guard, since it can be stolen without removing it.

Erving Goffman

situations are usually defined in relation to *physical* settings: places,
rooms, buildings, and so forth. The theory developed here extends the
study of static situations to the study of changing situations, and extends
the analysis of physically defined settings to the analysis of the social
environments created by media of communication.

This book is about the roles we play and witness in our everyday lives
as they are increasingly played before new audiences and in new arenas—"audiences" that are not physically present and "arenas" that do
not exist in time and space. It is about the ways in which individuals and
groups have changed their behaviors to match these new situations.

The situational analysis offered here describes how electronic media
affect social behavior—not through the power of their messages but by
reorganizing the social settings in which people interact and by weaken-
ing the once strong relationship between physical place and social
"place." The structure of social settings is shown to be a key element in
all group identifications, in transitions from role to role, and in the ranks
of social hierarchies. The study describes how, as we lose our old "sense
of place," we gain new notions of appropriate social behavior and identity. This book suggests that *change in behavioral settings* is a common
element linking many of the trends, events, and movements of the last
three decades. This analysis of the new situations, or "information-systems," shaped by new media is not intended to provide a complete explanation for social change or for all the current characteristics of our society,
but it is meant to suggest that changes in media may have much more to
do with recent social trends than is generally thought. The larger purpose
of the book is to offer a new approach to studying both media effects and
social change—not only for the study of the present but also of the past
and the future.

The book first develops general principles concerning the relationship
among media, situations, and behavior and then explores the potential
effects of a shift from "print situations" to "electronic situations" on a
broad range of social roles. Finally, three detailed "case studies" are presented on changing conceptions of masculinity and femininity, childhood
and adulthood, and political heroes. The first chapter of the book intro-
duces the major arguments and approach; the last chapter summarizes
the theory and discusses its implications for the future. The appendix discusses key concepts and their interrelationships.

The book is intended for general readers and for scholars and students
in several fields. Different readers may wish to approach it differently.
After reading the first chapter, some readers may wish to skip to the "case
study" chapters and then return to earlier chapters to see how the arguments are developed. Although the case studies grow out of, and build
on the earlier chapters, I have tried to make them comprehensible on their
own. With the different needs of different readers in mind, I have also
divided the footnotes into two categories. Those on the bottom of pages
are general comments, examples, or research and poll statistics that

should be of interest to most readers. The much more numerous scholarly references, qualifications, and comments are contained in notes in the back of the book.

I think my parents unintentionally started me thinking about some of the issues raised in this book when they steadfastly refused to "rush" into purchasing the new "toy"—television—that was spreading through our neighborhood. It seemed as if nearly every family we knew owned a television before we did, but my parents resisted, saying that "they haven't perfected it yet." (To this day, my parents have not bought a color television for the same reason.) As luck would have it, the set we finally did buy—a large console model with doors covering the screen (so that it could pass for a radio)—was a "lemon," thereby justifying my parents' fears. The set seemed to be broken as often as it worked, and my parents rarely hurried to get it fixed.

The on-and-off exposure I had to television as a child made me sensitive to how different the view of the world was to a child with television compared to one without. Although I didn't give it much thought at the time, I responded to television as if it was a "secret revelation machine" that exposed aspects of the adult world to me that would have otherwise remained hidden. My primary response to television was *not* imitation of the behavior I saw on it, nor was it to be persuaded that I needed to own the many products advertised. Rather, the information I received about social interaction on television affected my own willingness to accept other people's behaviors and claims at face value. Television educated me and my friends about certain aspects of adulthood that no longer allowed our parents to "get away" with some traditional parental behaviors. It also affected our views of members of the other sex and of teachers, police, politicians, and other "authorities." As silly as much television content was, its close-up views of strange people and places shaped my evaluation of the social performances of those I knew and met. Television changed the ways in which the walls of my home formed and limited my social experience.

Many years later, when I began studying for my master's degree, I was interested in analyzing the interaction of media and interpersonal behavior. I was surprised to discover how independently the two areas were being researched. Certainly, people looked at how media affected real behavior and how real behavior related to the content of media, but there were few models that dealt with both systems of communicating as part of a continuum rather than a dichotomy. Most of the concerns were about people *imitating* behavior they saw on television, or about the inaccurate *reflection* of reality as portrayed in television content—real life *as opposed to* the media. Few studies examined both media and interpersonal interaction as part of the same system of "behaving" or responding to the behavior of others. Few people seemed to be studying the ways in which new patterns of access to information about social behavior might be affecting people's ability to play old forms of roles.

As I describe in the first chapter, a few of the frameworks I studied in college suggested the possibility of piecing together such a theory. In my master's thesis at Queens College, I took a first step toward creating a new bridge between media theory and interpersonal behavior theory by looking at structural similarities between rules of interpersonal behavior and conventions of television production.[7] I began working on the broader theory developed in *No Sense of Place* in 1976 and presented an early draft as my doctoral dissertation at New York University in 1978 (University Microfilms, 1979). After letting the ideas ferment for a while, I began in 1981 to revise and expand the work for the present book.

Some of the ideas developed here have appeared elsewhere in various forms. Versions of Chapter 14 appeared in *Et cetera* in 1977 as "The Rise of 'Middle Region' Politics" and in *Psychology Today* in July 1984 as "Politics in the Video Eye: Where Have All the Heroes Gone?" A conference paper based on Chapter 13, "Television and the Obliteration of 'Childhood,'" is included in *Studies in Mass Communication and Technology*, volume one of the selected proceedings of the 1981 International Conference on Culture and Communication, edited by Sari Thomas (Ablex, 1984). An essay drawn from Chapter 13 was published in the Summer 1984 issue of *Daedalus* as "The Adultlike Child and the Childlike Adult: Socialization in an Electronic Age." A very brief form of the same chapter also appeared in *Newsweek* in August 1982 as "Where Have the Children Gone?"

Many people have contributed to this study and I would like to mention some of them here. The most concrete assistance came to me from colleagues who agreed to read and comment on parts or all of the manuscript. Jan Alberghene, Larry Baron, Bill Beeman, John Kelly, Tom Kochman, Jack Lannamann, Paul Levinson, Sheila McNamee, Bob Mennel, Ed Wachtel, and Mark West offered extremely useful comments and suggestions. My many debates and discussions with psychologist Carolyn Mebert helped sharpen the arguments in Chapter 13. David Leary also deserves special thanks, for reading and commenting on the manuscript, for easing me into the world of "word processing," and for being an enthusiastic and supportive colleague in more ways than are easily described.

Susan Rabiner, my editor at Oxford University Press, provided many insightful suggestions and comments and much appreciated enthusiasm for the project. As research assistants, Joanne Hollands, Russ Lawson, and Thomas Zack exhibited more patience than I could have mustered at hunting down books and articles, and the staff of the University of New Hampshire's Dimond Library—including its valuable interlibrary loan office—never balked once at my frequent and, at times, exotic requests. I

would also like to thank three of my former students—Karen Reisch,
Deirdre Wilson, and especially Tad Ackman—for criticizing drafts and for
digging up a number of interesting references that have enriched this
study. Laura Lee Leonard, Rhonda Mann, Beth Orzechowski, and Rose-
marie Thomas assisted with proofreading. Dozens of other friends and
colleagues—unfortunately too numerous to mention, but also too helpful
to forget—offered clues, references, and ideas that have improved this
work over the eight years I worked on it.

The research for this book was supported in its final stages by a Central
University Research Fund grant from the Research Office at the University of New Hampshire and by a Summer Faculty Fellowship from the
graduate school of the same institution. Dean Stuart Palmer and department heads Wilburn Sims and Jean Brown helped make this book possible in less tangible, but equally important ways by establishing working
environments that have fostered creativity and growth.

Most of all, however, I would like to thank my wife Candice Leonard
and my daughter Janna who give me love and support and who continually offer me perspective on the relative importance of people and writing. Candice also provided detailed criticisms and suggestions, numerous
references, and ideas. And Janna, who was born during the tense period
of completing the final manuscript, has provided me with a whole range
of new emotions and experiences I could not have previously anticipated
or understood. Together, Candy and Janna continue to give me a firm
sense of place and permanency in an ever-changing world.

Somersworth, N.H.   J.M.
October, 1984

Contents

   A Case Study in Changing Role Transitions   226
      The Adultlike Child and the Childlike Adult   227
      The Myth of Age-Determinism   231
      Television and Child Integration   235
      Mixed Grades for the School   253
      Literacy and the "Invention" of Childhood and Adulthood   258
      Reflections in Black on White   265

14 Lowering the Political Hero to Our Level
   A Case Study in Changing Authority   268
      The Merging of Political Arenas and Styles   269
      Political Ritual as Political Reality   276
      Great Performances Require the Perfect Stage   279
      Media and Presidential Mortality   283
      From "Private-Public" to "Public-Public"   287
      Watergate and "Cartergate"   292
      The Presidency in the Eye of Television: Reagan and Beyond   301

Part V   Conclusion

15 Where Have We Been, Where Are We Going?   307
      No Sense of Place   307
      Order, Not Chaos   313
      Hunters and Gatherers in an Information Age   315
      Good or Bad? / Real or False?   317
      Whither "1984"?   321
      New Generations of Electronic Media   324
      Controlling or Controlled?   328

      Appendix: Discussion of Terms   331

      Notes   341

      Bibliography   374

      Index   391

1

Introduction

Behavior in Its Place

When I was a college student in the late 1960s, I spent one three-month summer vacation in Europe. I had a wide range of new and exciting experiences, and when I returned home, I began to share these with my friends, family, and other people I knew. But I did not give everyone I spoke to exactly the same account of my trip. My parents, for example, heard about the safe and clean hotels in which I stayed and about how the trip had made me less of a picky eater. In contrast, my friends heard an account filled with danger, adventure, and a little romance. My professors heard about the "educational" aspects of my trip: visits to museums, cathedrals, historical sites, and observations of cross-cultural differences in behavior. Each of my many "audiences" heard a different account.

The stories of my trip varied not only in content, but also in style. There were varying numbers of slang words, different grammatical constructions, and different pronunciations. The pace of my delivery, body posture, facial expressions, and hand gestures were different in each situation. Each description had its own unique mix of earnestness and flippancy. My friends, for example, heard a speech filled with "sloppy speech" and sarcasm.

Did I "lie" to any of these people? Not really. But I told them different truths. I did what most of us do in everyday interaction: I highlighted certain aspects of my personality and experience and concealed others.

At the time of my trip, I was not even aware of this variable feature of my behavior. Like most people, I thought of myself as a unified "me" who always behaved in roughly the same way. I focused, as I now realize, only on what was *constant* in my behavior across situations. I concentrated on my choices within a given situation, rather than on the overall constraints. I thought of my range of possible comments in a seminar, for example, and neglected to notice that I did not, as a student, have the option of getting up and leading the discussion (just as now, as a professor, I do not have the option of sitting quietly and blank-faced through a class). I did not consider that in some situations it was normal for me to sit silently and passively (while listening to a religious sermon, for example) and that in other situations the same behavior would be interpreted as strange or hostile (dinner with a friend). And although I and everyone I knew unconsciously changed behaviors from situation to situation, I thought (in keeping with the sentiments of the times) that "playing roles" was something done by people who were either dishonest or not in touch with their "real selves."

My perceptions of my behavior, and of social interactions in general, changed the next semester when I became familiar with the work of sociologist Erving Goffman. Goffman describes social life as a kind of multistaged drama in which we each perform different roles in different social arenas, depending on the nature of the situation, our particular role in it, and the makeup of the audience. Goffman's work reads like anthropology, but instead of focusing on a strange or primitive culture, his observations illuminate our own society and behavior. Goffman made me aware of perceptions and actions that are normally intuitive and unconscious. He made me aware of things I knew, but did not know I knew.

Although Goffman gave me a whole new perspective from which to view social behavior, I felt that something was missing from his view of social life. It was the height of the turbulent 1960s, and Goffman's frameworks—first developed in the 1950s—were unable to account for the *changes* in social roles that were taking place.

The general picture of social interaction that Goffman presents is one of people actively involved in many different dramas: People are constantly changing costumes and roles, learning and adhering to a complex matrix of conventional behavior, and working hard to maintain their performance in each ongoing situation without undermining or threatening their *different* behaviors in *other* social situations. Goffman's social scenario is very dynamic on the surface. But the dynamism usually rests in the kind of activity needed to adjust to a relatively stable social order with fixed rules, roles, social occasions, and institutions. Individuals must absorb the social conventions, must practice, rehearse, and maintain their performances, but the scripts and stages are relatively unchanging. In Goffman's social world, the dynamism is mostly in the projection of figures against a static ground. Behavior may change from place to place, but the ways in which it changes, as well as the situations for which it changes, are usually constant.

This stable view of social life did not correspond to the events of the time. Although people in the late 1960s were still "playing roles," they were not playing the same roles they had played in the past. In Goffman's terms, the performers seemed to be mixing up their performances and their styles of interaction. Things that were once kept in the "backstage" area of life—such as sex and drugs—were now being thrust into the public arena. People were dressing and speaking in public as if they were at home. Many journalists and scholars were abandoning the public ideal of "objectivity" and were incorporating their personal experiences and subjective feelings into their work. There were pressures to break down old segregations of behaviors and audiences and to treat people of different sexes, ages, races, and professions more alike. Nuns were shedding their habits and moving from convents to the community. Female secretaries were refusing to make coffee for their male bosses. A "youth culture" arose across class, race, religious, and even national lines. Children were calling parents and teachers by their first names as if they were peers. Men and women were abandoning old forms of courtship and marriage. The President of the United States showed his operation scars to the nation as if all the people in the country were his intimate friends. There was a new distrust of government, politicians, and corporations. Centralized authority seemed to be giving way to "community control." Amidst these and many other changes, Goffman's stated quest for a "minimal model of the actor" that would allow us to "wind him up, stick him in amongst his fellows, and have an orderly traffic of behavior emerge" seemed illusory.[1]

Another theorist I was studying, Marshall McLuhan, offered one possible source of explanation for widespread changes in social behavior: changes in media of communication. McLuhan's work reads more like epic poetry than traditional scholarly analysis, but, in his own way, McLuhan predicted the behavioral changes of the late 1960s more effectively than Goffman did. Writing in 1961 and 1963, McLuhan drew a surprisingly accurate picture of what would be happening in the streets of New York, San Francisco, Washington, and other American and European cities between 1967 and 1972. McLuhan wrote of widescale social change, of "retribalization," of the decline of traditional feelings of nationalism, of the demand on the part of youth and minorities and others for "in-depth" participation, and of the distrust of distant authority. The long hair, beards, nudity, tribal music, and chants against the "Establishment" seemed to fulfill McLuhan's prophecy.

McLuhan attributed such changes to the widespread use of electronic media. But the mechanism through which electronic media bring about widespread social change is not made very clear in his work. McLuhan describes media as extensions of the senses, and he claims that the introduction of a new medium to a culture, therefore, changes the "sensory balance" of the people in that culture and alters their consciousness. But McLuhan offers few specific clues as to why people with different sensory balances behave differently.

As a college student trying to integrate all that I was learning and experiencing, I was disturbed by the incompleteness of these two theories and yet intrigued by both their visions of the social order. Goffman and McLuhan each provide a different clue to understanding social behavior.

Goffman offers one factor that molds behavior: the "definition of the situation" as it is shaped by particular interactional settings and audiences. Yet Goffman explicitly ignores *changes* in roles and the social order. McLuhan, on the other hand, points to widescale change in social roles resulting from the use of electronic media, but he provides no clear explanation of *how* and *why* electronic media may bring about such change.

This book has grown out of more than a decade of interest in weaving these two strands of theory into one whole cloth. I suggest that Goffman and McLuhan have complementary strengths and weaknesses: Goffman focuses only on the study of face-to-face interaction and ignores the influence and effects of media on the variables he describes; McLuhan focuses on the effects of media and ignores the structural aspects of face-to-face interaction. These oversights may stem from the traditional view that face-to-face behavior and mediated communications are completely different types of interaction—real life *vs.* media. This study explores a common denominator that links the study of face-to-face interactions with the study of media: the structure of social "situations." I suggest that the mechanism through which electronic media affect social behavior is not a mystical sensory balance, but a very discernible rearrangement of the social stages on which we play our roles and a resulting change in our sense of "appropriate behavior." For when audiences change, so do the social performances.

Consider, for example, what would have happened to the various accounts of my European vacation if, on my return, my parents had decided to throw a surprise homecoming party to which they invited all my friends, relatives, professors, and neighbors. What would have happened to my description of my trip if I could not have separated my audiences? If my parents had ushered me to the center of a large circle comprised of all these people and asked me to give a fifteen minute talk on my trip, what could I have said?

Had I begun to give the "safe" description that I would have given privately to my parents, my friends would probably have been bored or might even have started to giggle. Had I reported on my dangerous or romantic adventures, my parents and the neighbors might have felt uncomfortable. Clearly, almost any account designed for a specific audience would probably have offended or bored parts of the combined audience. So I might have become tongue-tied or I might have been able to adapt quickly to the combined situation and devise a new, synthesized account that said a little bit to each segment of the audience, but was bland enough to offend no one. But no matter what I said, the situation would have been profoundly different from the interactions I had with isolated audiences.

The point is that when distinct social situations are combined, once appropriate behavior may become inappropriate. When a particular private situation becomes more public by being merged into other situations, behavior style must adapt and change. A combination of situations changes the patterns of role behavior and alters the texture of social reality. The situation I would have faced at such a homecoming party serves as a rough analogy for the situations that are created by electronic media of communication.

The combination of many different audiences is a rare occurrence in face-to-face interaction, and even when it occurs (at a wedding, for example) people can usually expect the speedy resumption of private isolated interactions. Electronic media, however, have rearranged many social forums so that most people now find themselves in contact with others in new ways. And unlike the merged situations in face-to-face interaction, the combined situations of electronic media are relatively lasting and inescapable, and they therefore have a much greater effect on social behavior. If, for example, I could *never* get away from the mixed group at my return party, those things I wanted to say only to my friends would have to be spoken in the presence of my parents and professors—or never said at all. Further, if my parents and professors could never leave the mixed audience of the party either, then my friends and I would likely begin to see and hear aspects of their behavior—arguments, illnesses, doubts, anxieties, sexual behaviors, and so forth—that they had once kept hidden from us. The new merged patterns of behavior might lack the extremes of the previously distinct encounters, but they would also contain many behaviors that were once considered inappropriate in "mixed company."

Similarly, I argue in this book that while there are still many private forums, electronic media—especially television—have led to the overlapping of many social spheres that were once distinct. In contrast to face-to-face conversation and books, for example, radio and television now make it more difficult for adults to communicate "among themselves" because they are often "overheard" by children. In a similar way, electronic media have heightened men's and women's knowledge of each other's social performances for the opposite sex. And the merger of different audiences and situations through radio and television has made it difficult for national politicians to say very specific things to particular constituencies or to behave differently in different social situations. The theory developed here suggests that such restructurings of social arenas and social performances are at least a partial reason for recent social trends, including the blurring of conceptions of childhood and adulthood, the merging of notions of masculinity and femininity, and the lowering of political heroes to the level of average citizens.

Put very simply, the basic argument here is that many of the traditionally perceived differences among people of different social "groups," different stages of socialization, and different levels of authority were supported by the division of people into very different experiential worlds. The separation of people into different situations (or different *sets* of situations) fostered different world views, allowed for sharp distinctions between people's "onstage" and "backstage" behaviors, and permitted people to play complementary—rather than reciprocal—roles. Such distinctions in situations were supported by the diffusion of literacy and

printed materials, which tended to divide people into very different informational worlds based on different levels of reading skill and on training
and interest in different "literatures." These distinctions were also supported by the isolation of different people in different places, which led
to different social identities based on the specific and limited experiences
available in given locations. By bringing many different types of people
to the same "place," electronic media have fostered a blurring of many
formerly distinct social roles. Electronic media affect us, then, not primarily through their content, but by changing the "situational geography" of
social life.

Perhaps the best analogy for the process of change described in this
book is an architectural one. Imagine that many of the walls that separate
rooms, offices, and houses in our society were suddenly moved or
removed and that many once distinct situations were suddenly combined.
Under such circumstances, the distinctions between our private and public selves and between the different selves we project in different situations might not entirely disappear, but they would certainly change. We
might still manage to act differently with different people, but our ability
to segregate encounters would be greatly diminished. We could not play
very different roles in different situations because the clear spatial segregation of situations would no longer exist.

In one large combined social situation, for example, students would see
their teachers falling asleep in front of the television set, blue collar workers would see corporation presidents being yelled at by their own children, voters would see politicians have one drink too many, women
would overhear men talking about strategies for interacting with women,
and children would see the sometimes childish behaviors of their parents.
As a result, many types of behavior possible in the past would no longer
be feasible. It would be difficult, for example, to plan strategies for dealing
with people while those very people were present. We would have trouble projecting a very different definition of ourselves to different people
when so much other information about us was available to each of our
audiences. Certain behavior patterns that never existed before, therefore,
would come into being. In the combined setting, some behaviors that
were once kept in the "backstage" of each performance would, of necessity, emerge into the enlarged "onstage" area. We would be forced to say
and do things in front of others that were once considered unseemly or
rude. The behavior exhibited in this mixed setting would have many elements of behaviors from previously distinct encounters, but would
involve a new synthesis, a new pattern—in effect, a new social order.

An outside observer from the old social order might conclude that the
people in this new social system had lost their sense of etiquette and even,
perhaps, their morality and sanity. Yet that observer would, in fact, be
witnessing the effects of a merger of social situations rather than a conscious decision to behave differently.

The use of this architectural analogy to describe the effects of electronic media is, of course, overstated. Walls, doors, gates, and distances still frame and isolate encounters. But electronic media have increasingly encroached on the situations that take place in physically defined settings. More and more, the form of mediated communication has come to resemble the form of live face-to-face interaction. More and more, media make us "direct" audiences to performances that happen in other places and give us access to audiences that are not physically present.

While Goffman and many other sociologists tend to think of social roles in terms of the *places* in which they are performed, I argue that electronic media have undermined the traditional relationship between physical setting and social situation. Electronic media have created new situations and destroyed old ones. One of the reasons many Americans may no longer seem to "know their place" is that they no longer *have* a place in the traditional sense of a set of behaviors matched to physical locations and the audiences found in them.

This book explores a new conception of social situations that includes both physical settings such as rooms and buildings and the "informational settings" that are created by media. For media, like physical places, include and exclude participants. Media, like walls and windows, can hide and they can reveal. Media can create a sense of sharing and belonging or a feeling of exclusion and isolation. Media can reinforce a "them *vs.* us" feeling or they can undermine it. This book attempts to describe who and what we are becoming as our social situations change and as, in response, our behavior takes on new forms and meanings.

The first part of the book (Media as Change Mechanisms) develops a general framework for studying media and social change. Chapter 2 describes the limitations of the traditional focus on the effects of media content and then discusses two seemingly incompatible perspectives, each of which offers partial clues to a new approach to the study of media effects: the "medium theory" (of McLuhan and others) and the "situationism" (of Goffman and others).

Chapter 3 uses the concept of "information-systems" as a common denominator to link the study of media environments with the study of face-to-face situations. The chapter outlines the general ways in which social behavior changes when new media or other factors merge or divide information-systems. Starting with the notions of "backstage" and "onstage" behavior, I describe how the merging of previously distinct situations leads to "sidestage," or "middle-region," behavior, and how the division of one situation into two or more situations leads to "deep backstage" and "forefront stage" behaviors.

Chapter 4 analyzes "behavior" in more specific terms by discussing three general role categories: group feelings (group identity), role transitions (socialization), and authority (hierarchy). Each of these categories is shown to be dependent on a particular configuration of information-systems, and, therefore, susceptible to change in a predictable direction when a culture adopts new media of communication. I argue that the number of distinct group identities, stages of socialization, and levels of authority in a society is linked to the number of distinct public spheres, the sharpness of the division between backstage and onstage settings, and the strength of the relationship between physical location and social experience.

Part II of the book (From Print Situations to Electronic Situations) details three significant ways in which electronic media affect the information-systems found in a print society. Chapter 5 describes how differences in the "access code," "physical characteristics," "conditions of attendance," and the degree of explicitness with which information is available lead print media to foster segregated information-systems, while electronic media foster integrated information-systems. Thus, many types of information that were technically "public" in a print culture, yet largely inaccessible to many sectors of the population, are now available to most people through electronic media. Chapter 6 describes how differences in the form of information (pictures vs. printed words, for example) and differences in the way messages are encoded and decoded, lead print media toward more formal, impersonal communications, while electronic media tend toward informal, intimate, and expressive messages. Electronic media, therefore, tend to expose many features of what was formerly the "backstage" of social life. Chapter 7 details how electronic media undermine the traditional relationship between physical travel and social mobility, convey "live" information to those not present, and do not link experience to physical location. Electronic media thereby tend to redefine the notions of social "position" and social "place."

The chapters in Part III (The New Social Landscape) combine the principles developed in Parts I and II into a general theory on the impact of the "contemporary media matrix" on three decades of social change. I argue that because electronic media merge formerly distinct public spheres, blur the dividing line between private and public behaviors, and sever the traditional link between physical place and social "place," we have witnessed a resulting diffusion of group identities, a merging of different stages of socialization, and a flattening of hierarchies.

Part IV (Three Dimensions of Social Change) tests the plausibility of the general theory by examining in detail the recent changes in three sets of roles, one for each of the role categories examined throughout the book: masculinity and femininity (group identity), childhood and adulthood (socialization), and political leaders and followers (hierarchy). All three analyses suggest that electronic media have led to a blurring of previously distinct roles.

Part V (Conclusion) summarizes the book's arguments, offers some guidelines for evaluating the described changes and for predicting future developments, and suggests that, as a "placeless" culture, many of our new behavioral norms resemble those of nomadic hunters and gatherers.

Those readers who are accustomed to studies of media effects that discuss primarily the characteristics or content of *media* may be surprised at how much this book describes the structure of *interpersonal* behavior. The analysis of the dynamics of face-to-face interaction grows out of my belief that much media research has been limited to looking at narrowly defined responses to media content (such as imitation or persuasion) because researchers have largely ignored those aspects of everyday social behavior that make it highly susceptible to change when new media alter "who know what about whom." By examining changing patterns of access to information, this book suggests that the widespread use of electronic media has played an important part in many recent social developments, including the social explosions of the 1960s, the many "integration" movements (blacks, women, elderly, children, disabled, etc.), the rise of malpractice suits, the development of "halfway" houses for prisoners and the mentally ill, the decline of the nuclear family and the rise of the nuclear freeze movement, and the trends toward living alone and "living together." The theory suggests that a broad, seemingly chaotic spectrum of social change may be, in part, an orderly and comprehensible adjustment in behavior patterns to match the new social situations created by electronic media.

PART I
Media as Change Mechanisms

2

Media and Behavior:

A Missing Link

Almost everyone who has commented on electronic media, whether as casual observer or as scholar, whether in praise or in condemnation, has noted the ability of electronic media to bypass former limitations to communication. Electronic media have changed the significance of space, time, and physical barriers as communication variables. We can now speak to someone in Alaska while we are sunning in Florida, we can experience distant news events as they are happening or *re*experience images, actions, and voices of those long dead, and we can sit in any room in any house in the country and get a close-up view of a football huddle.

Yet neither the pervasiveness of electronic media nor the common awareness of their seemingly miraculous capabilities has spawned widespread analysis of the impact of such new patterns of information flow on social behavior. The overwhelming majority of television studies conducted in the United States, for example, has followed the dominant tradition in research on earlier mass media and has focused primarily on *message content.*[1] The potentially different effects of different types of media are largely ignored.

The focus on media messages grew out of early concerns that propaganda transmitted through the mass press or over radio could have a nearly universal effect on different people and could lead to a mass or mob reaction. The general failure of researchers to demonstrate clear and direct effects of media content on social behavior, however, has led to many modifications in theory and approach over the last sixty years. The old "hypodermic needle" theory (popular in the 1920s), which postulated a direct and universal response to a message stimulus, has been abandoned by almost all researchers. The tendency, instead, has been to put additional variables in between the stimulus and the behavioral response. Individual differences, group differences, the role of influential peers, stages of cognitive development, and other social and psychological variables are now seen as muting, changing, or negating the effects of the messages. But ultimately, the new models are still based on the concept of a response to a stimulus—the message.[2]

No matter how many intervening factors are taken into account, the vast majority of media studies do not stray very far from the original assumptions that media "inject" something into people and that the study of media effects, therefore, must begin with an analysis of *what* is injected. With a focus on media content, studies of television have examined what people watch, how much they watch, how they perceive and understand what they watch, and how what they watch affects what they later think and do. The concern is with media messages, not with the different patterns of information flow fostered by different media.

Even some studies that look beyond specific messages and claim to be studying the "environment of television" often turn out to maintain the traditional content focus. George Gerbner's "cultivation analysis," for example, examines television as a symbolic environment in which we live, an environment that cultivates a specific world view.[3] But the aspect of the environment that most concerns Gerbner and his associates is the image of reality as portrayed in television messages. Cultivation analysis focuses on the ways in which the totality of media content creates a mythology about women, minorities, crime, and so forth, a mythology that subsequently shapes viewers' perceptions of and response to their real environments.

Disenchantment with the limited knowledge that has been generated by the various "effects models" has led a number of researchers over the last two decades to embrace a different perspective: the "uses and gratifications" approach.[4] In this model, people, even young children, are not passive recipients of or reactors to media stimuli; rather they are purposive and conscious selectors of messages that fulfill personal needs (such as "keeping in touch with important events" or "escape from boredom"). This approach turns the old stimulus-response model on its head. It suggests that it is not so much that the media affect people, as it is that people selectively use, and thereby affect, the media. This model suggests, for example, that in order to survive, media such as newspapers or radio stations, or genres such as soap operas or situation comedies, must adapt to people's needs. While this approach rejects many of the old assumptions, it is very similar to the traditional studies in one key respect: Its focus is still on message content. It asks why people choose the messages they choose and it examines the functions that various types of media messages fulfill. Even when these studies look at which medium people use in order to gratify a particular need, the concern is rarely focused on the particular characteristics of different media of communication.

A number of political and economic critiques of media institutions (and of mainstream media research) appear to ask very different questions: Who controls the conduits of information in a society? And how are media institutions structured to further ideological, economic, and political ends?[5] But even these critiques often return to a content focus by asking how control over media institutions determines what gets on television and what does not. These are legitimate and extremely important questions, but they, too, often overlook the particular natures of various media. There is little discussion of how the same political and economic system might be affected differently by different media, or of the difference between attempts to control the content of newspapers and attempts to control the content of television.

While all these examinations of media content have much social significance, it is surprising that other types of questions about media are so rarely asked.[6] Indeed, most studies of the impact of media ignore the study of the media themselves. The content and control of television are studied the same way the content and control of newspapers, comics, movies, or novels have been studied. The medium itself is viewed as a neutral delivery system.

Scholars who study the effects of other types of technology have rarely taken such an exclusively narrow perspective. Few who have studied the effects of the Industrial Revolution, for example, would claim that the only important things to study are the specific goods that the new machines produced. Instead, historians, sociologists, and others have long noted that the important things to look at in the industrialization of society are the effects of the new means of production themselves on such variables as the balance of rural and urban life, division of labor, degree of social cohesion, structure of the family, value systems, perceptions of time and space, class structure, and rate of social change.

The research on television has been severely limited to the extent that it views electronic media merely as new links among pre-existing environments. That is, such research ignores the possibility that, once widely used, electronic media may create new social environments that reshape behavior in ways that go beyond the specific products delivered. While much concern with television, for example, has focused on the effects of violent or sexist content on the behavior of children, there has been almost no attention paid to the possibility that different *ways* of communicating cultural content may lead to different social conceptions of "childhood" and "adulthood" or of "masculinity" and "femininity." Like the person perusing the television listings in a newspaper, those who focus only on media content are more concerned with what media bring into the home than with the possibility that new media transform the home and other social spheres into new social environments with new patterns of social action, feeling, and belief.

To explore such a possibility further, we need to know at least two things: (1) how changes in media may change social environments, and (2) what effects a change in social environments may have on people's behavior. To come to a new understanding of the effects of electronic media on social behavior, this book fuses together two theoretical perspectives that have dealt with these issues: (1) "medium theory"—the historical and cross-cultural study of the different cultural environments created by different media of communication, and (2) "situationism"— the exploration of the ways in which social behavior is shaped by and in "social situations." These two fields have developed independently of each other and the questions explored in them have traditionally been far removed from the main concerns of most mass communication research- ers. Yet each of these areas of inquiry offers partial clues to a detailed theory of the effects of electronic media on social behavior. The remainder of this chapter summarizes these two perspectives, reviews their strengths and weaknesses, and describes the gap between them that needs to be filled before we can begin to see how changes in media may affect every- day social behavior.

Media as Cultural Environments

While social scientists have focused on the study of media messages, a few scholars in fields outside of communication, sociology, and psychol- ogy have taken a more historical and cross-cultural approach to commu- nication technologies and have tried to call attention to the potential effects of media apart from the content they convey. I use the singular, "*medium* theory," to describe this research because what makes it differ- ent from other "media theory" is its focus on the particular characteristics of each individual medium.

The observations of the medium theorists are often incomplete and dif- ficult to analyze and apply, yet they are of significance to this study because they suggest that media are not simply channels for conveying information between two or more environments, but rather environments in and of themselves. The best known and most controversial of these scholars are Harold Adams Innis and Herbert Marshall McLuhan.

A political economist by training, Harold Adams Innis extends the prin- ciples of economic monopolies to the study of information monopolies.[7] He sees control over communication media (such as a complex writing system controlled by a special class of priests) as a means through which social and political power is wielded. New media, however, can break old monopolies. The Medieval Church's monopoly over religious information (and thereby over salvation), argues Innis, was broken by the printing press. The printing press bypassed the Church's scribes and made the Bible and other religious materials widely available. The same content, the Bible, therefore, had different effects in different media.

Innis argues that different media have different potentialities for con- trol. A medium that is in short supply or that requires a very special encoding or decoding skill is more likely to be exploited by an elite class that has the time and the resources to gain access to it. Conversely, a medium that is very accessible to the common person tends to democra- tize a culture.

Innis also claims that every medium of communication has a "bias" either toward lasting a long time or toward traveling easily across great distances. He suggests that the bias of a culture's dominant medium affects the degree of the culture's stability and conservatism as well as the culture's ability to take over and govern large amounts of territory. "Time biased" media such as stone hieroglyphics, he argues, lead to relatively small, stable societies. Stone carvings, after all, are difficult to revise frequently, and their limited mobility makes them poor means of keeping in touch with distant places. In contrast, messages on "space biased" papyrus allowed the Romans to maintain a large empire with a centralized government that delegated authority to distant provinces. But papyrus also led to more social change and greater instability.

In *Empire and Communications* and *The Bias of Communication,* Innis rewrites the history of civilization as the history of communication media. He begins with the cradle of civilization in Mesopotamia and Egypt and ends with the British Empire and the Nazis.

Among the people Innis influenced before his death in 1952 was a scholar of medieval literature, Herbert Marshall McLuhan. To Innis's concepts of information monopolies and media "biases," McLuhan adds the notion of "sensory balance." He analyzes media as extensions of the human senses or processes, and he suggests that the use of different technologies affects the organization of the human senses.[8] McLuhan divides history into three major periods: oral, writing/printing, and electronic. Each period, according to McLuhan, is characterized by its own interplay of the senses and therefore by its own forms of thinking and communicating.

Oral societies, McLuhan argues, live in an "ear culture" of simultaneity and circularity. The oral "tribal" world of the ear is a "closed society" of high interdependence and lack of individuality. People in oral cultures, according to McLuhan, have a mythic "in-depth experience" where all the senses live in harmony. McLuhan claims that writing and, to a greater degree, print, break through the tribal balance, give oral people an "eye for an ear," make the sense of sight dominant, and distance people from sound, touch, and direct response. The break from total reliance on oral communication allows people to become more introspective, rational, and individualistic. Abstract thought develops. From the circular world of sound with its round huts and round villages, people move, over time, toward linear, cause-and-effect thinking, grid-like cities, and a one-thing-at-a-time and one-thing-after-another world that mimics the linear lines of writing and type. Allegiance to those one lives with and can hear, see, and touch shifts to allegiance to an abstract "nation" or to a "brotherhood" of a particular religion. To McLuhan, many of the characteristics of Western rationality and civilized behavior can be attributed to the influence of the printing press.

According to McLuhan, electronic media are like extensions of our nervous systems that embrace the planet. Electronic sensors return us to village-like encounters, but on a global scale. As a result of the widespread use of electronic media, everyone is involved in everyone else's business, and there is a decline in print-supported notions of delegated authority, nationalism, and linear thinking.

Innis and McLuhan are unique in terms of the breadth of history and culture they attempt to include within their frameworks. Other medium theorists, however, have looked at specific segments of the spectrum of media effects. J.C. Carothers, Jack Goody and Ian Watt, Eric Havelock, A.R. Luria, and Walter Ong have studied various aspects of the shift from orality to literacy.[9] They have argued convincingly (indeed, much more convincingly than Innis and McLuhan) that literacy and orality involve completely different modes of consciousness. They describe how the introduction of literacy affects social organization, the social definition of knowledge, the conception of the individual, and even types of mental illness.

H.L. Chaytor and Elizabeth Eisenstein have examined the significance of the shift from script to print.[10] Print is often thought of merely as the "mechanization" of writing, yet Chaytor argues that the shift altered conceptions of literary style, created a new sense of "authorship" and intellectual property, fostered the growth of nationalistic feelings, and modified the psychological interaction of words and thought. Eisenstein echoes many of these themes and presents an enormous amount of evidence and many cogent analyses to support the argument that the printing press revolutionized Western Europe by fostering the Reformation and the growth of modern science.

Walter Ong, Edmund Carpenter, Tony Schwartz, and Daniel Boorstin have looked at the effects of electronic media on thinking patterns and social organization.[11] Schwartz and Carpenter are generally McLuhanesque in content, method, and style. Ong and Boorstin, however, present more traditional scholarly analyses that support McLuhan's basic arguments but also go beyond them. Ong describes the similarities and differences between the "primary orality" of preliterate societies and the "secondary orality" that results from the introduction of electronic media into literate societies. He looks at the spiritual and psychological significance of the return of "the word" in an electronic form. Boorstin describes how new media "mass-produce the moment," make experience "repeatable," and join many other recent technological inventions in "leveling times and places." Boorstin also compares and contrasts political revolutions with technological revolutions and discusses the impact of new technologies, including electronic media, on our conceptions of nationality, history, and progress.[12]

The medium theorists do not suggest that the means of communication *wholly* shape culture and personality, but they argue that changes in communication patterns are one very important contributant to social change and one that has generally been overlooked. Their analyses of media and social change also suggest that the transformations are not sudden or

rords, in
sors, for
)ose and
listened
l memo-

as trans-
ng to the
ld means
se, but it
arly, tele-
elephone
of a new
of earlier
,ction and
s are now
ulting loss
alogy here
on social
society, but
duction of
stems the-
ory and ecology: When a new factor is added to an old environment, we do not get the old environment plus the new factor, we get a new environment. The extent of the "newness" depends, of course, on how much the new factor alters significant forces in the old system, but the new environment is always more than the sum of its parts.

Put simply, the medium theorists are arguing that the form in which people communicate has an impact beyond the choice of specific messages. They do not deny the significance of message choice *within* a cultural milieu. (McLuhan himself, for example, expressed a clear preference for certain programs, including "60 Minutes," saying, "There are certain things I just don't like to miss that's all"; as for other programs, such as "Star Trek," he added, "I don't give a damn."[16]) But these theorists are primarily interested in a higher level analysis—a cross-cultural and historical perspective.

This type of analysis in other fields is rarely controversial. If a political historian were to argue that it often matters less what the leader of a country says in his or her speeches than it matters whether the leader is an elected official in a democracy or a monarch who has inherited a throne, few would blink an eye. And while a barefoot peasant might prefer to get a pair of shoes rather than a hammer—regardless of whether the shoes and hammer are hand-made or mass-produced—an economic historian will note the ways in which a shift from manual to mechanical production of all goods affects many aspects of the society, including the proportion of the population that is barefoot.

Yet for a number of reasons, the medium theory perspective has failed to penetrate deeply into scholarly activity or the popular consciousness. For one thing, much of the funding for media research is generated from sources interested in the administration of existing media institutions or in the formation of public policy concerning media regulation and control. Further, the search—especially in the United States—for "scientific" evidence of media effects has led most researchers to focus on collecting data that can be quantified and analyzed statistically. Since the medium theorists' comparisons and contrasts of different media environments do not have much to say about how to run or regulate media *within* a specific technological environment, and since it is difficult, if not impossible, to "test" the medium theorists' broad historical and cultural theories through surveys, direct observation, or experiments, most media research has focused on much narrower questions. Similarly, one of the reasons the medium theorists have not attracted much long-term popular enthusiasm is that their attempts to avoid saying that one form of communication is "better" or "worse" than another sharply contrasts with many popular views such as the belief that reading books is inherently good and watching television is inherently bad.

Furthermore, there is a general tendency for people, including many scholars and researchers, to ignore or even deny the effects of the invisible environments of media simply because they are invisible. It is ironic that we often distinguish ourselves from the beasts in terms of our ability to communicate, yet many of us are very resistant to considering the impact of significant shifts in the means through which we communicate. Most people are much more willing to accept the widespread social and psychological effects of physical and material causes (such as industrialization, new means of transportation, drought, war, and economic depression) than they are willing to consider informational contributants to social change. It is generally simpler, for example, for people to consider the impact of a ten percent rise in gasoline prices than it is for them to consider the impact of a tenfold increase in the capacity of computer memory chips. Material changes are concrete and imaginable; informational changes seem very abstract and mystical. And even within informational changes, people are more likely to grasp onto those aspects of the information environment that are most visible: particular messages. Yet by concentrating popular and scholarly attention primarily on message content, our approach is often not that different from a hypothetical attempt to grasp the impact of the automobile by ignoring the issue of new patterns of travel and by focusing instead on a detailed examination of the names and faces of passengers.

Although many people are resistant to the types of claims made by the medium theorists, a number of the problems with the acceptance and further study of medium effects grow out of the limitations of the medium theory works themselves. Innis and McLuhan, for example, make broad claims concerning the impact of various media, but these claims lack the development of clear, linear arguments and evidence. Their books seem to be written in the midst of revelations, with both the excitement and the impatience caused by blinding flashes of insight. They run past details and skip over logical arguments as if they are certain that their widely spaced footsteps will lead the reader to the same conclusions.

Innis writes obscurely, condensing paragraphs into sentences, stating conclusions while omitting arguments and support. McLuhan's work leans heavily on aphorisms, puns, and metaphors. Indeed, many of McLuhan's greatest insights are invisible to the uninitiated reader because McLuhan offers his own nonlinear style as evidence for the strength of oral forms of reasoning. Innis' and McLuhan's analyses are most appealing to people who already believe their basic arguments. And even those who accept Innis' and McLuhan's arguments may have difficulty explaining the arguments to others in their own words. Like a mystical religion, "McLuhanism" seems like overwhelming truth to those who believe in it and like hogwash to those who do not.

Innis' and McLuhan's "findings" are in an unusual form and they are, therefore, not easily integrated into other theoretical research frames. Their observations have a direct, declaratory, and conclusive tone that makes them easy to accept fully or reject fully, but difficult to apply or explore further. McLuhan, for example, claims that electronic media have been "abolishing both space and time as far as our planet is concerned."[17] In the process, he argues, we have lost the ability to fragment our roles, to take a specific point of view, and we have begun to "live mythically and integrally" in a "global village."[18]

There is poetry in these descriptions of media effects that touches the soul yet distresses the mind. The powerful form of the statements makes them compelling, but it also exposes them to refutation by even the slightest qualifying argument or evidence. Have time and space, for example, really been "abolished"? Or have they simply been "demoted" from prime determinants of all direct intercourse to determinants of only certain forms of interaction?[19]

McLuhan suggests that traditional scholarly analyses are based on a false assumption that linear thinking is the only way to reason—an assumption, he claims, that was spawned by the lineality of writing and print and is now being undermined by electronic media. Scholars who approach McLuhan's work for evaluation, therefore, are faced with a peculiar paradox: They have to call on their traditional rational critical skills to criticize a work that questions the necessity and universal value of such skills. Ironically, but predictably, the response of many critics has been emotional, hostile, and, at times, *irrational*.[20]

McLuhan's provocative statements and unusual style made him, for a time, a household name. In 1967, NBC aired an hour-long program featuring McLuhan. In March 1969, he was interviewed by *Playboy* magazine. McLuhan was variously dubbed "the oracle of an electronic age," "the sage of Aquarius," and the "Dr. Spock of Pop Culture." His slogans and terminology ("the medium is the message," "global village," "hot" and "cool" media) became well known. The debates over whether anyone really understood his nonlinear, punny prose served as the basis for a sight-gag in a Woody Allen movie, *Annie Hall*, where Allen pulled McLuhan into a scene to tell a long-winded "explicator" of McLuhan's theories that "you know nothing of my work."[21]

Yet McLuhan's star burned as briefly as it burned brightly. The attention given to McLuhan's theories on television and radio, and in books, newspapers, and magazines served as a double-edged sword. It brought the idea of non-content media analysis to the consciousness of wide segments of the population in the late 1960s and early 1970s, but the equation of the study of medium effects with McLuhan's style turned many scholars away from serious attention to the subject. By the time of his death in 1980, McLuhan had lost on both fronts: Many of his terms still echoed—but without much understanding—in popular arenas, and his conceptual frameworks had been banished from most scholarly forums.

In contrast to Innis and McLuhan, the studies of Carothers, Havelock, Ong, Chaytor, Goody and Watt, Eisenstein, and others are, for the most part, traditional scholarly works that develop strong and convincing arguments built on historical research and field data. Yet perhaps because they are narrow and focused studies that have developed out of distinct disciplines (the classics, psychiatry, English, religion, anthropology, history, etc.), these works are not widely known, nor are they generally conceived of as being parts of one body of literature. With the exception of Ong, most of these scholars do not even explicitly state the general principle that *all* media are powerful shapers of culture and consciousness. Instead, they focus on the special problem before them: the consequences of literacy, the effects of differences among writing systems, and so on. Because of this narrowness of focus and also because the most generative and detailed works—Ong's later books and Eisenstein's massive study of printing—were written after the widescale rejection of McLuhan, these scholars have found no clear and waiting audience for their research.

But perhaps the greatest problem with the medium theory works is that ultimately they provide more of a *perspective* for studying the effects of media on behavior than they present a detailed *theory*. The insights, observations, and evidence they collect point to the need to study media environments in addition to studying media messages, but they do not form a clear set of propositions to explain the means through which media reshape specific behaviors. McLuhan's discussion of sensory balance is rich in insights and intuitions that ring true; Ong adds strong evidence concerning the ideas of a shifting sensorium and changing modes of consciousness. But discussions of "media biases," "sensory balance," and "new modes of consciousness" are very abstract. They identify important processes, but in the end, they mystify the effects of media even as they seem to clarify them. How, exactly, does a new sensorium or a new mode of consciousness affect one's behavior? Eisenstein offers a concrete analysis of the effects of the new diffusion of information caused by the printing press. Yet her detailed discussion of the Reformation and the Scientific Revolution does not offer us much information about the ways in which media, *in general*, affect culture, nor even about the specific effects of the printing press on the behavior of individuals.

Finally, perhaps because environments are most visible when one is outside of them, the studies on the effects of writing and print have tended to be much more detailed and scholarly than the studies of electronic media. McLuhan's difficult mosaics remain the richest source of hypotheses that relate specifically to the telephone, radio, and television. Ultimately, the medium theory literature offers little competition for the mainstream television content studies in terms of concrete, comprehensible effects of electronic media on *everyday social behavior*.

Part of what is missing from the medium theory studies is any real attempt to link an analysis of media characteristics with an analysis of the structure and dynamics of everyday social interaction. Most people would acknowledge that new media lead to new links among people and places, new ways of storing and retrieving social information. But a question that remains unanswered is: Why and how do technologies that merely create new *connections* among people and places lead to any fundamental shift in the structure of society or in social behavior? One potential answer to this question rests in the ways in which *dis*connectedness—the separation of social situations and interactions—shapes social reality.

The theory developed in this book, therefore, attempts to bridge the gap between the perspective offered by the medium theorists and the sociological perspective, outlined in the next section, on the relationship between "social situations" and social roles. At first, the discussion of situational determinants of behavior may seem to have nothing to do with the effects of electronic media; and indeed, most of the people who have developed and studied this perspective have little or nothing to say about media. Yet by describing the social significance of *limited* access to each other through the *separation* of situations, the situationists offer a framework that can, with some work, be adapted to study the effects of new patterns of interaction brought about by new media.

Situations and Behavior

Social situations form the hidden ground for our figures of speech and action. When we speak of "where" something happened, or say to someone "you had to be there," or suggest that someone is interpreting behavior "out of context," we are alluding to the elusive variable of "social situation." Similarly, when we chastise someone for acting "inappropriately," we are implicitly paying homage to a set of unwritten rules of behavior matched to the situation we are in.

Early in this century, sociologist W.I. Thomas suggested the paradox of social situations: "If men define situations as real, they are real in their consequences."[22] In other words, *we* construct social situations, but the arbitrariness of our definitions for situations does not make them any less binding on us.

Situational rules stand somewhere between objectivity and subjectivity. Within a cultural group or subgroup, situational rules and roles appear "objectively" real because the expectations are often shared. The rules, however, often have little or no basis in nature, and would not necessarily make any sense to people in other cultures or groups. At the same time, the definitions of situations are not merely "subjective"; because they are real to most people within the same culture or group, such shared social meanings have been labeled "*inter*subjective."[23]

Each defined situation has specific rules and roles. A funeral demands behaviors different from those at a wedding, a party has rules different from those of a classroom, a job interview entails roles that are distinct from those in a psychiatric counseling session. Anyone who believes that situational definitions and situationally defined roles have no "reality" should attempt to behave in the first of each of these pairs of situations as they would normally do for the second.

Each situational definition also prescribes and proscribes different roles for the different participants. When a patient goes to speak to a psychiatrist, the situation determines the range of behaviors for each person. Only one of the two participants, for example, is "allowed" to cry. Similarly, a minister at a funeral must behave differently from the relatives of the deceased.

When people enter any given interaction, therefore, the first thing they need to know is "what is going on here?" They need to know the "definition of the situation."[24] The definition of the situation is a simple concept that is used to describe the complex dynamics of encounters and the rules that govern them. As Erving Goffman suggests in *Frame Analysis*, the variation in situational definitions can be quite convoluted. A situation can have a "primary framework" (such as "fighting") and yet be overlaid with various "keyings" ("playing at fighting" or even "actor portraying a play fight").[25] Yet while analytically complex, the perception of the definition on the part of native adult members of a society or group is apparently relatively intuitive and direct. Indeed, it is often much more difficult for researchers to identify, define, and study situational definitions than it is for the average citizen to navigate them.

One of the ways in which we adapt to social life is by learning our culture's stock of situational definitions. By the time we grow to adulthood in a given society, most of us have unconsciously mastered the broad outlines of many, if not most, of our society's definitions of situations. To be "improperly socialized" is, in part, to be unable to negotiate successfully the demands of various situations. The worker who acts like a colleague to his or her boss, the person who tells jokes at a funeral or starts a poker game at a wedding reception—these people are either unable to grasp the situational definitions or perhaps so keenly aware of them that they feel they must constantly challenge them. For "normal" passage through social interactions, most of us semiconsciously adapt to situations without giving them much thought. Studies have shown that children as young as four change speaking styles depending on the situation and the "audience."[26]

Little conscious calculation is needed to adapt to most situational definitions within a culture because, at any given time, a society's situations tend to be highly conventionalized and finite in number, rather than idiosyncratic and infinite. Indeed, one can conceive of the general range of appropriate and inappropriate behaviors for most situations by using brief labels, such as "first date," "birthday party," "organizational meeting," and so forth. And one can narrow down the range of behaviors by combining various labels (for example, "birthday party at the office for a co-worker whom I plan to ask out soon"). In a sense, every situation has an "agenda," though for informal gatherings, such as parties or "hanging out with friends," the implicit agendas often include the provision that there will be no formal or explicit agendas.

Usually we give situational agendas little conscious thought unless something goes wrong: a lawyer at a divorce settlement begins to sing his favorite love songs, or a close friend begins speaking to you as if you were one of her employees. Even when something like the above goes wrong with the situation/behavior match, we are likely to attribute the strangeness to the person rather than to the definition of the situation.[27] It rarely occurs to us that each of these behaviors is, in a sense, "normal," and that the problem is in the relationship between the behavior and the situation. Looking to the person for the problem is especially damaging in cross-cultural encounters, where participants often begin with the best intentions and end with the assumption that the members of the other culture are rude or crazy.[28]

The effects of situational definitions (as well as the reasons for their general invisibility) can be made clearer by thinking of three categories of situational behavior: behaviors that almost *always* happen in the given situation, behaviors that almost *never* happen in the situation, and behaviors that *sometimes* happen in the situation. At a job interview, for example, the interviewer almost always asks the interviewee some questions. Almost never, however, do the interviewer and interviewee play checkers or embrace sexually. There is a third category of behavior that contains those things that sometimes happen at interviews: jokes are told, some flirting goes on, a job or an applicant is turned down. In a different situation, however, the contents of the three categories shift. Things that might never happen at an interview, for example, might happen at a party or in a park; indeed, the behavior of the same two people would be completely different in different situations.

One of the reasons that the situational determinants of behavior often go unnoticed is that we tend to concentrate more on the third category—things that sometimes happen in given situations—than we concentrate on the "almost always" and "almost never" categories. We tend to take the situational frames for granted and focus instead on the range of choices within the overall constraints.

Another reason that the power of situations remains invisible to us much of the time is that most of us tend to see ourselves as the prime unit of analysis in our social experiences. We tend to focus on what is consistent in our behaviors from situation to situation and are rarely fully aware of the ways in which we change behavior as we change situations. When we choose something to wear, for example, or say something, or take any action within a situation, we focus more on what we *decide* to do than on the limits of decision that the situation imposes on us. Freedom within a range of choices, therefore, is often mistaken for absolute freedom.[29] In a sense, we each have different personalities in different situations, yet we often choose to focus on the higher level personality that emerges from the consistency in the strategies we use for adapting to different situations.

We are not entirely powerless in the face of the situations that exist in the culture we are born into. Since situations are created by us, they can also be changed by us. People, especially people in positions of authority, can define new situations. Legislators, judges, and administrators frequently do so. Similarly, individuals often make contracts with each other to define or to redefine their interactions. Nevertheless, once we define a situation, such as a marriage or a business relationship, we are bound by its definitions as well. Furthermore, while each of us can define and redefine *some* situations, *most* of the situations we encounter in everyday life cannot be easily changed by individuals. Most social situational change is slow and unconscious (change in courtship rituals, for example). And, as I argue in this book, the evolution in social situations often comes about as the unintended consequence of technological innovations. Even when a situation is changed suddenly by law (such as the end of school segregation) or other means, it is generally only after the new situation is "inherited" by several subsequent generations that it comes to be seen as natural or, put differently, that it is seen as so "normal" that it is barely seen at all.[30]

We often complain about having to fulfill various "social obligations" or having to follow certain rituals in social situations (such as making small talk with people we do not like at business lunches or renting a tuxedo for a wedding). At the same time, most of us do not usually appreciate too much ambiguity or uncertainty in the definition of situations. We choose to go to a specific restaurant or club, or register in a certain type of hotel, because of the relative certainty of the type of experience we will have there. When we select a place to eat, we usually have some idea of the likelihood of there being screaming children or barking dogs to compete with our dinner conversation (or we have some advance clue to how other diners may react to *our* child or pet). Even when we want to have a "wild adventure," we usually select an environment where such an adventure—as opposed to more routine activities—is most likely to take place. Few people would feel comfortable coming to a situation not knowing anything at all about it. As many mysteries and detective dramas suggest, the largely undefined situation can be a source of great tension and anxiety.

Social behavior and communication, then, involve much more than people bouncing "messages" off each other. To a large extent, behavior is shaped and modified by the socially defined situations in which people find themselves. While there remains much individual variation within a given situation, there is also a larger consistency in the patterned variations most people exhibit as they move from one type of situation to another.

Because of the lack of full awareness of situations, situations have remained a minor part of social inquiry until recently. In social psychology, for example, the unit of analysis has usually been the individual and his or her behavior. To study behavior, social psychologists have often pulled people out of the matrix of socially defined situations and placed them in the "controlled environment" of the laboratory. The purpose has been to isolate aspects of behavior for more accurate observation and analysis.

In recent years, critics of the laboratory method have argued that rather than studying "raw behavior" in isolation from extraneous variables, psychologists have actually been studying the way people behave in a newly defined situation—the psychological experiment. Among other things, research has shown that subjects in experiments try to please the experimenter, that people who volunteer to be in experiments differ in a number of significant ways from the general population, and that the expectations of the experimenter often unintentionally influence the results of an experiment or the researcher's perception and interpretation of the results.[31] Initially, some of these studies were seen as means to perfecting the methodology of experimentation, but the more that the effects of the experimental situation have come to seem unavoidable, the more such work has become a critique of the experimental method itself, especially as it has been applied (to the near exclusion of other methods) to the study of many aspects of social behavior. Psychologist Ralph Rosnow, for example, has called for a more "pluralistic" social psychology that embraces a variety of methods and approaches, including more "contextualist" studies that examine "where, when, and before whom the behavior is performed."[32]

In recent years, there has been a dramatic increase in the examination of social "episodes," "settings," and "contexts."[33] Studies, theories, and critiques have suggested that personality measures are often poor predictors of everyday social behavior and that behaviors such as anxiety reactions are largely shaped by situational factors.[34] One disturbing study found that otherwise normal students who were randomly assigned to be "guards" in a simulated prison began to display uncharacteristic cruelty, aggression, and sadism. Indeed, a hostile guard-prisoner relationship developed so quickly and with such intensity that the experiment had to be abandoned in less than a week.[35] Researchers have also begun to examine the ways in which situational definitions affect a person's accent, vocabulary, and other linguistic variables.[36] Psychologists have been experimenting with teaching people to control compulsions and addictions by monitoring the situational cues that stimulate the behaviors. This approach has been used with overeating, drug abuse, alcoholism, and smoking.[37] Other research and theory suggest that "competence" and "skill" are situationally defined.[38] Ethnomethodologist Harold Garfinkel has developed a method of making situational conventions visible by breaking the rules of situations and then observing the resulting confusion and the process of reconstruction that follows.[39] Philosopher Rom Harré and psychologist Paul Secord have argued that people's own accounts of the rules of social situations should be used as the foundation of a new scientific approach to the study of social behavior.[40] Although psychology has long focused on individual traits or responses to isolated stimuli, Adrian Furnham and Michael Argyle have suggested that as a result of "disillusionment and limited success" with old perspectives and methods, the "social situation, rather than the individual, may develop into a new unit of psychological research."[41]

The situationist whose approach may indirectly provide the most clues to the impact of new media on social roles is Erving Goffman. Goffman describes social life using the metaphor of drama.[42] He sees us each playing a multiplicity of roles on different social stages. For each "audience" we offer a somewhat different version of ourselves.

Goffman suggests that such role performances are necessary for the ordinary and smooth flow of social life. In any given interaction, we need to know what to expect of each other. We do not want doctors in an emergency room to tell us that they do not feel like looking at our wounds today, nor do we want a waiter in a restaurant to sit down and eat with us. We expect people to follow the definitions of situations and their roles within them. Even with our friends, we expect some general consistency of style and behavior. Yet each person must exhibit very different behaviors in different settings. Psychiatrists would be considered strange if they spoke in detail about their own emotional problems with their patients, yet they would anger their spouses and friends if they did *not* speak about their own problems and feelings.

Goffman suggests that when we enter a social setting, we want and need to know something about the situation and the other participants. We need to know whether the situation is formal or informal, happy or sad. We need to know the various roles of the other people, whom we should speak to and whom we should avoid, and whether or not we are welcome. Conversely, people in the situation need to know something about us. What is our reason for being there? What role will we play in this situation?

Goffman notes that much of this information is not "naturally" available. It may take years to know a person fully, to understand the true complexities of a particular social situation, or to learn how a given group of people function in a specific social institution or establishment. And yet most social interactions require instant judgments, alignments, and action. As a result, Goffman suggests, people are constantly mobilizing their energies to create socially meaningful "impressions." Through dress, gesture, muscle tonus, and arrangement of furniture and other props, we set the stages of our lives and define general roles for ourselves and for other people. Thus, when we walk into a store or office or school, we are usually able to get an immediate sense of the overall structure of the situation and who is in what role.

Even a person who appears to be "doing nothing," Goffman suggests, is usually mobilizing his or her energies in a particular way. When in the presence of others, people often have an "interaction tonus," which suggests that they are ready to begin an encounter should the need arise. Also, people often carefully control their posture and glances to avoid appearing threatening, dangerous, or odd. Complete relaxation or staring off into space—especially when it is prolonged—is often taken as a sign of hostility or insanity.

For Goffman, the performance of any social role is literally a performance, that is, a selected display of behavior that cannot go on continuously and which must, to some extent, consciously or unconsciously, be planned and rehearsed. And, just as in a play, the stage must be properly set, the actors must carefully control their actions, and the roles in one drama must be kept separate from roles in other dramas.

In keeping with the metaphor of drama, Goffman suggests that any individual's behavior in a given setting can be broken down into two broad categories: "back region," or backstage behavior, and "front region," or onstage behavior. In front regions, the performers are in the presence of their "audience" for a particular role, and they play a relatively ideal conception of a social role. Waiters, for example, are in a front region when they serve people in a restaurant dining room. In the front region, waiters are usually polite and respectful. Their appearance and manner is one of cleanliness and efficiency. They do not enter into the dinner conversations of restaurant patrons. They do not comment on their customers' eating habits or table manners. They rarely, if ever, eat while in the sight of patrons.

When waiters step from the dining room into the kitchen, however, they suddenly cross a line between the onstage and backstage areas. In the kitchen, waiters are in an area that is hidden from the audience and they share this area with others who perform the same or similar roles vis-à-vis the audience. Here, then, waiters may make remarks to each other about the "strange behavior of the people at table seven," they may imitate a customer, or give advice to a "rookie" on methods of getting big tips. In the kitchen, food may be handled and discussed with somewhat

less respect than in the dining room, and waiters may "get out of cos-
tume" or sit in a sloppy position with their feet up on a counter.

While the waiter is a low status position in our society, the same distinction in behaviors is characteristic of high status positions such as doctor, lawyer, and judge. When "onstage," doctors tend to hide doubts,
ignorance, feelings of depression, and sexual responses to the sight of a
naked person. While not with patients, however, doctors may joke with
a nurse about the physical appearance or personality of a patient, ask a
nurse never to correct them within earshot of others (a "stage direction"),
or telephone a colleague to get advice on an unusual set of symptoms.
Virtually all role performers tend to have back regions where they and
their "teammates" (those who share the same role or work to foster the
same impression) relax, rehearse, develop strategies for future performances, and joke about their behaviors in front regions.

Such backstage behavior may, on the surface, seem more "real" or honest than front region behavior, yet the issue is not quite that simple. An
individual may "really be" a dedicated, compassionate teacher even
though she complains to colleagues about workload, and wonders aloud
if she should not have been an advertising executive, or jokes about an
occasional urge to strangle a particular student. Nearly everyone exhibits
contradictory behaviors in different situations. Indeed, even back region
behavior may be thought of as a kind of role, where teammates will not
tolerate formal, front region style. Social truth is an elusive and "situa-
tion-relative" concept.

Although we often believe that it is dishonest or immoral to "put on"
a character or "play a role," Goffman suggests that this is a naive belief.
Some people, it is true, may purposely give misleading impressions (con
artists, spies, undercover agents), but *all* individuals must give *some*
impression. Thus, while a dishonest judge may pretend to be an honest
judge, even an honest judge must play the role of "honest judge." All
judges—honest and dishonest alike—must avoid being seen in questionable places with questionable characters even if there is nothing inappropriate "actually" going on. Even honest judges must dress and behave
properly when "onstage," by wearing black, not pink, robes and by sitting behind the bench rather than cross-legged on the floor at the feet of
the jury.

"Impression management," therefore, serves as a kind of social shorthand through which people identify themselves and provide expectations
about their behavior—both to others and to themselves. What distinguishes honest from dishonest performers, suggests Goffman, is not the
need for performance, but rather the attitude of the performers toward
their own roles. In one sense, honest people are those who are at least
partially taken in by their own performances and come to think of themselves as the characters they portray.

Further, the staging of a front region role does not necessarily involve
"fooling the audience" because, to a large extent, audiences *want* only a

limited "version" of the performer. Of the wide range of behaviors exhibited by every person, we expect and accept only a small range of expressions within any given social setting. We expect to be treated differently in a restaurant than in a doctor's office. We expect the doctor to appear confident, concerned, patient, and professional—and slightly superior. We expect a waitress to be efficient, respectful, and nonintrusive. And we demand these differences in "character" even if the waitress is a student earning her way through medical school.

The stability of social interactions based on expression and impression is reinforced by the fact that we each gain a sense of ourselves through relationships with other people. While we often prefer to think of ourselves as autonomous individuals who make our own destiny, most of the concepts we use to define ourselves are relative and social. When we think of ourselves as being tall or short, smart or dumb, careful or bold, competent or incompetent, kind or harsh, we must compare ourselves to others. Indeed, even when we imagine or remember ourselves in a particular social situation, we often see ourselves from another person's viewpoint. For example, if you remember a situation in which you ran away from something menacing or gave a public presentation, you are likely to see yourself in the pictured scene. When we actually run down a street, we cannot see our faces or bodies; what we see are "bouncing" houses and cars. Yet we often forget our sensory experiences and recall, instead, the social experience of what we might have looked like to an observer.[43]

The selves we project are not simply masks we slip on, therefore, but personalities we become attached to. The longer we play a given role, the more the role comes to seem real, not only to our audiences, but also to ourselves. The first time a graduate student teaches a college class, for example, the student often feels like an imposter. But if the performance is "carried off" well, especially over several semesters, the person may feel "Yes, I *am* a teacher!" As Peter Berger has observed, "it is very difficult to pretend in this world. Normally, one becomes what one plays at."[44]*

---

*There are, no doubt, many exceptions to this rule, but there are also many dramatic affirmations of it. In November 1981, for example, a man arrested for shoplifting in Louisville identified himself as Pat Salamone, but he later turned out to be Patrick Livingston, an undercover FBI agent. After five years of pretending to be a Miami pornography dealer, Livingston became the part he played. He always introduced himself as Salamone, always behaved like Salamone, and kept bank accounts in his alias.[45] A "60 Minutes" report on the incident suggested that an unpublished FBI report had found a similar trend among other undercover agents. Similarly, kidnap victim Patty Hearst claims that at first she only *pretended* to join the "Symbionese Liberation Army" (her kidnappers), "but somewhere along the line I got lost. I got ... caught up with what they were doing. ... My reality became their reality."[46] In her year of eluding the FBI, Hearst passed up many opportunities to escape and, in one incident, fired a submachine gun in the air to facilitate the getaway of two of her "comrades." When arrested she raised her fist in a defiant salute and gave her occupation as "urban guerrilla."

While some people may argue that the key to freedom is to reject social roles, another view is to think of freedom in terms of the ability to *choose* roles, to control, to the extent possible, the types of audiences for our performances, and to be whoever we want to be where and when we desire. The contrast between these two views of freedom and self-expression may explain why Goffman's work has been seen both as a denial of self-hood and a celebration of it.[47]

Like all social theories and perspectives, situationism, as presented by Goffman and others, tells us only one part of the complex story of social life. Many situationists, for example, ignore or downplay those spontaneous aspects of the self that generate new realities, that resist the restraints of social conventions and roles.[48] Yet one way to conceive of the situational approach to behavior is as a balance to the common belief in the relative autonomy of self and to the research tradition of studying social behavior by observing personality traits or testing responses to an isolated "stimulus."

The recent work on social situations has led to a curious state of affairs, where many social scientists now agree with the need to study naturalistic social phenomena, but where relatively few people are doing it.[49] Part of the reason for this has been that the situational approach has offered few methodological alternatives to the laboratory experiment that are acceptable to mainstream social psychologists.[50] Even simple situations are so complex and involve so many different variables that they appear to be incredibly "messy" units of analysis to researchers accustomed to isolating and manipulating a few factors.

As of now, the research on situations has supported the plausibility of situationism more than it has advanced toward a general theory of situations and behavior. Although there have been many empirical and analytical studies of situations, most of this work has focused on describing situation-specific behaviors as they exist at a particular time in a given culture. There has been relatively little work explaining the general process through which situations affect behavior, there have been few attempts at generating propositions for predicting why and how social situations change, and there have been virtually no analyses of how behavior will change when situations change. Indeed, there is still no clear agreement on how to define a "situation" or describe its elements.[51]

Goffman's work is especially frustrating in this regard. His frameworks are developed with such a wealth of observation, minute detail, and insightful analysis that they seem to provide their own built-in proof. Yet there have been surprisingly few extended adaptations or applications of Goffman's principles. The reason for this, perhaps, is that in presenting a rich source of data on behavior, Goffman has presented countless observations and few integrating theories. It is very difficult to abstract principles from Goffman's writing, which some consider a stylistic merger of the scholarly monograph and the novel.[52] Indeed, his most important principles are often left implicit or are slipped in surreptitiously at the end of paragraphs. To complicate matters further, Goffman rarely integrates a new work with his earlier works, and most of his books have no subject indexes. When he died in 1982, Goffman was in the process of exploring new social terrains rather than explaining his life work.

Yet as problematic as situationism is at this time, it does provide a clear, useful, and interesting perspective from which to view social roles and rules. Further, Goffman's dramaturgical model, in particular, provides many implicit clues to the effects of new media on social behavior. For the model suggests that to "be" a certain type of person generally requires the appropriate social situations and audiences. Any factor that restructures social stages and reorganizes social audiences, therefore, would have a great impact on social behavior. If social reality exists in *distinct* sets of behaviors, if "truth" is situation-bound, if the more we know about individuals in general, the less clearly we may be able to see who they "are" as they stand before us in a given situation, then what a profound change in selves, society, and social reality we would witness when the situations in which people behave are somehow rearranged.

The Theoretical Gap: Media and Situations

There are a number of difficulties in attempting to integrate the work of the medium theorists and the situationists. On the surface, the two bodies of literature seem incompatible. They each suggest something about the social order, but they do not overlap. The medium theorists describe how media reshape large cultural environments and institutional structures, but they do not tell us much about the ways in which media reshape specific social situations or everyday social behaviors. For their part, most of the situationists are more concerned with describing situations and situational behaviors as they exist in a society rather than in analyzing how and why situations evolve. Such a static, descriptive approach is not very useful in analyzing or predicting social change. Further, the situationists focus almost exclusively on face-to-face interaction and ignore interactions that take place through media.[53]

Yet beneath the surface, both perspectives have some common elements. Both the medium theorists and the situationists reject the significance of studying only lower-level variations within a system (such as variations in content within a medium or variations among individuals' behaviors within a situation). Instead, they both focus on the overall effects of the larger structure of the environment. More important, the medium theorists and the situationists implicitly deal with a similar theme: patterns of access to each other. The situationists suggest how our particular actions and words are shaped by our knowledge of who has access to them, and the medium theorists suggest that new media change such patterns of access.

The largest problem in integrating these two perspectives is the theoretical gap in our understanding of the relationship between media and situations. The medium theorists discuss media as if they have little to do with the dynamics of face-to-face interaction, and the situationists barely seem to notice that media exist. In order to fuse these two approaches into a theory of the impact of media on social behavior, we must develop a common denominator concept that will link the discussion of media with the discussion of place-bound situations. We also need a framework that extends the description of relatively fixed role behaviors in static situations into an analysis of situational and behavioral *change*. Further, we need to discover how social roles, in general, are affected by changes in media and situations. These tasks are the work of the remaining two chapters in Part I.

3
Media, Situations, and Behavior

Beyond Place: Situations as Information-Systems

Situations are usually defined in terms of behaviors in physical locations. Goffman, for example, describes a behavioral region as "any *place* that is bounded to some degree by barriers to perception."[1] Roger Barker sees "behavior settings" as "bounded, *physical-temporal locales*."[2] Lawrence Pervin defines a situation as "a specific *place*, in most cases involving specific people, a specific time and specific activities."[3]*

It is not surprising that most of those who have studied the effects of situations on behavior have focused on encounters that occur in given places. Until recently, place-bound, face-to-face interaction was the only means of gaining "direct" access to the sights and sounds of each other's behaviors. The physical barriers and boundaries marked by walls and fences as well as the passageways provided by doors and corridors directed the flow of people and determined, to a large degree, the number, type, and size of face-to-face interactions.

Further, such physical settings continue to be very special. A given place, such as a room, takes on particular social significance because its walls and doors and location tend to include and exclude participants in a particular way. The walls of a room simultaneously permit focused interaction among some people while isolating the participants from other

---

*Of course, situationists also consider many other characteristics of situations, including: tasks, goals, rules, roles, traditions, temporal factors (season, month, day, time, and length of encounter), the characteristics of the people present (number of people, their age, sex, status, nationality, race, religion, degree of intimacy with each other), and the subjective perceptions of participants. But place often figures as an implicit or explicit part of the definition of situations, perhaps because situationists realize that so many of the other factors would be affected by a major change in the physical setting or its boundaries.

people. The size of a physical setting tends to set a minimum and a maximum number of people who can interact within it comfortably. A football field, for example, is not a very romantic spot for two lovers to interact, and a telephone booth is not a suitable place for a meeting of a board of trustees. The thickness of doors and walls, the size and location of windows (as well as the presence or absence of window shades), and the distance of the setting from other encounters in other locations, all serve to support or undermine various potential definitions of the situation.*

Although there are many logical reasons for the traditional focus on place-bound situations, a question that arises is whether behavioral settings must be places. That is, is it actually *place* that is a large determinant of behavior, or is it something else that has traditionally been tied to, and therefore confused with, place? There is another key factor besides place mentioned in Goffman's definition of regions that tends to get lost in most of his and other situationists' discussions of behavioral settings: "barriers to perception." Indeed, a close examination of the dynamics of situations and behavior suggests that place itself is actually a sub-category of this more inclusive notion of a perceptual field. For while situations are usually defined in terms of who is in what location, the implicit issue is actually the types of behaviors that are available for other people's scrutiny.

Goffman describes, for example, how waiters are in a "front region" when they are *in* a dining room, and in a "back region" when they are *in* the kitchen. The relationship between back and front regions in Goffman's analysis is often tied directly to physical location. Yet place is not the real issue. If there are no patrons in the dining room (before or after serving time, for example), then the dining room could clearly serve as a back region area of preparation, rehearsal, and relaxation. Conversely, if a customer walks into the kitchen, the kitchen would be transformed, for a time (and to the extent possible), into a front region. Similarly, if two waiters in the dining room surreptitiously exchange glances that mock the patrons they are serving, or if they whisper "stage directions" to each other, in passing, then they have had a back region interaction, even though they are physically "onstage."

It is not the physical setting itself that determines the nature of the interaction, but the patterns of information flow. Indeed, the discussion of the definition of the situation can be entirely removed from the issue of direct physical presence by focusing only on information access. If an intercom is mistakenly left on in the kitchen and a few patrons overhear the back region banter of their waiters, then the situational definition will

---

*Other physical variables *within* a given room—such as furniture arrangement, lighting, and temperature—also affect behavior. In a classroom, for example, freestanding chairs arranged in a circle obviously foster different types of interaction among those present than desks bolted to the floor in straight rows. Similarly, the distance between a receptionist's desk and the chair of a waiting client may determine whether the receptionist and client feel that they "have to" interact with each other.[4]

be affected even though no change in the physical place or in the physical locations of the participants has occurred. In the same way, social situations and social performances in society, in general, may be changed by the introduction of new media of communication. When literacy allows parents to spell words to each other to prevent their young and still illiterate children from understanding what is being said, the parents have established a backstage area even while they are in the presence of their children. Similarly, when two teenagers speak to each other on the telephone, they override physical distance and create a backstage area apart from the adults with whom they live.

To include mediated encounters in the study of situations, we need to abandon the notion that social situations are only encounters that occur face-to-face in set times and places. We need to look at the larger, more inclusive notion of "patterns of access to information."

"Information" is used here in a special sense to mean *social* information: all that people are capable of knowing about the behavior and actions of themselves and others. The term refers to that nebulous "stuff" we learn about each other in acts of communication. This type of information is the heart of news, gossip, political campaigns, courtships, as well as all personal and professional relationships and encounters. It is also the subtext of most primary education. Such information comes in many forms including words, gestures, vocalizations, posture, dress, and pace of activity. At base, the information of concern here deals with social behavior—our access to each other's social performances.

This definition of information differs from some of the common uses of the term to refer to "facts," in general, or to quiz show type trivia such as "What is the capitol of Nebraska?" or "Who was the first female member of Congress?" Similarly, it does not refer to objective statements about the workings of the universe that exist prior to, and apart from humanity. In this analysis, information relates to the social, not the natural order. The concern is more with "social experience" than general "knowledge."*

Another way to think about a social situation is as an "information-system," that is, as a given pattern of access to social information, a given pattern of access to the behavior of other people. This definition is not in contradiction to the definitions presented by most situationists, but it extends the study of situations beyond those interactions that occur in place-bound settings.

The notion of situations as information-systems allows for the breakdown of the arbitrary distinction often made between studies of face-to-

---

*As is discussed in Chapter 4 and the Appendix, however, knowledge—or what might be called "technical information" or "objective fact"—which supposedly exists beyond the subjectivities of social interaction, often turns out to be very much about people, behavior, and the social order. When Galileo peered into the heavens, for example, he retrieved "facts" that threatened the Catholic Church and the role structures of his day. Technical knowledge, therefore, often functions as social information in disguise.

face interaction and studies of mediated communications. The concept of information-systems suggests that physical settings and media "settings" are part of a continuum rather than a dichotomy. Places and media both foster set patterns of interaction among people, set patterns of social information flow.

Thus, while places create one type of information-system—the live encounter—there are many other types of situations created by other channels of communication. This wider view of situations as information-systems, rather than as places, is especially relevant to the study of *electronic* media because electronic media have tended to diminish the differences between live and mediated interaction. The speech and appearance of others are now accessible without being in the same physical location. The widespread use of electronic media leads to many new social situations.

New Media, New Situations

We all know from everyday experience that electronic media override the boundaries and definitions of situations supported by physical settings. When two friends speak on the telephone, for example, the situation they are "in" is only marginally related to their respective physical locations. Indeed, the telephone tends to bring two people closer to each other, in some respects, than they are to other people in their physical environments. This explains the almost jealous response on the part of some people who are in the same room with someone speaking on the phone. They often ask "Who is it?" "What's she saying?" "What's so funny?" or "Come on, get off the phone already!" Or they try to participate by throwing in remarks from the background and by attempting to elicit a response from the person on the other end of the phone. Ironically, to participate fully in the phone conversation of someone you are "with," you often have to leave that person and go to another room to pick up an extension phone.

There are many rough parallels between the flow of information through media and the flow of information in physical settings. A phone conversation, for example, is roughly analogous to the situation that occurs when four people go to a lecture or a play together and sit side by side in one row of seats. In this situation, the people on the two ends often feel isolated from each other and from conversations that take place between the two people in the center. Conversely, the two people in the center may feel that they share a small conspiracy and can say things to each other that are not fully accessible to the other two people.

In the same sense, when salespeople ring a doorbell and then quickly check the neatness of their hair or clothing, they are in a situation roughly analogous to salespeople who dial a telephone number and then clear their throats before the phone is answered. Before the door is opened and before the phone is answered, the salespeople remain backstage. The dividing line between backstage and onstage is informational, not necessarily physical.

Most interactions through media can be described using an interpersonal analogue.[5] Watching television is somewhat like watching people through a one-way mirror in a situation where the people know they are being watched by millions of people in isolated cubicles; radio listening is like listening to people through a door or wall with a similar awareness on the part of participants; and so on. The point is that while mediated and live encounters are obviously very different in some ways, they can be analyzed using similar principles. The patterns of information-flow, whether direct or mediated, help to define the situation and the notions of appropriate style and action.

When we find ourselves in a given setting we often unconsciously ask, "Who can see me, who can hear me?" "Who can I see, who can I hear?"* The answers to these questions help us decide how to behave. And although these questions were once fully answered by an assessment of the physical environment, they now require an evaluation of the media environment as well.

As "information-systems" rather than physical settings, a society's set of social situations can be modified without building or removing walls and corridors and without changing customs and laws concerning access to places. The introduction and widespread use of a new medium of communication may restructure a broad range of situations and require new sets of social performances.

Interaction settings themselves, of course, are not the only source of situational definitions. The shared meanings of situations develop over time and through social traditions. Religious ritual, social custom, and legal codes all contribute to the stock of situational definitions, and they guide people's use of available settings. A change in settings alone, therefore, will not bring about immediate or complete change. Nevertheless, while the social "scripts" develop through many sources, appropriate "stages" are necessary for the social dramas to be performed. If the settings for situations merge, divide, or disappear, then it will be impossible to maintain the old definitions of the situations.

Perhaps one of the reasons that theorists of situations and roles have tended to view social situations as relatively stable is that it is extremely rare for there to be a sudden widespread change in walls, doors, the layout of a city, or in other architectural and geographical structures. But the change in situations and behaviors that occurs when doors are opened or closed and when walls are constructed or removed is paralleled in our

---

*In live settings, we also often ask "Who can touch or hurt me?" Indeed, one of the things that distinguishes mediated communication from live communication is the lack of risk of physical harm or involvement. The aggressive or erotic style of some telephone and CB radio conversations may be attributable to the odd mixture of intimacy and distance afforded by these media.

times by the flick of a microphone switch, the turning on of a television set, or the answering of a telephone.

To understand more fully the potential impact of electronic media on behavior, we need to look more closely at the relationship between behavior and "situation segregation" with an eye toward seeing what happens to behavior when situational boundaries move.

New Situations, New Behavior

As you sit reading this book, there are probably people somewhere who could very much use your help or advice. An elderly relative may need assistance changing a light bulb. A depressed friend might be cheered to hear your voice. If you are a trained professional, there are, no doubt, many people in dire need of your professional skills. If any one of these people was with you in the *same room*, you would probably put this book down and interact with them. Yet by being in a place *away* from the people and situations in which your help is needed, you are more easily able to behave in a manner that might be considered inappropriate, rude, or hostile if the people needing your help were in the same space with you.*

Truly different behaviors require truly distinct situations. This principle explains why restaurant managers often find it difficult to "dine out" in their own restaurants. For even if they are technically "off duty," they are too aware of, and concerned about, possible problems. Similarly, hospital interns who want to read or eat while off duty usually do not do so in the corner of the hospital emergency room. When in the same space with a bleeding patient, it is difficult for doctors to say, and for patients to hear, "Sorry, I can't help you, I'm off duty." In general, when people are "on their own time," they usually try to be "in their own space" as well.

The ability to accept each other in terms of specific roles in a given situation often depends on our lack of awareness of each other in *other* situations. A man, for example, would be very uncomfortable to discover that the marriage counselor he and his wife have made an appointment to see is one of his former wives. Similarly, a young woman may be quite hesitant to undress in front of a doctor whom she recognizes as a boy who had a crush on her in high school. The lack of sufficient insulation between a new and an old situation in each of these examples makes it difficult to accept the new definition as the "real" one. For these reasons, there is often mutual embarrassment when people who know each other in one situation run into each other in other situations. What does one say to one's gynecologist at a cocktail party?

It is very difficult to respond to one situation as if it were another. Parents' exhortations that a child must finish all the food on a plate "because

---

*Ironically, however, the longer and better we know people, the more easily we are able to ignore them even when they are in the same space with us. As we will see later, this may be an analogy for the long-term effects of our electronically heightened awareness of national and international problems and issues.

children are starving in Africa" are usually ineffective because so rarely are there any starving African children peering through the window. Separation of situations allows for separation of behaviors. It is through the separation of situations that even dedicated doctors and teachers are able to rest and be merry in certain times and places—even though somewhere *else* there are surely patients dying for lack of care and children condemned to ignorance.

For every moment of our lives, there are things happening someplace that would upset us, that would involve us, that would drain our energies and engage our feelings. There are more things that—if present and in our view—we would feel compelled to respond to or do something about than could possibly fit into the sane experience of a single lifetime. Situation segregation, however, acts as a psycho-social shock absorber. By selectively exposing ourselves to events and other people, we control the flow of our actions and emotions. Compassion, empathy, and even ethics may be much more situationally bound than we often care to think.[6]

But what would happen to our social behavior if there was a sudden widespread change in our society's overall pattern of situations? Unfortunately, most of those who have studied situations have little to say on the subject. For Goffman and many other situationists, situations and their matching roles are relatively stable. The boundaries of situations sometimes break down, but the disruptions are generally seen as unusual and temporary. Someone may say or do something inappropriate, inconsistent behavior or information may "leak" into one situation from another situation (causing confusion and embarrassment), or two distinct situations may temporarily merge—but ultimately, the old definitions are reasserted.[7]

Young children, for example, may wake up and emerge from their bedrooms into the midst of a party given by their parents, thereby causing some embarrassment on the part of those adults who may feel they have been overheard or observed saying or doing things not usually said or done in front of children. Or a young executive may be embarrassed when her parents come to see her office and insist on telling everyone they meet about some of the "cute" things she used to do as a child. But once the children go back to bed and once the executive's parents leave the office, the old definitions generally regain their hold.

Even in extreme cases, where individual performers are disgraced and permanently lose credibility, similar situations and similar performances continue unchanged. Thus, when a supposedly distinguished professor appears at a national conference too drunk to deliver a keynote address, conferences and professors, in general, nevertheless remain largely untouched. Similarly, unprofessional remarks or behaviors on the part of a few individual executives, doctors, or judges do not necessarily undermine the basic social definitions of corporations, hospitals, and courtrooms.

What has interested many situationists up to this time is how the definitions of situations are protected from such disruptions and how those situations that are disrupted are repaired. What we cannot tell from such analyses is what happens to behavior when changes in situations are relatively *permanent*—and this is precisely the type of information we need to know if we are to study the behavioral impact of new media by examining their effects on the boundaries of situations.

To explore the effects of media on behavior, we need to convert the static and descriptive model of behavior in situations into a variable and predictive one. We need to come up with some general principles that allow us to describe the *dynamics* of situations and behavior. The remainder of the chapter develops a few such principles: the importance of "situation pattern" as opposed to "behavior sum," the general need for a single definition of a situation, the rise of "deep back," "forefront," and "middle region" behavior as situations divide or merge, and the interdependency of all an individual's onstage and backstage performances.

Variable Situation Pattern

Social reality does not exist in the *sum* of people's behaviors, but in the overall *pattern* of situated behaviors. Therefore, when the dividing line between two distinct situations is moved or removed, social reality will change. Contrary to what much of the situational literature often seems to imply, the pattern of situation segregation and integration is a variable rather than a static aspect of an individual's or a society's existence, and there are potentially infinite degrees and patterns of situation overlap. Patterns of situation segregation and integration can be modified by individual life decisions, by chance, and by other forces, including a society's media use.

While we usually tend to think of situations in terms of what and who is in them, situations are also defined by what and who is outside of them. Behavior in an environment is shaped by the patterns of access to and restriction from the social information available in that environment. The way male high school students speak in a locker room, for example, is determined not only by the presence of other male students, but also by the absence of female students, parents, teachers, and principals.

A key factor in determining the extent to which a situation is isolated from other situations is the nature of the *boundary* line that divides the situation from other situations. The membranes around social situations affect behavior not only because they often fully include and exclude participants, but also because they can partially include and exclude participants. A person may be visually excluded from a situation by a wall, yet aurally included by the thinness of the visual barrier. In the same way, media may affect the definition of situations by bypassing traditional physical restrictions on information flow. Richard Nixon, for example, found that a tape recorder in the Oval Office led to his private "locker room" conversations being evaluated as public pronouncements.

By changing the boundaries of social situations, electronic media do not simply give us quicker or more thorough access to events and behaviors. They give us, instead, new events and new behaviors.

McLuhan writes, for example, that "Jack Ruby shot Lee Oswald while tightly surrounded by guards who were paralyzed by television cameras."[8] Although McLuhan does not elaborate, perhaps he means that the guards could not respond appropriately to the immediate situation because the television cameras blurred the guards' role function and the identity of their "audience." Were they performing their roles for those present or for those watching television? Were they there to intimidate the crowds and respond quickly to physical disorder? Or were they there as mute and rigid symbols of authority for the television collage?

The example is extreme, but it is indicative of the situations faced by many Americans as they find that they are acting in new arenas, with new audiences, and that they have access to others and others have access to them in new and confounding ways. And these changes are affecting everyone from Watts to the White House.

When Black Power advocate Stokely Carmichael found himself attracting media attention in the late 1960s, for example, his access to a larger social platform turned out to be a curse rather than a blessing. In the shared arenas of television and radio, he found himself facing at least two distinct audiences simultaneously: his primary audience of blacks, and an "eavesdropping" audience of whites. In personal (unmediated) appearances, he had been able to present two completely different talks on Black Power to black and white audiences, respectively. But in the combined forums of electronic media, he had to decide whether to use a white or black rhetorical style and text. If he used a white style, he would alienate his primary audience and defeat his goals of giving blacks a new sense of pride and self-respect. Yet if he used a black rhetorical style, he would alienate whites, including many liberals who supported integration. With no clear solution, and unable to devise a composite genre, Carmichael decided to use a black style in his mediated speeches. While he sparked the fire of his primary audience, he also filled his secondary audience with hatred and fear and brought on the wrath of the white power structure.[9]

Similarly, when a reporter meets with the President and his wife before television cameras, how should the President and First Lady behave? Is this encounter an intimate social meeting among three people or is it a public performance before the nation? The answer is that it is both, and, therefore, that it is neither. The President cannot act as if he and his wife are totally alone with the reporter, nor can he act as if he is addressing a crowd at Gettysburg. To the extent that actions are shaped to fit particular social settings, this new setting leads to new actions and new social meanings. In this sense, we have not only a different situation, but also a different President, and—in the long run—a different presidency.

But what exactly happens to the definition of old situations when the patterns of situations change? When situations merge or divide for extended periods of time, do we get completely new behavior patterns or simply a sum or fraction of old ones? Perhaps we get no significant change at all. Or perhaps we simply get confusion. One key to the answers to these questions is our apparent need for a *single* definition for most social situations.

The Need for a Single Definition

As described in Chapter 2, when people are asked to come to a party, meeting, or other social gathering, they want to know whether the occasion is joyous or solemn, casual or formal, personal or professional and whether the interaction will be between superiors and inferiors or among equals. But this is not merely a matter of curiosity. The "definition of the situation" helps to determine participants' dress, posture, speech pattern and style, energy level, mood, and so forth. Even though the situational definition is often out of the participants' awareness, it serves as the glue that binds many elements of an interaction together. Further, because each participant must dress, speak, and behave in one generally consistent pattern, there seems to be a need and a demand for a *single* primary definition of each social situation.

The need for a single primary definition for most situations helps us begin to understand what usually happens when situations merge or divide. When two situations merge, we rarely get a simple combination of situations. Instead, a single new situation with a single new set of rules and roles often evolves. When two couples pair up to double-date, for example, the situation that emerges is not the sum of the two separate dates, but a new, third situation. Indeed, a common pattern of interaction on a double-date involves one conversation between the two males and another conversation between the two females. Similarly, when a romantic couple move in together, they do not get their romantic interactions *plus* the day-to-day necessities of life. Instead, they get a whole new interactive system; both their lovemaking and their billpaying habits are transformed.

There is a big difference between the effects of short-term and long-term mergers of situations. A sudden, temporary merger of very distinct situations causes a disruption in behavior. Without a clear definition for the situation, everyone may be embarrassed, confused, and/or angry. If, for example, someone at a party opens the door of a bathroom to find someone already there who has forgotten to lock the door, there is likely to be a moment of great embarrassment for both people.

While temporary breakdowns lead only to confusion and disruption, however, permanent or long-term breakdowns lead to the birth of new behavior patterns. When people routinely perform bodily functions in the same physical place, for example, a new, stable definition of the situation must arise. This is what happened to the Peruvian soccer team whose plane crashed in the Andes. The book *Alive*, which details their ordeal, describes the conversations that they had concerning each other's bowel movements.[10] Similar situations occur among longtime roommates or couples who live together for many years.

There is a certain "cultural logic" to the nature of the merger of situations. Indeed, the new definition of a combined situation sometimes makes so much "sense" that we often do not see that the former situations no longer exist and that a third situation has arisen. Yet the new situation is usually one where many behaviors can take place that could not have taken place in the two distinct situations and vice versa. An employer who marries an employee, for example, will find that just as there are newly permissible behaviors, so are there many requests that can no longer be made and behaviors that are no longer appropriate. The new relationship is neither "husband and wife" nor "boss and worker."*

All separate relationships among relatives, friends, and business associates may include complaints and jokes about absent members; that is, they involve behavior that would be inappropriate or rude when all are present. These same principles apply to the situation mergers and divisions that are created by media.

Although we often say that we want people to be "consistent," what we often mean by this is that they should be "situationally consistent." That is, we generally demand consistency of treatment from others *within* a situation, but we are less concerned with consistency of treatment *across* situations. Shoppers, for example, will tolerate paying more for an item one day than the next. They will even tolerate paying different prices for the same item on the same day in different stores. But they will generally not tolerate paying a higher price than other people in the same store at the same time and place. Similarly, college students generally accept the fact that professors modify course requirements from semester to semester, but there would be an uproar of protest if a professor established different requirements for different students in the same class. Changes in

---

*Because mergers of situations destroy old definitions, there are many implicit and explicit rules about keeping situations separate. Psychiatrists are not supposed to become emotionally or sexually involved with their patients. The military strongly condemns "fraternization"—a friendly or romantic relationship between superiors and subordinates. Similarly, teachers are not supposed to date their students. There are many vulgar sayings about how unwise it is for business associates to become romantically involved. For whether the personal relationships prosper or end poorly, it becomes difficult, if not impossible, to maintain the old business relationships. Besides the moral problems with some role mergers, the relationships are confusing, and the motives of the parties involved are often ambiguous. Indeed, one explanation for the incest taboo is that it allows for a very special type of unambiguous relationship—a loving, caring, and nurturing bond that is not sexual.[11] Of course, people often break the implicit and explicit rules. As a result of past and present personal relationships, for example, many workplaces are teeming with animosities, and there often exists a whole network of unwritten rules and behavior patterns that do not appear on organizational charts.

the boundaries of situations, therefore, can change people's perceptions of equality and fairness and lead to social unrest. As discussed later, changes in situation boundaries as a result of changes in media may have much to do with the recent rise of feminist and minority consciousness.

In general, it can be argued that: (1) *behavior patterns divide into as many single definitions as there are distinct settings,* and (2) *when two or more settings merge, their distinct definitions merge into one new definition.*

These principles suggest that the dynamics of social systems are, in one sense at least, very similar to the dynamics of physical systems. Both social and physical systems can divide into as many distinct states as there are distinct systems, and yet merged systems tend to blend into a relatively consistent state. It is possible, for example, to keep two separate, but adjacent rooms at vastly different temperatures, let us say forty degrees and four degrees. If the wall between the two rooms is removed, however, then the entire joined space will, after a short while, reach a relatively consistent temperature. The temperature, however, would not be forty four degrees (the *sum* of the two distinct temperatures), but some temperature in between. In the same way, people can develop distinct behavior patterns in two distinct situations, but if the two situations merge, then they often get one new, synthesized definition. The physical analogy can be extended even further. For just as there is some variation in temperature from the top to bottom of a room and from the center to the edges, so are there different degrees of commitment to the definition of a social situation. At a wedding, for example, there will be people who are deeply involved in the ritual and there will be those who are less involved and have their thoughts and emotions in other places.

"Middle," "Deep Back," and "Forefront" Region Behavior

Given the idea that the merging of previously distinct situations leads to a new single situation, is there any way to describe the new situation in relation to the old? What is the relationship between the old behaviors and the new behaviors?

While Goffman's model of back and front region behaviors describes a static set of stages and is limited to face-to-face interaction, the principles implicit in it can be adapted to describe the changes in situations and behaviors brought about by new media. Implicit in the region model is the interdependence of back and front regions. Individuals' onstage performances depend on the existence of a backstage area, isolated from the audience, where performers can learn their roles, rehearse them, discuss strategies with teammates, or simply relax or lapse into inexpressiveness. Thus, if performers lose the ability to keep their back region behavior separate from their front region behavior, they not only lose aspects of their privacy, they also lose the ability to play certain parts of their front region roles. When actors have no place to rehearse lines in private, they cannot build to a performance that excites and moves the audience. People who live together, for example, often help each other rehearse for onstage roles on *other* social stages, but they often have little private space and time to rehearse for and impress each other.

This either/or conception of the dramatic aspects of social performance—having a backstage area or not having one—can be extended into a continuous and variable model of the interplay of onstage and backstage styles. In general, *whatever aspects of the rehearsal become visible to the audience must be integrated into the show itself; whatever backstage time and space remain hidden can still be used to perfect the performance.* When the dividing line between onstage and backstage behaviors moves in either direction, the nature of the drama changes accordingly. The more rehearsal space that is lost, the more the onstage drama comes to resemble an extemporaneous backstage rehearsal; when the backstage area is increased in size, then the onstage behavior can become even more formal.

Using the concepts of back and front region as a base, the new behavior that arises out of merging situations could be called "middle region" behavior. Conversely, the two new sets of behaviors that result from the division of situations could be called "deep back region" behavior and "forefront region" behavior. Middle region behavior develops when audience members gain a "sidestage" view. That is, they see parts of the traditional backstage area along with parts of the traditional onstage area; they see the performer move from backstage to onstage to backstage. To adapt, the competent performer adjusts his or her social role so that it is consistent with the new information available to the audience. A middle region, or sidestage, behavior pattern contains elements of both the former onstage and offstage behaviors but lacks their extremes. "Deep back" and "forefront" region behavior develop when performers gain increased isolation from their audience. The new separation of situations allows for both a coarser backstage style and a more pristine onstage performance.

In middle region behaviors, the extremes of the former front region are lost because performers no longer have the necessary backstage time and space; the control over rehearsals and relaxations that supported the old front region role is weakened. The new behaviors also often lack the extremes of the former backstage behavior because the new middle region dramas are public (that is, performed before an "audience") and, therefore, performers adapt as much as possible to the presence of the audience, but continue to hide whatever can still be hidden.

If children come to an adult party, for example, conversations about death, sex, and money may stop until the children leave. If the children stay for a long time, however, some new compromise style of behavior is likely to arise where "adult" topics are discussed in front of the children, but with neither the explicitness characteristic of an adult-adult party nor the innocence once deemed appropriate for an adult-children party. Indeed, the longer the adults and children stay together, the more the children will see the childish side of adulthood, and the more the children will be exposed to and talk about adult topics. As we will see later, this serves as an analogy for what happens to child and adult roles as electronic media begin to merge child and adult information-systems.

In one sense, middle region behaviors are simply *new* front region behaviors. But if we think of them merely as front region behaviors, we lose the ability to see the nature and direction of the behavioral change. By describing the new behaviors as "middle region" or "sidestage," we are able to compare the new behaviors to the old behaviors, and we can observe the synthetic nature of the new drama. Further, the idea of middle region behaviors explains the process that brings about the new public style: a shift in the dividing line between traditional back and front region behaviors.

The middle region style seems to have a "back region bias." This bias is partly due to the fact that the back regions of our lives encompass things that cannot disappear: sleeping, eating, elimination of bodily wastes, sexual activity, depressions, anxieties, and doubts. Front region behavior, in contrast, is more flexible and variable. While we can each make up a very different front region style, back regions tend to involve many of the things we all have in common. Another reason the back region aspects of middle region behavior are most evident is that it is always easier to see what has newly arrived as opposed to what has recently disappeared. The first time that we spend the night at a new friend's house, for example, we are more likely to notice that the friend snores or burps than we are likely to notice the loss of some of the more formal aspects of the friend's speaking style.

The back region bias of middle region behavior is even more evident over time. For a brief period, a revealed back region can be converted into a relatively traditional front region performance. The less performers can control and restrict others' access to themselves, however, the more back region behavior must come to light. A normally sloppy teenager, for example, may clean his room when his aunt comes to dinner on Easter Sunday. But if Aunt Mary stays for six months, she will undoubtedly witness a different drama. Similarly, televised tours of the White House that reveal previously unseen rooms and meetings can, for a time, be changed into front region dramas (as, for example, was Eisenhower's scripted and televised "cabinet meeting."[12]) Yet, when television reveals even one full day of "live" proceedings, the performance must change. Thus, in a television special on the Carter White House, the audience heard Jimmy Carter tell President Anwar Sadat of Egypt that they were going into a long meeting and that Sadat might want to go to the bathroom first. The longer and more closely people are observed, either in person or by camera and microphone, the more their behavior is stripped of its social symbols and posturing.

When a situation divides into two or more distinct regions, exactly the opposite process takes place: behavior in each sphere becomes more specific and more extreme. When children move out of their parents' homes, for example, the privacy of their own residence offers both the parents and the children the possibility of developing more idiosyncratic private styles of behavior, as well as revised, "cleaner" fronts for each other. Similarly, the more privacy political leaders can maintain, the sharper the potential contrast between an informal backstage style and a front of "distinguished leader." When the dominant media in a society foster many distinct information-systems, therefore, they will also tend to support forefront and deep backstage behavior styles.

One of the reasons that the dynamics of region behavior and the effects of media on them are largely invisible in everyday interactions is that people very quickly adapt to the new definitions of situations. Generally, role performers control whatever backstage information can be controlled. But if damaging backstage information escapes into a front region, it is often integrated into the performance. If a dinner guest arrives earlier than expected, for example, and the guest witnesses an argument between the hosts and their children as well as the last minute attempts to clean the house and prepare the dinner food, the hosts will find it impossible to play the same front region role they would have played if the guest had come on time. As a result, middle region comments are likely to be made about "raising kids these days" or the impossibility of keeping a large house clean. Since the idea that there is no calculated "performance" is itself part of many social performances, it is important that audience members not become too aware of attempts to hide back region information.

The process through which "deeper" back region and more "forward" front region behaviors develop is even more invisible to audiences than the development of "middle region" behaviors—for, by definition, that which can no longer be seen is not there for scrutiny. When newly private situations develop, people usually give little thought to the effects of the structural change; instead, the new behaviors are often attributed to changes in personality or motivation. When young adults "go away" to college, their family and neighbors may begin to see them as "more mature." Similarly, national politicians who temporarily retire to the "privacy" of local politics may later be able to re-enter the national arena appearing more "presidential."

In similar ways, significant and widespread changes may occur in patterns of social interaction as a result of the use of new media of communication without people being fully aware of the degree or nature of the changes. In each given interaction, individuals will feel they are merely adapting to the demands of the particular situation they find themselves in. People may wonder why behavior patterns seem to have changed (or, more likely, why "people" have changed), and be unaware of the fact that the changes are related to a shifting line between backstage and onstage settings.

The Interdependence of All Behavioral Systems

The back region/front region model is usually used to analyze behavior in a single setting such as a restaurant or hospital. Once we go beyond a single setting, it is difficult to apply the model literally. The front/back distinction is too simple. What, for example, is the relationship among several different front region performances on the part of the same individual?

The dramaturgical model can be adapted even further, however, to consider the interdependency of *all* performances and behavioral settings. An individual's front region behavior in one role is, after all, an indirect back region to other roles. In a sense, each front region performance depends on a multiplicity of front and back regions. The ability of a person to perform well as a trial lawyer, for example, not only depends on good courtroom performance and a backstage area to prepare briefs and discuss strategies with colleagues, but also on the past and present ability to perform relatively well (and inconspicuously) in other roles such as student, taxpayer, parent, spouse, and so on. None of these roles may be as clearly and directly related to courtroom style as a strategy meeting with colleagues, but a performance as a lawyer still depends on these other roles, and also on the performance of them in segregation from the role of lawyer. A lawyer's credibility in the eyes of a judge and jurors may be undermined by information about the lawyer's driving habits, marital relationship, and parenting style.

Because most of us attempt to present ourselves as relatively consistent personalities for each one of our audiences, any information that an audience has about our behavior from other situations has to be taken into account when we execute a given performance.* The concept of "middle region" behavior, therefore, can be extended beyond the merger of the backstage and onstage behaviors for a single role. Middle region behavior can refer to the behavior that results from the merger of any two or more previously distinct situations. Conversely, "deep back region" and "forefront region" behaviors develop whenever any situation divides into two or more distinct situations, or whenever there is an increase in the distance between situations. Middle region behaviors result from the new overlapping of situations and audiences, and deep back region and forefront region behaviors result from the new possibility of "purer" or more extreme versions of behavior matched to more specialized and isolated contexts.

In general, *the more distance there is between two or more situations, the more an individual's behavior can vary from one situation to the next.* Con-

---

*One exception to the desire for consistency among all available information is in a relationship of true intimacy, where two people accept the variations in the other's behavior as easily as they accept the variations in their own. Ironically, although the language of romance suggests that love makes "two people into one," perhaps it is really that love allows one person to be many people—in at least one intimate social sphere.

versely, *the less distance there is between situations, the more similar the behaviors in them.*

Take, for example, the distinction between the student role and the teacher role. A person cannot be both a docile student and a strict teacher at the same time. Yet often the same person is asked to play both these roles. If a very competent college student, John, is asked by Ms. Smith, the teacher, to lead a class discussion while the teacher attends a professional conference, John must develop a new, synthetic role. This "student/teacher" must now play a role that is neither the role he played as student among his peers, nor the role played by the "real" teacher. For if John played only his old student role while the teacher was away, he would have little or no effect on the class, and if he played a typical "real" teacher, he would probably be mocked or resented by his classmates who know too much about him to accept him in that role. (Here, ironically, his well-performed front region student role becomes potentially damaging back region behavior when he tries to play "teacher.")

This situation can be varied to illustrate how the degree of distance between situations affects behavior. If Ms. Smith asks John to take over a different class in the same school, John can now play the role of teacher somewhat more fully. And if Ms. Smith herself is a student for an advanced degree in a different school, then the distinctions between Ms. Smith's teacher role and her student role can be very great. The distance between situations contributes to the degree of separation in behavioral style. Such "distance" is determined by both time and space. All teachers, for example, were once students, but temporal insulation allows for these roles to be very different.

Such changes in face-to-face situations and behavior can be viewed as analogies for the ways in which new media may help bring about social change by merging or dividing social situations. New media that tend to divide existing social information-systems will allow individuals to develop both "deeper" backstage and more "forward" onstage behavior styles; new media that tend to merge existing information-systems will lead to more "sidestage," or "middle region," behaviors.

We remain one step away from a basic framework for studying the potential effects of media change on everyday social behavior. We need to look beyond changes in individuals' behaviors in specific settings and consider how and why social roles, in general, will change when there is widespread and systematic change in all, or most, of a society's situations.

4

Why Roles Change
When Media Change

Patterns of information flow are a constitutive element of social status. People of the same status in a society generally have access to similar situations, or information-systems. People of different social statuses usually have access to different situations. Children, for example, have traditionally been restricted from access to certain types of situations and the information available in them. Similarly, men and women have traditionally been segregated into different social spheres. The widespread rearrangement of social settings as a result of the use of new media (or other factors such as industrialization, war, or natural disaster), therefore, should have an effect not only on many individuals' behaviors, but also on the behaviors of whole categories of people. By changing the types of situations to which each social category has access, new media may change our conceptions of a wide range of social roles.

It would, of course, be impossible to discuss every social role in a single chapter. Therefore, I analyze three broad *categories* of roles: roles of affiliation or "being" (group identity), roles of transition or "becoming" (socialization), and roles of authority (hierarchy).

In everyday life, these three types of roles overlap. Most individuals function in all three categories at once: identified with a number of groups, at various stages of socialization into new roles, and at some particular rank or ranks within one or more hierarchies. Further, the categories themselves overlap and a specific role may not fit neatly into a single slot. Being a "rookie," for example, is primarily a function of socialization, but it also involves issues of group identity and hierarchy. Being a member of an elite class has elements of both hierarchy and group identity.

Although the role categories are interrelated, each has its special characteristics. Unlike the other categories, group identity allows for "separate but equal" statuses, where members of different groups may stand in no particular hierarchal or developmental relationship. Socialization is unique among the three categories in that it involves the process of "becoming," that is, the transition from role to role. Unlike members of separate groups (doctors vs. lawyers, for example), a child is expected to develop into an adult, a medical student is expected to become a doctor. And in contrast to both group identity and socialization, hierarchal roles encompass a "separate and unequal" dimension.

These three categories of roles were not chosen because they are mutually exclusive, but rather because, in combination, they are socially inclusive; that is, taken together, they cover virtually every facet of every social role. Realignments in group identities, socialization stages, and ranks of hierarchy would change the entire structure of social life.*

This chapter presents a relatively traditional view of social roles with one very important variation: It translates the features of each type of role into terms compatible with the common denominator concept discussed in the last chapter—information-systems. While roles are often analyzed simply as static sets of "appropriate" or "expected" behaviors, this chapter describes roles in relation to what people know and experience compared to other people. Each role category—affiliation, transition, authority—is discussed in terms of three variables: relative access to social information, backstage/onstage distinctions, and access to physical locations. By showing how all three types of roles rest on these situational variables, I attempt to show how the structure of a society's social roles is susceptible to change as a result of shifts in the use of media of communication. This chapter does not present a detailed analysis of the effects of electronic media on social roles. That is left for later chapters. The major purposes here are to outline the "mechanism," or process, through which changes in media may change social behavior and to indicate the general direction in which roles will change when media change.

Group Identity: Shared but Secret Information

Shared but secret behavior will cement any group into a conspiracy.— Germaine Greer[1]

"Our" Experience vs. "Their" Experience

Many adventure, spy, and monster movies are based on a common theme. An unacquainted man and woman are thrust into a situation of extreme danger. At first, they do not especially care for each other; indeed, sometimes they actively dislike each other. But in the midst of their terrifying fight to survive, to recruit the help of disbelieving or uncar-

---

*The concepts of role, status, group identity, socialization, and hierarchy are discussed further in the Appendix.

ing outsiders, or in their battle to destroy some social menace, they fall in love and make a permanent commitment to each other.

This familiar scenario may be mythic in its dimensions and details, but it nevertheless highlights a significant element in all human associations and groupings: the need for shared yet special experience.

A group is held together by what is special about it, and this "specialness" consists of information that members have in common with each other and do not share with members of other groups. Further, while we often think of groups in terms of people who at least occasionally meet together in the same time and place, the same informational factors play a part in the individual's sense of identification with groups, or social categories, that never meet as a whole. Veterans of the Vietnam War, for example, share the experience of having been soldiers in an unpopular war. This experience unites them and simultaneously separates them from other people.

Unfortunately, group identity always involves the notion of "otherness" concerning those not in the group, those who do not share the same situations. For a group to be an "us," there must also be a "them." Simone de Beauvoir expresses the ease and frequency with which such including/ excluding group feelings arise. "If three travelers chance to occupy the same compartment, that is enough to make vaguely hostile 'others' out of all the rest of the passengers on the train."[2]

Any common experience, information, or role that separates two or more people from others will give them a sense of common identity. Yet because social experience, information, and roles are situation-bound, group identities will change with variations in situations or with a shift in participants' perspectives concerning "insiders" and "outsiders." Two New Yorkers who meet in Georgia may feel an immediate bond that unites them "against" Georgians. At the same time, however, a Georgian and a New Yorker who meet in Italy may feel a similar connection with each other because they are both American. In both instances, conversations may dwell on chauvinistic group topics: the praising of "home" and the mocking of "the foreigners." Similarly, two black people who are arguing with each other may suddenly feel united when a white passerby calls out a racial slur. Conversely, a once small and unified group may divide into factions after an influx of many new members.

Individuals often have overlapping group identities. Doctors, for example, may see themselves as being sharply distinguished from nurses, and yet in relation to a patient on an operating table, both doctors and nurses may feel part of a single "operating team." Members of the Navy, Army, and Air Force compete among themselves but have a sense of unity in relation to civilians. Even soldiers in combat may, at times, experience a bond with "the enemy" resulting from their similar roles relative to others.[3] Similar cross-team bonds may also occur among lawyers on opposing sides of a case, secretaries for competing firms, or children of feuding families.

Neither the complexity of the overlapping of groups nor the suddenness and simplicity with which temporary associations and groupings can arise makes the existence of such groups any less real or significant. In weaving our way through the fabric of social interactions, we find ourselves bound in multiple and nonlinear ties with others. Yet there is a similarity in all "groupings" in terms of the process that binds them together and simultaneously sets them apart. The nature of ties and associations—both shallow and deep—can be related to access to similar situations and experience in contrast to other people.

Therefore, while we tend to think of our group affiliations simply in terms of "who" we are, our sense of identity is also shaped by where we are and who is "with" us. A change in the structure of situations—as a result of changes in media or other factors—will change people's sense of "us" and "them." An important issue to consider in predicting the effects of new media on group identities is how the new medium alters "who shares social information with whom." As social information-systems merge or divide, so will group identities.*

Backstage Teaming

The shared experience that is the basis of group cohesiveness can also be related to the distinctions between backstage and onstage behaviors. Members of the same group tend to share the same roles or to foster the same performance. The power of a shared backstage can be seen even in quickly formed groups. Thus, passengers in a train compartment—to adapt de Beauvoir's example—may be from different countries and professions, and yet they share the role of "passengers in Number Seven." And these passengers are likely to find themselves presenting a unified front if they are accused of being too noisy or if a drunken man tries to enter their compartment after the passengers have already spent most of a trip together.

The passengers become a "team," in Goffman's sense. Members of a team are distinguished from members of the audience by their perspective

---

*Charles Horton Cooley's notion of the "looking glass self" and George Herbert Mead's concept of the "generalized other" help to explain the power of information access and its relationship to personal identity. Individuals, according to these two thinkers, develop social selves as they incorporate the views of others and begin to judge themselves as others would judge them.[4] The values and standards of *those we are exposed to*, therefore, have a great impact on our perceptions of self. For this reason, the influence of a primary group is inversely related to the amount of access an individual has to competing points of reference. "Strangers" and "outsiders" are often viewed as threats by many groups because they are potential "significant others" from whose perspective group members may start to view and judge themselves differently. (Similarly, parents are often very concerned over a child's choice of friends.) Books, movies, and electronic media also provide information about alternative role behaviors which compete with information learned in face-to-face interactions at home, church, or school. The power of competing social perspectives is so great that even victims of lengthy kidnappings may, after a time, come to judge themselves from the perspectives of their kidnappers.[5]

on the situation and by the amount of information they have concerning the performance.[6] Team members know more about the performance than audience members because they have access to both backstage and onstage behaviors. Team members tend to foster each other's performances and to work as a unit to protect the projected definition of the situation. Very strong team bonds develop among most people who live or work together for long periods of time.

The notion of "team" can be extended and used as an analogue for all groups, even those where members do not share the same specific performance or backstage. All priests, for example, tend to have roughly similar types of information about their religion and their roles even though they do not practice in the same parish. Indeed, all members of the clergy—regardless of religion—tend to share similar staging contingencies, problems, and possibilities.

Just as a shared backstage allows a group or team to act together or to act in a similar fashion, so do a group's onstage actions require that members of other groups or of the "audience" *not* have access to the group's backstage rehearsals and relaxations. Complementary roles always depend on restricted access to backstage situations and the information available in them. If two people have access to the same staging information, it is much more difficult for them to enact very different roles for each other. A traditional lawyer/client relationship, for example, depends on different group identities for the client and the lawyer. A teacher/student relationship also depends on such distinctions. A lawyer, therefore, often makes a "poor" client for another lawyer. He or she knows too much about the staging of the lawyer role to go through the normal ritual. Similarly, when an experienced teacher takes a course taught by another teacher, both may be uncomfortable.

Since a clear sense of "us" depends on the sharing of each other's backstage behavior, and because a clear sense of "them" depends on not having access to other groups' backstage behaviors, a change in media may rearrange a society's group identities by offering new ways of revealing or hiding the backstage behaviors of many groups.

"Our" Place vs. "Their" Place

Because of the traditional relationship between places and situations, group identities have usually been closely linked to shared but special access to physical locations. Individuals gain similar experiences by being "isolated together" in the same or similar places. The relationship between group identity and physical location explains the otherwise confusing statement: "I'm so glad *we* are finally *alone*."

The awesome power of the shared but special experience that comes from long-term sharing of the same environment is hinted at in brief gatherings at professional conferences, summer camps, and "retreats." These situations arbitrarily bring people together suddenly and then disperse them after a short period of time, yet they usually work very successfully to pull strangers into a single group and, simultaneously, to separate them from the outside world.

The relationship between group identity and group territory is tied to the traditional relationship between place and information access. To be "in" a group—to share its experience and information—one once had to be in the proper place. By being isolated together in the same or similar places, members of groups have generally lived in their own informational worlds. The traditional information characteristics of physical places have insulated participants and created the type of shared but special information-systems that unite group members and separate them from "outsiders." Access to a group's territory was once the primary means of incorporation into the group.

Another way to predict the effects of a new medium on group identities, therefore, is to examine the ways in which the medium supports or undermines the traditional relationship between distinct physical locations and isolated information-systems. By severing the traditional link between physical location and social situation, for example, electronic media may begin to blur previously distinct group identities by allowing people to "escape" informationally from place-defined groups and by permitting outsiders to "invade" many groups' territories without ever entering them.

Role Transitions: Controlled Access to Group Information

> *Every person in his first trip to a foreign country, where he knows neither the people nor the language, experiences childhood.*—Shulamith Firestone[7]

We'll Tell You When You're Older

Socialization is the process of "becoming," the transition from one role to the next. Socialization, therefore, is closely related to the information characteristics of group identity discussed above. In a sense, the goal of any socialization process is to acquire the "shared but special" information of the reference group.[8]

The individual being socialized into a group is excluded from the full information complex of the group. A child, for example, is excluded from many of the "secrets" of adult life, including the full definitions of adult situations. What distinguishes the individual being socialized into a group from a complete outsider (i.e., a member of a different group), however, is that the exclusion from group secrets is not permanent or even absolute. The individual being socialized *is* given access to the information of the group, but the access is usually gradual and often carefully timed and sequenced.

Although most attention to socialization focuses on the child, socialization continues throughout life. All socialization processes—bachelor to husband, woman to mother, immigrant to citizen, sorority pledge to sorority member, student to graduate, and so forth—involve the exposure of the individual to new situations and new information. The exposure to a group's set of situations slowly brings the individual into the group. Simultaneously, socialization involves the *regulation* of the amount and speed of exposure to the group's information. In reference to any particular group, therefore, roles of socialization are distinct from both the roles of outsiders (members of other groups) and the roles of bona fide members of the group. A company's sales trainees, for example, are treated more like insiders than are customers or salespeople from another firm, but they are not given many important secrets until they become full-time (and possibly long-term) employees.

The pattern of providing gradual access to the group's information is a social convention, but it is not quite as arbitrary as the outright restriction of information from members of other groups. To become a member of the group, the individual may have to learn a great deal of complex knowledge (as does an engineer or economist). The complexity and amount of technical data may "naturally" require a socialization period of some length. Similarly, the mental and physical capacities of the individual may set outside limits to the amount and speed of learning. A high school student being trained as an Olympic boxer has to develop physical strength and endurance. And in child socialization, the individual's social development is supported by physical maturation and cognitive growth, which cannot always be accelerated by situational factors.

Nevertheless, the complexities of the task and the limited capacities of the individual are only partial explanations for lengthy socialization processes and rituals. The specific stages and the exact length of the socialization period are often determined by arbitrary conventions. They exist, in part, because they protect the group. Through socialization of new members, the group continues or strengthens its existence. But new members are also a threat. They may not share the full set of beliefs and values held dear by the group. They may reveal the group's special information to outsiders. Socialization periods are a means of arbitrating between the need for new members and the desire to maintain the "specialness" of the group. To protect the group, socialization periods tend to become much more than "educational" experiences. The rite of passage from outsider to insider is heralded as a change in the person, rather than a mere change in access to information.

Stages of socialization and movement between them affect the identity of the individual even though the stages are largely arbitrary, social, and information-bound. The point at which medical students are incorporated into the group, or "become doctors," is an arbitrary point in their development. Nevertheless, most people—from the students' parents, who can now exclaim, "My child the doctor!" to the Commissioner of Motor Vehicles, who now offers "the doctors" a different type of license and license plate—recognize a change in the students' characters and identities. The change is "real" in the sense that all social behavior and attitudes are real; the movement from one social category to another "causes" a change in an individual's behavior and in the response of others. This type of social change, however, is often mistaken for a change *within* the individual, and, as a result, the arbitrary situational variables that foster the change often remain invisible.

Even rites manifestly based on biological stages of development are at least partially conventional. The particular stages that are chosen as pertinent, the number of such stages selected, and the specific rituals surrounding each transition are all socially defined. The number and type of stages within childhood and adulthood, for example, vary across cultures and within the same culture over time. Even the timing of such transitions as puberty rites, which are supposedly based on biological timing, may be partially arbitrary. In his classic study of "rites of passage," Arnold van Gennep distinguishes between "physiological puberty" and "social puberty" and argues that because the two "only rarely converge," initiation rites should not be called "puberty rites."[9]

Ashley Montagu has gone even further, claiming that "terms such as embryo, fetus, baby, infant, child, adolescent, maturity, and old age all reflect quite arbitrary meanings that correspond neither to biological nor to developmental realities."[10] Montagu suggests that what we traditionally do in conceiving of all development is take continuous and overlapping "phases" and arbitrarily redefine them into sharply bordered, discontinuous "stages." As a result, we mistake culturally defined situations for natural ones. We divide people who may be quite similar into different social worlds with different obligations, rights, and roles (18-year-olds and 17-year-olds, for example) and we combine people who are very different into one stage of life (a girl at menarche and a woman whose reproductive system is fully developed, for example).[11] Such arbitrary distinctions may be necessary for the smooth functioning of a society, but they blind us to the continuous nature of individual growth and to the potential for widespread changes in socialization stages.

Transitions between social categories, therefore, are "real, yet arbitrary," and patterns of access to situations, or information-systems, often play a larger part in establishing and maintaining social character and identity than do "natural" stages. The number of possible stages of socialization into groups depends on the number of possible isolated information-systems. One way to predict the impact of a new medium on socialization roles is to examine its potential for dividing people of different ages and backgrounds into different informational worlds. The more people's access to group information can be divided into distinct stages, the greater the number of possible stages of socialization into adulthood and other social groups. Conversely, the more people tend to share very similar information, the fewer distinct stages of socialization.

Peeking Behind the Curtain

Socialization can also be discussed in relation to increasing access to a group's backstage behaviors. A socialization process often begins by separating individuals from their old groups and plunging them into a very active, but relatively unrevealing group sphere. The "basic training" for new roles often involves difficult, time-consuming—and comparatively unimportant—work. This first phase of socialization forces prospective members into the group's situations and perspectives without at first giving away much of the group's backstage information. And the difficulty of the tasks tends to filter out those who are not committed to joining the group.

Through most socialization processes, individuals are associated with the new group before they have enough backstage information to discredit it. And by the time trainees do have enough information to do serious damage, any attempt to discredit the group or reveal its secrets would also undermine their own status. While third-year law students are not yet lawyers, they have enough information to embarrass lawyers. To do so, however, would also be to jeopardize their own status as "law students" and to pollute their future status as "lawyers." The length and difficulty of the socialization process (and the sometimes relatively meaningless tasks that are required) protect the group from potential revelations on the part of individuals with no personal commitment to the group.

New media, therefore, may also affect the socialization process by affecting the extent to which many groups are able to control access to their backstage behaviors. The more a medium tends to allow for very private backstage areas, the more it will support slow, sequenced stages of socialization. The more a medium tends to reveal areas of group activity that might otherwise be private, the more it will undermine slow, staggered socialization processes.

Place and Promotion

The relationship between a change in status and access to new information explains the traditional link between social passage and physical passage. A group's shared but special information was once accessible primarily to those in a shared but special location. Socialization into a new group, therefore, has traditionally been linked with new access to the group's territory and to the knowledge and information available in it. Further, each distinct stage of socialization has traditionally been associated with its own place or with its own degree of access to various group locations. Students move from classroom to classroom and school to school as they climb the educational ladder. Individuals gain greater access to the inner reaches of hospitals as they move from pre-med students to medical students to interns to residents.

Physical relocations, however, affect social status only to the extent that they actually remove people from one social world and place them in another. A social "debut," for example, was designed to be both a physical passage and an informational passage. Traditionally, the young lady's "coming out" was just that, a literal entrance into the larger social world. James Bossard describes the account of a woman who had her debut in the 1920s: "Before her début, she says, she never had had a 'date.' She never had gone out on the street unless escorted by her elders, or in the company of a maidservant. Her introduction was a definite and exciting crisis which, overnight, brought a drastic change in her relationships with her whole social group and immediately gave her new privileges, responsibilities, and a new status."[12]

The significance of a debut changes dramatically when the ritual no longer marks a true informational passage into adult life. As one of my students reports: "Today, many young women make fun of their debut because it no longer has any meaning. I heard about one group of 'socially elite' debutantes who smoked pot before, and went skinny-dipping after, the ceremony. One woman wore sneakers under her gown."

The changes in status that come with physical relocation are reinforced and given physical reality by new forms of dress, new names, new activities and games, new appropriate gestures and postures. One individual at different stages of socialization may be called Nancy, Nan, Ms. Smith, Nancy Smith Brown, and Attorney Brown. As a college student, Nan may be allowed to slouch in her seat, wear paint-stained jeans, and grimace at the remark of a fellow student. As an attorney, Nancy Smith Brown may feel compelled to sit up straight, wear clean and respectable clothing, and reply straight-faced to a client's every question and comment.

The number of different transitions in a socialization process is partly determined by the number of different "places" in which people can be isolated. In order for people to "pass" from one stage to another, with distinct behaviors for each, the situations in which they play each of their roles must be distinct. One cannot maintain clear distinctions between fifth and sixth graders, for example, if they are not separated into different classrooms. One cannot sharply distinguish the language of children from the language of adults if children and adults always share similar places. Each socialization situation has its single definition with appropriate language, dress, and behaviors. In this sense, Nancy cannot "be" both "student Nan" and "Attorney Brown" in the same setting at the same time.

Another way that new media may work to reshape socialization roles, therefore, is by affecting the traditional relationship between physical location and access to social information. The more a medium supports the relationship between physical isolation and informational isolation, the more it supports the separation of people into many distinct socialization "positions." The more a medium allows people to gain access to information without leaving old places and without severing old affiliations, the more it fosters the homogenization of socialization stages.

Authority: Mystery and Mystification

Hierarchy is always based on some notion of exclusiveness, and as we enact our hierarchal positions in society, we depend greatly on hierarchal mystifications to impress those beneath us with our exalted glory.—Hugh Dalziel Duncan[13]

One way to view society is as the interaction among superiors, subordinates, and equals.[14] While we often think of high status as being closely tied to the wealth, possessions, or inherent abilities of individuals, the hierarchal order often has much to do with communication patterns in specific situations. People not only pass from status to status through lifelong socialization processes, but they change status in different situations every day. A corporation president, for example, occupies different statuses when in interaction with his or her employees, spouse, children, friends, and parents. Such distinctions in status are dependent on distinctions in situations and on limits on the amount of information available to various audiences.

Most high status roles involve performance and appeal rather than being and command. Indeed, recent leadership studies suggest that "leadership" may not be the proper term. For the word incorrectly suggests that the leader is free to choose his or her own style and actions, and that as a result of the leader's forceful personality, great intelligence, or special skill, others will simply follow. As Murray Edelman suggests, the new focus in studies of leadership is on the "willingness of followers to follow."[15]

There is a great difference, then, between "power" and "authority."[16] Power refers to one's ability to coerce others (through physical, economic, or other means) to do one's bidding. One can *possess* the means of power: physical strength, armaments, and money. But authority must be *performed*. Authority refers to one's ability to gain the trust and willing obedience of others. While power rests on intimidation, authority survives through inspiration.

To be perceived as a "great leader," one cannot simply *be* great, one must *behave* like a great person. And the measure of the success of such behavior lies not in the leader's actions, but in the response to them. Leadership is not something an individual "has." It is something that exists in specific interactions and rituals in specific social situations. We have no other way of seeing and experiencing "greatness." If people were all naked and mute, we would not have a social hierarchy, only a biological one based on shape, size, muscle, and impulse.

The successful appeal for authority rests on the appropriate staging of the hierarchal drama. Relative mastery of hierarchal performances can be expressed in terms of several types of variable control over situations and the information available in them.

Exclusive Access to Knowledge

High status is demonstrated and maintained through the control over the knowledge, skill, and experience relevant to the role. A large measure of the high status of physicians, for example, is obviously related to their assumed knowledge of anatomy, diseases, tests, and treatments. The status of ambassadors in a foreign country rests heavily on their knowledge of their governments' policies and intentions; in their own countries, the status of ambassadors rests on familiarity with foreign governments. Even the authority of a car mechanic—to the extent that a mechanic has "authority"—rests on a special knowledge of cars.

The specific situation will often define the relative significance of different types of social information and knowledge, and the situation will therefore define the relative status of those present. A mechanic with stomach pains will have less status than the doctor he goes to visit. But a world famous neurosurgeon with an immobilized Mercedes 450 SEL may be at the mercy of the nearest mechanic. Further, knowledge access in itself is not enough to justify authority. One must have *more* access than the other people in the situation. The boundaries of the situation further shape relative authority by affecting who else is "there" to compete with.

The status of superiors may be undermined when inferiors gain access to relevant knowledge. A dedicated hypochondriac may outdo a doctor in medical research on supposed ailments and thereby disrupt the typical patient/doctor relationship. Similarly, a doctor may annoy a mechanic by offering advice on the specific repairs needed for a car and the appropriate cost of parts and labor. To preserve status, knowledge is often protected by encoding it in jargon or by restricting access to it in other ways. (A *Physician's Desk Reference*, or *PDR*, for example, which lists the uses and misuses of currently available drugs, was, until recently, a very difficult book for the average citizen to gain access to. Similarly, auto parts are often marked with code numbers that must be "broken" with a code book; mechanics sometimes use one catalogue to decode the part number, another to check its list price and repair shop discount, and yet another to locate a dealer.) In general, authority is enhanced when information-systems are isolated; authority is weakened when information-systems are merged.

Thus, while we can distinguish between the concepts of "social information" (information about behavior and role performance) and "technical knowledge" (facts and data about things in general), the two are closely interrelated. Control over technical knowledge is itself part of the social information complex; that is, control over knowledge gives one the "right" to perform a particular type of role.

High status that is not based on special control over knowledge is often seen as arbitrary and may be revolted against. Sensing such a threat, perhaps, the fifteenth century Catholic Church moved to suppress translations of the Bible into the vernacular. Indeed, the Church was much more concerned with translations of the Bible and heretical writings than with obscenity.[17] Exploiting the same principle, Luther and Calvin forwarded their reforms by encouraging personal reading of the Bible. As Harold Innis has described, changes in communication technologies have helped swing the balance of power back and forth among monarchs, priests, and other sectors of the population.[18]

In keeping with the unequal control over information, the higher status person is generally the one to initiate interactions with subordinates. Teachers begin classes, not students, and doctors initiate the examination of their patients. The right to begin an interaction is supported by greater initial control over knowledge and social information. If not given due respect, the high status person may restrict the disclosure or application of pertinent and vital knowledge. At the same time, however, the right to solicit information without giving any in return further enhances status by increasing relative control over information. A teacher can ask a student a type of question that the student cannot ask in return; a doctor is allowed to ask a patient a personal question or examine the patient's body without submitting to a similar examination. Only in the equality of children's play are the doctor/patient roles alternating.*

Movement from nonreciprocal toward reciprocal interaction generally reflects a change in relative status and information control. Interaction between a parent and a child, for example, often becomes more reciprocal as the child grows into an adult. Similar evolutions occur in some teacher/student and boss/worker interactions as a student moves from undergraduate to graduate, and perhaps to colleague, and when a worker is promoted or becomes a boss's friend, lover, or spouse. Thus, the fading of the custom of male initiation of courtship interactions is one significant indication of the move toward more equal gender roles.

The more a medium of communication tends to separate what different people in a society know, therefore, the more the medium will allow for many ranks of authority; the more a medium of communication tends to merge informational worlds, the more the medium will encourage egalitarian forms of interaction.

Hiding the Existence of a Backstage

More than any other type of role, hierarchal roles depend on the shielding of backstage rehearsals, practice, and relaxations. Doctors, for example, generally do not read medical reference books in front of their patients, nor do they readily display their sexual feelings or admit doubts, fears,

*Nonreciprocal access to information may grant de facto authority to individuals in roles that are not officially high status positions. Thus, even car mechanics gain status to the extent that they have the right to query customers on their driving habits. Similarly, secretaries, receptionists, and nurses often wield much more power than their salaries and job descriptions would suggest.

and anxieties. Judges, lawyers, and political leaders similarly try to shield their backstage areas. The greater the ability to hide the time and effort needed to maintain a high status role or rest from it, the greater one's seeming power and omnipotence.

The need for a carefully staged performance is made clear in many "training manuals" for high status positions. Balthasar Gracian, the seventeenth century rector of the Jesuit College, for example, advised priests to "Mix a little mystery with everything" because mystery "arouses veneration."[19] Similarly, Machiavelli suggested that since most princes cannot possess all the ideal princely qualities, they should at least make an effort to *appear* princely, "for men in general judge more by the eyes than by the hands, for every one can see, but very few have to feel."[20]

The performance aspects of hierarchy and high status often go unnoticed or unexamined because the notion of their being "no act" is itself part of the high status act. In other words, many persons of high authority must control their images so carefully that they do not seem to be controlling their images. Hierarchal roles, therefore, have a somewhat different relationship to information and knowledge than do group identity and socialization roles. Group identity and socialization rest on *explicit* control over information and knowledge. Many of us realize that a member of a group or a person being socialized into it has access to knowledge and experience kept secret from an "outsider." Yet while this special access is true of high status people as well, hierarchy also often involves a "meta-control," that is, control over the need for control. More than roles of group identity or socialization, hierarchal roles often demand a metaphysical dimension; that is, they require an *appearance* of innate qualities that transcend humanity and mortality. The gulf between superiors—especially very high status superiors—and subordinates is made to seem much more than a simple difference in knowledge and experience. The information possessed by very high status people must appear to be not only "unknown," but "unknowable." In this sense, roles of hierarchy involve both mystery and "mystification."*

The ability to play hierarchal roles depends greatly on restriction of information and on limiting subordinates' access to all but a few onstage situations. The higher the status, the more the need for such control. To hold awe in the eyes of followers, leaders must often hide their eccentricities and weaknesses, their early training and mistakes, their bodily func-

---

*Hierarchal mystification holds great dangers. It can be used to support evil governments and to maintain the power of unworthy people. Even the discussion of mystifying techniques may be disturbing and seemingly immoral. For his advice, Machiavelli's name has become synonymous with treachery and deceit. Yet such techniques are necessary for most, if not all, leadership. Good governments and worthy people must make use of them as well. And to ignore a study of such techniques may leave us helpless in the face of their abuse. As Duncan suggests, "We must learn to *confront* the mysterious power of hierarchy. If we can do this, it may be possible to make conscious use of hierarchy for good ends. All magic is not black."[21]

tions and malfunctions. Unlike group and socialization roles, hierarchal roles depend not only on keeping backstage behaviors private, but also on the denial of the existence of a backstage.

An examination of hierarchal roles suggests that all people are, in a sense, "ordinary." An image of greatness, however, can be maintained by not allowing one's ordinariness to show. Or, put differently, there are "great people," but their greatness manifests itself only through controlled social performances in suitable social situations. High status depends on conscious or unconscious strategies for controlling situations. The high status person can maintain his or her status only by carefully controlling information and by hiding the need for, and the techniques of, control. Yet if one's strategies for appearing important are exposed, one loses one's image of importance. All techniques of creating awe, therefore, bring with them the danger of shame—shame caused by the potential revelation of the need for technique.

The reliance of authority on privacy suggests that hierarchies are usually supported by media that foster a clear distinction between leaders' personal behaviors and public actions. Hierarchies will be undermined by new media that expose what were once the private spheres of authorities.

Places of Authority

The need for secrecy in roles of authority explains the traditional link between degree of status and degree of control over territory. Land ownership may symbolize wealth, but such ownership also plays a role in the social drama by allowing an individual to be physically isolated. The more remote a person is, the more the symbolic abstraction of a social role can take precedence over the person's concrete (and "ordinary") physical existence.

Because of the high status person's need to project only the proper image, subordinates must be kept away from any situation where the high status person is likely to display inappropriate behavior. "Inappropriate" may mean simply relaxing, playing cards, or laughing uncontrollably. For moderately high status persons, such as surgeons, this control may be necessary only in certain situations. The surgeon may have to behave one way in the hospital and yet be given more leeway at a cocktail party or on the golf course. Very high status figures, such as Popes and Presidents, however, may be expected to be "on" and "in character" at all times and in all situations.

High status positions, however, are not supported by the lack of back region behavior, but by its general invisibility. Indeed, high status positions generally require a deeper backstage area in order to build up to very formal front region roles. Further, even very high status figures will be expected by their closest friends, relatives, and advisors to behave in a "normal" manner—yet such behaviors could be very damaging if they

are "leaked" to the general public. As a result, high status has traditionally been correlated with physical inaccessibility.

Inaccessibility as a measure of status is reflected in the arrangement of
offices. A private office is a greater status symbol than a shared office.
Further, the relative status of two people can often be measured not only
by the relative amount of territory they each control, but also by the relative degree to which they each have access to the other's territory. If you
can come into my office without knocking, but I have to make an appointment to see you, you are of a higher status. Control over territory and
ownership of property not only allows for restricted access to oneself, but
also for the option of easy access to anyone living or working within one's
"domain."

Although high status has traditionally been associated with territorial
control, it is not "territory" alone and in itself that fosters social authority,
but rather the informational control that has traditionally come along with
it. The idea that information access is the larger, more inclusive category
is suggested by eye behavior rules. A person of high status often has the
right to look at a lower status person for a long time, even stare him or
her up and down, while the lower status person is expected to avert his
or her eyes. This nonreciprocity of information flow associated with relative status is also reflected in seating arrangements. The end of a rectan-
gular table is a high status position because the person sitting there can
watch all the other people at the table without turning his or her head.[22]
Similarly, there is a rough parallel between the old testament rule of not
looking into the face of God and the consequences of the traditional
arrangement of the psychoanalytic couch. The high status of both God
and psychotherapist is protected through invisibility.

Changes in media, therefore, may also affect hierarchy by altering the
accessibility of high status figures. Media that support the relationship
between physical isolation and social inaccessibility will support hierarchal mystifications; media that undermine that relationship may work to
lower many high status roles.

PART II
From Print Situations to Electronic Situations

Regardless of the ways in which new media change a society, the resulting new social order must grow out of the old one. New media have an effect by being *different* from older media and by changing those aspects of society that depended on earlier means of communicating. The printing press, for example, was able to spur both the Reformation and scientific inquiry because it bypassed the relative monopoly of information created by the slow, tedious writing of the scribes.[1] The potency of a new medium emanates not only from its own uses and inherent characteristics, but also from the ways in which it offsets or bypasses the uses and characteristics of earlier media. The same media, therefore, may have different effects in different societies. The impact of electronic media in many third world countries, which have not yet become widely literate, is no doubt quite different from the impact of electronic media in our own country.[2]

Yet while new media merely become part of the existing spectrum of older media, it is still meaningful to ask how the "media matrix" in a particular society is altered when a new medium (or new *type* of medium) is added to it.* To explore the impact of electronic media in the United States, this part of the book examines the differences between electronic media and print media as they have been used within our particular cultural and economic context.

Within the category of print, I include media such as books, newspapers, magazines, and pamphlets. Within the category of electronic media, I include technologies such as television, radio, telegraph, telephone, tape recorder, and computer. Unfortunately, it would be impossible to com-

---

*The idea of a "media matrix" and the related issue of the limited sense in which an "electronic society" is purely electronic are discussed further in the Appendix.

plete a detailed analysis of each of these media in this one section of the book. I have focused, therefore, mainly on a prime medium within each category: the book and television. In many ways, these two media are the quintessential representatives of their respective categories. It is around the book that traditionalists rally in the face of threats from new media; and among electronic media, it is television that continues to be most besieged by criticism and controversy. But since all media used in a society interact with each other, and because all print media share certain characteristics that distinguish them from all electronic media, I bring in many relevant examples from other media as well.

As in the rest of the book, the approach taken here is that media are types of social settings that include and exclude, unite or divide people in particular ways. This discussion of changes in media, then, is analogous to the study of architectural or geographical change, or to the effects of migration or urbanization. The focus is on the ways in which a new medium or a new type of medium may restructure social situations in the same way that building or breaking down walls or physically relocating people may either isolate people in different situations or unite them in the same or similar situations. Within this situational analysis of the differences between print and electronic media, the relevant types of questions are: Who in society has access to the information in this environment and who does not? To what extent do people of different ages, sexes, races, and educational backgrounds have access to the same or different information-systems because of this medium? How does the type of information available in this environment differ from the information available in other social situations? In general, in what ways does the widespread use of this medium affect "who knows what about whom"?

Part I described how behavior changes when the boundaries of situations change. In addition, we have seen that the number of distinct group identities, stages of socialization, and ranks of hierarchy is closely related to the number of distinct social information-systems, the extent to which "backstage" behaviors are kept separate from "onstage" behaviors, and the relative strength of the link between physical location and social experience. This part of the book, therefore, is divided into three chapters based on three major questions concerning the differences between "print situations" and "electronic situations":

1. To what extent does the medium tend to divide or unite different types of people into different or similar informational worlds?

2. To what extent does the medium allow for great distinctions between people's informal, private "backstage" behaviors and their formal, public "onstage" behaviors?

3. To what extent does the medium support or weaken the traditional relationship between social situations and physical locations?

New media need not destroy or replace older media in order to have a significant effect on the structure of social information-systems. The discussion here details how electronic media have tended to merge many formerly distinct social situations, blur the dividing line between private and public behaviors, and tear apart the once taken-for-granted bond between physical position and social "position."

5

The Merging of Public Spheres

Perhaps the primary characteristic of any medium is its ability to impinge on our senses and connect with our processes of thought and expression. If no one has access to a medium, then no one can send or receive its messages. This idea is almost too obvious to mention. What is less obvious, however, is the related fact that the type of access and the steps needed to achieve access are different for different media. Different media tend to establish different types and numbers of social information-systems. The widespread use of a new medium, therefore, may increase or decrease the "sharedness" of social information. One medium may tend to create separate information-systems for different people; another medium may tend to include many different types of people in a common set of situations. This chapter describes and discusses the characteristics of electronic media, particularly television, that tend to lead to a breakdown in discrete information-systems for different sections of the population.

As a number of media critics have observed, part of the reason for television's heterogeneous audience is that the economic system of television is based on "selling" viewers to advertisers.[1] While viewers often think of television programs as "products," themselves as the "consumers," and advertising as the "price" paid to watch the programs, the true nature of the television business is quite different. The products are the viewers who are sold to advertisers. The more viewers a program draws, the more money advertisers are willing to pay to have their message aired. Because of this system, network broadcasters have little interest in designing programs that meet the specialized needs of small segments of the audience.

A basic rule of network programming is "Least Objectionable Programming" (LOP). That is, the key is to design a program that is least likely to be turned *off*, rather than a program viewers will actively seek out. After all, any program that will delight one segment of the population (opera, advanced auto mechanics, hard core pornography, Shakespeare, introduction to quantum physics, etc.) is likely to turn off—and be turned off by—most of the rest of the population most of the time. And if the cost of producing and distributing the program and commercials exceeds what advertisers are willing to pay to reach the number of viewers the program draws (or if another program of the same cost can draw more viewers), then the program will almost certainly go off the air. Most television programmers, therefore, consciously try to design programs that will reach as large an audience as possible.

The economic structure of broadcasting, however, does not fully explain the relative heterogeneity of television audiences compared to book readers. Without making any excuse for the poor quality of television entertainment or for a dubious use of public airwaves, we can still discuss other factors that lead to homogenized information-systems in electronic media.

Media "Access Codes"

The skill and learning required to encode and decode messages in a medium determines, to a large degree, who in a society can use the medium to send messages and who has access to the information the medium carries. Even within a given form of communication, such as writing, different coding systems can have significantly different social consequences. Complex writing codes tend to support a literate elite that controls cultural information and ritual. The Chinese, for example, use a "logographic" writing system in which one symbol represents a whole word. This system requires the learning of up to 5,000 symbols for basic literacy and the mastery of as many as 20,000 symbols for scholarly pursuits. Such a system clearly limits the number of people who have full access to the medium.[2]

Other codes, such as the syllabaries of the Phoenicians and the Hebrews are simpler to learn, but because they lack vowels, they still require special reading skills. In a syllabary, the same written syllable, "B," for example, can be pronounced in many different ways, including "bā," "bē," and "bō." A given group of written letters might be used to represent a number of completely different words with different pronunciations and meanings. To read these codes accurately, a person must have some previous knowledge of the text and its subject matter.*

The greater the ambiguity in a writing system or the more symbols that must be memorized, the smaller the number of people who can master it. Syllabaries, then, are more "democratic" than logographic writing, but

---

*If our alphabet were a syllabary, the written symbols "wtr wth brd" could stand for "waiter with beard," "water with bread," and many other combinations of words (whiter, bird, breed, brood, bride, etc.). Such a symbol system is best interpreted by someone who already has some "inside knowledge" as to what is likely to be in it.

more elitist than truly phonetic alphabets. In addition, if the written material is in limited supply because of slow production or high cost, then only a limited number of people will have full access to the communication that the writing system offers.

The phonetic alphabet minimized the ambiguity of many written codes, and the spread of printing made books accessible to those who could not afford hand-written manuscripts. Yet even with relatively plentiful and inexpensive printed books, reading and writing have remained both means of access to, and restriction from, social information. In a print society, a person has to read and write well in order to gain full access to the society's stock of knowledge and communication networks. Even a dime novel requires minimal reading proficiency; a short note to a friend requires some writing ability. Because we begin to learn to read and write when we are very young, we often forget that reading and writing are incredibly complex skills that require years of learning and rote practice.[3]

Reading and writing involve an abstract code of semantically meaningless symbols that must be memorized, internalized, and then forgotten— forgotten in the sense that when literate people read and write letters of the alphabet, they *hear words* rather than focus on the shape and form of the written symbols.[4]

Further, reading is not mastered "all-at-once"; it requires years of practice and involves many discrete stages of proficiency. The sequence of the stages is based on increasing linguistic, grammatical, and stylistic complexity. One has to read simple books before reading complex books. Even among adults in the most cultured and civilized of societies, the literacy rate has never reached 100%.* And even among those who are literate, only a small percentage reaches the highest levels of reading and writing skill. *Any* writing system is more selective and exclusive than spoken language.

The skills needed to read and write affect access to print in two ways: Communication through writing and books is "automatically" restricted to those who know the required access code, and—even among those who have knowledge of the basic code—messages can be directed at different groups by varying the complexity of the coded message. Young children and illiterates, therefore, are excluded from all printed communication, and society is further divided into many distinct sets of information-systems on the basis of different levels of reading ability.

In contrast to reading and writing, television viewing involves an access code that is barely a code at all. Television by no means presents "reality," but television looks and sounds much more like reality than sentences and paragraphs do. Even two-year-old children find television accessible, and this explains why television is so readily used as a "baby-

---

*It has been estimated that at least 23 million and perhaps as many as 72 million American adults are "functionally illiterate," that is, unable to read a want ad, understand a bus schedule, fill out a job application, or address a letter so that it reaches its destination.[5]

sitter." Children aged two to five watch over twenty-five hours of television per week.[6] These active television watchers are of an age when the letters of the alphabet are little more than odd shapes and lines—except perhaps those dynamic letters that are pictured for them on television's "Sesame Street."

Television's code of electronic signals, which produces facsimiles of everyday sights and sounds, has basically one degree of complexity. Once you know how to watch and listen to one television program, you essentially know how to watch and listen to any television program. You may not understand all that you see and hear—just as you may not understand all that people say and do in a real-life situation—but you need not penetrate a complex superimposed filter of printed symbols to "enter" the communication situation.*

Many television "techniques" are based on natural experience. The low angle shot, for example, wherein the camera "looks up" to the subject, is generally used to give the subject dominance and power. But surely this is not simply an arbitrary convention. All of us as children have craned our necks to see those adults for whom we have felt love, respect, and fear—people we literally "looked up to." There are many other strong relationships between the structure of television sequences and the structure of everyday face-to-face interaction.[8] Such relationships suggest that learning to understand televised sequences is far simpler than learning to understand the arbitrary codes of reading and writing.

In general, there is no set sequence in which television programs must be watched. A person does not necessarily have to watch "simple programs" before watching "complex programs." Adults who have watched television only for a few months probably understand television approximately as well as adults who have watched television for many years. Whatever differences might exist are minimal compared to differences between adult illiterates and adult readers. There are no specific "prerequisites" for watching a television program, as there are prerequisites for

---

*There are some television techniques that require more learning than others. Flashbacks, dissolves, and parallel editing (cutting back and forth between two or more simultaneous sets of action) are conventions that must be learned. Also, studies have shown that very young children do not always realize that an object pictured in a close-up is the same object that was pictured in a long shot.[7] But even these conventions are probably learned in a "gestalt" rather than in set stages. Once you understand the idea of "flashback," you understand all flashbacks. Once you learn that a dissolve is used to show a passage of time or a change of location, you do not need to "practice" understanding other sequences using the same technique. The key points are that *compared to the code in print*, television's coding elements are limited in number, one does not have to go to school for many years to learn and master them, and, most important, one can "experience" television without fully understanding them. In contrast to the content of books, whatever behaviors and words are on television will be accessible to most people regardless of their age and level of education. Of course, both print and television also have "content codes," such as the structural elements of various genres and forms, which are not immediately grasped even after gaining basic access to the medium.

reading *Ulysses*. While the complexity of the *content* of television may vary, the ways in which the content is *encoded* in different television programs is relatively constant: pictures and sounds. The often-used phrase "visual literacy," therefore, is a misnomer.[9] Understanding visual images has nothing to do with literacy.

It is not surprising that people of all ages, educational backgrounds, and income levels watch many of the same television programs. In recent years, for example, children have enjoyed the adult soap opera "Dallas," and adult viewers have found pleasure in a children's puppet show, "The Muppets." Indeed, in 1980, both of these programs were among the most popular shows in *all* age-groups in America, including ages two to eleven.[10]

While the coding variable in print has its most noticeable impact on the information made available to children, the same variable also subtly shapes the organization of adult knowledge and experience. The different levels of complexity in the print code offer a seemingly natural means of segmenting information. All fields develop "introductory" books and texts. These books generally must be read before moving on to "intermediary" and "advanced" texts. Knowledge is compartmentalized; readers are segregated. An expert in one field may direct messages to other experts in the same field simply by writing in a complex shorthand that assumes a great deal of prior training and reading. Specialized terms and phrases, names, and quotations in foreign languages are used in "advanced" texts without explaining them or placing them in context. The increase in the complexity of the content is often accompanied by the use of longer words, smaller type, fewer pictures, and more complex grammatical constructions. I remember being frustrated when I was a child by the prefaces to many schoolbooks; they were addressed "to the teacher" and were written in small print and long words that made them difficult for me to decode.

The coding of print does not make all such compartmentalization necessary, but it makes it possible and expedient. What would be rude in interpersonal communication—addressing only part of the audience—becomes the standard, efficient, and appropriate style of communicating in print. The complexity of the code and the effort needed to read bring only certain people to certain books. Books "gather" specific readers to specific information-systems.

The growth and maintenance of distinct information-systems in print over several centuries have fostered the growth of implicit assumptions and specialized jargon that are not comprehensible to "outsiders." In print situations, people cannot easily cross from one field into other fields. As a result of such a system, philosophers, sociologists, anthropologists, and psychologists now discuss similar phenomena in different "languages." The communication patterns encouraged by print make it difficult for experts in one discipline to communicate with experts in other disciplines. Outsiders who want to gain access to a discipline must often become neophytes all over again and work their way up a new ladder of segregated information-systems. Barriers of time and pride generally keep people within the confines of their own "field." Such a system allows for many interactions that might be called "private-public," that is, the situations are technically public, but functionally restricted to members of a single group. Medical specialists, for example, can communicate with other medical specialists without being "overheard" even by other members of the educated population.*

The complexity of print's code, therefore, separates information-systems both within and among age-groups. The stages of learning required to master complex information in print support many distinct groups, many stages of socialization into each group, and many levels of status and authority.

Despite our familiarity with this system, there is nothing "natural" about such divisions and stages of knowledge. In normal oral discourse, for example, there is no clear sequence of difficulty. The idea of stages and sequences of texts was an innovation that followed the spread of printing.[11] Education in oral cultures involves relatively few "sequences" of courses and little separation of people into many different groups based on age and years of learning. School systems in literate societies, however, are usually designed to divide people into groups based on differences in reading ability. How well one reads is used as a guide to one's intelligence and one's capacity for understanding new ideas. This system makes sense in a print culture, but it is not the only logical means of organizing information or categorizing people. Electronic media, including the telephone, radio, television, and even the computer, have fewer stages and compartments of knowledge. Unless one places the content of print directly into these other media, the messages of electronic media are closer to the nonlinear information of sounds, pictures, and actions.

Some information that might be found only in "advanced" books, such as medical texts, may be presented on television in a form accessible to a wide audience. A thirty-minute program I watched recently, for example, offered detailed instruction in "Cardio-Pulmonary" Resuscitation (CPR). This emergency procedure to revive heart attack victims was described with words, pictures, and actions. The doctor on the program emphasized several times that, contrary to earlier medical thought, one needed no special training or prior knowledge to learn this procedure. It was so simple,

---

*This system of dividing knowledge has become so ingrained in our consciousness that new, interdisciplinary areas of study, such as "American studies," "popular culture," and "communication," are sometimes considered to have no substance because they do not attempt to carve out an isolated territory or to horde knowledge and because the questions asked are often too easily comprehensible to people in other disciplines. Sadly, in order to defend themselves against such attacks, some scholars in these fields develop their own specialized jargon and narrow methods in order to appear mysterious—and therefore valuable—in the eyes of other scholars. Yet such defensive actions destroy the original value and usefulness of the interdisciplinary approach.

he said, that even a child could learn it—indeed, his eight-year-old daughter had already mastered it.

I am not suggesting that a television program on CPR is equivalent to reading an advanced medical text. The CPR program is presented in a vacuum. The information is not tied to more basic medical information and is not a step toward developing more complex knowledge. The logical linking of pieces of information into large, complex, and connected treatises and theories is a feature of writing and print.[12] In this sense, the CPR television program is far inferior to a print lesson on the same technique. Yet what involves complex coding and decoding in a book may be presented more simply and perceived more directly through television. Information that would have been limited to, and divided among various sets of specialists if presented only in books is accessible to the average television viewer.

Books and television have their own individual strengths and limitations. The complex, step-by-step nature of print allows for the development of extended and connected descriptions and analyses, but it also tends to create sharp divisions between those who have access to a given information-system and those who are restricted from it. The linear structure of print's code leads to different specialists following different "lines" of inquiry. Television breaks down the barriers among different fields, but it favors discrete clumps of information rather than long connected arguments and analyses.

Throughout history, the vessels in which ideas have been stored have come to be seen as the shape of knowledge itself. Yet to understand the impact of new media, we need to distinguish between the inherent complexity of specific ideas and processes and the superimposed complexity of the means through which we encode and describe them. It is conceivable, for example, that if the only way people learned to tie their shoelaces was through descriptions in print, tying shoelaces might be viewed as a skill that was "naturally" restricted to the highly educated.

Because of differences in coding, electronic media have led to a breakdown of the specialized and segregated information-systems shaped by print. There is now much greater sharing of information among different sections of the population. What many people learn and experience through electronic media have relatively little to do with their age, traditional education, and social position. In terms of what and how much people watch on television, for example, the similarities among various age groups, races, sexes, and classes are much more striking than the differences.*

*Recent studies reveal, for example, that households with incomes under $10,000 watch an average of 47 hours and 3 minutes of television per week; households with incomes over $30,000 watch television 47 hours and 50 minutes per week. The amount of television college-educated viewers say they watch is close to 90% of the time reported by viewers overall, and men and women watch approximately the same amount of television per week. The biggest differences in viewing habits occur between age groups. Teens watch

Unlike print, television offers its content to all members of the population. Television, therefore, does not readily support an information elite that completely controls interpretation of the culture's stock of knowledge, nor does it lend itself to segregated systems of discourse. The content of television can still be manipulated and controlled by powerful economic and political forces, but controlling television is not the same as controlling print. While different people read different books, whatever is on television tends to be accessible to anyone who can make sense of it. Unlike books, television cannot readily be used by elites to communicate only among and about themselves.

Just as television messages are easy for the viewer to decode, so is it relatively simple for information to be encoded for presentation on television. Once the complex paraphernalia are set up, the presentation of messages is relatively simple. Almost anyone can stand in front of a television camera or tape recorder microphone and "send a message." Indeed, in recent years, the most expensive television content—advertising—has turned more and more to the use of "hidden camera" interviews of "real people" and to commercials in which corporation heads hawk their own products. Similarly, shows such as "Real People" and "The People's Court" are a new type of television variety show that replaces traditional forms of talent and performance with the everyday behavior of unusual, yet still very "ordinary" people.

These commercials and programs are produced, directed, and edited by trained professionals, but the strips of content can be produced by almost any willing adult or child. The relevant point is that while print requires encoding of information by people with very special skills, radio and television messages can be produced by the "person-on-the-street," even the child-on-the-street. In some ways the average person is preferable to an actor because he or she looks and sounds "authentic." For these reasons, perhaps, the technique of interviewing the common person has also become the staple of television news and documentaries. Many broadcast journalists travel to the streets to get on-the-spot-reactions, while print journalists seek out "experts" to get "statements" of official policy and informed opinion. A reader interested in eating disorders or divorce would probably read books written by doctors and psychiatrists, but the

the least television with an average of "only" 22 hours, 30 minutes a week, people over 55 watch the most television with an average of 35 hours, 6 minutes a week. But even here, the main point is that *every* age group—from 2-year-olds to the elderly—watches a great deal of television, more than 22 hours a week. And many of the same programs are watched by all age groups and social categories. In contrast to such similarities in television viewing, there are great differences in reading habits among those of different ages, incomes, and education levels. In 1971, for example, the Gallup Organization found that 50% of college-educated adults had read a book in the last month compared to only 18% of those with a grade school education; 39% of those between the ages of 21 and 29 had read a book, while only 16% of those 50 years or over had. In addition, book reading itself is a kind of "private club." For the polls suggest that, on average, almost 75% of adults have *not* read a book in the previous month.[13]

television viewer interested in such topics often watches people who have experienced the problems themselves.

Using a camera or microphone to record events is also quite different from using a pen and paper. While there is a great gulf between a home videotape of your cousin's wedding and a professional documentary film on the event, the gap is not as great as between a letter written about the wedding by a seven-year-old and a professional writer's account of it. Even a small child can turn on a video camera and "capture" many aspects of reality. In fact, a surveillance camera can capture strips of action without *any* creative human intervention.

Although broadcast television provides much information to average viewers, the average person does not have many opportunities to communicate to others through television as it now exists. Television's accessible code, therefore, now has more of an impact on the messages the average person is exposed to than it has on the channels through which the average person sends messages. The increasing use of interactive television, CB radios, home video equipment, and computers, however, is changing this balance. In the meantime, the same variation in coding that sets television apart from print, sets the telephone apart from letter writing. Just as television plugs people of all ages and classes into a single information-system, so does the telephone give the young and illiterate a new kind of social "mobility." It is not unusual for parents to allow their very young children to answer or even initiate telephone calls; it would be impossible for very young children to participate in the family's social or business correspondence.

Getting the Message

Physical Characteristics

There is a relationship between a book and its message that need not always exist in electronic media. In addition to being a medium of communication, each book and its particular contents also form an independent physical object. As objects, books must be purchased or borrowed *individually*. Each particular message or set of messages must be actively sought out, actively carried into the home.

Although the same thing is true of some electronic messages (audio and video cassettes, discs, and records), electronic media also have the potential for an entirely different relationship between medium and message. Thousands of different electronic messages can be received through a single acquired object such as a radio, television, or computer. Further, the characteristics of the electronic medium do not vary with changes in the characteristics of the message. While a long book is heavier than a short book, a television set stays the same size regardless of whether it projects a ten-second promo or a ten-hour version of *War and Peace*. The programs on television are not experienced as physical objects with independent physical dimensions or existence. A person who owns one television set, telephone, or radio need not purchase or borrow any specific messages. Once these electronic media are in the home, the messages are able to flow constantly and indiscriminately.*

The need to select books and magazines individually, along with the time and expense involved in locating them, leads to a highly selective diet of information through print. One goes after printed messages that are worth the trouble. One's collection of books often represents select sets of messages painstakingly gathered over time. A personal "library" usually ties the individual into the information network of a group or a small constellation of groups. The personal library, therefore, also tends to isolate the individual from other groups and their information. Since one needs to search for individual books, one tends to "find" books on topics one already knows about and is interested in.

Many electronic messages are chosen with less care and discrimination. We often spend more time deciding over the model of a radio or a television set than we do selecting the particular broadcast program. People tend to choose a *block of time* to watch television rather than choose specific programs.[14] According to one recent study, for example, more than half of the programs watched by viewers are selected on the spur of the moment, and only one-third of the audience for typical hour-long programs remains until the end of the hour.[15] Similarly, studies in Britain and the United States have found that while the ratings for programs are often relatively constant from episode to episode, the composition of the audience changes dramatically. "On average only about *half* the audience on one day also watch the same programme on another."[16] Surprisingly, this massive abandonment and adoption occurs even for the conclusion of a two-episode cliff hanger. Such "content disloyalty" is probably more striking in radio. Such habits suggest that people are much more likely to stray outside their traditional fields of interest when attending to television and radio than when reading books or magazines.

As with the coding variable, the contrasting physical characteristics of books and television have their greatest impact on children. A child is restricted in many ways from getting certain books because of their size or cost, where the child must go to find them, where in the library or store they are kept, and who the child must ask to get them. Even the height of a shelf can dramatically limit the information a child has access to in print. *Each* book has its own special information. *Any* television set is capable of exposing children to a wide spectrum of "adult" information.

---

* In relation to physical characteristics, the cinema is more like a book than it is like a television or radio program. *Each* motion picture is an independent physical entity. A person has to seek out a specific movie and go someplace to view it. Similarly, while it is simple for a warden to restrict a book or a movie on "How to Fool Burglars" from a prison library or theater, it is much more difficult to censor a similar type of program from prison televisions and radios. Thus, even though movies and television have a similar visual code, television may have social effects that the motion picture does not.

The different relationship between content and medium in different media has generally been overlooked by those who embrace the tradi-tional concern with media content. Historian Theodore Roszak, for exam-ple, attacks McLuhan's interest in media rather than messages by saying that such interest reminds him of "Jean Harlow's quip when asked what she wanted for her birthday. 'Don't buy me a book; I gotta book.'"[17] But Roszak has not followed through on his own example. With respect to television, radio, or computer, Miss Harlow's plea would be quite logical: "Don't buy me a television, I already got a television" does indeed make sense. Different media may have different effects on "who knows what about whom" because of the different degrees to which access to one specimen of the medium (*a* book vs. *a* television) leads to access to only one or to many sets of messages.

The Association Factor

As an object, a book is more than a medium of communication; it is also an artifact and a possession. As such, it serves not only as a channel to provide information but also as a symbol of self and identity. Just as we choose styles of clothing not for utility alone, so do we choose books that "appropriately" project our image and sense of group affiliations.

Each book we choose to "associate" with takes up part of our physical environment. It must be physically carried into the home and stored somewhere, whether on a coffee table or under a mattress. A book is a belonging. Although records, tapes, and disks are also belongings, broad-cast television and radio content is evanescent; it is consumed and leaves no tangible evidence. Watching a program on television, therefore, is like stopping to watch an event in a public park. One does not have to take it into one's home, place it among one's possessions, and make it part of one's self. Indeed, watching television is even less of an affiliation than stopping in the park because watching something in the park is a public gesture of association, but watching something on television is often a private act that involves no public commitment of any kind and no expressed support.

Because of a difference in the "association factor," people will watch things on television that they would be unlikely to read about in a book or magazine or to pay to see in a movie theater. Many people who would be uncomfortable going into a bookstore and buying a magazine on trans-vestites would have no qualms about watching a program about trans-vestites on television. Talk show hosts such as Phil Donahue have built their careers on this dual response to the same content in different media.

The bond between the message and the medium in print gives specific types of books and magazines specific situational definitions. We may describe a particular book as "serious" or "silly," we may describe a par-ticular magazine as "good" or "bad." But a specific television set is virgin territory until some content comes through it. Perhaps this explains why

Jerry Falwell, the head of the Moral Majority, sued *Penthouse* magazine
for ten million dollars for publishing an interview he gave to two free-
lance writers,[18] even though Falwell has no similar qualms about sharing
the television forum with "immoral" people—including publishers of
such magazines and the women who pose for them. (Finding Falwell in
Penthouse is like finding him in a red light district, but finding him on
television is like meeting him in a metaphysical arena that is neither here
nor there.)

Conditions of Attendance

Even in private, reading a book demands more personal commitment and
affiliation than watching a broadcast television program or video cassette.
A book has to be held in one's hand and actively interacted with. The
television set, however, is flicked on and backed away from; the images
wash over the viewer.

Reading is hard work even for the literate. The black shapes on this
page, for example, must be scanned, word after word, line after line, paragraph after paragraph. You are working hard to receive this message. To
read these words, your eyes have been trained to move along the lines of
print the way a typewriter carriage moves a piece of paper. When you get
to the end of the line, your eyes dart back to the left margin and move
down one line. And just as musicians often hum the notes they see on
sheet music, many readers tend to sub-vocalize the sounds of the words
they are reading. Because of the energy involved, people will not bother
to read every book that comes to their attention. People are more likely
to search for specific books in which they are actively interested and that
justify all of the effort of reading them. Electronic images and sounds,
however, thrust themselves into people's environments, and the messages are received with little effort. In a sense, people must go after print
messages, but electronic messages reach out and touch people. People
will expose themselves to information in electronic media that they would
never bother to read about in a book.

With electronic media, therefore, people may represent themselves by
the type of equipment they have (or by the fact that they do *not* have any),
but people are less likely to represent themselves in terms of all the programs that are transmitted through the equipment into their homes.

Further, although many people believe that light television viewers are
more selective than heavy television viewers, studies have found this to
be untrue: Light viewers usually watch the programs that "everyone"
watches, while heavy viewers often make up most of the audience for
"special interest" shows simply because they will watch almost anything
that is on.[19] As mass communication researcher Dennis Howitt explains,
"for a programme to be very popular it has to attract people who switch
it on especially. A minority programme gains an audience simply from
those who do not bother to switch off."[20]

Because access to messages in books tends to be discriminatory and selective, messages encoded in print generally travel from members of one section of the population to other members of the same section of the population. Or, put differently, the selective flow of information may *create* "sections" of the population by dividing people into very different information-systems. Those who know nothing about the things you know, write, and read about seem very "different." Although television and radio may not markedly increase people's true understanding of many issues, they provide large segments of the population with at least surface familiarity with a broad range of topics and with people in very different life situations.* This familiarity helps to decrease the strangeness and "otherness" of others.

There are many exceptions, but as a rule, people read things that reflect their personal and group identity. Both the content and the writing style of a book tend to limit the number and type of readers. A book detailing poor conditions in a state hospital is likely to be read primarily by specialists and those personally concerned with the subject. A book on the experiences of Jews in Nazi concentration camps would probably be read by a similarly narrow audience. Television, however, rarely divides its viewers so clearly. A 1972 television documentary on New York's Willowbrook State Hospital, for example, reached a large audience and led to public embarrassment and reform. Similarly, the television miniseries, "Holocaust" reached 120 million people, most of whom had never read a book on the same subject.[21]

The writing style and promotion of some books may allow them to reach a wide readership that extends beyond those who have a traditional interest in the "topic." But even best sellers reach a relatively select readership. A book can usually find a place on the lists of the top 25 fiction or nonfiction best sellers for the *year* with only 115,000 hardcover sales,[22] or about one twentieth of one percent of the population. A successful prime time show, in contrast, is expected to draw between 25 and 40 million people to *each* of its episodes,[23] or between eleven and eighteen percent of the population. The lowest rated prime time program is likely to reach an audience that exceeds the wildest dreams of most authors.

Even the biggest best sellers reach only a fraction of the audience that will watch a similar program on television. It took forty years to sell 21 million copies of *Gone With the Wind*, but about 55 million people watched the first half of the movie on television in a *single evening*.[24] Similarly, in 1976, the television program "Roots" was watched, in part or whole, by approximately 130 million people in only eight days.[25] Even

---

*Just a few of the recent topics that have been discussed on the nationally popular "Donahue" show are: men who like to dress in women's clothes, bishops against nuclear war, child prodigies, idiot savants, teenage alcoholics, porno movie stars, male strippers, and people with herpes. Through such programs, viewers have "met" and listened to people in these and many other social categories.

with the help of the television-spurred sales, fewer than 5 million copies of *Roots* sold in eight years.[26]

The point is that there is almost no book that is capable of reaching as wide an audience as many television programs. Perhaps the closest thing to the universality of television programs is the Bible—and even the Bible has sat in many homes more as a symbol than as a frequently read book.* Finally, even if millions of people read the same book over a long period of time, the impact on group identity may be negligible compared to the impact of *simultaneous* viewing of events on television. In recent years, the viewing of a number of single programs has reached over eighty million people. The final episode of "M*A*S*H," for example, was watched by 130 million people, or almost 60% of the population.[28] After such "events," one is likely to find that more than one out of every two people one sees on the street the next day has had a similar experience the night before. And while some critics attribute this massive sharing of information wholly to the economic and political system that encouraged the growth of broadcasting, they often overlook the fact that such a widespread sharing of information is almost impossible in print media.

In print, there are women's books and men's books, children's books and adult books. Indeed, there is a different set of books for every age group of each sex. Each age/sex category tends to be contained in its own informational world. It is embarrassing to be seen reading a book designed for a person of another age or sex. Not long ago, a boy who read *Nancy Drew* mysteries instead of *Hardy Boys* mysteries might be mercilessly teased by friends and accused of having ambiguous sexual tendencies. Such distinctions in gender-appropriate material are much less clear on television. The Hardy Boys and Nancy Drew, for example, have appeared on television as one combined series. Television, therefore, may be affecting many group identities, stages of socialization, and ranks of authority by changing the patterns of information access established by distinctions in reading habits.

The shared nature of the television environment creates many new problems and concerns over media content. Content that would be appropriate and uncontroversial in books directed at select audiences becomes the subject of criticism when presented on television. When television portrays the dominant and "normal" white middle class culture, minorities, subcultures, and "deviants" protest their exclusion. Yet when television portrays minorities, many members of the majority begin to fear that their insular world is being "invaded." The nature of the portrayal of minorities becomes a catch-22. If, for example, homosexuals are portrayed in a negative and stereotypical fashion, gay rights groups protest.

---

*In surveys taken in the 1950s, for example, the Gallup Organization found that 85% of men and 81% of women had never read the Bible all the way through, 51% of those asked could not correctly identify the name of the first book of the Bible, 79% could not name a prophet mentioned in the Old Testament, and 53% could not name any of the first four books of the New Testament.[27]

If homosexuals are portrayed as "normal" people who simply have a different sexual preference, however, many viewers object to television "legitimizing" or "idealizing" homosexual life.

Similarly, television cannot exclusively present content deemed suitable only for young children because adult viewers demand more serious and mature entertainment and news. Yet when truly "adult" and "mature" programs are placed on television, many parents complain that their children's minds are being defiled. Ironically, many talk shows include discussions of what is appropriate television content for children; yet these shows themselves may be considered "inappropriate" because they reveal many adult secrets to the children who are watching them (including the secret that adults are confused and anxious over how to raise children).

Even a choice between happy endings and "realistic" endings becomes controversial on television. When programs end happily, critics argue that serious issues are trivialized through 30- or 60-minute formulas for solving major problems. Yet when realistic endings are presented—a criminal escapes or good people suffer needlessly—critics attack television for not presenting young children with the ideals and values of our culture.

When looked at as a whole, then, it becomes clear that much of the controversy surrounding television programming is not rooted in television content per se, but in the problems inherent in a system that communicates everything to everybody at the same time.

As a shared environment, television tends to include some aspect of every facet of our culture. Fairy tales are followed by gritty portrayals of crime and corruption. Television preachers share the airwaves with male strippers. Poets and prostitutes appear on the same talk shows. Actors and journalists compete for Nielsen ratings. However, there is little that is new about any of the information presented on television; what *is* new is that formerly segregated information-systems are integrated. Information once shared only among people of a certain age, class, religion, sex, profession, or other sub-group of the culture has now been thrown into a public forum—and few are satisfied with the mishmash.

It should be clear by now that the integrated nature of information-systems created by television is "overdetermined." That is, there are a number of factors, each sufficient to make a difference on its own, that work together to make television messages more inclusive than print messages.

Not recognizing all these factors, some observers suggest that new technologies will soon return us to the segregated information-systems of the past. These predictions are based on the belief that the relatively homogenized diet of electronic messages has been determined primarily by the limited number of television channels and the narrow choice of programs and will therefore be undermined by the new and expanding spectrum of options. Cable television, video cassettes, and videodiscs, it is true, have already begun to widen the range of choice through elec-

tronic media. And fiber-optics (thin glass "wires" that carry many channels of information), direct satellite-to-home broadcasts, and the marriage
of computer, television, and telephone will no doubt continue the process.
But it is unlikely that the result will be a return to the *same* segregated
systems of discourse fostered by print.

The simple perceptual mechanics of attending to various media suggest
that even hundreds of choices of television programs will not return a
family to the segregated situation that exists in the traditional picture of
Mom, Dad, Billy, and Susan gathered in the family den, each reading his
or her own book. The interaction with a book, magazine, or newspaper
is very personal and private. You hold it close to you, touch its pages, and
sometimes write in its margins. No one, not even a person looking over
your shoulder, knows for certain what word or line you are reading. Television, however, is not held in one's hand and a television message is
usually shared by everyone in the room.

Even if each family member goes off to his or her own room (or uses a
TV wrist watch), there is no complex code to restrict young children from
watching "adult" programs. Further, the lack of a strong "association factor" in many electronically perceived messages continues to lead people
to cross traditional informational boundaries.

Even when the content of electronic media is as specialized as book
content, it tends to reach a more general audience than similar content in
books. One of the unpublicized facts of cable programming is that many
stations whose content is specialized do not reach only specialized audiences. According to one extensive market research study, ABC/Hearst's
Daytime—which airs diet, fashion, cooking, exercise, and discussion programs aimed at women—draws an audience that is one-third male.[29]
(This is even more significant when one realizes that most of the available
audience during the day is female.) Similarly, although the magazine
Sports Illustrated is read primarily by men, the same study found that
more than one-third of the Entertainment and Sports Programming Network (ESPN) audience is female.[30] And while *Playboy*'s magazine subscribers are mostly men, 40% of the viewers of "The Playboy Channel"
are men and women watching together and, even more surprising, 20%
of Playboy's television audience is composed of women watching alone.[31]
As a result, the producers of "The Playboy Channel" are now trying to
modify the programs to appeal more to women without simultaneously
losing the men.[32] It might make sense for Helen Gurley Brown or Hugh
Hefner to teach people strategies for dealing with (and, at times, misleading) the other sex in books or in magazines such as *Cosmopolitan* or *Playboy*, but such advice on television may backfire because so many members
of the other sex are there to overhear it.

New technologies, therefore, are certain to break up the monolithic
power of network television, but they are unlikely to divide the audience
into clear and traditional categories of age, sex, religion, class, and education. The increase in electronic sources of information will not return us

to the segregated systems of print because almost every person will be able to attend easily to almost any source. New subgroups may develop, but they will be less distinct, less stable, and less recognizable.

Perhaps most overlooked by those who see a return to the segregated systems of the past is the fact that television, as it has existed, is not simply an inefficient alternative to delivering custom-designed programs to individual groups of viewers, nor is it only an economic system developed to distribute goods. Whether by design or accident, television's single web of information has also created a new "shared arena." And this shared arena has its own effects and uses apart from the viewing of specific programs and advertisements. The publicness of television, combined with the fact that television programs have no physical dimensions, do not take up any space in the home, and are passively consumed, has led to an "impersonal" use of television that distinguishes it from most book reading.

Many people read books to tie themselves into a particular network and to reinforce their special identities. That is, they read things that are of special interest to them. Although people likewise watch things about their special interests on television, they also often watch television simply to see what "other people" are interested in or doing.* Summarizing the findings of several "uses and gratifications" studies, for example, John Murray notes that books often serve specific needs related to "personal identity," but television and radio serve much more generalized needs such as escaping boredom, killing time, having something to talk about with others, and keeping in touch with main events in the world.[34] In this sense, reading is often used to enhance and crystallize one's *internal* reality; but television is often used as a means of monitoring *external* reality. Although many of the functions of television and reading overlap, television has more of a tendency to plug people from distinct reading circles into one public realm.[35]

Television has joined the marketplace and the street corner as another environment to be monitored, but not necessarily identified with. Even though many people watch television alone, television is capable of giving the viewer a sense of connection with the outside world and with others who are watching. At the same time, people take much less "responsibility" for what they watch on television than for what they read in books. With television viewing, people often feel they are merely observing what the outside world is like. It is not unusual for a person to watch avidly a television show and yet comment, "My God, I can't believe what the world is coming to!" Ironically, the ability of viewers to

* People also read newspapers to monitor outside events, but even here there is a difference from television. People are generally extremely particular about *which* newspaper they bring into their homes. The writing style, typeface, format, advertising, and so forth are all expected to reflect the reader's personal identity. Further, for the past two decades, polls have shown that Americans feel they get both "most" of their news and their most "trustworthy" news from television.[33]

dissociate themselves from the content of television allows for the most widespread sharing of similar information in the history of civilization.

A great part of the social significance of television, therefore, may lie less in what is *on* television than in the very existence of television as a shared arena. Television provides the largest simultaneous perception of a message that humanity has ever experienced. Through television, rich and poor, young and old, scholars and illiterates, males and females, and people of all ages, professions, classes, and religions often share the same or very similar information at the same moment. Through television, Americans may gain a strange sort of communion with each other. In times of crisis—whether an assassination attempt or the taking of American hostages—millions of Americans sit in the glow of their television receivers and watch the same material over and over again in an effort, perhaps, to find comfort, see meaning, and feel united with all the other faceless viewers.

Such times of large-scale sharing of information may be rare, perhaps only a few times a year, yet the knowledge of the existence of the shared arena is in many ways like the knowledge of the existence of the "family home" where relatives can spontaneously gather at times of crisis or celebration. It does not have to be used every day to have constant presence.*

Recognition of television's role as a new public arena solves a number of mysteries surrounding television viewing, including: why people complain so bitterly about television content but continue to watch so much of it, why many Americans say they turn to television for "most" of their news even though—by any objective standard—there is remarkably little news on television,† and why people who purchase video tape machines often discover that they have little interest in creating "libraries" of their favorite television programs.[37]

The shared forum of television is an arena for the declaration and confirmation of the "reality" of events. Protests, scandals, and disasters that have not been reported on radio and television do not seem to have "happened." The Watergate scandals became "real," not when the *Washington*

---

*For this reason, there is a big difference between listening to a cassette tape while driving in a car and listening to a radio station, in that the cassette player cuts you off from the outside world, while the radio station ties you in to it. Even with a local radio station, you are "in range" of any news about national and world events. Our radio and television antennae are like feelers we use to monitor the wider environment. Even "ordinary" messages on television or radio are significant messages that implicitly say: "We are not at war, no public official has been shot, no disasters have occurred. . . ." Perhaps one of the reasons Americans feel so much trust in television news, and yet do not support extending the news from 30 to 60 minutes, is that the "real news" comes in the first few minutes, sometimes seconds, of a broadcast. If the lead story is not earth-shattering, then Americans can comfort themselves with the thought that the earth will probably not be shattered for at least another day. Even in the event of a real crisis, a longer daily news is not necessarily desired by viewers because they know that a crisis will generate many late-night news specials.

†The script for an average evening network news broadcast, for example, would fill only about two columns of the front page of *The New York Times*.[36]

Post reported the stories, but when network television news reported that the *Washington Post* reported the stories. Similarly, civil rights demonstrations and Vietnam War protests became social realities, not when demonstrators took to the streets, but when the disturbances were viewed on television. Despite the distortions inherent in any brief selection of news, the reality of television news is a kind of self-fulfilling prophecy. When Walter Cronkite proclaimed "And that's the way it is" at the end of every CBS news broadcast, his statement was true to the extent that whatever is perceived simultaneously by so many people becomes a social reality— regardless of its relationship to an "objective" reality. People will watch things on network television they would not ordinarily choose to read about, therefore, because they feel they are keeping in touch with other Americans and with what is "happening."[38]

Implicit vs. Explicit Access

There is a final, subtle but very important point to be made about the different patterns of access to information established by different media: A change in the degree of *explicitness* with which information is made available to different members of the population will affect behavior even if there is no other change in what information people have access to.

One could argue that electronic media do not dramatically change the patterns of access to information available in print. For while print media have many restrictions and segregating tendencies, they can be overcome, and they often are overcome. A bright child, for example, often gets hold of difficult books or magazines on "adult" subjects, a specialist in one field may read books from another field, women may read a magazine directed at men, and a black person may read a pamphlet for white supremacists. In a print culture, therefore, information-systems are not entirely isolated and secure. Even when there were separate "languages" for adults and children and for men and women, children and women did know many of the "forbidden" words and topics.

What is not taken into account in these arguments, however, are the vastly different implications for social behavior between (1) simple access to information and (2) knowledge of that access on the part of others. New access to information will not necessarily affect social interaction unless everyone involved knows about the access. Or, put differently, knowledge of people's access to information is itself a significant piece of social information.

If children gain access to a book on sex, for example, this new access to information will not necessarily affect parent-child discussions, unless the parents *know* that the children have read the book (perhaps by finding it in a child's room). Even then, no dramatic change may occur unless the children know that the parents know about the book (perhaps by being there when it is found). Without full awareness, everyone may give everyone else the "benefit of potential ignorance" and never bring the subject to the surface.

Traditional distinctions among information-systems for different sexes and ages once led to numerous distinct behavior patterns. In adult/child relationships there were three distinct behavioral arenas: adult-adult interaction, child-child interaction, and child-adult interaction. Similarly, in male/female relationships there were also three distinct forums: female-female, male-male, and male-female. Lack of explicit knowledge of exactly what the members of the other group knew helped to maintain distinctions in adult and child behavior and in male and female behavior. Parents did not know what their children knew, and children did not know what their parents knew they knew. Similarly, a person of one sex could never be certain of what a member of the other sex knew. Children, adults, men, and women may have always cursed and spoken among themselves about taboo topics, but they did not usually speak of such things in front of each other.

Television undermines such behavioral distinctions because it encompasses children and adults, men and women, and all other social groups in a single informational sphere or environment. Not only does it provide similar information to everyone, but, even more significant, it provides it publicly and often simultaneously.

Television removes much of the doubt as to what subjects one's children or parents know about. Any topic on any popular situation comedy, talk show, news program, or advertisement—be it death, homosexuality, abortion, male strippers, sex-change operations, political scandals, incest, rape, jock itch, or bras that "lift and separate"—can be spoken about the next day in school, over dinner, or on a date, not only because everyone now knows about such topics, but also because everyone knows that everyone knows, and everyone knows that everyone knows that everyone knows. In fact, it almost seems strange *not* to talk and write about such things. The public and all-inclusive nature of television has a tendency to collapse formerly distinct situations into one. In a society shaped by the segregated situations of print, people may secretly discuss taboo topics, but with television, the very notion of "taboo" is lost.

Compared to print, television tends to include people of all ages, educational backgrounds, sexes, professions, religions, classes, and ethnic backgrounds into a relatively similar informational world. The differences between "types" of people are muted. To the extent that traditional distinctions in group identities, socialization stages, and ranks of hierarchy were based on the isolated situations fostered by print, such distinctions are likely to be blurred by the widespread use of electronic media.

6

The Blurring of Public and Private Behaviors

The impact of electronic media on social situations is not limited to a simple reshuffling of already "public" information. Electronic media do much more than take the information that was once available only in print and deliver it to new audiences. Print media and electronic media also differ in the *type* of information they convey.

Electronic media further integrate information-systems by merging formerly private situations into formerly public ones. In terms of the dramaturgical concepts discussed in earlier chapters, the shift from print media to electronic media is a shift from formal onstage, or front region, information to informal backstage, or back region, information, a shift from abstract impersonal messages to concrete personal ones. And this shift is not related directly to what "subjects" are discussed or to which particular people are placed in front of microphones or cameras, but to basic differences in the *form* of the information presented.

Information Forms

The differences between the types of information conveyed by electronic media and print media can be explained in terms of three dichotomies: communication vs. expression, discursive vs. presentational, and digital vs. analogic.

In one of his analyses of social interaction, Erving Goffman makes a distinction between "expression" and "communication."[1] Although Goffman uses this distinction to suggest what is special about face-to-face encounters, this dichotomy is helpful here because it points to the differences in the type of information conveyed by different media.

"Expression," as defined by Goffman, refers to gestures, signs, vocalizations, marks, and movements produced by the *mere presence* of a person in an environment. The expressions exuded by the individual do not present any explicit "statement" or "argument" about things in general, but they do provide information about the expressing organism. The tone of voice and facial expressions of a person being interviewed, for example, give us some sense of the way the person is feeling and is responding to the interviewer's questions. The information received from expressions is always tied to the expressor and to the specific ongoing situation. Individuals' expressions were once accessible primarily to those in their immediate physical presence.*

In contrast, Goffman narrowly defines "communication" to mean the use of language, or language-like symbols, for the intentional transmission of a "message." In this special sense, "communication" involves purposeful symbolic utterances or written statements about things, events, and ideas. Unlike expression, communication can be abstract. A person writing a book, for example, can communicate about events in other countries, activities that took place in the past or are planned for the future, or unobservable abstractions such as "freedom" and "happiness."

In terms of this distinction, one can start and stop communicating at will, but one cannot stop expressing. Communications are consciously given, but expressions are unconsciously "given off." Expressions are constant and much less controllable than communications. Further, while communications can be about anything, expressions, in one very important sense, are always "about" the individual giving them off. Expressions are personal and idiosyncratic; we look to them to discover how a person feels and what he or she is "like." For these reasons, most important decisions concerning relationships rely much more heavily on expressions than on communications. Few companies will hire new executives without meeting them first, and it is the rare person who chooses to marry someone merely on the basis of a résumé or a writing sample. Communications may provide important "facts," but expressive information is used to form basic "impressions."†

Although Goffman makes no explicit connection between the communication vs. expression dichotomy and the distinction between back and front regions, they are clearly related. Communications, because they are more controllable and manipulable, may be said to have a "front region bias," while expressions, because they reveal personal and private feelings, may be said to have a "back region bias."

One of the major differences between print media and electronic media is that print media contain only communications, while most electronic

---

*A few exceptions to the need for direct physical presence are the scent left by an animal or person, a pattern of footprints in the sand, or the style of handwriting in a letter—all of which may provide information about an organism's emotional state.

†Most communication theorists use the term "communication" to include both of these types of information. Thus, although I adhere to Goffman's special, limited notion of communication in this discussion, I use the term in the more typical, generic sense elsewhere in the book.

media also convey personal expressions. Electronic media make public a whole spectrum of information once confined to private interactions. Electronic media reveal information once exchanged only among people under each other's direct and close observation. In this sense, print media have a "front region bias," while electronic media have a "back region bias." A number of "dating services" have capitalized on the personal nature of electronic media by videotaping their clients for each other's consideration.

For the purpose of comparing print and electronic media, there is a strong parallel between Goffman's distinction between expression and communication and another dichotomy described by philosopher Susanne Langer: discursive vs. presentational symbols.[2]

Langer distinguishes between discursive symbols, such as language, and presentational symbols, such as pictures. The relationship between a discursive symbol and what it stands for is always different from the relationship between a presentational symbol and its referent. Discursive symbols are abstract and arbitrary; they bear no physical resemblance to the objects and events they describe. The word "dog," for example, does not look like a dog. In addition, discursive symbols are composed of discrete units, such as words, each of which has a meaning independent of the particular arrangement of the elements. The same words can be arranged in different sequences to mean different things ("The dog bit the cat" or "the cat bit the dog"). Making sense of any arrangement of words also involves an agreed upon grammar that has little to do with the things described. If, for example, I try to describe in words two things that have happened simultaneously, I must still mention one of them after the other ("The cat bit the dog just as the man walked out of the house"). There is a structure to discursive symbols that has nothing to do with the structure of reality.

Langer contrasts the form of discursive symbols with the form of presentational (or nondiscursive) symbols, such as pictures or photographs. The presentational symbol has a more direct link with the thing it is about. A picture of something looks like the object; there is a direct physical resemblance. The picture imitates aspects of the real world: shapes, proportions, shadings, colors, and textures. Even stick figures of people look more like people than the word "people" does. Pictures of people and the word "people" are not equivalent symbols.

The elements that make up a picture are much more numerous than the elements of language, but the elements of a picture have no independent meanings. In isolation, for example, dark and light specks of photographic grain are only "blotches." The light and dark specks gain "meaning" only when they are arranged in a pattern that reflects the shape of *real* objects or people. Sentences, in contrast, have meaning only when they are arranged according to the *arbitrary* rules of a given grammatical code.

Because presentational symbols must take a form that resembles reality, they are much less "editable" than discursive symbols. One can describe a landscape in many different words and sentences, but one would not normally cut up a picture of a landscape and rearrange it in different patterns in order to describe it in different ways. Because a photograph is not composed of discrete units strung out in a linear row of meaningful pieces, we do not understand it by looking at one element after another in a set sequence. The photograph is understood in one act of seeing; it is perceived in a gestalt.

The meanings of words and sentences can be explained in other words and sentences, but the "meaning" of one picture cannot be conveyed by viewing another picture. Words can describe other things (including pictures and other words); pictures merely present themselves. The Declaration of Independence can be paraphrased and even translated into other languages, but the essence of pictures such as the Mona Lisa, or of the American Marines placing the flag at Iwo Jima, or of little John Kennedy, Jr. saluting the passing casket at the funeral of his father, or, for that matter, any family snapshot, can be only weakly conveyed in words. "Paraphrasing" is a peculiarity of language. One can express the same thoughts in different words. But it is difficult to express the same picture in different ways. Each picture conveys a unique message. Although I can use my own words to explain Langer's words, it would be impossible to present my own picture to convey an image of Langer.

A presentational symbol cannot be used to "discuss" a specific abstract idea. "Respect," "patriotism," or the theory of gravity cannot be pictured easily. In viewing a picture, we may be reminded of such ideas (i.e., the pictures may bring certain *words* to mind), but language is needed to conceive of them in the first place.

Langer contends that discursive language is not our only articulate means of communicating. Nondiscursive symbols are another equally important form of mental activity and another "intellectual" means of describing reality. Yet, notes Langer, presentational symbols are often devalued because they cannot be translated directly into discursive language. Symbols such as pictures, sounds, and music simply "present" feelings and emotions without the benefit of words.

The discursive/presentational dichotomy offers another means of distinguishing print and electronic media. Print strips messages of most of their presentational forms; it conveys only discursive information. But most electronic media convey a rich range of presentational information along with discursive symbols. Radio conveys sounds and vocalizations. Television adds visual forms. Like expressions, presentational information is directly tied to specific objects or people in specific contexts. More than print, electronic media tend to unite sender and receiver in an intimate web of personal experience and feeling.

The presentational/discursive distinction is similar to another dichotomy—digital vs. analogic—discussed by Paul Watzlawick, Janet Beavin, and Don Jackson in *Pragmatics of Human Communication*.[3] Digital symbols are discrete units such as numbers or words. Digital systems are based on discontinuities—either/or. A number is either a 3 or a 4, but not both. A word is either one word or another. Analogic messages, in contrast, are continuous; they are based on the principle of more or less.

The difference between digital and analogic forms is exemplified in the two different types of watches and clocks now available. A digital watch presents the time in discrete units. It is either 12:57 or 12:58 (or some discrete unit in between, such as 12:57 and 10 seconds as opposed to 12:57 and 11 seconds). With an analogic watch, however, time is continuous. A person who sees the time as "12:57 and 10 seconds" on a digital watch, may see the time as "about one o'clock" on an analogic watch. A similar difference exists between a digital calculator and the analogic slide rule. The slide rule is excellent for making "approximations," but it cannot yield precise digital data.

Human communication can also be broken down into digital and analogic systems. The words we speak or write in a letter are digital messages. Words and sentences are discrete units with relatively specific meanings. The blank in the sentence, "I _____ eating fish" might be filled with the word "like" or "hate," one word or another word. But a hug or a handshake or a smile involve analogic expressions. There are no isolated units with independent meaning within a smile; there are no discrete degrees of sincerity in a handshake.

Watzlawick and his colleagues suggest that digital communications convey "content" messages, while analogic expressions convey "relationship" messages. That is, digital communications can be about things in general, while analogic messages tend to reveal how the persons emitting them feel about people and things around them or about the digital messages they are speaking or hearing.

This dichotomy also helps to distinguish between the form of information conveyed in print and electronic media. Print conveys digital information; most electronic media convey both digital and analogic information.

Personal vs. Impersonal Response

The three dichotomies summarized above offer a means of explaining why our responses to print media and to electronic media are so different. Print's communicative-discursive-digital messages and electronic media's expressive-presentational-analogic messages have different possibilities and limitations.

The messages in print and electronic media are about different things. Television, for example, can "present" an object or person in a manner in which verbal descriptions cannot. Thus, if the police hope to capture a fugitive, a verbal description would be much less helpful in identifying the fugitive than a videotape of the fugitive. Similarly, few people would trade an only photograph of a lost loved one for a poem about the loved one. But presentational messages are severely limited in their own way because they cannot convey abstract ideas or concepts. Thus the *idea* of "fugitive" or "justice" cannot be expressed in a videotaped image. It is possible to photograph two people eating together, but it is impossible to picture the concepts of "kindness," "friendship," or "love." It is possible to present a picture of *a* specific woman, but it is impossible to picture "femininity." One can present a picture of a ball or of a wedding ring, but the ideas of "toy," "roundness," or "continuity" must be discussed in words. The abstract idea of "great leader" can be spoken about in language, but a picture of a President is only a picture of a specific person.

Further, unless words are used to explain expressions and presentational symbols, their meanings are often ambiguous. Expressive messages have no qualifiers to specify which of several possible interpretations is the correct one. "There are tears of sorrow and tears of joy, the clenched fist may signal aggression or constraint, a smile may convey sympathy or contempt, reticence can be interpreted as tactfulness or indifference."[4] Similarly, people often rely on a picture's verbal caption to determine the picture's specific meaning.

Ironically, electronic media's analogic messages are both more direct and more ambiguous, more "natural," yet less precise. The analogic message comes directly from the sender/subject; it suggests how the sender/subject "really feels." Yet one cannot base a contract on a smile and a wink. Words must be exchanged if the exact meaning of the message is to be understood.

Electronic media's presentational messages have no equivalents to linguistic grammar or syllogistic logic. A person's gestures or tone of voice cannot be rearranged and edited the way words can be manipulated because gestures and tone of voice are not divided into discrete units. Expressive messages have no logical links, such as "if-thens" or "either-ors." Expressive messages cannot be used to distinguish between the past, the present, and the future, and they cannot be used to make propositional statements that are capable of being proven true or false ("It will rain tomorrow" or "I have three hands"). The thesis of this book could never be developed in a series of television images. Ideas live through language.

Yet the discursive means through which authors convey their messages are highly "impersonal." The words on this page, for example, tell you very little about my personal existence. I may speak with a lisp or a heavy accent. I may have shifty eyes and I may constantly mispronounce words. I may be tall or short, young or old, mischievous or sober. But you cannot tell any of this from the words I write. Even an awkward phrase or a misspelled word cannot be attributed directly to me. Perhaps an editor or a typesetter made the mistake. Print offers shared responsibility, and a printed page is a shield behind which human idiosyncrasy and frailty may hide. After thirty seconds of face-to-face interaction between us (or after seeing me on television), however, you would know things about my *personal* being that you could not discover from reading everything I have ever written.

The impossibility of translating many of the presentational messages on television into discursive language may explain why television is often looked down upon by many "intellectuals." Yet while most of the messages in television entertainment are hardly "realistic" or "educational" in conventional (discursive) terms, they do present viewers with realistic images and sounds of people and places. These presentational symbols feed our store of "experience" rather than our store of discursive knowledge, arguments, and ideas.

Discursive and presentational forms are so distinct that they are apparently produced and perceived primarily by different hemispheres of our brains.[5] In most right-handed people, the left hemisphere is the language center and the right hemisphere deals with tasks related to visual and spatial patterns. The left hemisphere is dominant in the handling of linear, sequential, and discrete symbols, but the right hemisphere is the primary realm of images, shapes, feelings, insights, and intuitions.[6]

As a result of all these differences, the messages in television tend to be "about" something different from those of print. Our response to a verbal message (such as a speech printed in the newspaper) is often to ask whether it is true or false, whether the arguments are logical, and whether it is well-written. Print messages can be "issue"- and concept-related. But expressive messages on television often lead to a different response. They are more personal, more tied to the speaker. Expressive messages constantly tell us something about the expressors' orientations to the situation, how they are feeling, and what their emotional response to their own behavior is. A common response to a speech on television, therefore, is to think about the speaker rather than the speech. While watching a politician on television, it is not unusual for people to think or say: "He seems nervous"; "She looks like she's going to cry"; "I don't trust him"; or "She's tough!"

One can choose, of course, to write about very personal matters—as in Augustine's *Confessions* or in letters to *Penthouse* magazine—but unlike presentational media, one's physical self is completely absent. Even when printed words are about intimate matters, the form in which the message is conveyed is impersonal and abstract. Relatively little about the flesh and bones *person* is ever revealed in print. On television, in contrast, one can speak about very impersonal matters, and yet be unable to escape sending, along with the abstract "topic," a broad range of personal cues.

Much more than print media, television thrusts the personal, private realm into the public arena. Television provides the type of information we are accustomed to responding to when we are with family members and friends. Compared to print, television provides a rich personal profile of the communicator. The separation between private emotion and public communication is blurred. The sudden loss of breath, the welling of tears in the eyes, the voice that cracks with emotion or moves steadily through a difficult passage—all these convey information that is not discursive, digital, or communicative, but presentational, analogic, and expressive. When presidential candidate Edmund Muskie stood on the steps of the Manchester *Union Leader* in 1972 to denounce a newspaper story attacking his wife, the response to the televised message was based primarily on his expressive behavior rather than on his communicated verbal message. Most people remember that Muskie cried; few can remember what he said.

A good example of the differing importance of verbal and nonverbal messages in different media comes from George E. Reedy, who served as Press Secretary for President Johnson. In a 1977 article on Jimmy Carter's use of television, Reedy suggests that, "at the very least, [Carter] has demonstrated that one need not resort to words to put across rather sophisticated points." Reedy suggests that the best example of this comes from Carter's "fireside chat" on the energy crisis.

> I have discussed this with individual Americans in many parts of the country and, except for news reporters who had to write stories about it or public officials who had to react to it, I have found no one who can remember anything he said. The fact that he wore a sweater while delivering the statement, however, has become legend and, significantly, everyone to whom I have talked ascribed a complex meaning to the act.[7]

The presentational nature of television affects our response to presidential debates and elections. The campaigns on television are rarely about issues; they are about personality and style. Media advisors often play more important roles in campaigns than political advisors and speech writers. In general, it is important for politicians to avoid getting upset or looking angry during television appearances. A politician's demeanor on television is often more important than his political programs. On the night of the Carter-Reagan debate, Reagan aide James Baker passed Reagan an index card with one word of advice: "Chuckle!"[8] When most people think back on such televised debates they tend to remember the general style and emotional state of the participants rather than their specific verbal arguments.

There is no great mystery to the focus on the expressive aspects of television's messages. It is not as if television deadens people to verbal messages to an "abnormal" degree. The same focus on expressive information exists in many interpersonal encounters. Anthropologist Albert Mehrabian's studies of nonverbal behavior suggest that the relative weight people give to messages in face-to-face encounters is 7% to the verbal, 38% to vocal inflection, and 55% to facial expression.[9] If these figures are accurate, more than 90% of the meaning of a message is derived from expressions rather than "communications." This explains why, when two people go out on a first date, they carefully monitor each other's expressions to get a sense of how good a time the other person is having. The formulaic verbal messages ("That was a very good movie" or "I had a very nice time") provide relatively little pertinent information.

It is primarily in written language that the words themselves become all-important. Without nonverbal cues, careful construction and rewriting are needed to capture the correct "feeling." Sarcasm, teasing, and other nuances of meaning are easily lost in letters and books. This is why even intimate love letters tend to have a "formal" quality, while many business meetings or telephone conversations seem quite intimate and personal.

In face-to-face encounters, the significance of the verbal message is inversely related to the amount of available vocal and gestural information. When nonverbal information is weak or absent, the verbal information becomes more dominant. The attention to a speaker's verbal message, therefore, varies with interpersonal distance. The closer the distance between people, the less attention paid to the verbal message.[10] A group of friends tightly clustered around a restaurant table rarely produces a conversation that would be fully understandable from a transcript of the words they have spoken. In intimate encounters, sentences are not completed, there are changes in tense, and numerous grammatical errors are made. Less care is taken to construct and to listen to words when other sources of information are available.

There are several reasons why the focus on expressive messages may be even greater on television than in face-to-face interaction. Although very close physical proximity is the exception rather than the rule in live encounters, the opposite is true on television. There are few, if any, people to whom a viewer is supposed to respond who are not seen extensively in close-up. Further, the one-way direction of information flow allows the viewer to do something that is generally considered impolite in face-to-face interaction—*stare*. Finally, in live interactions, a person cannot devote all his or her energy to monitoring the behavior of others because he or she is also deeply involved both in producing expressions and communications and in thinking about how other people are monitoring those behaviors. But with television, the viewer can slump in a chair and focus exclusively on the expressive behavior of those televised. The viewer remains unobserved and relatively inexpressive. (Indeed, for all these reasons, television may have been a stimulus to the recent growth of the field of nonverbal communication.)

Because of the rich expressive dimensions of television, interviews on television are completely different from print interviews. On television, even a "no comment" or a long pause is a meaningful and significant "answer." It is rich in expressive information. It shows the speaker's response to the situation and to the content of the question, even though the response is essentially nonverbal. One of the most popular programs on television, "60 Minutes," often uses footage of interviewees pausing between words or stammering. Very tight close-ups are often used, so tight, in fact, that any move of the head makes it appear that the subject is trying to escape scrutiny. Such shots seem to suggest that the interviewee is hiding something or is dishonest. (In a sense, the use of such shots may itself be a kind of deception, because sudden head movements or the expressive signs of discomfort do not necessarily mean deception; they can simply signify excitement, nervousness in front of a camera, tiredness, a lapse in memory, or an upset stomach.)

Although some analysts attribute the new "personal" coverage and exposure of political leaders to a conscious decision on the part of journalists and editors, it is more likely that the new bias is supported by the ability of electronic media to "capture" personal attributes. It now seems fair (and necessary) literally to "expose" the personalities of leaders because the revealing behavior emanates from the leaders themselves, and unlike quotes in a newspaper, expressive behavior cannot be easily rearranged or edited.* If a politician cries while speaking a certain sentence, it is not necessary to mention it in print, but you cannot play a tape of the words without also conveying the crying. It is fitting that in the jargon of broadcast journalism, taped reports and interviews are called "actualities"; the expressions are allowed to "speak" for themselves.

For a number of reasons, the decisions surrounding the broadcast of a videotape of a person are different from the decisions to quote someone in a newspaper. If I overhear a politician swearing, and I print the words, *I* seem to take some responsibility for them as well. If, however, I record the words and expressions on audio or videotape and then broadcast them, the words and expressions seem to come more directly from the speaker, and my responsibility (though arguably the same) seems greatly diminished.

In this sense, when magazine editors printed a picture of Vice President Nelson Rockefeller making an obscene gesture in response to hecklers in 1976,[11] the editors deferred responsibility for the gesture's appearance in their magazine to Mr. Rockefeller. Yet had no photographer caught the event on film, it is unlikely that the same editors would have printed an artist's rendering of the gesture or a detailed verbal description. The ability to capture personal expressions through cameras and microphones increases the extent of their incorporation into the public record.

---

*Films and videotapes can, of course, be "edited" in the sense that strips of action can be arranged in any sequence or cut to any length. But one cannot manipulate a person's actions and speech on videotape or film quite as freely as one can edit words on a page. In print, an editor may add words, delete words, change punctuation, and perhaps alter the spellings from American to British (in a sense, changing the author's "accent"). With film and tape, however, the deletion of a word is often obvious, the addition of a word almost impossible, and a sentence cut off in the middle sounds odd. To edit out a whole phrase or sentence, videotape editors must often cut to another shot (such as an interviewer nodding) so as to avoid a "jump cut" in which a person's head, body, and hands suddenly jump to a new position. Even the smoothest editing job, however, cannot change the cadence of a person's speaking or edit out a tone that smacks of conceit or uncertainty.

The expressive nature of electronic messages offers one explanation of why the public is no longer offended by the idea of political ghost writers. Presidents and politicians once wrote (or claimed that they wrote) all their own speeches. After all, if most people in the country can only *read* what you have to say, they will want to believe that you really wrote the words yourself. If someone else wrote the words, there would be no message directly from or about you. The expressions accompanying a speech over radio or television, however, are so personal and revealing in themselves, that the authorship of the words is now less significant.* Indeed, a politician speaking on television could probably please an audience even by reciting a collection of quotes from others' essays and poems that reflected his or her philosophy. Conversely, a politician might alienate an audience by having someone else *deliver* a media speech—even if the words were written by the politician. On television, expressions usually dominate words.

The personal and emotional response to expressive cues on television explains some otherwise baffling findings in political polls. In recent years, pollsters have found a split between the voters' political views and their personal feelings toward politicians. In February 1982, for example, only 47% of the national population approved of "the way Ronald Reagan is handling his job as President," yet 70% approved of him "as a person."[13] Another poll found that nearly a third of those interviewed disapproved of Ronald Reagan's policies, yet personally "liked him."[14] In an electronic age, therefore, it is quite possible that many people will vote for candidates with whom they largely disagree, or vote against candidates who share their political philosophy. Such voting behavior would be unthinkable if the voters only had access to transcripts of the candidates' speeches and policy statements, it only makes sense when the voters feel they "know" the candidates personally.

The programs that thrive on television depend heavily on expressive rather than communicative content. The transcripts of talk shows such as the "Tonight" show and of game shows such as "Family Feud" would make boring and unenlightening reading. Talk shows do not succeed because of talk. And in spite of the common belief that quiz shows are "educational" in a traditional sense, little or nothing is "communicated" in these shows. Game shows, however, are rich in expressions. People are placed in situations of stress and they react and respond. (Indeed, potential contestants are screened for their expressiveness.[15]) The "learning" in these programs comes from the "truth" and "reality" inherent in human behavior and experience.

---

*Although I have focused on media such as radio and television, the loudspeaker also has had a tremendous impact on the style of public address. With a microphone and amplifier, for example, a speaker could speak more softly and intimately, and more nuances of expression could emerge. It is probably no coincidence that the first use of amplifiers for presidential addresses, the birth of broadcasting, and the formal addition of a "speechwriter" to the President's staff all took place in the same year.[12]

The most expensive content on television—advertising—also relies much more heavily on expression than on communication. Few campaigns for nationally advertised products present a formal, logical, verbal "argument" for buying their product. Instead, they present people in highly expressive situations: smiling, laughing, hugging, kissing, singing, running, playing, or diving into water (often in slow motion). The implicit nonverbal arguments are that buying the advertised product will make you feel good, make you more huggable and lovable. Even when verbal messages are used, they often push discursive words as far as possible toward nonlinear presentational messages ("Have a Coke and a smile"; "Me and my RC"; "Coke is it!"). The expressive messages of advertising are almost impossible to regulate. As nondiscursive presentations, they cannot be proven true or false. If a diet soft drink commercial *said*, "Drink this and you'll be beautiful and have beautiful friends to play volleyball with on the beach," they could be prosecuted for fraud. But commercials rarely make such verbal claims. They do not appeal to rationality, but to the emotions and the senses.

It is not surprising that advertisers would want to circumvent rationality, but it is upsetting to realize that television news and documentaries often do the same. Transcripts of television newscasts often contain surprisingly little "information," and they seem strangely informal compared to newspaper reporting. The style of television news is often more suited to the neighborhood coffee shop than to the newspaper column.* Videotaped segments on the news frequently contain much more expression than communication. A microphone and camera thrust in the face of an airplane crash survivor or a mother who has just heard that her son has been killed yield very little communicated information, but offer viewers a rich source of expression.

---

*I still remember my surprise the first time I read a transcript of the "CBS Evening News with Walter Cronkite." The news program was aired on October 25, 1972, and began as follows: "Good evening. North Vietnam today stepped up its propaganda war over the subject of peace. Hanoi said President Nixon is tricky, and crafty, and the real stumbling block to peace in Indo-China, not President Thieu of South Vietnam. In Paris meanwhile, the Viet Cong said a cease-fire could come within hours, but not until Mr. Nixon either dumps Thieu, or gets him to accept a coalition government." These words *sound* fine when read out loud, but they are very different from the reporting style of respected newspapers. Note the informal constructions and the use of words such as "tricky," "crafty," "dumps," and "gets." Later in the same broadcast, Cronkite opened another serious story with the line, "More of those deadly little letter bombs turned up today." The next day's *New York Times* reported the same events quite differently. The mention of the Communists' accusations was buried deep within the story on the cease-fire and began as follows: "The Communists' statements from various quarters concentrated . . . on warning that they would fight on to victory if a settlement was not reached. There were renewed accusations that peace reports were a 'political trick' by the United States designed to 'dupe public opinion.'" One of the two newspaper stories on the letter bombs began, "Explosive devices sent by mail critically injured an Arab postman and a secretary here today, and other letter-bombs exploded or were intercepted in Algeria, Libya and Egypt."[16]

The informality of television news content is often supported by a chatty style and informal interaction among newscasters. (This is especially true for local news programs.) Indeed, the perceived quality of the relationship among television news "teams" is often the key to the success or failure of a news program. The quips and interchanges are generally low-level communications, but they are meaningful expressions. They are intended to make the viewer feel that the newscasters are "nice people" and that they are friends off the set.

One of the oddities of television news is the fact that the newscasters become part of the news in a way that newspaper reporters rarely do. Broadcast reporters and interviewers are also personally exposed on television. Because we experience their personal expressions and responses to events, they are now as prominent as the public figures and stories they report on. After revealing the personalities and homes of many world leaders and celebrities, veteran interviewer Barbara Walters felt it only fair and sensible that she do a television program on her own home and personal life. Similarly, Walter Cronkite's retirement from the "CBS Evening News" was itself a major news story.

If, as discussed above, expressions are ambiguous and imprecise, why do so many television programs, including news shows, rely heavily on them, and why are viewers apparently so accepting of them? Expressions are powerful and effective because they seem more natural and real than words. Expressions come directly from a human being, and the sender has significantly less control over them than over communications. A person can lie verbally much more easily than he or she can "lie" nonverbally.[17] An unethical person could say or write the false statement: "I love you." But it is much more difficult to *express* the same feeling nonverbally—especially over an extended period of time—unless it is true. Even beyond the issue of truth and falsity, however, is the basic sense that one has "met" or "knows" the persons one sees on television because one experiences their personal expressions.

It is also very difficult to have people change or manipulate their expressive behavior on demand. A threat or a twisted arm might force someone to write something he or she does not believe (such as a confession to a crime), but it is much more difficult to coerce someone into "sounding sincere." Further, expressive messages are so "personal" that it is very difficult for most people to "forge," or accurately mimic, another person's expressions. As an April Fool's prank, you might type a letter to a friend and sign it with the name of the friend's employer. If you do a good job, your friend may take the letter at face value. Yet if you call your friend on the telephone and pretend to be the employer, your task is much more difficult because you must capture the vocal style of the employer. And if you come to the door of your friend's house (or send a videotape) and pretend to be the employer, your chances of fooling your friend are very slim.

While words carry more precise meanings than expressions, they are often untrustworthy or insufficient when they are isolated on a page. When words are seen on a printed page, it is impossible to tell if they are composed out of fear or confidence, spoken with humility or conceit. It may be difficult to ascertain the true authorship of words, and it is impossible to check the sincerity of a statement by looking to expressions for evidence of deception. Even accurate quotes in a newspaper may be denied later by their speakers.

For all these reasons, expressive "evidence" on videotape is very powerful. Many police departments have found that videotaped confessions yield higher rates of conviction than written confessions because it is more difficult for defendants to deny such a confession or claim that it was forced out of them.[18] Similarly, the FBI's Abscam videotapes of U.S. Congressmen accepting bribes presented much stronger evidence than would have been provided by verbal accounts of witnesses. For the same reasons, the "living will"—a videotape of a person speaking his or her own last will and testament—is growing more popular. It is difficult to contest a will in which your wealthy Uncle Harold leaves you only a spare tire, when you see and hear Harold himself bestowing that gift on you.

The relative difficulty of controlling or forging expressive messages explains why electronic media are more intimate, personal, and revealing than print media. The rich range of expressive information in television suggests a reason for the claim by many Americans that they find television the most "trustworthy" of all sources of news.* For even though the news on television is highly packaged, with much information coming from the same sources used by newspapers and radio, at least there is someone you "know personally" speaking it to you. The power of expressive messages is also probably the source of the credibility of "hidden camera" interviews, person-on-the-street interviews, and such shows as "Real People."

Different electronic media vary in terms of the range of expressive cues they transmit. Radio, for example, conveys only vocal expressions. Those who are capable of managing their vocalizations well may be able to use the medium very effectively—even if they cannot control other expressions simultaneously. A nervous speaker may be able to control his or her voice, but not the nervous shaking of a leg or swaying of the body. Radio is more revealing than print, but radio remains an active filter of any expressive cues that are visual.

The trend from print media to electronic media (and from radio to television), therefore, is a trend from formal and social front region messages to informal and personal back region messages. Print media present crafted, stylized messages, while electronic media present spontaneous

*According to the Roper surveys, television has been viewed as the most believable source of news since 1961. Since 1968, it has held better than a two-to-one margin over the next most believable source, newspapers.[19]

and "natural" messages. Even when the "content" of news and entertainment programs is tightly scripted and planned, the expressions of the individuals in them present a "slice of life" view that is not comparable to printed messages. All other things being equal, electronic media tend to merge personal and public spheres.

The merger of personal and public has a dual effect on the information-systems associated with people of different ages, professions, and educational backgrounds. The expressive nature of electronic media of communication both homogenizes *access* to information and merges the general types of images *projected* by different people into the public realm.

Expressive messages are more equally accessible than verbal and printed messages. As Watzlawick and his colleagues note, young children, mental patients, and animals can accurately assess the general meaning of expressions, even when the linguistic cues are not meaningful to them.[20] Similarly, two researchers of nonverbal behavior, Paul Ekman and Wallace Friesen, note that a lay person's interpretation of expressive messages often coincides with those of experts.[21]

Although people could never learn a strange foreign language from reading a book written in that language, they can generally make some sense of the information presented by foreigners interacting on television. The "language" of action, vocalization, and interaction is rich in meaningful expressions. Lech Walesa, leader of the Polish workers' union, Solidarity, became an international hero through television even though many of his admirers could neither understand the words he spoke nor comprehend the complexity of the issues his union dealt with. Similarly, the average American may not understand all the implications of a politician's policy statements, but anyone can grasp the "meaning" of a campaign advertisement that shows a politician eating breakfast with his or her family, and anyone can sense the implications of an FBI sting film that shows a politician stuffing money in his or her pockets.

The expression/communication distinction sheds more light on the differences between reading habits and television viewing habits, as discussed in the last chapter. A book on a mental hospital may contain specialized discursive data which can be understood only by those with training in the subject. But while a television show may *discuss* similar specialized topics, the program usually *presents* very nonspecialized information as well. In one sense, all television programs that present the behavior of people are about the same thing: human gesture, feeling, and emotion. The expressive quality of television makes almost any television program accessible to the average viewer.

The heavy reliance on expressions in electronic media also tends to equalize the types of messages sent by different people. While some people have more pleasant and persuasive expressive styles than other people, there are no clear graded levels of expressive competence. One does not learn "to express" by going to Harvard. Even animals and children can express "effectively"—though not necessarily to the effect desired.

There may be ways to teach people to express more pleasingly, but our educational system takes that realm of behavior for granted.*

Every organism exudes expressions, and children and illiterates may be, at times, more pleasing expressors than renowned scholars and poets. The writing styles of people of different ages and educational backgrounds vary much more predictably than their presentational styles. While essays, articles, and books must be composed by trained "authors," the content of a video "essay" can be provided by almost any passing man, woman, child, or animal. In these terms, there is an underlying similarity among the messages presented by different people on television—a similarity that does not exist in any other form of communication except face-to-face interaction. Groups of people who were excluded from the public forum created by print because they lacked the requisite entry skills are now able to participate in the public arena created by electronic media.

There are, of course, expressive "superstars," people whose personal styles are pleasing to large sections of the population, people who are not only *able* to express (as we all are), but able to express in a way that many people find exciting. Talk show hosts such as Phil Donahue obviously have exceptional expressive abilities that can make them public "personalities," but, ironically, part of the appeal of Donahue's programs is that almost any member of his show's studio audience seems capable of providing some comedy or drama.

Further, those people who are excellent expressors are not necessarily excellent "communicators." The charismatic Lech Walesa, for example, is a powerful expressor in person and on television; but he would not command much attention in printed speeches or books. As *Time* magazine reports:

> His working-class Polish is rough and often ungrammatical. . . . His speeches frequently are riddled with mixed metaphors and skewed analogies; Solidarity's leaders admit that Walesa . . . is more intuitive than intellectual. He rather defiantly claims that he has never read a serious book in his life.
>
> Yet Walesa got through his message of hope to his countrymen. Said a Warsaw journalist: "Sometimes he doesn't even make any sense, but he is always reassuring."[22]

The accessibility of expressions compared to the elitism of discursive communications may explain why most people feel that they do not need political experts to help them interpret and understand televised political "speeches." And the "truth" and "reality" of all people's expressive mes-

---

*Actors are among the few people who consciously study expressive skills. In contrast to the stage, however, television "acting" often means learning how to behave "naturally" and pretending that no camera is present. Many business leaders now take training in speaking into television cameras so that they can address their employees through videotapes (or star in their companies' TV commercials). But again, a major part of their training is learning how to be comfortable about the presence of a camera. We know from the television series "Candid Camera" how good many unselfconscious "performers" can be.

sages explains, in turn, why the televised reactions of the person-on-the-street are so acceptable in news programs and documentaries.

The information form of electronic media is changing our perceptions of the world and its people. And through electronic "documents," future generations will experience a new sort of past. "History" was once a discursive script written and acted by the rich, the powerful, and the educated. Because of their discursiveness, historical sources were also filled with arguments, propositions, ideas, and ideals. The growing archives of audio and video tape, however, thrust the common person into history; simultaneously, they reveal what is common even about our leaders. And the "language" of these records is the expressive-presentational-analogic form of gesture, feeling, and experience. It is not surprising that in the last three decades many historians have discovered a new vacuum in our understanding of the past—the everyday experience of the common people who did not write down their thoughts and who did not make history, but who only occupied it. A whole new historical industry has developed that involves analyzing parish documents, gravestones, and other traces of "the world we have lost."[23]

"Imprint of" *vs.* "Report on"

All media act as filters that exclude aspects of "reality." Each medium, however, is a different type of filter. The more abstract, obtrusive, and slow the encoding process, the less messages resemble the things they are about. And the less messages resemble reality, the more the medium can be used to present stylized and idealized images of events. Conversely, the more the medium simply "captures" what is happening in a situation, without any particular effort on the part of those present, the more messages will closely resemble the behavior they are about. And the more messages are tied to real behavior and events, the less they can be manipulated and controlled. In this sense, slow, obtrusive media have a "front region bias," while fast, unobtrusive media have a "back region bias."

Written and printed messages tend to be more formal than electronically conveyed messages. Sitting down to write a letter involves an abstract, obtrusive code. It is difficult to forget about the intervening medium because you must "translate" information into its form. But sitting down in front of a microphone or television camera does not involve a complex recording activity. You simply "behave," and a "message" is automatically "captured."

The informality of electronic messages is heightened when the medium is bidirectional and interactive. Speaking to someone on the telephone, for example, is so natural that we almost forget about the intervening medium. (We often say "I spoke to _____ last night," not even thinking to add that it was a telephone conversation. We rarely say "I spoke" when we mean that we wrote someone a letter.) Because of the unobtrusiveness of the medium and its code, the telephone conversation is much more spontaneous and much less contrived than most letters. Letters to a close friend are often more stylized than telephone conversations with a stranger. People often rewrite letters several times, but rarely does one say on the telephone: "Let me start this conversation again."

This analysis also explains why one post-print medium—the telegraph—tends to be even more formal and less expressive than print. The telegraph's Morse Code is a code of a code. A student's letter asking for money from his or her parents would contain less expressive information than a telephone call involving the same request. But a telegram would be the least expressive of all three. It, like a hieroglyph, deals with stock communicative phrases ("IN TROUBLE STOP SEND FIVE HUNDRED DOLLARS STOP LOVE BOB"). For the same reason, computer messages can be rather "stuffy" when the computer is used for discursive communication rather than presentational information.

The striking difference in formality of the telegraph compared to the telephone is suggested by the first messages that have commonly been attributed to these media. Morse's first telegraph message is said to have been either "What Hath God Wrought?" or "Attention Universe!" Both messages are highly formal and abstract; they are clearly front region messages. They convey little personal expression or affect. The first telephone message, in sharp contrast, is reported to have been "Watson, come here, I need you"—a personal, back region message.

If the content of a medium requires complex encoding, then the encoder needs time and effort to formulate messages. The encoding energy and time pull the sender out of live, ongoing situations. In live interactions, one can compliment a cook while eating a meal, but to write about a delicious meal, one must usually wait until the meal is over.

The burden of writing, however, can also be a blessing. The time a person *must* take to write something can be used to facilitate the more careful crafting and molding of the final message. The time can be used to eliminate mistakes, resolve ambiguities, and hide the fact that one needs time to construct and edit the message. Thus, we may feel that a postcard written to hosts a week after a visit may better convey our thoughts about the visit than the spontaneous thank you's mumbled as farewells were said.

The great traumas of writing are hidden by the delays inherent in the medium. Just transcribing and proofreading an essay take a great amount of time. Anxieties, revisions, doubts, sweating, and swearing can all be concealed within this buffer time zone. Writing not only excludes all expressive behavior, it also conceals the physical process of producing the message. A final essay, therefore, can have a tone of confidence and formality foreign to the first fumbling drafts.

The more slowly messages are encoded, sent, and received, the more formal their typical content. Slow messages must "summarize" events; instantaneous messages can present a "transcript" or an "imprint" of events. A moment-by-moment account is less organized, involves many insignificant details, and contains many aspects of behavior that role performers would often prefer to keep secret. An instantaneous message is "messier" and more back region in flavor.

In writing a letter to a close friend, for example, you might summarize events of the last few weeks or months. You might tell your friend how the weather has been, that your child has begun to talk, or that you have been growing your own vegetables. Yet if in the middle of your letter writing, the same friend calls you on the telephone, the type of information you convey often changes. While the letter provides a general summary of the past, the telephone conversation often deals with the specifics of the present. You may look out the window and comment on the wind blowing your lawn chairs over, or you may have to get off the phone for a moment to tell your child to stop screaming in the next room. On the phone, your tone of voice might reveal that you are tired today, and you may feel obligated to explain that your stomach is a bit upset from eating a bad tomato. Even when the subject matter is the same—you and your life—the letter tends to present a more formal front region view, while the telephone conversation includes informal, moment-to-moment, back region experiences.

In the same manner, television's live coverage of events is more back region in style than newspaper accounts. Television reports of hostage situations, assassination attempts, union negotiations, and airport accidents include the stream of moment-to-moment rumors, suggestions, indecisions, anxieties, and incorrect assumptions. The choppy, disorganized, and mostly uninformative live coverage of a man's threat to blow up the Washington Monument in 1982 demonstrated how little police and reporters actually knew about what was going on. The newspaper stories the next day presented a much cleaner image.

Similarly, when John W. Hinckley, Jr., attempted to kill President Reagan, the videotape recording showed the disorganized scuffle around the assassin and his victims. Television news then reported that Press Secretary James Brady was dead and carried an announcement by Secretary of State Alexander Haig saying that, according to the Constitution, he was in charge at the White House, pending the return of the Vice President. Then, television news reported that James Brady was alive and that Haig was mistaken in his claim of authority. Then, the misinformation and mistakes on the part of reporters and officials became news stories themselves.[24]

Most television news is not "live," but unlike other media, television has the constant potential for instantaneous visual and aural coverage. In times of crisis, therefore, we expect television to use this potential. The videotape of the Hinckley assassination attempt went on the air four minutes after the first shot was fired.[25] The speed of the spread of news forced other actions to occur quickly. According to later reports, Alexander Haig rushed to speak to the press because he feared that silence from the government would be interpreted at home and abroad as a sign of confusion and leaderlessness. The result was that he literally ran to the press room, and came before the cameras out of breath and sweating, thereby contributing to the impression he hoped to forestall.[26] Similarly, television reporters felt the pressure to confirm or deny the rumor of Brady's death quickly. In one instance, CBS correspondent Lesley Stahl saw White House aides "dissolved in tears," which she suggested to viewers probably meant that Brady *had* died. Unknown to her at the time, the White House aides had just heard the false report of Brady's death on another television network![27]

In a sense, the instantaneous coverage of television created some of these "events." In an earlier time, the slower reporting would have filtered out many of these stories. The rumor that James Brady was dead, for example, might never have been reported, and then, certainly, the fact that there were mistaken reports concerning Brady's death would not have become a significant news event. The small details, mistakes, and confusions would have been hidden and forgotten in the invisible backstage fostered by the slower print media (just as the letter to your friend would probably not mention overturned lawn chairs, a screaming child, a bad tomato, and tiredness on a particular afternoon). Further, because government officials would have been unable to give an instantaneous response to the nation, a few hours delay could not have been interpreted as a sign of confusion.

Slowness, of course, is not a guarantee of accuracy (witness the headline "Dewey Defeats Truman"), but the speed of encoding in television, combined with its wide spectrum of nonverbal information, leads to a new degree of exposure of the many details, fluctuations, and uncertainties that were traditionally filtered out in newspaper reports. What was once part of the backstage area of life is now presented as "news."*

Thus, while much of the *content* of news is shaped by journalistic decisions and by political and economic factors, the *form* of the news is often greatly affected by the nature of the medium. For whether one believes that television news in the United States is biased or unbiased, controlled

---

*Motion pictures stand between print and electronic media in terms of this variable. Film must be developed before it is projected. Filmed newsreels and interviews can be screened and edited in the backstage created by such necessary delays. But the telephone, radio, and television permit (and therefore, in a sense, demand) instant "live" coverage and transmission. If John Hinckley's attack on Ronald Reagan had been filmed instead of videotaped, for example, there would have been time for the Secret Service and the FBI to request a screening of the film before it played on television. There would have been time for authorities to ask for a delay in its showing or to decide that parts were too graphic to display on television. And the public need not have been informed of such control and censorship since films can *never* be shown immediately. Because electronic images can be transmitted instantly, any attempts at control or censorship become difficult and apparent. Such "biases" of electronics sometimes operate even in countries where the press is tightly controlled by the government. When the Pope visited Poland in 1983, for example—in part to criticize the government—the *possibility* of covering his trip "live" seemed to demand at least some live coverage. As a result, the Polish people heard serious criticism of their government on the government's own radio and television.

or free, censored or uncensored, its style remains very distinct from print news.

The speed with which messages can now travel from senders to receivers limits the rehearsal and preparation time for many social performers (and makes whatever backstage time *is* taken more apparent). Even when one sits down to write a letter "immediately," several hours may be spent preparing the message. But if one is interviewed on the telephone, radio, or television, the message may have to be developed on the spot. The beginning of a sentence must be spoken before the end of the sentence is fully formed. The apparent inarticulateness of many of our leaders today may be related more to this change in media than to a decline in our leaders' basic intelligence.

Regardless of the specific symbol system used, all written messages separate behavior from reports of behavior. Electronic media, however, present behavior and experience much more directly. Many of us are willing to share with our friends detailed verbal or written descriptions of our experiences. But we would not necessarily want our friends to be present during all the situations we describe. Similarly, few of us would want even our closest friends to monitor constantly our behaviors and interactions through a video and/or sound system.

A written or verbal account of an event can be "packaged" and "cleaned up." An executive may tell his or her spouse that a training session for employees went "very well." The executive may forget to mention that at one point he or she tripped over a chair. And the executive may be largely unaware of the degree to which he or she made speaking errors, paced back and forth, or left out steps in a sequence of arguments. Clearly, whatever the executive later *says* about the event is not equivalent to the spouse having experienced the event directly. Thus, even in a technically "public" performance, such as a talk before one's employees, there may be many "back region" idiosyncrasies and mistakes that performers do not care to have publicized beyond the situation of their occurrence. A videotape of the executive's performance, however, would tend to carry such situation-specific behaviors beyond the live setting.

Electronic media, of course, do not simply "present" an event. Whenever you aim a camera or microphone in one direction, for example, you inevitably ignore things in every other direction. But electronic imprints of events do not allow for a clear separation between the "stream of behavior" in a situation and the information about the situation made available—later or simultaneously—to those not physically present. (Indeed, a videotape of an event may even shock and upset participants in the event who are not accustomed to seeing themselves "as others see them.") Cameras and microphones tend to force people to have memories and accounts of events that resemble the electronically captured images and sounds. As many politicians have discovered recently, it is impossible to deny quotes once they have been preserved on audiotape.

For these reasons, no doubt, many judges and legislators are hesitant to permit the televising of trials and legislative sessions. A written statement or a brief public appearance allows for a highly controlled performance. But it is much more difficult for someone to sustain a good "onstage" performance during many grueling hours of a trial or legislative debate. A camera at such events may capture public officials looking tired, getting angry, yawning, scratching an itch, picking their noses, or not paying attention. It is interesting to imagine how our image of great leaders of the past would change if we had thousands of hours of videotape of them instead of having only transcripts of their speeches and glowing (and sanitized) descriptions of their actions.

The live, ongoing nature of most electronic communications makes it much more difficult (and at times, impossible) to separate the public thread of experience from the private one. A wide spectrum of behavior is conveyed through electronic media. Emotions and feelings "leak out" through television. A depressed person may be able to write a cheerful note, but unable to make a cheerful telephone call. Not only does the nature of electronic media make it simple to forget that one's behaviors are mediated, but it also leaves one few options even if one remembers. For when the camera captures how you behave, then how you choose to act *for the camera* is also how you *really* behave in the situation, and how you behave in the situation is how the camera captures you. When a wedding is videotaped, or when the reunion of hostages and their loved ones is televised, the record of the event is an imprint of the behaviors themselves. Clearly, there is a relationship between private behavior and public message in electronic media that does not exist in print media.

Given the principles developed in Part I, this discussion offers another reason why the widespread use of television and other electronic media may be having a profound effect on social behavior. To the extent that traditional distinctions among various group identities, different stages of socialization, and different ranks of authority were dependent on pre-electronic distinctions between public messages and personal, expressive behaviors, we would expect significant changes in a wide spectrum of social roles.

This analysis has suggested that electronic media lead to a form of interaction that was once found exclusively in immediate physical interaction. All that has been discussed, therefore, brings us to the threshold of the subject of the final chapter in this part of the book. For when electronic media begin to provide the information once available only when participants met in the same place at the same time, then electronic media begin to reshape the meaning of "place" itself.

7

The Separation of Social Place
from Physical Place

The book of Genesis tells of God's visit to Abraham and Sarah when they are old and childless. God tells Abraham that within a year Sarah will give birth to a son. Sarah overhears this promise from inside her tent, and she laughs to herself because she is already well past menopause. Since Sarah is alone in her tent, she assumes that her laughter will go unnoticed. But God quickly asks Abraham: "Wherefore did Sarah laugh? . . . Is anything too hard for the Lord?" So surprised is Sarah by the exposure of her private behavior that she denies that she laughed.[1]

Our awe and surprise over such eavesdropping feats has diminished greatly in an age of electronic media. Being "alone" in a given place once meant that one was out of range of others' scrutiny. For people to experience each other directly, they had to travel through space, stay through time, and be admitted through the entrances of rooms and buildings. And these rules of physical place pertained to tents and palaces alike.

Although oral and print cultures differ greatly, the bond between physical place and social place was common to both of them. Print, like all new media, changed the patterns of information flow *to* and *from* places. As a result, it also changed the relative status and power of those in different places. Changes in media in the past have always affected the relationship *among* places. They have affected the information that people *bring* to places and the information that people have *in* given places. But the relationship between place and social situation was still quite strong. Electronic media go one step further: They lead to a nearly total dissociation of physical place and social "place." When we communicate through telephone, radio, television, or computer, where we are physically no longer determines where and who we are socially.

Physical Passage and Social Passage

The relationship between physical place and social situation still seems so natural that we continue to confuse physical places with the behaviors that go on in them. The words "school" and "home," for example, are used to refer both to physical buildings and to certain types of social interaction and behavior.

Before electronic media, there was ample reason to overlook the difference between physical places and social situations. Places defined most social information-systems. A given place-situation was spatially and temporally removed from other place-situations. It took time to travel from situation to situation, and distance was a measure of social insulation and isolation. Since rooms and buildings can be entered only through set doorways, people once could be included in and excluded from situations in clearly observable and predictable ways. Electronic media, however, make significant inroads into the situations once defined by physical location.

Communication and travel were once synonymous. Our country's communication channels were once roads, waterways, and railroads. Communication speed was limited to the speed of human travel. Even the legendary Pony Express took ten and a half days to communicate a message from Missouri to California.[2] The invention of the telegraph caused the first break between information movement and physical movement. For the first time, complex messages could move more quickly than a messenger could carry them.[3] With the invention and use of the telegraph, the informational differences between different places began to erode.

Just as students today are less anxious about attending a faraway college when home is only a phone call away, so did the telegraph greatly aid in the settlement of the Western frontier. The telegraph brought East and West closer together informationally. Physical distance as a social barrier began to be bypassed through the shortening of communication "distance." The mutual monitoring of East and West made the country seem smaller and other places and people closer.

Movement from situation to situation and from social status to social status once involved movement from place to place. A place defined a distinct situation because its boundaries limited perception and interaction. Like all electronic media, the telegraph not only defies limits formerly set by distance, but also bypasses the social rite of "passage," that is, the act of moving both physically and socially from one "position" to another.

If people are to behave very differently in different social situations, some clear form of movement from one situation to the next is needed. If a celebration and a memorial service take place in the same place and time, there can be no distinct behaviors for each situation. Entrances and the rites associated with them, whether formal (carrying a bride over the threshold) or informal ("Please knock before you enter my room"), have traditionally allowed for orderly transitions from situation to situation and from behavior pattern to behavior pattern.

The boundaries marked by walls, doors, and barbed wire, and enforced by laws, guards, and trained dogs, continue to define situations by including and excluding participants. But today such boundaries function to define social situations only to the extent that information can still be restricted by restricting physical access. And while much social information is still accessible only by going to a certain place or by meeting people face-to-face, the once consonant relationship between access to information and access to places has been greatly weakened by recent changes in communication media.

The messages in all early media—stone, clay, papyrus, parchment, and paper—have physical volume and weight. When they are heavy or unmovable, people have to go to a specific place to experience them. Even when they are portable, however, they still have to be physically transported from place to place, and they move with the people who possess them. They have to be carried into places, stored in places, and carried out of places. These media, like the people who carry them, are subject to the restraints of social and physical passage.

Electronic messages, however, do not make social entrances; they steal into places like thieves in the night. The "guests" received by a child through electronic media no longer can be stopped at the door to be approved of by the masters of the house. Once a telephone, radio, or television is in the home, spatial isolation and guarding of entrances have no effect on information flow. Electronic messages seep through walls and leap across great distances. Indeed, were we not so accustomed to television and radio and telephone messages invading our homes, they might be the recurring subjects of nightmares and horror films. Whether the effects of such media on our society are good, bad, or neutral, the reprocessing of our physical and social environment is revolutionary.

As a result of electronically mediated interactions, the definition of situations and of behaviors is no longer determined by physical location. To be physically alone with someone is no longer necessarily to be socially alone with them. When there are other people "there" on the telephone, or radio, or television, intimate encounters are changed.

By altering the informational characteristics of place, electronic media reshape social situations and social identities. The social meaning of a "prison," for example, has been changed as a result of electronic media of communication. Prisons were once more than places of physical incarceration; they were places of informational isolation as well. A prisoner was not only limited in movement but also "ex-communicated" from society. The placement of prisoners in a secure, isolated *location* once led to both physical and informational separation from society. Today, however, many prisoners share with the larger society the privileges of radio, television, and telephone.[4] Whether this is good or bad is difficult to say, but it is different.

Prisoners' access to the world changes the social environment of both those inside and outside prison. Those outside prison cannot use television as a "private" forum in which to discuss problems of crime and crime prevention, and prisoners can "enter" society through the wires of the telephone. One survey of 208 inmates indicated that nine out of ten prisoners had "learned new tricks and improved their criminal expertise by watching crime programs."[5] Special publications such as *The Prisoner's Yellow Pages* have been prepared to help prisoners contact law libraries, counseling services, and employment agencies.[6]

For better or worse, those prisoners with access to electronic media are no longer completely segregated from society. The use of electronic media has led to a redefinition of the nature of "imprisonment" and to a de facto revision of the prison classification system: The communication variables of "high information" prisons versus "low information" prisons now have been added to the physical variables of "high security" and "low security."

The example of prisons may be extreme, but the impact of electronic media on prisoners is paralleled by the effects of electronic media on children, women, the poor, the disabled, and other groups whose social place was once shaped, at least in part, by physical isolation from the larger world.

Electronic media bring information and experience to everyplace from everyplace. State funerals, wars, hostage crises, and space flights are dramas that can be played on the stage of anyone's living room. And the characters in these dramas are experienced almost as if they were sitting on the living room sofa.

Communicating through electronic media is certainly not equivalent to traveling from place to place and interacting with others in live encounters, but the information transmitted by electronic media is much more similar to face-to-face interaction than is the information conveyed by books or letters. And "relationships" with others through electronic media are accessible to virtually everyone without regard to physical location and social "position."

Media ''Friends''

Electronic media's encroachment on place is suggested in one of the clichés of the broadcasting industry: "This show is brought to you *live* from . . ." Once, physical presence was necessary for the experience of a "live," ongoing event. You "had to be there" to experience an informal and intimate interaction. Place once defined a very special category of communication. Electronic media, however, have changed the relative significance of live and mediated encounters. Through electronic media of communication, social performers now "go" where they would not or could not travel, and audiences are now "present" at distant events.

What sort of relationship is formed between people who experience each other only through electronic media? In a perceptive article on media written in the 1950s, Donald Horton and R. Richard Wohl suggest that even when the communication is unidirectional, such as in radio and television, a special relationship develops that did not and could not exist in print media. What is unusual about the new mass media, they suggest, is that they offer the illusion of face-to-face interaction with performers and political figures. "The conditions of response to the performer are analogous to those in a primary group. The most remote and illustrious men are met *as if* they were in the circle of one's peers."[7]

Horton and Wohl suggest that the new media lead to a new type of relationship which they call "para-social interaction." They argue that although the relationship is mediated, it psychologically resembles face-to-face interaction. Viewers come to feel they "know" the people they "meet" on television in the same way they know their friends and associates. In fact, many viewers begin to believe that they know and understand a performer better than all the other viewers do. Paradoxically, the para-social performer is able to establish "intimacy with millions."

Horton and Wohl's framework explains the popularity of talk show hosts such as Jack Paar, Johnny Carson, and Dick Cavett. These are people, according to Horton and Wohl, who have no traditional performance skill; they are not singers, musicians, actors, or even professional-quality comedians. The content of their "performance" is mostly small talk and running gags. Yet they are likeable and interesting in the same way that a close friend is likeable and interesting. The viewer can rely on them to be "themselves." As Horton and Wohl suggest, the pure para-social performer is simply "known for being known." Within this framework, it makes sense that stories about Johnny Carson's threats to resign from the "Tonight" show, his arrest for suspicion of drunk driving, and his divorce settlement have been reported on the network news and in front page headlines.

Even performers with traditional skills often exploit the intimacy of the new media (or find that they cannot avoid it). As a result of close personal observation, many athletes, musicians, journalists, and politicians are now judged not only on the basis of their "talent" but also on the basis of their personalities. The para-social framework may explain why many singing stars turn to more and more personal lyrics and themes as their careers develop and why public officials often add more private information to their public speeches as they become more widely known. The theory can also be extended to actors playing fictional roles. For many viewers, soap opera and other television characters are real people to whom they can turn for inspiration and advice. During his first five years on network television, the fictional "Dr. Marcus Welby" received a quarter of a million letters, most requesting medical advice.[8]

Horton and Wohl do not link their framework to an analysis of the impact of electronic media on physical place, but they do offer observations that support such an analysis. They note, for example, that the para-social relationship has its greatest impact on the "socially isolated, the socially inept, the aged and invalid, the timid and rejected."[9] Because electronic media provide the types of interaction and experience which were once restricted to intimate live encounters, it makes sense that they would have their greatest effect on those who are physically or psychologically removed from everyday social interaction. (One researcher has found that the strength of the para-social relationship increases with the viewer's age, that many elderly people think of newscasters as their friends, and that some older viewers "interact" with newscasters by responding to them verbally.[10]) Even among "average" people, the para-social relationship takes its place among daily live interactions with friends, family, and associates. Indeed, "real" friends often discuss the antics of their para-social friends.

The para-social framework is extremely useful in analyzing many phenomena not specifically discussed by Horton and Wohl. The framework explains, for example, why it is that when a "media friend" such as Elvis Presley, John Kennedy, or John Lennon dies or is killed, millions of people may experience a sense of loss as great as (and sometimes greater than) the feelings of loss accompanying the death of a relative or friend. Even an awareness of the para-social mechanism is not enough to permit escape from its "magic"; the death of John Lennon, for example, was strangely painful to me and my university colleagues who had "known" him and grown up "with" him. Sociologist Candice Leonard has suggested that such mediated relationships lead to a "new genre of human grief."[11]

Unlike the loss of a real friend or relative, the death of a media friend does not provide traditional rituals or clear ways to comfort the bereaved. Indeed, the mourning for a para-social friend is filled with paradox and helplessness. Attempts to comfort the dead person's family with words or flowers are intrusions by strangers. And intensely felt personal grief is simultaneously strengthened and weakened by the extent to which it is shared with the crowd. In order to banish the demons of grief and helplessness, therefore, thousands of people take to the streets or hold vigils near the para-social friend's home or place of death.

Ironically, but appropriately, the media provide the most ritualized channels of mourning. Radio and television present specials and retrospectives. And many people use the telephone to contact real friends who shared the intimacy with the para-social friend. But the final irony is that, in some ways, the para-social performer does not die. For the *only* means through which most people came to know him or her—records, films, and videotape—are still available. The relationship is frozen, rather than destroyed. In part, it is the potential and hope for increased intimacy that dies, and the never to be face-to-face consummation of the relationship that is mourned.

The para-social relationship has also led to a new form of murder and a new type of murder motive. Police generally distinguish between two types of murders: those committed by a person who knows the victim, and those committed by a stranger. Yet, there is now a third category: the para-social murder. While the media and police noted that John Lennon's murderer was a "complete stranger"—meaning that the two had never physically met—they overlooked the powerful para-social ties between them. Mark David Chapman knew John Lennon so well that for a time he thought he *was* John Lennon.[12] A similarly bizarre relationship existed between would-be presidential assassin John Hinckley and actress Jodie Foster. Hinckley committed his "historic act" in order to cement a "personal" relationship with Foster.[13]

In both love and hate, normal and bizarre, the para-social relationship is a new form of interaction. It has some of the traditional characteristics of both live encounters and communication through books, but it is, in fact, neither.

In formulating the notion of para-social interaction, Horton and Wohl point to the differences between "old" and "new" media. But they overlook the overall evolutionary trend, even within each type of medium, toward a shrinking of the differences between live and mediated encounters. Writing systems have evolved toward greater replication of spoken sounds (from hieroglyphs to the phonetic alphabet) and photography and electronic media have evolved toward fuller representations of face-to-face sensory experiences.

Media theorist Paul Levinson has detailed the long-term evolutionary course of media.[14] He argues that the trend is toward fuller replication of the means of communication that existed *before* media and technology. Levinson's theory gives substance to our intuitive sense that one form of a medium is "better" than another. The addition of voice to the telegraph, or sound to silent movies, or color to television, he suggests, is perceived as an "improvement" simply because the medium becomes less like a medium and more like life.

Levinson uses his theoretical framework to reject the criticism of many social theorists who suggest that media are distorting the human condition by taking us further and further away from "reality." Levinson argues, in contrast, that human beings use media to recreate as "natural" and as "human" a means of communicating as possible, while at the same time overcoming pre-technological limitations to communication (lack of permanent records, impossibility of speaking or seeing across vast distances, impossibility of being in two places at once, and so on).

Levinson's fascinating description of media history shows how an early form of a medium first gives up aspects of the "real world" in order to overcome a spatial or temporal limitation and how later forms of the medium then recapture aspects of natural communication. The telegraph, for example, gave up speech in order to travel quickly across the continent and globe; but then the telegraph evolved into the telephone which regained the human voice.

A major problem with Levinson's framework, however, is that he completely overlooks the ways in which the original spatial and temporal "limits" help to define the nature of social interaction. In suggesting that media recreate reality, Levinson defines "reality" in terms of sensory functions of communication —seeing, hearing, speaking. He ignores the ways in which the substance of human interaction changes when the barriers among situations are removed.

The theories of Levinson and of Horton and Wohl are helpful here because they suggest that face-to-face interaction is no longer the only determinant of personal and intimate interaction. The evolution of media has begun to cloud the differences between stranger and friend and to weaken the distinction between people who are "here" and people who are "somewhere else." These frameworks suggest that electronic media are unique in that they mask the differences between direct and indirect communication. What is missing from these theories, however, is an appreciation of how much social behavior changes when people are able to communicate "as if" they were in the same place when they are, in fact, in different places.

The Binding of Message to Context

The discussion thus far has suggested that electronic media weaken the significance of physical place as a determinant of social situations. Interestingly, many electronic media also strengthen one aspect of the relationship between messages and physical locations. For just as expressive and presentational messages are always about the emitting person, so are they tied to the physical location of the sender. Quotes in a newspaper may have nothing to do with the place in which the words were spoken, but a recording of a speech also captures aspects of the physical environment in which the speech was made.

Teddy Roosevelt's meetings with the press often took place while he was being shaved in the White House.[15] If he desired, Roosevelt could formulate a formal, impersonal "statement" for public release. Such a statement would be discursive and devoid of personal expression. It could be completely context-free (that is, have nothing to do with shaving). But electronic messages are usually context-bound. A President can lie in bed and write a formal statement to send to a newspaper, but a President would probably choose to get up, wash, and dress to deliver a similar statement for television. Further, for television, some background must be chosen—an office, or a fireplace, or a national monument. Even radio and telephone transmit background sounds from the sender's environment. Communication over electronic media, therefore, is similar to live interaction to the extent that it binds both people and their messages to the originating environment. And just as viewers may sense that they have "met" a person they see on television, so may they feel that they have "visited" the places they see. (Indeed, the millions of unrecalled "experiences" each of us has with things, places, and people through television may be the source of many feelings of *déjà vu* if we eventually experience them in real life.)

Another way to describe the difference between a printed "statement" and a television message is that television combines the situation of production of the message with the situation of presentation of the message (and often with the situation of reception of the message as well). In a print interview, for example, the interviewer and interviewee are in one place and the resulting interview is presented and received in another "place." In an interview designed to be printed, the interviewee can distinguish between "on" and "off" the record; he or she can establish one type of interaction with the interviewer and another type of interaction with the readers of the interview. A good example of this comes from a magazine interview of Barbra Streisand. Describing the process, the interviewer, Lawrence Grobel, writes:

> The interview sessions became, at times, a battle. When I touched on subjects that weren't comfortable for her, she would answer evasively or glibly and I would tell her what I thought of her answers—and get on her nerves. . . .Things often got emotional.
>
> For the next few weeks [after the interview sessions ended], she would call regularly to add another thought she'd had. I would fumble for my tape recorder, attach it to the telephone and we'd be off again.
>
> . . . She clearly regarded this interview as something special. It was going to be her definitive statement, she said, in which she would talk about subjects that had been rumored but neither confirmed nor denied.[16]

This description suggests that, during the long preparation for an interview to be printed, the private relationship with the interviewer ("a battle," "answer evasively") is clearly separated from the public relationship with readers ("her definitive statement").

The "place" inhabited by the interviewer and interviewee on television, however, is often the same one experienced by the television viewer. The interview subject must speak to the interviewer and the audience at the same time, and a new situation and behavior style arise. The strange mixture of formality and informality, of intimacy and distance in television interviews is the result of the merging of formerly distinct social situations.

Print allows for segregation of situations. The experience one has and the experience one writes about are different. Print media preserve the sanctity of place and the clear separation of different strains of behavior. Electronic media, however, play with place in a strange way. They violate its boundaries and change its social significance, yet they also use place as a backdrop for social events. Electronic media bind expression to physical settings but also merge many formerly distinct behavioral settings.

Time and Space "Saturation"

With its natural insulation, physical place was once the prime determinant of the definition of a situation. The spatial and temporal isolation of a physical location allowed for *one* definition of the situation to "saturate" the time/space frame. Goffman discusses "saturation" as a characteristic of Anglo-American societies where social performances tend to be given indoors and where "the impression and understanding fostered by the performance will tend to saturate the region and time span, so that any individual located in this space-time manifold will be in a position to observe the performance and be guided by the definition of the situation which the performance fosters."[17]

Any medium can pull a person out of the definition of the situation. Print media and electronic media, however, differ in their impact on the definitions of situations and on the relationship between situations and places.

Print media tend to create new, totally absorbing definitions. Reading is best done alone, in a quiet place, and to the exclusion of other activities. Indeed, special places are designated for reading. These places are designed to separate people, often into single-person cubicles. A reader, of course, is "connected" with other people by reading what they have written or what has been written about them, but the reader tends to be removed from those physically present. (Indeed, even when someone hands you a greeting card, you must ignore them for a moment in order to read it.) In this sense, reading is "anti-social"; it isolates the reader from live interactions. Reading is linear and absorbing. It is difficult to walk, talk, eat, exercise, make love, or drive an automobile while reading. Yet most of these activities are possible while watching television, and all are possible while listening to the radio.

In these ways, electronic media invade places, yet do not "occupy" them in the way that other media such as books do. Television not only changes the definition of the situation in places, but it does so in an unstable and inconsistent manner.

The funeral of Senator Hubert Humphrey, for example, was "brought" to the American home on January 14, 1978. Not only was this situation ("funeral of popular politician") combined with whatever situation existed previously in the home ("eating Sunday dinner," for example), but the new situation could also be lost and regained simply by changing channels. In the New York City area, the Humphrey funeral was broadcast live on ABC and NBC; Channel 9 carried a monster movie with hundreds of people being killed; Channel 5 broadcast a music and dancing program, "Soul Train"; Channel 11 provided a dubbed Japanese monster movie; Channel 2 showed a Tarzan cartoon; and Channel 13 broadcast "Zoom," showing at one point a boy helping his father to catch fish. Not only was the average viewer not required to travel to any specific place to see the Humphrey funeral (and all the types of accompanying expressions that were once accessible only to those present at such events), but the experience of the funeral was not allowed to saturate the time/space frame. Further, the nature of the combined situation (eating dinner during funeral) was itself unstable. The viewers could easily change their "place" by flipping channels.*

The "disrespect" for place and occasion inherent in the use of electronic media was even more dramatically demonstrated when one network stopped covering the Humphrey funeral in the middle of the service to broadcast an important golf match. Similarly, one network's offering during Anwar Sadat's dramatic peace mission to Israel involved alternating "live" coverage of Lod Airport in Israel with "live" coverage of the Ohio State-Michigan football game.

Electronic media destroy the specialness of place and time. Television, radio, and telephone turn once private places into more public ones by making them more accessible to the outside world. And car stereos, wrist-watch televisions, and personal sound systems such as the Sony "Walkman" make public spaces private. Through such media, what is happening almost anywhere can be happening wherever we are. Yet when we are everywhere, we are also no place in particular.

"Home is wherever there's a telephone," says one telephone company ad. This analysis suggests, as well, that "anywhere there's a telephone is no longer the same home." Those entering many places no longer find them informationally special. Places visited for the first time now look familiar if they (or places like them) have already been seen on television. And places that were once very different are now more similar because nearly every place has a television set, radio, and telephone. With electronic media, most places—from the child's room to the priest's home to the prisoner's cell—now have a strong common denominator. Those aspects of group identity, socialization, and hierarchy that were once dependent on particular physical locations and the special experiences available in them have been altered by electronic media.

---

*One recent study of television habits found that more than a third of the viewers of a typical hour-long television program do not watch the program to the end, that about 40% of viewers in cable households "always" or "often" search for another program during commercial breaks, and that 40-50% of television viewers are eating, washing the dishes, talking on the telephone, or reading while "watching television."[18]

PART III
The New Social Landscape

This section of the book looks at the potential changes in a broad spectrum of roles as a result of electronic media's reorganization of social situations. It weaves together the strands of theory developed in Parts I and II. Each of the three types of roles examined in Chapter 4 (group identity, socialization, and hierarchy) is analyzed in terms of each of the three major characteristics of electronic situations outlined in Chapters 5, 6, and 7 (the merging of public spheres, the exposure of back regions, and the undermining of place). This analysis leads to a reinterpretation of a broad field of social conflict and role change.

Each of the first three chapters deals with changes in one of the three role categories. The fourth chapter presents an analysis of the ways in which the impact of electronic media is made visible and is enhanced by subsequent adjustments in notions of "appropriate" behavior, in media content, and in rules of access to physical locations. This analysis of "effect loops" suggests that while such adjustments are often perceived as spontaneous *causes* of social change, they themselves may be *effects* of changes in media and situations.

Television is currently the most potent medium in merging public spheres, exposing back regions, and separating physical place from social place. The emphasis here, therefore, is on the last three decades of social change as they may have been influenced by the "contemporary media matrix," a matrix that has been dominated by television.* To deal exclusively with television, however, would be to distort its impact and to ignore the other electronic media that often function in tandem with it.

---

*A reasonable starting point for the study of the effects of a television-dominated media matrix is 1954, the first year that more than half of the households in the country owned television sets.[1]

Since the telephone and radio continue to be a part of the current matrix of media, and since the computer is beginning to reshape the media experiences of millions of Americans, these media also play a part in this analysis of electronic media and social change.

In many ways, it is absurd to argue for the widespread social impact of any single variable in isolation from others. The world is complex, and thousands of significant factors work to affect every personal and group action. Yet the isolation of variables and the search for cause-and-effect relationships are at the heart of most scientific inquiry and popular curiosity. In a laboratory, variables can be isolated and the strongest empirical evidence of causality can be demonstrated. But the strength of laboratory findings concerning social behavior—the isolation of variables—is also a great weakness. For in interpreting experimental studies, one must take into account the unnatural setting of the experiment and the cold fact that real life does not offer isolated variables. In defending the cause-effect linking of variables in all experimental findings, one must use the qualifier, "all other things held constant." The researcher using an analytical methodology must often use a similar disclaimer when discussing the effects of a single variable.

By logically isolating the variables of media, situations, and social roles, my analysis suggests that electronic media have specific types of effects on social behavior. I outline the *direction* of change brought about by the widespread use of electronic media—all other things held constant. But other things are never constant, and I do not deny that many factors have influenced the situations I describe, and I know that other factors have acted to counter or mute many of the effects of electronic media.

Most readers are likely to have pet theories and beliefs concerning the genesis of the many behaviors, movements, and trends I analyze in this part of the book. I ask them merely to accept the possibility that the situational changes I describe may be important contributing influences to these events as well. This analysis is not meant to obliterate other explanations any more than other analyses would necessarily obliterate this one.

Put differently, the subject of the discussion here is not "social behavior and all its causes," but rather "electronic media and the potentially wide spectrum of its influence." My "findings" should be interpreted the same way findings in an experiment on the effects of a chemical, known to have been added recently to drinking water nationwide, might be interpreted. This chemical may be found to increase heart rate and metabolism, for example, but such a fact does not mean that there are no other drugs that have the same effect, nor does it mean that there are no other drugs or foods or personal habits that might moderate or offset the effects of the chemical.

In this section of the book, I try to paint a picture of recent social changes. To be viewed clearly, however, the picture must be viewed through the lens of the situational theory of change pieced together in

Parts I and II. I have tried to answer the question: If all the above analyses are correct, what trends, events, and movements of the last three decades might they help explain? I have found it stylistically awkward to include in every sentence a "may be," "possibly," or "if we believe the above." Although my sentences are, for the most part, simple declarative statements, the discussion is meant to set forth a tentative theory rather than present hard and fast conclusions.

8
New Group Identities

The Merging of Group Experiences

As discussed in Part I, group identity is based on "shared but special" information-systems. The greater the number of distinct social information-systems, the greater the number of distinct "groups"; the smaller the number of distinct information-systems, the smaller the number of distinct group identities. The merging of many formerly distinct situations through electronic media, therefore, should have an homogenizing effect on group identities.

As a result of the widespread use of television, for example, the social information available to the ghetto family now more closely resembles the information available to the middle class family. Information available to women now more closely resembles information available to men. Formerly distinct groups not only share very similar information about society in general, they also share more information about each other—information that once distinguished "insiders" from "outsiders." As a consequence, traditional group bonds are weakened and traditional distinctions among groups become partially blurred.

The change in the information characteristics of traditional groups leads to two complementary phenomena: the decreasing importance of traditional group ties and the increasing importance of other types of association.

The homogenized information networks fostered by electronic media offer individuals a comparatively holistic view of society and a wider field within which to measure their relative lot. To use George Herbert Mead's term, electronic media alter one's "generalized other"—the general sense of how other people think and evaluate one's actions. The "mediated generalized other" includes standards, values, and beliefs from outside tra-

131

ditional group spheres, and it thereby presents people with a new perspective from which to view their actions and identities. The new mediated generalized other bypasses face-to-face encounters in family and community and is shared by millions of others.*

One result of this shared perspective and more common set of situations is that members of formerly isolated and distinct groups begin to demand "equal" rights and treatment. This analysis, therefore, offers one possible explanation for the recent, sudden rise of "minorities" as potent social and political forces. Blacks, women, hispanics, Native Americans, gays, children, prisoners, and the disabled are all groups composed of people who now feel or are seen as isolated in a corner of the larger environment, restricted and disenfranchised.

The rise of minority consciousness, according to this analysis, actually indicates the demise of one aspect of minority status in the traditional sense. Minority affiliations were once based on *isolated* information-systems and very *distinct* group experiences. The demand for full equality in roles and rights dramatizes the development, in a way, of a mass "majority," a single large "group" whose members will not tolerate any great distinctions in roles and privileges.

Today's minority consciousness is something of a paradox. Many people take renewed pride in their special identity, yet the heightened consciousness of the special group is the result of being able to view one's group from the outside; that is, it is the result of no longer being fully *in* the group. Members of today's minority groups are united in their feelings of *restriction* from certain rights and experiences. People sense they are in a minority group because they feel excluded from the larger reference group. The diminutive connotation of the term "minority" does not refer to the small number of people in the group, but rather to the limited degree of access the members feel they have to the larger society. The term "minority" as it is sometimes applied to women[1]—the majority of the population—is meaningless in any other sense.

The importance of information restriction in shaping current group identities is clearest in extreme examples of "minority groups," such as those formed by families of soldiers missing in action or in the "Adoptees Liberty Movement Association" (ALMA), whose members want to learn the identities of their real parents.[2] As in many current minorities, the members of these groups are united in their "special" desires to dissolve

---

*The role that media play in forming our generalized other and in teaching us about "average" and "normal" behavior suggests an explanation for the structure and content of many popular television game shows such as "Family Feud." Many of the questions on such shows have little to do with "objective fact" and much to do with intersubjective group beliefs, customs, and behaviors ("ways to punish children," "items found in a first aid kit," "something wives do to gain their husbands' favor," "something kids have a favorite one of," and so forth). Further, the source for determining the correctness of answers is not a set of highly trained or educated "experts," but simply members of a studio audience—people like you and me.

into the mainstream, to know what everyone else knows, and to experience what everyone else experiences.

In this sense, many minorities consciously proclaim their special identity in the unconscious hope of losing at least part of it. When gays, for example, publicly protest for equal treatment under the law, including the right to teach and the recognition of homosexual marriages, they are not only saying, "I'm different and I'm proud of it," they are also saying, "I should be treated as if I'm the same as everyone else." So there is a paradoxical call for both consciousness of differences and blindness to them.

Ironically, the sense of restriction felt by many minority group members may be the result of the sudden *increase* in access to a larger, more inclusive information environment. For to know about and be constantly exposed to places you cannot go and things you are not allowed to do makes you feel more isolated than you were before. My uncle has told me many times that when he was young, he did not realize how poor his family was because everyone he knew was poor. Through television, today's ghetto children have more points of reference and higher standards for comparison. They see what they are being deprived of in every program and commercial.

Information integration makes social integration seem more possible and desirable. Distinctions in status generally require distinctions in access to situations. The more people share similar information-systems, the greater the demand for consistency of treatment.

The merging of information-systems, however, does not necessarily lead to instant integration or to social harmony. In fact, the initial outcome of information integration is increased social tension. On its own, information integration heightens one's awareness of physical, social, and legal segregation. The formerly excluded no longer accept "their place"; they try to gain equality, while many of the privileged try to maintain the old exclusionary ways. It is not that surprising, then, that tension over racial and other forms of integration peaked as television completed its invasion of the American home.*

This analysis suggests that the "social consciousness" of the 1960s was, in part, a "mediated consciousness." Formerly local issues became national problems through television. When previously isolated situations are presented in a public forum, people often feel they must take a stand on them. Parents who have ambivalent feelings concerning premarital sex, for example, may carefully avoid discussing the topic with their children. Yet they may feel compelled to "give a ruling" when confronted with explicit information concerning teenage sexuality—especially if the information is presented in front of their children, friends, or

---

*Although the correlation of two events does not prove that there is a causal link between them, the civil rights movement and television followed a strikingly similar curve of growth. The civil rights movement began in earnest in the early 1950s, grew in significance in the 1960s, and, along with the black power movement, peaked in the late 1960s. Similarly, television spread from only 9% of American homes in 1950 to 96% in 1970.[3]

neighbors. In an analogous manner, the national disharmony of America in the 1960s can be understood in terms of people feeling forced to choose sides publicly on many social issues that were once "kept in the closet."[4] Ironically, *dis*unity may have been the result of a new unified information-system. The phrase "the whole world is watching"—chanted by demonstrators at the 1968 National Democratic Convention in Chicago—offered a literal description of television and a clue to its impact on moral and political stance.

The shared information environment fostered by electronic media does not necessarily lead to identical behavior or attitudes among all individuals. It does lead, however, to a common awareness and greater sharing of *options*. The choice of dress, hair style, speech patterns, profession, and general style of life is no longer as strongly linked as it once was to traditional group ties. Another outcome of the homogenization of information networks, therefore, is the development of many new, more superficial, and temporary groupings that form against the now relatively unified backdrop of common information. People traditionally divided into groups that corresponded primarily to social class, ethnicity, race, religion, occupation, and neighborhood, but current groupings also develop on the basis of wearing similar clothes, participating in similar sports, owning the same type of computer, appreciating the same type of music, or attending the same class. Many sub-groups are now formed through the exercising of similar options. (And many "minority groups" form on the basis of a common sense of being restricted from some or all of the generally available options.)

The development of relationships and groupings on the basis of brief encounters and the sharing of superficial experiences is not new. What is new about our current social groupings is that such superficial and haphazard patterns of sharing experience now have relatively greater social impact. For people who meet in such ways already have much in common from similar exposure to mass media, and relationships between people from very different traditional groups have a better chance of lasting beyond the initial encounter. The once typical feeling that some people who meet casually at school or elsewhere cannot sustain long-term relationships because they "come from different worlds" is now muted. Personal incompatibility has replaced group identity conflict as a prime justification for ending relationships. Indeed, one of the current difficulties of maintaining long-term love relationships and marriages, even with members of one's own traditional group, is that there now seem to be so many other people with whom one has so much in common. Ironically, love may less frequently last forever because so many other people seem to be potential candidates for eternal love.

The sharing of situations by many formerly distinct groups produces a tension to develop a single "citizen" status to be shared by all. Even in the long run, however, the size of the "group" created by electronically shared information is too large to sustain traditional group cohesion, and it includes too many people to give members a sense of what makes them special and unique. Metaphors aside, it is impossible to consider the whole country or world as one's "neighborhood" or "village." Subgroups develop or continue to exist, therefore, on the basis of sub-sets of shared experience, but their boundaries are blurred by the massive sharing of information through electronic media. Indeed, people must now make a conscious effort to maintain distinctions in group identities that were once taken for granted. Contrary to general belief, the recently popular search for "roots" and "ethnic identity" may not be a sign of rising group identity in the traditional sense, but an indication of its decay. Extremely powerful group identities are unconscious and intuitive. The active search for ancestry and background may suggest a conscious identity crisis and a sense of relative rootlessness. Further, the search for one's *unique* background is now couched in terms of the *shared* right of everyone to his or her own heritage.

There are, of course, many groups of people whose religious traditions and beliefs make them resistant to changing their behavior to match new situations. It is not surprising, for example, that fundamentalist religious groups should begin to stand out against the backdrop of rapidly shifting group identities and other social change. For just as a quickly moving bird stands out against the still sky, so does a fixed boulder stand out in a quickly moving stream. The Moral Majority has risen in protest against most of the changes that are described in this chapter, and it has used the airwaves to make its views known. In one sense at least, however, even the Moral Majority has acted like many other "minority" groups; for it has demanded its "equal opportunity" to influence "human rights" legislation and to express its own special identity within the shared arena of television. As Richard Viguerie writes in *The New Right: We're Ready to Lead*: "Liberals are now complaining about conservative ministers who are just doing what liberal ministers have been doing for decades."[5]

The Exposure of Backstage Group Behavior

Electronic media have exposed parts of the traditional backstage behavior of many groups. Information once available only to group members has become available to outsiders as well. As described earlier, one of the major differences between electronic messages and print messages is that electronic media such as television present "expressive" information that was once accessible only in intimate face-to-face encounters. Through television, each American has "access" to the personal expressions of people from all over the country and world, and he or she receives much information that once was available only to members of other groups. Through electronic media, groups lose exclusive access to aspects of their own back region, and they gain views of the back regions of other groups.

The exposure of the back region of another group may have one of two opposite effects on attitudes, depending on the nature of one's initial opinions concerning the other group. Groups that were highly admired may lose some of their luster from the exposure of the "ordinariness" of their members. Groups that were hated and feared, however, may seem less dangerous and evil—because their members seem more human.

Access to back region *expressive* information of an enemy sometimes diminishes the hostility toward that enemy even when the content of *verbal* communication is explicitly hostile. This principle suggests a common element underlying some diverse and otherwise baffling shifts in public attitudes. As historian Erik Barnouw has noted, when Nikita Khrushchev began appearing on American television in the late 1950s, his humanness weakened the potency of the State Department's anti-Soviet propaganda and forced a change in U.S.-Soviet relations—even though Khrushchev's words were often very anti-American. "With somewhat baggy pants, outstretched hand, jovial manner, he looked more like a traveling salesman than a mysterious dictator."[6]

Similarly, the televising of the Vietnam War may have been a double blow to the support for the war as it was being conducted. First, television gave Americans an unprecedented intimate view of the "enemy." In radio and newspaper stories, the words "enemy" and "friend," or "communist" and "freedom fighter" are quite distinct. But on television, our friends and our enemies in Vietnam looked very much alike. This made it quite difficult to maintain a traditional "them vs. us" attitude about the Vietnam War. (During World War II and Korea, the images in comic books and feature movies were carefully shaped to create archetypes of good and evil.) Encounters that take place at intimate distance—or in closeup—are not necessarily positive, but they are very personal and intense. The desire among some Americans to "blow the Gooks off the map" (which often included our "allies" in South Vietnam) and the pleas of other Americans to "stop the genocide" can both be explained, in part, by the closeness of television's view of Vietnamese.

Second, television revealed a back region view of *our* army and of warfare in general. The disorganized and bloody view of fighting may have been even more damaging to the war effort. The fighting pictured on television seemed very different from a war fought the way John Wayne would have fought it. The you-are-a-soldier view offered by television cameras gave little sense of overall action or movement. There were no clear "fronts," no feelings of "advance." Instead of verbal abstractions such as "fierce battle" or "victory" or "fighting for democracy" (once offered by newspapers and radio), there were concrete images of wounded soldiers and civilians, screaming children, defoliated jungles, and scared refugees. On television, "saving a village from communists" often meant counting the dead bodies of prepubescent Viet Cong or burning a village so that no one would care about it. This shift from discursive to presentational, from front region reporting to back region exposure, may have intensified dissatisfaction with "our boys" and with the conduct of the war on the part of both hawks and doves.[7] Some people wanted to fight a "normal" war and bomb North Vietnam out of existence; others wanted to stop interfering in the "civil war" in another land. But after a significant amount of exposure to Vietnam on television, few people were satisfied with the war as it was.*

The same dynamic may have been at work in the ambivalent American reaction to the 1979 Iranian takeover of the American embassy and the holding of American hostages. For alongside the dominant and predictable hostile, patriotic response, some Americans began to develop a strange sympathy for Iranians. The incident brought about the first widespread public discussion of American wrongs in Iran (the overthrow of an elected government, among other things). A prominent presidential candidate commented that the deposed Shah had ruled "one of the most violent regimes in the history of mankind" and had stolen billions from the Iranian people, and a ten-member delegation of Americans, headed by a former U.S. Attorney General, defied President Carter's ban on travel to Iran in order to attend a conference on Iranian grievances against the United States.[8] Both these actions were condemned by many as destructive of American unity, yet they were significant indications of an unusual lack of traditional "them vs. us" feelings. And there were other signs of sympathy. American schoolchildren, for example, responded positively to Iran in the midst of the crisis by requesting a record number of Iranian pen pals.[9] Iran may have made its biggest tactical blunder by later expelling all Western journalists. It is much easier to create devils (and angels) at a distance.

Of all electronic media, television offers the most potent merging of formerly private and public spheres. Radio and telephone stimulate the visual imagination, but they do not provide accurate pictures of people and events. Through television, strangers are experienced as intimates. Since the information environment created by a new medium is likely to have its greatest impact on those who grow up within it, we should expect major group realignments to have taken place when the first generation of television children reached adulthood.†

---

*This is probably one reason why both the British and the American military did not permit full coverage of their recent forays into the Falkland Islands and Grenada, respectively. In the absence of backstage images, those actions could simply be remembered in terms of an onstage verbal label: "rescue missions."

†Exactly which age cohort should be considered the "first TV children" is not clear. But one reasonable suggestion is the first age group that had televisions in at least half of its households before entering school and being introduced to literacy and print—in other words, the age group that was 4 years old in 1953 (the year that households with children under 5 passed the 50% television saturation mark[10]). The members of this group were 18 in 1967, the approximate time that the "integration movement," with its exclusive concern with civil rights, yielded to the "youth movement," with its wider protests against the war and its general rejection of the traditional American way of life. One could also make a case for a slightly older group (those who were in the first to third grades in 1953 and could appreciate how much information television was giving them compared to their school texts) or for a slightly younger group (who were exposed to television long before entering school). In any case, there is a striking correlation between the coming of age of all these "television children" and the heating up of social conflicts in the mid- to late 1960s.

This analysis offers a new explanation for the sudden social explosions that took place in the late 1960s and that continue to ripple through our culture. In the late 1960s, two sequential generations stood face-to-face, yet worlds apart in their conceptions of appropriate social roles and of the balance between public and private behavior.

Many of the unusual characteristics of the 1960s can be related to the influx of traditionally backstage behaviors into onstage spheres. A common theme underlying many of the issues that led to protests was the "credibility gap." This "gap" may have been related to the imbalance between front region behaviors and (newly exposed) back region behaviors. "Credibility" involves consistency among all *visible* behaviors. Yet since all people display inconsistent behaviors in different spheres, and since television merges previously distinct situations, the generation that grew up with television kept catching its elders in what seemed to be acts of deception and immorality. This led to widespread disrespect for parents, government officials, and authorities in general. If one reads between the lines of reports on student unrest, the potential impact of television becomes clear. A report on the disturbances at Columbia University in 1968, for example, noted:

> The present generation of young people in our universities is the best informed, the most intelligent, and the most idealistic this country has ever known. This is the experience of teachers everywhere.
>
> It is also the most sensitive to public issues and the most sophisticated in political tactics. . . .
>
> The ability, social consciousness and conscience, political sensitivity, and honest realism of today's students are a prime cause of student disturbances. As one student observed during our investigation, today's students take seriously the ideals taught in schools and churches, and often at home, and then they see a system that denies its ideals in actual life. Racial injustice and the war in Vietnam stand out as prime illustrations of our society's deviation from its professed ideals.[11]

Many of the items in this statement can be related to television ("best informed," "most sensitive to public issues," "sophisticated in political tactics," "honest realism," and "they see a system that denies its ideals in actual life"). Television exposure is a common element underlying social consciousness and social conscience. Television juxtaposed traditional ideals with vivid scenes of racism and war. Perhaps the young generation in the 1960s was perceived and perceived itself as unusually "idealistic" because more was exposed to them than to earlier generations and they therefore demanded that all the behaviors they saw be brought into balance. The striking inconsistency among exposed social spheres may have been a prime source of the protesters' moral exhortation and utopian politics.

This analysis of the issue of "credibility" and consistency offers a logical explanation for a 1960s slogan that does not make much sense in any other context: "Don't trust anyone over 30!" This plea was often quoted by the older generation as evidence of the short-sighted and illogical nature of the youth movement. For didn't the people who chanted it understand that they too would soon be over thirty? But the phrase may have referred only to those who were *at the time* over thirty, those who came of age in a pre-television era,* those who tried to maintain clear separations between traditional backstage and onstage behaviors. These people seemed untrustworthy as soon as contradictory behavior or, even more commonly, *attempts at control* became visible. The youth generation, in contrast, "let it all hang out." the trust slogan may have had more to do with a generational difference in behavior than a simple difference in chronological age.

The blurring of onstage and backstage regions, then, is the common denominator linking the protesters' political stance and their behavioral style. The intense solidarity felt by participants in what was called "the Movement" was the result of a sudden sharing of much information that once was exchanged only among family members and close friends. What delighted many "insiders" was the public display of formerly back region features such as informal dress, obscenity, nudity, intimate self-disclosures, emotions, and admissions of vulnerability. The comfortable intimate sphere had suddenly been expanded. In a sense, the "flower children" went out into the streets in their pajamas and embraced strangers as if they were their brothers and sisters playing in the family den. The disgust felt by "outsiders" at this display was based on the same dynamic: the movement of back region behaviors into the front region. For, as Erving Goffman suggests, there is a strong parallel between back region behavior and regressive behavior. Indeed, Goffman's general description of appropriate back region behavior, written in the 1950s, could serve as a description of many of the "shocking behaviors" of the protest marches and sit-ins of the late 1960s.

> The backstage language consists of reciprocal first-naming, co-operative decision-making, profanity, open sexual remarks, elaborate griping, smoking, rough informal dress, "sloppy" sitting and standing posture, use of dialect or sub-standard speech, mumbling and shouting, playful aggressivity and "kidding," inconsiderateness for the other in minor but potentially symbolic acts, minor physical self-involvements such as humming, whistling, chewing, nibbling, belching, and flatulence.[12]

Goffman wonders whether backstage interactions allow people to regress or whether clinical definitions of regression are actually defined situationally—that is, that regression is backstage behavior acted out in situations or for motives that are not socially sanctioned. In either case, what outsiders saw at sit-ins and happenings was apparently regressive behavior, seemingly indicative of a decline in civilization beginning with the new

*People who were 31 in 1967, for example, were already 18 in 1954, the first year that more than half of American households owned television sets.

generation. And the displeasure and discomfort were reinforced by the mysterious origins of this new behavior. Like a strange plague, the new spirit of the 1960s changed behavior without respect to religion, race, or other forms of manifest upbringing.*

The bonds among members of the The Movement seemed very natural to insiders, and the intense negative response of outsiders only reinforced the "them vs. us" feeling that is the basis of all strong group ties. Insiders shared their food, money, cars, fears, and affections; outsiders seemed old, cold, stuffy, and unfeeling.

The *social* movement of the 1960s, therefore, may have been a direct result of the new patterns of *information* movement. People now knew more about the private behaviors of others, and they felt that they might as well drop the old masks and act as if they knew.

In this sense, the 1970s and 1980s have been a continuation, rather than a reversal, of the 1960s. The "gestalt" of the 1960s may be gone, the utopian political and social rhetoric may have disappeared, but the basic situational dynamics continue to lead to adjustments in social behavior to match information access. Former back region behavior continues to flow into front regions. Sit-ins, T-shirts, slogans, demands for freedom, equality, and justice are still everyday sights and sounds, but there is no longer any amazement or shock. These tactics are used by the police, handicapped, rednecks, farmers, homosexuals, and the elderly. *The* Movement is dead; but it lives on its many diverse offspring. Now the single massive line of confrontation (and solidarity) is gone. It is no longer young versus old, yippies versus "pigs," hippies versus rednecks. As one cross-country traveler noted in 1978:

> Vanished are the days in the '60s and early '70s when hirsute travelers were thrown into sheep-dip vats in Wyoming and shot at in Georgia . . . .
> "If you'd a come through here five years ago," I was told by a friendly Oklahoma housewife who invited me in for lunch, "they'd a got you down and cut your hair. But now, all of them that was doin' it, they have long hair themselves."[13]

Contrary to many claims, the former protesters have not simply settled down or "sold out"; instead many of their "offensive behaviors" and "unpatriotic beliefs" have been incorporated into the system. The 1960s

---

*It is important to remember that there was a significant shift in the style and rhetoric of protests in the mid- to late 1960s. Many of the civil rights marchers of the late 1950s and early 1960s were short-haired people wearing jackets and ties who demanded that "Negroes" receive a piece of the American pie. The protests of the late sixties, however, were much more back region in flavor, and the protesters demanded fundamental changes in the workings of the American political system and in social sensibilities. Again, such a shift is in keeping with this analysis. Many of the early demonstrators may have been moved to protest certain *issues* by the new images of the nation and the world offered by television, but their sense of appropriate private and public *behavior style* had already been conditioned before television. The full effect of television was not felt until the younger generation changed the style in which the same and other issues were handled.

"counterculture" was characterized by its antiwar protests, its distrust of authority, its looser sexual mores, and its use of illicit drugs. Many of these behaviors and beliefs have become part of mainstream America.

At the beginning of 1967, for example, only 32% of the American public thought that the U.S. had made a mistake in sending troops to Vietnam. By May 1971, polls indicated that 62% agreed with the antiwar protesters.[14] By 1978, the percentage was even higher and the sentiment stronger: 72% agreed that "the Vietnam war was more than a mistake, it was fundamentally wrong and immoral."[15]

In 1966, only about 25% of the public felt that the "people running the country don't care what happens to people like me." By 1977, that figure had jumped to sixty percent. Over 55% of those polled in 1958 agreed that they "can trust the government in Washington to do what's right." By 1978, fewer than 30% had similar faith in Washington.[16]

In 1967, 85% of the public felt that premarital sex was morally wrong. By 1979, only 37% felt the same way, and more than 50% of those polled felt that living together without marriage was "not morally wrong."[17]

In 1962, only a small percentage of the population (4%) had ever used an illegal drug. By 1982, about a third of all Americans, 12 years of age and older, had used marijuana, cocaine, heroin, or another illegal substance.[18] The National Institute on Drug Abuse found that a staggering 66% of the high school graduation class of 1981 had used an illegal drug.[19] Most significant, although the drug culture was initially a "dropout" culture as well, *Newsweek* has recently reported on the "explosion of on-the-job drug taking by perfectly respectable professionals," and *The New York Times* has observed that the "level of public tolerance of the use of illegal drugs is continuing to rise in all levels of American society."[20]

In many ways, then, the Movement and the Establishment have merged into a "middle region" system that has elements of both. Radicals of the 1960s run for political office, and judges and corporate executives smoke marijuana and use cocaine. Congress finishes some of the work started by the protesters who camped at the Washington monument: It investigates the abuses of the CIA and FBI, intimidates a President into resigning from office, and tries to curb the government's covert operations against other countries. Blacks take over the mayoralty of major cities such as Atlanta, Chicago, Philadelphia, and Los Angeles, and former racist politicians beg blacks for forgiveness and support. And the basic distrust of government and authorities, which characterized The Movement, has now spread throughout large segments of the total population.*

---

*Current trends not only suggest a merging of the politics of radicals and conservatives, but also of behaviors traditionally linked with differences in social class. Premarital sex, high illegitimacy rates, "shacking up," and drug use were once associated primarily with the lower socioeconomic groups of society. These behaviors have now spread upward through all levels in society. In the early 1970s, for example, it was possible to predict differences in teenage sexuality on the basis of race, socioeconomic status, religion, and residence. By the end of the decade, however, many of these distinctions had disappeared.[21]

Many elements of the "racism" and "imperialism," which were the objects of protest, remain unchanged, but there has been a marked change in overt style and a clear attempt to bring all visible behaviors into balance. The brutal images of southern police attacking blacks with firehoses and dogs or of Chicago's finest viciously clubbing protesters at the 1968 Democratic Convention are no longer visible on our television screens. Gone, too, are shouts to "kill the pigs." Protesters are now often gingerly removed on stretchers. David Dellinger, one of the "Chicago Seven" charged with inciting riots in Chicago, is still on the front lines of protest. But now Dellinger apologizes to the police officers who carry him away, and he smiles for the press cameras. Dellinger says, "No one is calling cops 'pigs' anymore. Today the protesters often have a friendly word for the police, and the response is often positive."[22]

In the mid-1960s, the slightly long "Beatle haircut" caused a furor of protest among adults (80% of those polled by Gallup in 1965 thought schools should ban it[23]). Today's "punk" hair and dress styles and the androgynous appearances of many rock stars suggest how far youth must now go in order to appear "different." And the relatively low-key response among the older generation suggests how little people are now shocked by oddities of dress or appearance. In the late 1960s, long-haired male youths were often ridiculed for their "unmanly" appearance by some police officers, construction workers, and other "real men." But things have changed. In New York City, for example, the male police officers in the 44th precinct in the Bronx recently complained about the lack of electrical outlets for their hair dryers, and a number of them wear earrings.[24]

If the members of the current generation of youth seem apathetic, it may not be only that *they* are different from the "60s generation" but that society has changed as well.

With the loss of the great confrontations between generations has come a complementary change in social ideals and issues. Most protests have turned away from a wide range of national and international concerns and have moved in two opposite directions at once. One direction is toward a large, single global issue—nuclear disarmament—that led in 1982 to the largest protest rally in American history.[25] The other direction is toward very concrete, specific, and often local and self-oriented issues. The young people who took over "People's Park" in Berkeley in the 1960s claimed to be fighting unfair authority, racism, war, and imperialism, but the people—including many elderly—who "sat-in" a decade later to reopen "People's Firehouse" in Northside, Brooklyn were working to save Northside, Brooklyn.[26]

The manifest emotions and ideals of the 1960s are long gone, but the underlying social dynamics are very much the same: massive realignment of behavior to match new patterns of information flow. The continuing shift in the balance of public and private group spheres has two effects on group actions. As a result of increasing exposure of backstage behaviors through electronic media, some "private" group behaviors are pushed back into a "deeper," more invisible back region. At the same time, the group's real image and behavior may change. When women gain access to once exclusively male back regions, for example, some jokes about women may be forced into even more isolated all-male situations. At the same time, however, men *actually* begin to treat women differently in the now mixed situations. All structural changes in situations tend to be followed by real changes in behavior.

The generally increased exposure and awareness of the back region of a group leads to a new "middle region" alternative behavior. The behavior in the newly mixed situation is not the former onstage behavior, nor is it the former backstage behavior. The Ku Klux Klan, for example, surely one of the most extreme of social groups, has recently developed a new image. The Grand Wizard of one of its factions, David Duke, is a young, average-looking college graduate who rationally and calmly proclaims the need for a group that protects the rights of white Americans. The Ku Klux Klan, he suggests, is just another human rights group that looks after its own interests.[27]

The increased awareness of the back region activities of many institutions has forced a change in their processes and procedures. Marine training programs, for example, have had to reduce boot camp brutality as a result of increased access to the inside by outsiders and increased access to the outside by insiders.[28] The drive toward a single set of standards and ethics has extended beyond the boundaries of the United States (as is reflected in the current controversy over the proper role of "human rights" issues in the formation of U.S. foreign policy), and even beyond human environments (as is reflected in the popularization of the concern over the treatment of animals in the laboratory[29]). In connecting everyplace to everyplace, electronic media have changed the rules that were once particular to specific social situations.

The Undermining of Group Locations

Electronic media have had a tremendous impact on group identity by undermining the relationship between physical location and information access. Many categories of people—women, ghetto dwellers, prisoners, children—were once "naturally" restricted from much social information by being isolated in particular places. The identity and cohesion of many groupings and associations were fostered by the fact that members were "isolated together" in the same or similar locations: homes or offices, ghettos or suburbs, prisons or stores, playgrounds or bars. Such physical segregation worked to create social segregation for as long as place and situation were still closely linked. Now, however, electronic messages on television, telephone, and radio democratize and homogenize places by allowing people to experience and interact with others in spite of physical isolation. As a result, physical location now creates only one type of information-system, only one type of shared but special group experience. Electronic media begin to override group identities based on "co-presence," and they create many new forms of access and "association" that have little to do with physical location.

Electronic media have an impact on group identity by distancing people from traditional group perspectives. The use of the word "perspective" to mean both what one sees from a given location as well as one's social attitudes suggests the strong traditional relationship between physical place and social belief. Shared physical location fosters a shared perspective which, in turn, reinforces group solidarity. A shift in physical position generally leads to a shift in attitude. A common example is the change in our perception of a street or intersection as we switch from pedestrian to driver. The same principle, however, provides the basis for one of the subtlest techniques of cinematic persuasion and propaganda: the shifting of perspective and position rather than the altering of content. In the celebrated film *The Godfather*, for example, we are not asked to believe that the mafia family members are good people; we are simply "put" in their home and given their view of the world. As a result, we find ourselves in the unusual position of rooting for the criminals and cheering when government agents are killed. Similar techniques are used in war movies and westerns where, regardless of "plot," viewers tend to take the side of those whose perspective they are shown.[30]

Through visual portrayal of real and fictional events, television presents most members of our society with a crazy-quilt pattern of perspectives. Regardless of physical location and traditional group ties, people experience how the world looks and feels from other places and other role perspectives. Television's views are, to be sure, distorted and incomplete, and often they are purposefully biased for political or economic reasons. Nevertheless, television "removes" viewers from their physical locales and offers them alternative views of other people and the physical environment. The "view from no place" that television permits may have been a stimulus for the growth of such groups as Amnesty International, for the increasing awareness of ecological issues, and for the growing demand for nuclear disarmament. Such issues require an "overview," an overriding of traditional group concerns and a bypassing of needs as seen from one's particular place. (Ironically, the "liberalizing" effect of the multiple perspective view may still give a political advantage to conservatives, reactionaries, and special interest groups. After all, multiple perspectives often lead many people to an overabundance of empathy and, therefore, to political ambivalence and inaction.)

The impact of electronic media on group identity may be most apparent in large cities where traditional community ties are often already weak, where people do not know all their neighbors, nor speak to everyone they see. But small towns too are experiencing a change in perspective. Media ties compete with family, church, school, and community. Media create new "communities," and a large portion of their content is shared by most people in the country. Many jokes, phrases, expressions, and events heard and seen on television provide a common set of "experience" for people across the land.* It is not surprising, therefore, that what sociologists refer to as the "urbanization" of America includes not only population shifts to large cities but also a general urbanization of attitudes and behaviors throughout the country.[31] Electronic media move people informationally to the same "place."

The homogenization of regional spheres is, of course, only a matter of degree. Different places are still different, but they are not as different as they once were. The psychological distinctions between states and regions were once very great. As late as the 1940s, one coast of America was something of a mystery to the other. A cross-country trip was a true adventure into the unknown.[32] But television has removed much of this sense of mystery.

The telegraph began the breakdown of communication barriers between different places. But it presented terse coded messages that had to follow the telegraph lines. Radio enhanced the process, first by sending Morse Code through the air rather than through wires and later by adding the human voice. But radio merely *reported* verbally on events in other parts of the world or country. The information was still descriptive and "second-hand," a linguistic abstraction. Radio provided "word-pictures," but the pictures had to be redrawn in each listener's imagination. It is difficult to imagine something new and mysterious without picturing it as some variation of what one has already seen. Further, with radio, each listener creates his or her own unique and subjective picture. Television, in contrast, seemingly allows the viewer to experience distant events and places directly and "objectively." It is significant that when Edward R. Murrow's radio program "Hear It Now" became television's "See It Now," the premiere show featured a live hookup between California and New York; viewers saw the Golden Gate Bridge and the Brooklyn Bridge simultaneously on a split screen.[33] With television, the final demystification of other parts of the country began.

Electronic media, of course, are not the only causes of merging situations. High speed travel and mass production of identical clothes, appliances, and other products also have had their impact. As Daniel Boorstin's history of America suggests, the development and use of electronic media may be part of a larger trend of the homogenizing of here and there.[34] But electronic media have an effect that goes beyond other variables. Travel allows people to get from *place to place*. Identical products give *different*

---

*Past examples include: "Goodnight, Chet; Goodnight, David" (from "The Huntley-Brinkley Report") and "I can't believe I ate the whole thing" (from an Alka Seltzer commercial). More recent examples are: "But Noooooo" (from the first cast of "Saturday Night Live"), "Good answer, good answer" (from "Family Feud"), "How _____ (hot, cold, etc.) was it?" (from the "Tonight" show), "Kiss my grits" (from "Alice"), and "Where's the beef?" (from a Wendy's hamburger commercial). Such phrases come and go quickly, their content being less important than their use as a common, and ever-changing, "tradition."

places the same surface look. These changes are physical not information. Electronic media, in contrast, eat away at the very meaning of distinct places: shared but special *experience*. To be "with" other people is
very different from using the same products or eating similar foods.

It is common for people who travel to a distant location to adapt, at
least in part, to the behavior style of the "natives." New York executives
who fly to California to complete contract negotiations, for example,
expect to do business "California style" while there. But electronic media
create new placeless situations that have no traditional patterns of behavior. When New York and Californian business executive "meet" via video
teleconferencing, they behave in a mixture of Californian and New York
style that is both yet neither.

The millions who watched the funeral of John F. Kennedy, the resignation of Richard Nixon, or the assassination of Anwar Sadat were in a
"place" that is no place at all. Similarly, the millions of Americans who
watch television each evening (nearly one out of every two people in the
country) as well as the millions who listen to the radio every day as they
work or drive (about 80% of the population)[35] are in a "location" that is
not defined by walls, or streets, or neighborhoods, but by evanescent
"experience." How does one behave in such "places"? Electronic media
affect social roles because they bypass the communication networks that
once made particular places unique. More and more, people are living in
a national (or international) information-system rather than a local town
or city.

Television's "national embrace" has an effect on local media content
and local behavior. National weather reports, for example, are now
included even in local news programs. And a disaster in another state—
such as California mud slides or sink-holes in Florida—often receives
more attention in local news and conversation than a house fire in one's
home town. One result of this national and sometimes international view
is that the total strangeness of "strangers" as well as the special meaning
of "neighbor"—both important elements in the "them vs. us" feelings of
group identity—have been muted.

It is difficult to isolate oneself from the metaphysical arena created by
television. In the early days of television, the low quality of programming
made it embarrassing for professors and other "highbrows" to admit that
they even owned a television set, let alone that they spent any valuable
time watching it. Today, however, the massive saturation of television
into virtually every American home imbues the activity of watching television with multiple levels of social significance (and therefore offers con-
venient justifications as well). To watch television is now to hook into part
of the "American experience." One can watch popular programs, not
merely to see the program, but to see what others are watching. One can
watch, not necessarily to stare into the eyes of America, but at least to
look over the shoulders of Americans and see what they see. Television
watching may not allow you to keep your finger directly on the pulse of

the nation, but it does allow you to keep your finger on the pulse the nation is keeping its finger on.

Television today has a social function similar to the weather. No one takes responsibility for it, often it is bad, but nearly everyone pays attention to it and sees it as a basis of common experience and a source of topics of conversation.

The ease and speed with which one can tune into the national television forum or be in touch with other people through the telephone make it more difficult for people to isolate themselves in specific places. With electronic media, one is always "in range," others are always "within reach." To be "out of touch" today is to be abnormal. Many people now carry portable radios, or even television sets while on vacations or "retreats," and many isolated camping sites advertise that they have a TV room and a telephone. Similarly, for a person to live or vacation in a place that has no telephone is often thought to be an implicit insult to friends, relatives, and co-workers. Taking one's phone off the hook may be seen as a mark of a misanthrope. In some occupations, people are expected to wear "beepers" that make them accessible at any time wherever they are and whatever they are doing. Thus, many of the traditional behavioral characteristics of "place"—those dependent on isolation—are overridden. Indeed, electronic media have given insularity of thought and place a bad name. It now seems unnatural to be completely unaware or inaccessible. This may partially explain why the television set and the telephone recently have become fixtures even in the recreation rooms of convents and in the formerly silent halls of the Trappist monks.[36]

Electronic media create ties and associations that compete with those formed through live interaction in specific locations. Live encounters are certainly more "special" and provide stronger and deeper relationships, but their relative number is decreasing. Many business, social, and even intimate family encounters now take place through electronic media ("Long distance is the next best thing to being there.") Although close physical ties in the home are important enough to compete successfully with a small number of electronic links, the many contacts through radio, television, and telephone begin to outweigh personal interactions through sheer number. Indeed, many "family encounters" now take place in front of the television set. Whether media have actually affected the *amount* of family interaction may be less of an issue than the fact that they have changed the *uniqueness* of what goes on in the home. Because many electronic messages within a given home are also experienced simultaneously by many other families, the shared but secret behavior of the family unit is further diluted. A person's psychological affiliation with his or her nuclear family is weakened when the families of friends, co-workers, and relatives share much of the same information at the same time. The common backdrop of social experience provided by electronic media creates broader (and therefore shallower) ties and associations.

Electronic media's impact on the uniqueness of family interactions suggests a common element underlying both the 1960s fad of communal liv-

ing and the stronger current trend toward single-member households.*
Both communal living and living alone represent a breakdown of traditional family ties; both represent treating large numbers of others with
equal intimacy. The commune movement involved treating strangers like
family; living alone involves treating even family members like partial
strangers. In an electronic society, it makes sense that the single-member
household arrangement has become the stronger of the two trends. Living
alone more closely reflects, in physical terms, the patterns of association
fostered by electronically created information-systems. Communes, like
extended families before them, involve deep, long-term, place-bound
commitments with a stable group of others. In both electronic communication and single-living, however, the options of association are large and
shared, but the choice is individual and idiosyncratic. Just as electronic
interactions do not saturate a time/space frame, so now do many live
relationships take on an ephemeral and sporadic quality.

The integration of social spheres does not simply give people new
places to play their old roles; it changes the roles that are played. As place
and information access become disconnected, place-specific behaviors
and activities begin to fade. The psychological and social distance among
physical places is muted. As a result, dress codes in schools and restaurants have come to seem antiquated or phony. And when people do
"dress up" today, it is more likely than in the past to be viewed as a "cos-
tume" rather than as a clear sign of personal identity. Further, people are
less likely to wear the once "appropriate" dress for their role in a given
place because places and roles no longer seem that distinct. Presidents
wear jeans in public and nuns shed their habits.

As different places become informationally similar, the social definitions of different locations begin to merge. Factories and lavishly deco-
rated residential lofts can coexist in the same buildings because location
now has much less to do with group identity and interaction. The workplace begins to move back into the home because business interactions
and information flow are now less dependent on the physical presence of
co-workers and clients. As previously distinct situations are combined,
formerly distinct behavior patterns merge. One of the contingencies of
establishing an office at home, for example, is the need to develop a new
social role that is neither "executive-in-office" nor "spouse/parent-at-
home."

Traditional groups were formed on the basis of long-term shared locations and live experience. Workers in a factory, women at home, children
in school, and shoppers in a store often defined themselves in terms of
the physically defined "group": the factory, the family, the school, the
neighborhood. Problems with a supervisor, a husband, a teacher, or a

---

*Between 1960 and 1981 the number of people living alone in the United States nearly tri-
pled. In 1982, the U.S. Bureau of the Census reported that nearly one out of every four
households in the United States consisted of a person living alone.[37]

shopkeeper were once likely to be considered personal problems between individuals. Today, however, the mediated "view from above" redefines many problems into "social issues" and into battles between "social categories." When a promotion is denied, it is now likely to be linked to sex discrimination or racism; a problem with a spouse is likely to be defined in terms of spouse abuse or sexism. A child's problem in school may end up as a court battle over educational malpractice, and an interaction with a shopkeeper may be seen as a "consumer" issue. I am not suggesting that these perceptions are necessarily "false," only that they certainly are *different*. While interactions continue to occur in specific places, they are now conceived of as taking place in a much larger social arena.

Many of today's groupings are based on single, superficial attributes shared in common rather than on an intimate web of complicated interactions and long-term shared experience. The current battles over the rights of "smokers" versus "nonsmokers,"[38] for example, suggest how removed many current groupings are from traditional place-bound group ties.

Audiences for particular group behaviors are no longer determined by physical presence, and the performance of roles on all social levels shifts as a result. Police who negotiate with the city "through the media," for example, can no longer clearly distinguish their front region image of dedicated and selfless protectors of the people from their back region haggling for more sick days, vacation time, and higher salaries. Similarly, when the U.S. Senate's debate on the Panama Canal Treaty was broadcast live in Panama, there was a merging of the back region of American-American dealings into the front region of American-Panamanian interaction. The United States could no longer conduct its internal arguments with all due intensity and bitterness without insulting Panamanians, nor could it present a unified and diplomatic front to Panama without diminishing internal debate and discussion. Thus, the undermining of group locations leads to the dilution of traditional group behaviors and the development of "middle region" compromise behavior patterns.

9

New Ways of Becoming

The Overlapping of Socialization Spheres

Socialization involves controlled access to the information of a group. The greater the number of distinct social information-systems, the greater the possibility for establishing and maintaining clear stages of socialization into groups. The information characteristics of print, for example, allow for carefully structured steps of socialization for children, immigrants, and other "outsiders." As discussed earlier, the complexity of print requires a long learning period simply to grasp the basic access code. The young child, the illiterate, and, to varying degrees, the immigrant, are therefore excluded from most communication that takes place through print. Further, different sets of messages can be directed at people with different degrees of reading competence. Through print, what people learn and the rate at which they learn it are "automatically" controlled.

With electronic media, however, these socialization stages are less marked. Unlike print, the presentational form of television does not allow it to be used to distinguish clearly between the information available to the preschooler, the sixth grader, and the adult. The distinctions on television are relatively vague and ambiguous. Indeed, many of the same programs are watched by all age groups. In 1980, for example, "Dallas," "The Dukes of Hazzard," "Love Boat," "M*A*S*H," "The Muppets," and "Happy Days, Again" were among the most popular network and syndicated programs for *every* age group in America, including ages two to eleven.[1] The significance of this fact for child socialization becomes clear when one considers that even the oldest members of the child group—the eleven-year-olds—are only in the sixth grade in school. Books and lessons aimed at the sixth grader generally present a much more distant and idealized view of adult life than is presented in "Dallas" or "M*A*S*H."

Books have a built-in censor that television does not share. While print isolates children from adults and separates children of different ages from each other, television thrusts everyone into one common information-system. Television, of course, does not obliterate the stages of reading, but it does destroy the nearly total insularity of the distinct information-systems established by print. Although there is certainly much that children still need to find out from books, reading skill alone no longer determines the order and sequence in which "adult" information is revealed to children. An information-system is only as secure as its smallest opening. The door to book information is still thick and strong, but television now provides children with a large keyhole through which to view the adult world.

A child's age was once a prime determinant of what he or she knew. Very different types of children were exposed to similar information because they were in the same age *group*. Now, children of every age are presented with "all-age" social information through electronic media. Much more than in a print culture, children are now thrust back on their *individual* cognitive and social development as a means of attaining their social status. Strict age-grading of activities and roles and knowledge no longer seems as appropriate or necessary.

The change in the structure of information-systems affects not only young children but people of all ages. The physical properties of print, the conditions of attendance, and print "gatekeepers"—such as librarians, teachers, and book dealers—further restrict information to "appropriate" life stages. A boy of sixteen would be unlikely to buy a book on infant care or the problems of aging, even though he could probably read such a book with no difficulty. Similarly, a recently married young woman would be unlikely to buy a book on menopause or divorce, and a great-grandmother would probably not buy a book on the latest contraceptive techniques. Even when people are interested in reading a book about a distant phase of their lives, they may be embarrassed to show that interest in front of a store clerk or librarian. The phases of life grow more distinct as people become isolated in the separate information-systems of print. Similarly, any profession or trade that is learned through books, rather than through relatively nonlinear observation and imitation, tends to develop stages of initiation and promotion that follow the steps of reading difficulty and the mastery of advanced texts.

Books provide vast areas of knowledge, but the isolated information-systems of print also often foster insularity of thought and experience. Electronic media's homogenized information networks, in contrast, lead to a less selective diet of information and therefore to less distinct sets of knowledge and perspective at different life stages. Any active television viewer is exposed to discussions about marriage, infertility, divorce, menopause, child and spouse abuse, old age, sickness, and death. As a result of increased awareness of the experiences and problems of being in another phase of life, many of the clear distinctions in the roles, rights, and responsibilities of different life stages are becoming relatively blurred. The more one learns about how people of another stage of socialization behave, the more one can select aspects of that behavior for oneself. As we all learn about the definitions of situations we have not yet experienced directly, it seems less important to "act one's age" or to "act one's stage" in a socialization process.

The thrust toward an homogenized social status, regardless of age, was most visible in the "youth revolt" of the 1960s. The children of the Woodstock generation were at once more childlike and more adult than previous generations. Their manifest behavior style was free and loose, pleasure-oriented, and egocentric. They eschewed traditional adult values and responsibilities. Yet at the same time, they were, at times, highly disciplined, socially and morally conscious, and intellectual. They listened to music for its social "message," and they acted on the basis of a conscious and altruistic philosophy. These child-adults could gather by the thousands at impromptu events without violence and internal strife. As parents and police fumed, they could march silently with raised candles, demonstrating for peace by demonstrating that peace was possible.

Bob Dylan became a powerful symbol for the protesters of the 1960s, perhaps because his early songs and singing embodied this mixture of childhood and adulthood. He was young and shabbily dressed, and his style was unsophisticated, yet he had the craggy voice, insights, and "reminiscences" of a wise old man.

Thus, although the manifest social tensions of the 1960s suggested an isolation of age-groups, the latent dynamics involved a merging of behaviors traditionally associated with different life stages. The protesters demonstrated that one could be both practical and idealistic, both reckless and responsible, both a child and an adult at the same time.

While the 1960s are often perceived as a long-gone aberration, the homogenization of socialization stages has continued in our culture. When compared to the 1960s, the changes are nearly invisible because they are so widespread. Behaviors of adults and children continue to merge. The revolt in age-status has expanded on both sides with the "children's rights movement" and the "gray lib" movement. It has been pushed to the edges with pleas for gentleness to the newborn because they are "feeling human beings"[2] and by the growing momentum of the "death awareness movement," which is bringing the subject of death, as well as the dying themselves, closer to the center of social activities.[3] Magazines such as *Newsweek* feature cover stories on "Growing Old, Feeling Young" and "Bringing Up Superbaby."[4] The first story shows old people climbing mountains and running in a marathon; the second pictures infants and toddlers being "taught" about mathematics, music, computers, and the structure of the brain. The advancement of the retirement age, the lowering of the voting age, and the extension of due process rights to children are all indications of the strength of the drive toward a single all-age behavior style and role conception.

These changes must be viewed as parts of a single process in order to be fully understood. Looking at isolated changes distorts the meaning and significance of the overall trend. On the surface, maintaining old people in the work force and in social activity in general may seem to reflect a renewed respect for the elderly. But this is clearly not the case in the traditional sense. Old people today are not generally appreciated as experienced "elders" or possessors of special wisdom; they are simply seen as sometimes remaining competent enough to be included in the unitary role category of "active citizen." Old people are respected to the extent that they can behave like young people, that is, to the extent that they remain capable of working, enjoying sex, exercising, and taking care of themselves.

As more and more social statuses are homogenized, the controversial "integration" issues move further toward the social fringes. Abortion, nursing home scandals, and the "right to die" movement have become foci of political and social concern and controversy because they each involve people who are not yet, or no longer able to be, "active citizens." As a result, there is controversy over the appropriate status and rights of fetuses, the very old, and the terminally ill. The question of capital punishment versus life imprisonment for murderers involves a similar conflict between the "civil rights" of the murderers and their minimal capacity to be integrated into the general society. All these issues can be seen as related to our increasing inability to see life as divided into clearly demarcated stages and categories.

Backstage Access and Blurring Role Transitions

The merging of formerly public and private spheres blurs the distinctions among full group membership, stages of socialization into a group, and outsider status. Generally, individuals being socialized into a group learn about the group's ideals first (i.e., front region behavior) and then gain more access to back regions as they become more fully socialized. Through electronic media, however, the sequence and amount of information have changed. Individuals learn much about a group's back region behavior before they become full members of the group. As a result, stages of controlled access are bypassed. Partially socialized members and outsiders gain enough "damaging" information to undermine group roles and behaviors. Furthermore, because partially socialized members have not fully invested themselves in the group, they have little or nothing to lose by "exposing" group members. As group members become aware that their shared but secret information is being revealed to outsiders, they find it more difficult to play traditional group roles. Thus, traditional roles for group members as well as for those being socialized into the group begin to disappear, and new, synthesized roles develop.

Children, for example, learn more about adult life through electronic media than they did through print. Indeed, television is the first mass medium to present young children with a detailed back region view of parents. Yet children have no commitment to the adult group. An early outcome is a revolt against many adult roles by children; a later result is the feeling among adults that they cannot maintain their traditional adult performances. In the long run, both adult and child roles shift toward a "middle region," all-age role.

Through print, children of the past were given an onstage view of adulthood. Parents and other adults were presented as all-knowing, cool, calm, and collected. The backstage areas of adulthood—doubts, anxieties, fears, sexual behaviors, arguments, illnesses, preparations for "adult" behaviors, and childish impulses—were all kept secret. Children were also shielded from the knowledge of the size and depth of the backstage area. For the most part, they saw the onstage role of adults as the single reality.

In a print culture, this system could be supported and maintained easily. Traditional children's books presented stylized, idealized, and stereotyped versions of adult behavior: See Mommy cook dinner; See Daddy come home from work; See George Washington never telling a lie. In other words, children were presented with the way parents, and adults in general, attempted to behave in front of them. In going through the grades of school and the corresponding levels of printed material, children were slowly given more and more access to the behind-the-scenes life of adults. This *staggered* access supported role distinctions between adults and children. By the time people were let in on most of the adult secrets, they were already adults themselves, and they, in turn, protected their younger siblings and children from this information. The stages of reading literacy made this compartmentalization of information seem "natural" and necessary.

On the other hand, even very traditional television programs—such as the situation comedies of the 1950s—create a very different information environment. Many television programs present children of all ages with backstage views of adulthood. They reveal how adults *prepare* for and relax from parental roles. They show children how parents behave when they are *not* with their children. Similar backstage behaviors of teachers, police officers, politicians, and all adult authorities are revealed. In contrast to print-educated children, television children learn about depressed parents and crooked cops before they learn (the often contradictory) ideal role models at home or school. Public service announcements aimed at people who drink too much, at parents in need of the "parental stress hotline," or at those who have questions for the "VD hotline" are overheard by children. (In fact, some of the announcements implicitly suggest that children should initiate the distress signal in the home—by asking a father to stop drinking, for example.)

From this perspective, many types of programs that are generally excluded from discussion in the TV-and-children controversy probably have a tremendous impact on adult-child relationships. Traditional dramatic and comedy programs, news shows, documentaries, and public service announcements all reveal adult secrets to children. Thus, while most of what appears on television is low-level entertainment and hardly "educational" in the traditional sense, television nevertheless reveals to children many truths about the structure and content of adult behavior that were hidden from them in print.

Similarly, electronic media affect the perception of America held by new immigrants. Immigrants to any land often have an idealized image of the citizens of that country. Television alters that image. Before immigrants learn the language well enough to read newspapers or books, the abstract ideals of America—"land of the free and home of the brave"—are juxtaposed with images of racial strife, crime, political scandal, and drunk driving. Further, the feeling that Americans are "different" is muted by thousands of hours of close-up views of people who are, in many ways, like people everywhere.

Part of the mystique of any training or socialization process is the belief by the person going through it that when the process is complete, he or she will be "another person," a person with special qualities. The seminarian and the medical student remain somewhat in awe of priests and doctors—until they work very closely with them over a long period of time or become one themselves. In books, the abstract language of piety and respect keeps people of various occupations on pedestals. "Judge," "police officer," "lawyer," "doctor," "priest"—these are all respectful labels. On television, however, any one of these noble professions is represented in dramas, on the news, in documentaries, and on talk shows not by an abstract label but by a specific *person*—a person often seen in close-up with a particular face, a certain kind of nose, a specific dialect, perhaps someone who is a bit nervous or inarticulate. After many such portrayals, television may diminish the awe we feel for those who have gone through the socialization sequences we are beginning or considering. The end points of many socialization processes no longer seem so mystical or special, not because we know as much as those people, but simply because they appear to us now more as people than as abstract roles. Through television, people of all ages and all socialization stages are exposed to people of all other ages and stages.

Television's emphasis on personal expressive traits leads to "equalization" of many different types of people. Some people may appear more credible on television than other people, but the distinctions in credibility are not necessarily in line with traditional stages of socialization into groups or with the traditional ranking of different social statuses. On television, for example, a law student may not appear significantly different from a lawyer, a blue collar worker may outperform a corporation president. Television reveals the simple humanity, the ordinariness of almost everyone it "exposes" to an audience. And while this exposure may be reassuring and comforting in one sense, it is also demystifying and, at times, disappointing.

In books and on the theatrical stage, even the "bad guys" maintain a certain awe through distance and abstraction. But radio and especially television reveal the expressions, the frailties, the ordinariness of almost everyone we experience through them. We may like or dislike the people we see in television's close-ups, but it is difficult to think of them in terms of abstract roles categories. They are primarily people, people who happen to inhabit a role.

Television's exposure of backstage role information affects the general perception of socialization stages and personal identity. When not "onstage" in front of their primary role audience, people often explicitly distance themselves from their front region roles.[5] When they are among friends or family, for example, doctors, lawyers, and executives may make fun of certain aspects of their roles, or they may joke about the ways in which their "audiences" take them so seriously. Because television dramas, news shows, and talk shows present many social performers when they are not actually in front of their primary role audiences, many aspects of such back region behaviors begin to emerge.

Of course, "deep backstage" behaviors for real (vs. fictional) people are rarely revealed. We do not usually see people going to the bathroom, engaging in true backstage humor, or even meeting with colleagues in an actual back region interchange. (Two notable exceptions are the Watergate tapes and the FBI's Abscam videotapes.) Because television exposure is by definition "public," the role performers are still performing, but because they are on a different stage, the performances they give contain many behaviors that were once backstage to their traditional roles. Further, the revelation of the existence of an offstage—a time and place in which performers are not "in character"—affects the general perception of the relationship between roles and people. The exposure both of the relaxation from a role and of the preparation and rehearsals needed for a front region performance makes the onstage behavior of many social performers appear to be "only a role"—something separate from the person that can be slipped on and off.

The exposure of parts of the back region for many different roles removes much of the mystification surrounding role transitions. Both audience and performer are affected; people who change status no longer seem or feel that "different."

For all these reasons, perhaps, we are experiencing a more frequent and flexible movement into and out of life stages and roles such as marriage, priesthood, various professions, and relationships in general. People are now less surprised and shocked when others make these transitions because each socialization stage or passage is given less metaphysical reality. Similarly, there is less personal guilt or anxiety on the part of the individuals making such transitions. People now know much more about other roles and about other levels and types of socialization. Roles are seen as temporary phases chosen by an individual rather than as natural developments. Thus, while people still pass through many socialization stages, the stages are socially and personally less distinct and significant. The overall result is a generally more common set of language, dress, rights, roles, forms of address, and appropriate topics of discussion for all stages and types of socialization.

The Weakening of Socialization Places

Traditionally, each stage of socialization has been associated with its own physical location. Young children are separated from much of the adult world by being isolated in the home or classroom. In school, children of different ages are separated into different informational worlds by being separated into different classrooms or buildings. Law, medical, and seminary students are all physically isolated from their old worlds and placed together with their own kind. Movement from one stage of socialization to the next—matriculation in school, graduation, promotion in business—traditionally involves physical movement into a new place. The new physical access brings access to the information available in the new environment and causes isolation from the information and experiences available in other environments.

Electronic media, however, bypass the isolating characteristics of place and they thereby blur the differences between people at different stages of socialization and between people in different socialization processes. Children at home, for example, are no longer as fully isolated from other environments as were children in a print society. Indeed, through television, children today often have *greater* access to information from multiple environments than adults, because adults are often busy working. Young children once depended almost entirely on their parents and teachers as channels to information about the world, but today's children sometimes help adults keep in touch with outside events.

Electronic media make it difficult to isolate students and trainees from their old environments. Seminary students who take an hour break from their studies may suddenly find themselves plugged back into the world through radio, television, and telephone.

People may understand why a friend or relative has to "go away" to a special place to "become" a doctor, lawyer, officer, or priest. But because it is now so easy to contact others wherever they are, people expect to be able to use the telephone to stay in touch with friends or relatives who are trainees for various roles. One outcome of electronic media's homogenized information flow is that people in various socialization processes are partially reintegrated into the larger society in spite of their physical isolation.

By separating place and information access, electronic media have led to a general break in the relationship between social passage from role to role and physical passage from location to location. The idea of special places for special stages of life is fading; the idea that a status change requires a change in location no longer makes as much social sense. *Where* one is now has less to do with *who* one is because where one is now has so little to do with what one knows and experiences. The dissociation of social passage and physical passage is the common theme underlying the tendency in recent years for students not to care too much about attending their graduation exercises and the significant trend toward simply "living together" rather than getting married.[6] Not attending one's graduation involves making a social passage without going through the physical passage; living together involves going through a physical rite of passage but not a social one. Similarly, there are movements to bring both birth and death back into the home, to make hospital rooms look more like bedrooms in the home, to ease prisoners back into society through work-release programs, and to remove the mentally ill and retarded from special institutions and integrate them into the community. The high school "equivalency diploma" and educational programs that give credit for general "excellence at real life"[7] are further evidence of the declining importance of social passages based on particular locations and place-bound information-systems.

Although the manifest effect of the changing relationship between information and place is that people pass through stages of socialization without going through physical passages or that they gain access to places without changes in social status, the latent impact is the overall minimization of the importance of social transitions. The increased interest in adult socialization, "seasons," and "passages"[8] may seem to suggest that transitions are becoming *more* socially significant. But the surface rhetoric and stated concerns surrounding life stages have masked the underlying social dynamics. The ability to view one's life as a series of transitions requires a "view from above," a view removed from the perspective of any particular life stage. People are no longer confined within the information-systems of a given socialization stage. Television gives people at all stages of socialization a better sense of what it "feels" like to be at another stage of socialization. Paradoxically, people are more *aware* of life transitions because each stage of life is now less special, less all-encompassing.

The decline in the importance of social transitions has made our society more tolerant of ambiguous social categories. Being "of age" but unmarried, "living in sin," having sex without love, or being pregnant at one's marriage ceremony are no longer significant social stigmas. Similarly, graduating from college and then working as a manual laborer is not as strange as it once was. Even illegitimacy has gained a certain degree of de facto legitimacy in recent years. In 1955 only about 15% of the births to women under 20 occurred out of wedlock; by 1977, the percentage was 44%. Further, pregnant teenagers are no longer automatically expelled from school.[9]

The dramatic change in our attitudes toward social passages in recent years can be demonstrated by looking back to the recent past for old perceptions and beliefs. In 1968, for example, a story about a Barnard sophomore who lived, unmarried, with a man made the front page of *The New York Times*.*

---

*The story involved Linda LeClair who had violated Barnard housing regulations and was living with her boyfriend. The incident and its repercussions (including student protests over LeClair's threatened expulsion and student demands for new housing regulations) actually led to a total of twenty articles in *The New York Times* in 1968. Many of the articles, including the front page story ("Head of Barnard Asks Parents of Defiant Girl for Their Views"[10]), are quaint and paternalistic by today's standards.

10
Questioning Authority

The Blurring of High and Low Status Situations

Authority rests on information control. High status roles generally depend on access to and control over the dominant communication channels of the time. In *Preface to Plato*, Eric Havelock describes the interrelationship of communication and leadership in an oral society. Havelock discusses the important role of poetry in early Greek culture and argues that, as a result, the leaders were generally "those who had a superior ear and rhythmic aptitude, which would be demonstrable in epic hexameter. . . . The good performer at a banquet would be estimated not exclusively as an entertainer but as a natural leader of men, for he, like Achilles, was a superior 'speaker of tales.'"[1] Similarly, Harold Innis notes that in scribal cultures, scribes were often treated like royalty.[2]

Of course, not everyone who has access to the communication skills of an era will automatically be accorded high status, but those who wish to attain high status beyond a small interpersonal sphere will generally have to master such skills. All changes in media of communication, therefore, are inherently revolutionary. New conceptions of communication competence and new prerequisites for control over information tend to alter the relative political and social power of different people and various sectors of the population.

In a print society, most "significant" communication takes place through reading and writing. In nineteenth century America, for example, more people read a national politician's speech than heard it, and people kept "in touch" by reading newspapers and books and by writing and reading letters. Social and political status in such a society generally involved climbing—at least partially—the ladder of literacy. It was unthinkable in a print society to have nonliterates become actively involved in the governing process because they had neither access to the "public forum" created by books and newspapers nor the skill necessary to make a significant contribution to the "discussion."

As described earlier, electronic media highlight personal expressions and require only minimal coding and decoding skills. As a result, electronic media affect the social hierarchy in two ways: They change the skills needed by authorities and high status individuals (and thereby they often change those who can fill such roles), and they change the overall balance of power between leaders and followers (because the requisite skills are now less exclusive and mystifying).

More than in the past, authorities today must often "look and sound good" rather than write and reason well. But looking and sounding good are not learned the way one learns to read and write. The skills needed to encode messages in electronic media do not necessarily require years of training and practice, and they are generally more accessible to the "average" adult or child. The roving reporter with a camera and microphone can often collect from passersby oral statements at least as eloquent as those made by authorities. (And the pool of potential contributors to the public dialogue is now enormous.) When television journalists juxtapose the best of their person-on-the-street responses with political speeches and statements by "experts" (often *read* haltingly from a piece of paper), traditional authorities may suffer from the comparison. They seem stuffy, unnatural, and, sometimes, untrustworthy.

Electronic media put many traditional authorities at a disadvantage. The situation is most obvious in media forums such as talk shows or call-in radio and television programs where authors and experts are often outflanked by spirited and fast-talking audience members or callers. While electronic media are certainly not the only forums in which authorities are called on to play their roles, these forums do provide significant contact between high status persons and those in whom they are supposed to inspire trust and respect. Further, the same process of "equalization" is inherent in the simple everyday use of the telephone, where almost anyone can speak to anyone. Oral interaction on the phone bypasses both traditional writing skills and traditional linear hierarchal arrangements. Through electronic media, many authorities who once had a clear advantage over the average person are now often put on equal or lower footing.

Perhaps this analysis explains the drastic shift in conceptions of authority that occurred in the late 1960s. Students around the nation and the world revolted against traditional authorities and demanded more of a role in the workings of universities and government. When topical songwriter Phil Ochs penned a song about a student who rejects paternalistic college administrators and declares "When I've got something to *say*, sir, I'm gonna say it now,"[3] Ochs may have been unconsciously pointing to the resurgence of *oral* forms of discourse in the working of institutions and in political action: involvement of all participants regardless of level of education, immediate action and reaction, and rejection of distant authority.

The protests of the sixties may have quieted down, but perhaps only because there has been a dramatic shift in the balance of authority. Young students today *do* have more of a say in the workings of society. Most universities now take student evaluations into account for faculty tenure and promotion decisions, students serve on most university committees, and students have much more of a voice in where and how they live.* Many campuses have Public Interest Research Groups (PIRG's), student lobbies, and special interest groups such as the Black Student Union and the Campus Woman's Caucus. While '60s-style student demonstrations have largely (though not completely) disappeared, lobbying and litigation on the part of students have increased dramatically.[5] At its height of activity in the 1960s, the radical Students for a Democratic Society (SDS) had only 6,000 dues-paying members and another 30,000 locally affiliated members across the nation. A little over a decade later, a student group in one state alone, the New York Public Interest Research Group (NYPIRG), had 125,000 dues-paying members.[6] The relatively few broad social issues that led to protests in the 1960s have been replaced by more numerous local and self-oriented concerns, but the shift from altruism to "meism" has not been accompanied by an increase in passivity. Student *involvement* in the workings of society is still great, perhaps even greater than it was in the 1960s.[7]

Electronic media affect traditional hierarchies by altering the direction and patterns of information flow. A business analogy helps to clarify what is happening in our society in general. The rungs of status in a corporation ladder are supported by information "going through channels." If a corporation president directly informs a lowly secretary or janitor of a raise in salary, or if a clerk in the office mailroom is permitted to go directly to the chairperson of the board to complain about working conditions, the status and authority of all the intermediary administrators are weakened. To maintain a position in a hierarchy, individuals must have information from above pass through them to those below. The worst thing that can happen to an administrator in a traditional corporation is to be frequently informed of important pieces of corporate information by someone beneath him or her in the hierarchy. If people in a hierarchy get and give information in no set sequence or pattern, then the linear structure of the hierarchy will dissolve. To a significant degree, this has been the effect of electronic media on many of our traditional hierarchal roles.

---

*A recent Carnegie Council study reported that student attitudes concerning the part they should play in governing universities have changed very little since 1969. The significant change has been a dramatic rise in actual student involvement in campus governance. Students now hold seats on most committees at 96% of the schools visited in 1979. At 75% of the 600 colleges and universities studied in 1978, students participate in such powerful planning bodies as the educational policy committee. More than 60% of college presidents indicated that such student involvement has occurred since 1970.[4]

I have used the corporation as an analogy for general societal change, but since corporations are a part of our society as well, they too are being affected by the new patterns of information flow. There are significant moves away from traditional hierarchal secrecy and "lines" of authority. New techniques are being adopted such as "matrix management" (in which executives report to more than one supervisor) and "quality circles" (in which groups of employees who work in the same area meet to discuss and solve common problems—rather than depending on "orders from above"). Linear and segregated situations are yielding to circular and integrated information-systems. Furthermore, it is probably no coincidence that *electronics* companies such as Digital Equipment Corporation and Intel Corporation are leading the way in many of these innovations. In some high technology firms, there are few, if any, private offices or conference rooms, many executives report to multiple supervisors, and projects are often worked on by interdisciplinary "teams" composed of people from different offices. There is often significant "local decision power," with different branches of the same firm varying greatly in procedures, and there is extremely high mobility (in every direction—not just "up" the hierarchy), with employees often selecting the position they wish to move to next. Significantly, many of these changes are affecting not only upper-level management, but also those on what were traditionally the "lower rungs" of corporate status. Many high tech companies encourage workers to participate at all decision levels. Unions, therefore, have thus far found it extremely difficult to "organize" workers in computer industries. The workers do not have the traditional "them vs. us" attitudes concerning their employers.[8]

New patterns of access to information through electronic media bypass traditional channels and gatekeepers and undermine the pyramids of status that were once supported by print. Parents, teachers, doctors, corporation presidents, political leaders, and experts of all kinds have been losing the controlling elements that supported their traditional status in a print society. The status of many of these roles is therefore declining.

Once teachers and parents had nearly absolute control over the general social information available to the young child. This gave the process of socialization many aspects of hierarchy. Now these authorities are often placed in the position of explaining or responding to social information available directly to children through television. Attempts made by parents to discuss programs with their children,[9] or attempts by some teachers to adjust school curricula to incorporate programs that children watch on television,[10] suggest a new means of "leading" children by running after them as quickly as possible.

The loss of control over the direction and sequence of information flow also has led to a flattening of political status. The old linear party "machines," for example, have been losing their importance because information no longer travels in a set sequence through the party hierarchy. Party outsiders have a greater chance than ever of winning elections because they can bypass party channels and go directly to the people through telephone, radio, and television. People no longer inherit their political party along with their religion. The trend since the early 1970s has been toward issue and interest group politics over party politics.[11]

Voters once left politics to politicians. Studies of voting behavior in the 1950s reveal a very stable picture of politics, with a voter who felt a life-long commitment to a political party and who was largely satisfied with the political process. The studies also reveal that most voters were only "mildly involved" in politics, that they were "remarkably unsophisticated" in their view of political matters, and that they demonstrated very little consistency among their attitudes about different issues.[12]

Studies of voters since the 1960s, however, reveal an entirely different scenario: voters who are deeply involved in political issues and yet largely alienated from both political parties and the political process.[13] In the 1950s, there had been a dramatic difference between the "issue consistency" of political "elites" (those for whom politics was a career) and the consistency of attitudes among the masses. Later surveys revealed, however, that by the mid-1960s the average citizen demonstrated a more coherent structure of political opinion than had the political elites of 1958. Further, the changed voter attitudes were not correlated with increased education. While college-educated voters demonstrated the greatest issue consistency, the largest proportional increase in "sophisticated political evaluation" occurred among people with less than a high school degree.[14] Such changes may be related to the new patterns of access to political information fostered by television and to the resulting demystification of political leaders and political ritual.

Of all social roles, those of hierarchy are affected most by new patterns of information flow. The loss of information control undermines traditional authority figures. Further, because information control is an *implicit* rather than an explicit aspect of high status, the changes in hierarchy are surrounded by confusion and despair.

When low status persons lose the information that supports their function, the impact is comprehensible. If, for example, a salesman's customer list is stolen, his inability to earn a living can be directly attributed to his loss of information control. But as discussed previously, high status roles depend, in part, on hiding the importance of information control. High status is often made to appear to rest on the innate qualities of the individual. Even high status role performers themselves may come to see their roles as significant parts of their selves. When high status persons lose the control over information that assured their status, all concerned are likely to sense that a metaphysical change has taken place, a deterioration of the individuals and of society. If a doctor is not familiar with a recent miracle cure that his or her patient has seen on television, the assumption may be that he or she is no longer a good doctor—indeed, that doctors are not as good as they used to be. And this feeling may be felt by both patient and doctor.

The sudden rise of malpractice suits of all kinds (including educational and parental malpractice), as well as the first resignation of a President in American history, suggest a continued belief in the "greatness" of certain roles, but a fundamental disappointment in individual performers. Indeed, recent Gallup and Harris public opinion polls suggest that many people continue to have faith in social *institutions* (such as higher education, the military, and the medical profession) but not in the *people* who head them. Between 1966 and 1980, the public's trust in the authorities who head higher education declined from 61% to 33%; faith in the leadership of organized religion slipped from 41% to 20%; trust in the leaders of major companies fell from 55% to 19%; faith in the military leadership dropped from 61% to 33%; and confidence in the leaders of medical institutions plummetted from 73% to 30%.[15] In the long run, the continuing disappointment in many authorities may lead to a new, lower conception of most of our social institutions.

Not long ago, the natural bias of the communication environment was to limit information about politicians and other authorities. Politicians had to to *act* to get a message across. Indeed, the major role of public relations and advertising, in general, was once that of getting information *to* the public. The intent was to make certain aspects of people, institutions, ideas, and products visible. Other aspects were kept invisible through simple neglect. Now, however, public relations is becoming more and more an attempt to restrict information or to counteract information that is already available, as in recent oil and chemical company public relations campaigns. Similarly, politicians find that they have less control over information about themselves and national affairs in general. They often find themselves commenting on the information already available instead of making new revelations to the public.

It has been common to hear accusations about presidential "management" of news since the presidency of John Kennedy, yet the fact is that the news was always managed. "News" is a combination of substance and image, just as all social interaction involves controlling what is revealed and what is hidden. What has changed in recent times is not necessarily the "truth content" of political news, but the politician's control over information, and the control over the control. We are now more aware of the manipulation of public impressions.

Increased public access to information leads to more power for the public (relative to "authorities") and this, in turn, leads to even more access to information, and so on. In response to the pressure of special interest groups, the government itself has initiated and reinforced laws and policies of "openness" and "disclosure." In 1977, the House Committee on Government Operations published a guide to using the 1966 Freedom of Information Act and the Privacy Act of 1974. The purpose of the guide is to allow the average citizen "to learn what the Federal Government is doing in general and what it knows about citizens as individuals." The guide is written in plain language and is "designed . . . to make the workings of Government more transparent."[16] The trend is accelerating as the public demands greater access to government files and as advances in photocopying and computer technology make compliance feasible.

The high degree of accessibility to information through electronic media has led to demands that all information—whatever its source or form—be accessible to the average person. Highly specialized language or jargon is now frowned on. The Catholic mass is now performed in the vernacular, and consumers are demanding plainer language in legal contracts. Leaders in business, politics, and religion must now espouse their commitment to "openness" in order to appear trustworthy. In recent years, television cameras have exposed the interiors of both the White House and the Vatican.

Ironically, however, the more that is found out about what authorities do and know, the less they appear to deserve to be all-powerful authorities. From the doctor's knowledge of the body to the divine monarch's channel to God, high status is protected through special and exclusive access to information. Once authorities "give away" their information, their expertness and status may dissolve. High status that is not (or is no longer) based on special access to information is generally revolted against. Heads of state who lose their control over information sometimes lose their heads as well.

Leaders today, therefore, must play a delicate game of trying to appear open while also attempting to reassert control over information. Both Presidents Carter and Reagan have attempted to appear candid and "accessible," yet they have also worked hard to stop White House "leaks." Ironically, however, the White House is now so leaky at the seams that there have even been leaks concerning the attempts to stop the leaks. In April 1983, for example, *Newsweek* reported that both the leaks and some of the manifest attempts to control them are part of a calculated and condoned White House policy to "test public reaction, to send signals (often in code) to other players in the political process, to win favor with the press or simply, as one White House official says, 'to put our spin on things.'"[17] Apparently unable to stop the flow of information, authorities attempt to manage and use the flow as best they can. But even this management has become a topic of public discussion.

The new patterns of relatively open information flow have led to a general distrust of authority in America. *New York Times* reporter Richard Lyons notes the change, but is at a loss to explain it:

> Americans in growing numbers are turning a deaf ear to the pronouncements of public officials and eminent scientists. Many of them continue to smoke, refuse to wear seat belts, decline to immunize their children, protest a proposal to ban saccharin and believe laetrile to be effective in the treatment of cancer . . . .

The reason for this apparent public contrariness is not precisely known, but a sampling of the opinions of polltakers and scholars suggests that the cause may be a deepening suspicion of government in particular and authority in general.[18]

The new balance of access to information may be the reason why Americans are now very "involved" in politics and in political issues and yet also extremely disenchanted with most major candidates and the political process itself. As Americans have lost faith in distant authorities (who are no longer distant informationally), there has been a general trend toward "self-government," "community control," and "self-help." In obscenity cases, for example, there has been a move toward "community standards." Moreover, within the community, it is not necessarily community *leaders* who are asked to judge the obscenity standard. Concerning this issue, Cleveland, Ohio developed a questionnaire to survey average citizens.[19] There is also a growing trend toward "voter legislation," where citizens, rather than elected representatives, vote on the implementation of laws.[20] Citizens are constantly seeking information on their "rights" and looking for protection from potential encroachments by high status people, big business, or government. And the general trend toward "self-help care," the feminist critique of the medical establishment, the return of lay midwifery, and the rise of "alternative birthing centers" suggest the demystification of the once almighty role of the doctor.[21]

Backstage Visibility and the Decline of Authority

Roles of hierarchy are upset not only by the loss of exclusive control over knowledge directly relevant to role functions (medical data for a doctor, for example), but also by the merging of public and private situations. More than any other type of roles, hierarchal roles depend on performers restricting access to their personal lives. Much human activity is common to all individuals. If high status persons cannot segregate such behavior from their onstage high status performances, then they appear to be more like everyone else. By providing greater access to, and awareness of, backstage behavior, electronic media tend to undermine traditional abstractions of status.

The current drive toward intimacy with our leaders involves a fundamental paradox. In pursuing our desire to be "close" to great people or to confirm their greatness through increased exposure, we often destroy their ability to function as great people. "Greatness" manifests itself in the onstage performance and, by definition, in its isolation from backstage behaviors. Yet when we say that we want to see what authorities are "really like," we generally mean we want to see what they are *least* like, that is, both how they behave least often in the role they perform for us, and also the least they can be in social terms. In intimate spheres, people are often very much alike: They eat, they eliminate, they get tired, they sleep, they make love, they groom, they indulge in whims and self-involvements.

There is an inherent "vanishing truth" paradox in the use of television to give us a close-up view of our politicians, experts, doctors, psychologists, teachers, and other authorities. When we see our leaders in varieties of situations and locations, when we observe them as they respond to spontaneous interviews or as they grow weary from a day of work or campaigning, we do not simply learn more about them. By searching behind the fronts of performers, we also change the roles that can be performed and perceived—as well as the images that high status performers have of themselves.

The backstage exposure of our high status performers dramatically changes the relative flow of social information. With respect to our national leaders, for example, we have essentially reversed the nonreciprocal flow of information that traditionally supported their high status. Leaders once had easy access to others, but were able to control access to themselves. Before the 1920s, most people had never heard the voice of a President or received any direct evidence of his humanness or personality. Before the late 1940s, few reporters had access to portable voice recording machines that could be used to substantiate quotes from interviews (and therefore quotes could be denied). Indeed, it is somewhat startling to realize that as recently as the beginning of Eisenhower's presidency, the press was not allowed to quote the President directly without permission.[22] Through television, "the people" now have more access to the personal expressive behaviors of leaders than leaders have to the personal behaviors of the people. This reversed status is being reinforced by the current demands for "full disclosure" on the part of officials and the complementary demand by the public tor protection from government spying and for controls on government access to personal records.[23] With this new reversed nonreciprocal information flow, we are witnessing dramatic changes in our conceptions of Presidents, members of Congress, and the heads of intelligence agencies.

The irony inherent in most investigations of back region activity was very apparent in the Senate Watergate hearings. At the beginning of the process, the senators glowed brightly in their righteous indignation over White House back region misconduct. To many, these senators were America's new heroes. They would put things right and rule the land with a steady and honest hand. But as the days and weeks passed, the increasing exposure of the senators took its toll. Ultimately, the hearings were followed by investigations of members of Congress as well. As journalist Shana Alexander observed, the limelight was too bright for any old-style heroes.

> Washington has no heroes left. Not only has the spreading scandal destroyed our national leadership . . . but familiarity has rubbed the stardust from the shoulders of the men who did the job, the various lawyers, prosecutors, investigators and members of the Senate committee. . . .

I'm not complaining. It's necessary to toss out old heroes from time to time, spring cleaning of the mind. But we have hit a unique dead spot in the national cardiogram; the pulse is nearly flat. A few weak blips of admiration do appear on the scope, but they are not heroes.[24]

The disclosure of authorities' backstage behavior leads to shock and public demand for increased attention to ethics and standards. The change in the *structure* of information environments is often mistaken for a change in the *substance* of individuals' personalities and characters. In the long run, we must either re-establish distance and mystification or redefine downward many formerly high status roles.

The Severing of the Territory/Status Link

All past changes in media have affected social hierarchies by altering information flow and control. But electronic media have an impact on hierarchy that was not shared by any earlier media: They bypass the once strong relationship between high status and territory. Territory was once directly related to authority, not only because of the wealth and power that land control represented, but also because territorial control once allowed for control over information within one's territory and for the use of one's property as a shield against the scrutiny of others. A secure territory allowed for a private backstage rehearsal and relaxation area and therefore supported high status onstage role performances.

Isolated locations continue to support authority, but electronic media now bypass a number of the status characteristics of territory. One's physical position and territorial control no longer guarantee socially significant informational control. Ever since the assassination of John Kennedy, for example, television news has maintained what is gruesomely called a "death watch" on the President so that nothing will happen to the chief executive without full media coverage.[25] (The major record of the JFK assassination was a home movie.) The President is now watched whenever possible. Ronald Reagan's "vacations," therefore, often continue to be onstage performances as he is spied on by telephoto lenses; sometimes he feels the obligation to wave to the distant cameras while relaxing or riding a horse. No matter what he does, however, people are now much more aware that the President is not always "on the job."

The dissociation of physical and informational control affects all authorities, even those who are not as publicly visible as the President. An executive office with a view was once an important symbol of high status in business, but today such an office would be meaningless without a telephone (and increasingly without an on-line computer). Indeed, levels of corporate status are often correlated with degrees of free long-distance calling privileges (and, more recently, with degrees of computing power). Who one can "see" or "reach" is no longer determined primarily by physical placement and movement. A telephone or computer in a ghetto tenement or in a suburban teenager's bedroom is potentially as effective as a telephone or computer in a corporate suite. Conversely, walls, barbed wire, doors, guards, and outer offices no longer fully protect an executive from *being* reached. The telephone bypasses physical barriers. It is possible to shut oneself off somewhat with telephone receptionists or automatic answering machines, but the increased energy required suggests that there is a new balance of power at work.

The new balance of control over access and information is often obscured by the seemingly awesome power at extremes. As *Washington Post* editor Ben Bradlee describes, his friend John Kennedy was very proud of the ability of the White House telephone operators to locate anyone, anywhere they might be, at any time.

> Once, he dared Tony [Bradlee's wife] and Jackie and me to come up with a name of someone the operators couldn't find. Jackie suggested Truman Capote, because he had an unlisted telephone number. Kennedy picked up the telephone and said only "Yes, this is the president. Would you please get me Truman Capote?"—no other identification. Thirty minutes later, Capote was on the line . . . not from his own unlisted number in Brooklyn Heights, but at the home of a friend in Palm Springs, Calif., who also had an unlisted number.[26]

The range of a President's reach is dramatic. But it represents an impressive *amount* of access rather than an impressive *degree* of access. For the average person with a telephone can closely approximate many of the feats of the President's staff. The ability to reach Capote in a remote location in thirty minutes is less testimony to the great power of the presidency than it is testimony to the flexibility and reach of electronic media, *which are available to everyone*. With electronic media, the power of Presidents and other authorities is absolutely greater than it was before, but relatively decreased. When travel was the key to social access, even a President had to travel or send a messenger. But this nonmediated access still greatly favored Presidents and other high status figures. Only they had the resources and time to attain frequent access to many distant people. The average person was trapped in daily confines and routines. Through electronic media, access is simpler for everyone and the relative advantage of traditionally high status figures has been diminished.

The inability of high status persons to isolate themselves informationally by isolating themselves physically leads to an inability to separate situations and the behaviors appropriate to them. There is now a limit, for example, to the range of behavior a President can exhibit at different times and places. Presidents have greater difficulty hiding their behaviors in "private" locations and this leads to a necessary change in the image they project in "public."

Ironically, the more that electronic media undermine the status of leaders, the more many people perceive the behaviors of authorities as arrogant or haughty. As our leaders are informationally crippled by the uncovering of the backstage machinations of power, the exposed behaviors make it appear that our leaders are becoming too authoritarian. And so many people demand more control over information in order to fight "abuses of power."[27] Our leaders are now faced with the dilemma of having to gain and maintain high status by appearing ordinary, and yet they face criticism if they lack dynamism and power. The Watergate scandal and the general "crisis in confidence," therefore, may involve much more complex ethical and philosophical issues than is generally assumed.

The decreasing importance of place-situations has a direct effect on the linear communication lines which supported traditional hierarchy. Political information, for example, no longer travels from national leaders to local leaders to citizens; it now often goes directly from national leaders to the citizens' homes. As a consequence, many people do not know the names of their district leaders or members of Congress and would not recognize their "representatives" if they passed on the street.

In many instances, electronic media not only bypass local and regional representatives, they also bypass the national government. Americans once looked to their own government for information about other countries. Now, much international information reaches citizens directly. Radio could bring us closer to the British because we share a common language, but television can even bring us closer to Poles and Afghans. While political factors often influence the varying television exposure to other peoples, the form of whatever coverage we do see has also affected our political sensibilities. Among other things, we now find it easier to separate "the people" from "the government." Indeed, at times, we are even able to separate in our minds the head of the government from the ideologies his or her government represents, and we respond instead (both positively and negatively) to his or her personality. This has been the case with Khrushchev, Castro, Brezhnev, Sadat, Begin, Thatcher, and others.

To the dismay of seasoned diplomats, a number of foreign leaders and citizens since Khrushchev have been able to reach the American people directly, effectively bypassing many of the channels of international diplomacy and the American political hierarchy.[28] President Carter, for example, was among the many Americans who watched television as Anwar Sadat made his historic trip to Jerusalem, and President Reagan was too busy being inaugurated into office to follow along with other Americans the televised return of the hostages held by Iran. American leaders no longer convey all international information to the American people; in many instances, American politicians who speak to the public about foreign affairs are now placed in the weak position of describing events to eyewitnesses.

The impact of electronic media on international relations is most visible in confrontations between governments. Early in his presidency, Jimmy Carter attacked Fidel Castro for supporting a massacre in Africa; Castro replied in a television interview with Barbara Walters. The response was not filtered through American government channels. Carter, no doubt, had to watch the response along with other Americans. Moreover, the American attack and the Cuban reply were made in the same forum. Both leaders spoke "directly" to the American people and both spoke from the same "place" and "distance." The natural tendency to side with those who share the same "position" was muted. More than in earlier eras, Americans had the opportunity to accept and believe the "other side."

As information direction changes, traditional lines of hierarchy and traditional forms of negotiation are bypassed. The situation calls to mind an episode in the "Star Trek" television series. An alien leader makes a demand of Captain Kirk through the ship's television system. Kirk is not convinced by the alien's message and the alien therefore directly addresses Kirk's crew members (who also have access to the communication) and asks *them* to make the decision on their own. Whether such undermining of authority is ultimately good or bad deserves to be the subject of heated debate, but it is important to realize first the nature and dimensions of the change.

Ironically, in bypassing local members of a larger hierarchy, electronic media ultimately bring about a new type of local control. People are less likely to be in awe of physically distant leaders, partly because they have seen these leaders close-up and they do not appear to be worthy of special trust, and partly because many leaders have simply lost the control over information that made their positions necessary and viable. As a result, many local communities have demanded independent control over their own school boards and other community affairs. The new local control, however, is very different from old forms of local government. Local politicians were once steps in a linear hierarchy of representative government. Electronic media not only bypass many of the old channels, they also undermine the whole system of graded hierarchy and delegated authority. Electronic media have fostered the growth of a neo-feudal system of local political vassals and lords with a decline in the relative power and influence of central authorities. One of the ironies of an electronic age is that new media have made completely centralized control technically possible yet socially unacceptable.

11

Effect Loops

As I noted in the introduction to this part of the book, there are many other social factors beside the new electronic situations that affect the issues that are discussed here. Yet some of the factors that appear to be independent of electronic media may actually be closely related to them. This chapter briefly examines three significant processes that are often perceived as spontaneous human decisions that independently cause social change: changes in conceptions of "appropriate" behavior, changes in media content, and changes in the rules of access to places. Here I suggest that these apparent causes are themselves often responses to the new situations created by new media.

I refer to these three variables as "effect loops" for two reasons: (1) because they not only respond to changes in media but also enhance the effects of new media, and (2) because they act as "feedback loops" by working to establish a new balance between patterns of information flow and other social conventions; that is, these three variables change so as to return the social system to *structural equilibrium*, yet in so doing, they bring about *substantive change*.

The Etiquette Loop

One of the reasons it is difficult to see the relationship between electronic media and changes in behavior is that media do not function in a vacuum. Electronic media are not the ultimate molders of behavioral changes. Old role structures may be undermined by new patterns of information flow, but new role structures can never be created by media; they must be created by people. As Cooley, Mead, and Goffman suggest, individuals gain perceptions of their own behavior when they see themselves as "social objects," that is, when they envision themselves as others would see

them. New media may affect who performs before whom, where and
when the performances take place, and the type of control over information that can be exercised, but the performer and audience are still people, and behavior is still *socially* defined. New media may undermine the
viability of old behavior forms, but new roles must take shape in human
interaction and response.

For these reasons, the effects of media are often overlooked, and
changes in social behavior are often seen as spontaneous "modernizations." Changes in the notion of "appropriate" roles and behaviors, however, can often be traced back to structural changes in social situations. If
men and women regularly sit and watch the same television programs,
for example, our ability to distinguish "women's subjects" from "men's
subjects" or "women's language" from "men's language" diminishes
sharply. Once a great deal of information is shared and, even more important, shared explicitly, then men and women are likely to begin to speak
the same language and discuss the same topics and expect the same rights
and privileges. This behavior is made possible or necessary by new information-systems, but it must be developed and reinforced interpersonally.
In this way, television not only affects the behaviors and perceptions of
those actually *exposed* on television; it also changes the general notion of
appropriate behavior among many of those who *view* television.

Such changes not only reflect electronic media's breakdown of information-systems but also enhance it by spreading the results of information-system changes into interpersonal and place-bound situations. A
particular classroom may not be electronically monitored and it may have
no electronic receiving equipment. And yet the new information environments within which all the participants live *outside* the classroom may,
nevertheless, undermine the traditional role structures and purposes of
the school. An elementary school history lesson about the ideal functioning of the executive branch of government may be interrupted by a
youngster who has detailed information concerning the latest presidential
scandal. And this information may be available through television to a
child who would not yet be old enough to have access to this type of
information from other sources. Similarly, two young teenagers may
shock their parents with their language and sexual candor. The school-
child's and the teenagers' behaviors reflect and extend the merging of
information-systems fostered by electronic media. New media, therefore,
may have an effect on interactions in places in which media are neither
present nor thought about.

The traditional focus on media content and the concern over viewers'
imitation of it have made it difficult to see how new media may lead to
behavior that is not portrayed in media at all. How, for example, could
television have anything to do with the increased use of certain four-letter
words in "mixed company" when such words are almost never heard on
television? Yet television's general exposure of the back region/front
region structure of social interaction may make viewers more aware of the

existence of backstage behavior and more fascinated with its exposure. The apparent "hypocrisy" that television exposes in many of the discrepancies between role performers' back and front region behaviors (the woman who plays "hard to get," the man who acts as if he is confident when he is really fearful, and so on) may have a tendency to encourage viewers to develop a more consistent "middle region" style for themselves that includes many words and actions from their *own* backstage behavior—not necessarily from the idealized and sanitized backstage behaviors projected on television.

As social information-systems merge, formerly "taboo" topics are included in male-female and parent-child discussions, public figures include personal messages in their public presentations, and teachers discuss things with young students that were once considered inappropriate subjects for a classroom (such as drug use and sexual abuse of children).

Our new patterns of behavior and speech do not necessarily reflect a disregard for taste and etiquette. They do represent a *new* sense of propriety resulting from merged situations. As Amy Vanderbilt notes:

> In today's society almost any topic in the world is discussible, if there is reason to discuss it and if the discussion of it is conducted with taste and discretion. . . . The world has changed very much. . . . [Women] cannot continue to expect men's conversation around them to be geared to drawing room levels. . . . Tasteful conversationalists have absolutely no compunctions against discussing such things as pregnancy, abortion, divorce, separation, political and other scandal. . . . Not so very long ago, these things would have been considered very crass as subjects for mixed conversation.[1]

New media, therefore, not only affect the way people behave, but they eventually affect the way people feel they *should* behave. As suggested below, such changes in behavior and attitude further enhance the overall effects of electronic media by "feeding-back" into the system as the "updated" content of the shared media environment, thereby further breaking down distinctions between private and public information-systems.

The Media Content Loop

The changes in the structure of information-systems brought about by new media not only affect behavior directly, they also have an influence on the content of media. Changes in media content and changes in social behavior may often be correlated, therefore, not necessarily because of a direct causal link between them, but because they are both influenced by the same factor—the changing structure of social situations. The impact of electronic media on information-systems leads to several different types of change in media content.

Previously Distinct Varieties of Content Become Homogenized

As all groups tend to be exposed to relatively similar material through electronic media, the content of programs begins to follow the structure of the combined audiences and the merged arenas. Once everyone has seen a broad range of programs, each of which was designed for a select group, the content of individual programs begins to change. There are fewer and fewer distinctions made between "men's programming" and "women's programming" or between "adult programs" and "children's programs." It no longer makes much sense to have very distinct shows and topics because everyone has already been exposed to the whole spectrum of social information. Even cable shows aimed at women discuss car mechanics, and cable programs aimed at children discuss talking about sex with parents.[2]

The acceptance of shared topics for children and adults is reflected in a federal court's 1976 rejection of the concept of a "family viewing hour," which was intended to restrict sex and violence on television during the early evening hours when many children are watching television. David Rintels, then president of the Writer's Guild of America-West, explained why his group fought against the special programming for children. Implicit in his argument is the belief that children's knowledge of adult topics has already been markedly increased. Rintels stated: "I believe there is nothing on television which cannot now be watched without embarrassment, even by children; indeed, I think the opposite is much truer, that television is not nearly honest enough or frank enough about sex, that we should be able to delve far more deeply into the serious social and moral questions which sex raises, and that we could all become richer for it."[3]

The shared environment of television leads to a new "middle region" content for programs. Television content has evolved the same way that the conversations at a cocktail party might evolve if the guest-list were expanded to include people of all ages, classes, races, religions, occupations, and ethnic backgrounds. No issue from infant care to incest is left untouched, yet technical jargon and highly focused ideas and discussions are banished to more specialized arenas. In humor, the "mixed company" problem is handled in one of two ways: Either jokes are chosen that offend no ethnic group or large segments of the population, or conversely, jokes are told that offend everyone equally. (The latter technique was Norman Lear's innovation in "All in the Family" and other shows.) Both tactics reveal adjustments to the mixed audience of television.

New Role Behaviors Are Depicted as the Content of Programs

Changes in group identity, socialization, and hierarchy caused by changing information-systems are portrayed on television. The new social behaviors are aired on news shows, documentaries, talk shows, televised hearings, and other nonfiction programs. Further, to match the behavioral changes, fictional programs follow with a conscious "updating" of content. The "hippie" and the "liberated woman" become characters in situation comedies and dramas ("All in the Family" and "Maude," for example). Social trends such as "living together" and nontraditional households are portrayed ("Three's Company," "Different Strokes"). In addition, traditional roles are presented in a new "middle region" form, consistent with the new information available about roles and role performances in general. The doctors in "M*A*S*H," for example, are shown making jokes while performing surgery. And former distinctions between public and private situations and behaviors are presented as merging ("Mary Tyler Moore Show," "Hill Street Blues," "St. Elsewhere") or as completely merged ("Welcome Back Kotter," "Barney Miller").

The Content of Programs Evolves to Match the New Information Form

In contrast to print, television does not allow control over what is "expressed" along with what is "communicated." Television news programs, for example, cannot escape presenting a wide range of personal expressions in addition to "objective facts." Rather than attempting to fight this aspect of television news, producers have taken the parts of the back region that are difficult to hide and thrust them into the show itself. This is especially true of local news programs. Backstage expressiveness, personal feelings, informal interaction, and ad-libbed jokes have become an important aspect of the performance. Similarly, many television quiz and talk shows have abandoned attempts to hide microphones, camera operators, "applause" signs, and cue cards. One recent short-lived program went so far as to open and close the program with viewers listening to the voice of the show's director as he gave "cues" to the camera operators and other staff. Expressiveness, "personality," and offstage behavior have become the implicit subjects of so many news shows that a new "news" program—"Entertainment Tonight"—has made them its explicit subjects.

Similarly, televised sports competitions reveal so much backstage-style emotion along with the athletic feats that the emotion begins to take center stage. Olympic weight-lifters, for example, are followed into their "warming rooms" after an unsuccessful lift and are asked to describe their "feelings" about the failure. The emotional aspects of such competitions become so prominent that good "expressors" are substituted in some sports programs for real athletes. So "celebrity sports competitions" are presented as television entertainment, with performers who are only amateur athletes but professional expressors.

Flubbed lines and unintended clumsiness were once the bane of traditional actors and performers. Yet such mistakes are now so common and so public in "live" performances before vast radio and television audiences that they have become a part of the show itself. At first, anniversary

celebrations of programs such as the "Tonight" show or "American Bandstand" included "bloopers" and "great mistakes," and a number of records and television specials were devoted exclusively to outtakes and
bloopers. Now, there are several regular television shows that use bloopers as part of their weekly entertainment. Similarly, the Home Box Office
news spoof, "Not Necessarily the News," delights in using "news outtakes" of political figures and their families making mistakes in speeches,
saying or doing silly things, and tripping or falling down. The implications of this change in attitude toward backstage behavior, however, is
that many politicians and professional actors are almost never "backstage." An outtake from a movie may reappear as prime time entertainment; a transcript of presidential banter while testing microphone levels
before a speech may appear in a national magazine.[4] With the new knowledge of this potential outcome, such actors must begin to treat many of
their backstage rehearsals as indirect performances. Exactly where the
new line is between true back region behavior and the expanded front
region is difficult to discern, but such changes in media content (and in
real behavior) may be understood best by viewing them in relation to the
new social settings created by the use of electronic media.

Print Media Use Electronic Media as the Standard
by Which to Determine "Appropriate" Content

One indication of the dominance of television in our society is the fact
that print media now often emulate the type and form of information that
television provides. The traditionally more formal and abstract print
media have turned toward issues of "personality." New magazines such
as *People* explore the personal lives of public figures. Print journalists and
scholars have adopted a more personal and subjective style. Newspapers
now often describe events in a manner that simulates what one might
have seen and heard on television. Quotes in print, for example, are now
more likely to include "ums" and "ahs," and grammatical and other mistakes are more likely to be left intact. Indeed, descriptions of events in
print are now more likely to report on aural and visual phenomena that
might have gone unnoticed to most people *at* the actual event, but were
clearly perceptible to those who were watching television. The sweat on
a politician's brow, a tear running down a face, or a nervous twitch may
become part of the print description—because the "event" is now defined
in terms of how it appeared on television. From the written record alone,
it will appear to future generations that it was only in the mid-twentieth
century that our leaders were stricken with physical and verbal
clumsiness.

The inherently revealing television interview now sets the standard for
the style and content of many print interviews as well. In the early 1970s,
for example, Erving Goffman observed a surprising change in the balance
between "on" and "off" the record in print interviews. Goffman suggests

that it was once assumed that a large part of any interaction—even with a journalist—was meant only for the time and place of the conversation, and people being interviewed, therefore, usually split their flow of activities and words into two streams: one "for the record" and one "off the record." But "in the last five or six years . . . interviewers have come to serve as monitoring devices for relaying what they witness of matters ordinarily held to be off the record. Subjects then find, in effect, that they have been spied on."[5] Goffman offers no explanation for the change, but the idea of a reporter as a "monitoring device" suggests that print journalists now try to reproduce the "feel" of a television interview.

The "presumption of intimacy" created by electronic media has affected not only the print interview, but biographies and memoirs as well. It now seems more acceptable to write books about the very personal lives of great people, to reveal old secrets, and to betray old confidences. Indeed, memoirs *without* such intimate revelations about the writer or others now seem stuffy and unrealistic. In recent years, well-known actresses and politicians and members of their families have written revealing accounts of backstage encounters with domestic violence, alcoholism, drug abuse, and sexual obsessions. Commenting on the trend without explaining it, *Newsweek* reported:

> In the late '70s, privacy is a dirty word. . . . Confessing all used to be the recourse of has-beens whose humiliations had already been thoroughly aired in the tabloids. . . .
>   Now everybody's into it. The degree of candor varies, but the aim, at least, is to satisfy what has become a huge national appetite for personal revelation.[6]

In general, television makes the traditional line between back and front regions seem contrived. What was acceptable content for books in a print culture may be unacceptable in an electronic culture. In a print culture, children's books can contain any information about adult behavior that adults choose to include in them. Children can be presented with an idealized and stereotyped view of adults and with a sanitized image of social reality. Yet once much "adult" information is available to children through television, traditional children's books seem phony to children. In recent years, therefore, the content of children's books has changed to include many topics, such as sex and drugs, that were once taboo for children but are now known to them because of television.

Ironically, in *following* electronic media's pursuit of intimacy, print media often appear to *lead*. For the more private (and less regulated) nature of print forums allows books and magazines to reveal deeper back region behaviors. If an actress's cleavage is revealed on television, then a magazine may show her completely naked. If broadcast media tend to merge private and public realms and to suggest to people that the traditional distinctions between private and public behaviors are arbitrary and hypocritical, then the editors and publishers of books, magazines, and dictionaries feel more comfortable including four-letter words in their publications. (Similar changes occur in the relatively private motion picture, in *non*broadcast electronic media such as records and videotapes, and even in the semi-private world of cable.) Such changes in nonbroadcast content may feed-back into the system of broadcast media when the changes in children's books, the new pictorials in magazines, and other new content become the topics of television news, entertainment, and talk shows. Recently, for example, Phil Donahue has interviewed both pornographic movie stars and women who lost their jobs for posing nude in *Playboy*.

What is common to all these changes in media messages is the circular relationship between the structure of information-systems and their content. Any major change in the overall patterns of social information flow affects the content of all media.

The Territorial Access Loop

Although electronic media undermine the relationship between social situations and physical places, distinct places obviously still exist and place remains an important determinant of many types of interaction. Physical interactions—from lovemaking to murder—are rather limited over the telephone, even the videotelephone, and the "company" provided by a radio or television or computer can also be viewed as a new form of solitary confinement. Even if media provide much information that was once available only through physical presence, physical movement can still be restricted regardless of apparent access to other people through media. Women may share much more information with men and yet still be restricted from certain all-male situations; prisoners may be plugged into the outside world through media but still remain *in* prison; a child may have access to information from around the world and yet not be allowed to leave the house. The freedom provided by information access alone, therefore, is a very limited one.

Changes in information-systems, however, tend to be followed by changes in rules of travel and access to places. The shift in information flow seems to create an imbalance, a tension between individuals' enhanced informational status and their still limited physical mobility. New rules of physical movement and access are developed, therefore, as a means of aligning spatial configurations with the new patterns of information flow. As mental patients and prisoners gain more informational access to the social world, the concepts of "halfway" houses and work-release programs develop. As the disabled are increasingly able to monitor and interact with the larger environment despite their physical isolation, they increase their demands for corresponding physical access through special parking spaces, ramps, and sidewalks that slope down into the street. When—to paraphrase the telephone ad—people are able to let their fingers, eyes, and ears "do the walking" via electronic media, everyone in society gains relatively equal "mobility."

Electronic media offer previously isolated groups a new form of social access and movement. As a result, restrictions on physical access that once seemed normal and necessary now seem arbitrary and reactionary. Once women see hundreds of hours of men's interactions in all-male backstage situations on television, it no longer seems to make as much sense to women to have bars, clubs, and jobs that exclude women. Once children have seen a thousand deaths and funerals on television, it no longer seems as logical to exclude children from a family funeral.

To have information from an environment is to be partially "in" that environment. Information access opens the door to physical access. It is not surprising that one of the key forms of protest since the 1960s has been the "sit-in." The sit-in often involves physically taking over an environment that has already been demystified and "conquered" through informational access.

I noted in the "etiquette loop" discussion that television not only affects the perception of those behaviors exposed on television but also changes viewers' general sense of appropriate behavioral style. Similarly, television not only demystifies the places actually exposed on it but also promotes a new sense of access and openness to all places. As this new attitude results in a more open approach to many physical locations, the change in rules of access feeds-back into electronic media through the first-time exposure of various places on television (the House of Representatives, mental hospitals, the White House, courtrooms, emergency rooms, welfare offices, the Vatican, etc.). And these exposures further increase the demystification of "place."

The argument that homogenization of information leads to homogenized access to space gains some historical support from the fact that before print spread through Western Europe, there was no extensive separation of classes, sexes, ages, or activities into separate rooms and places.[7] Business was conducted in the home, rooms had no special function (except the kitchen), servants slept and ate in the same rooms as their masters, and the home was relatively open to the larger community. The specialization of rooms began with the middle class and nobility, the same classes that first became the most literate. This specialization "satisfied a new desire for isolation."[8]

Perhaps part of this new desire for isolation was related to the segregating tendencies of print. Once print allowed sub-groups to develop their own "private discussions," then separate physical environments may have been needed to maintain similar distinctions in live interactions. Once books established a set of information that was accessible to adults but generally inaccessible to children, adults may have felt a greater need to distinguish adult environments from child environments. Once princes and priests could read advice books (such as those by Machiavelli and Gracian) on how to present themselves to their "audiences," then perhaps there was a greater desire to maintain more distance and privacy, both for reading about and rehearsing for onstage roles and for relaxing from them.

Conversely, electronic media today may have a great deal to do with the trend toward fewer distinctions among places, not only because electronic media merge many social information-systems, but also because electronic media weaken the usefulness of places as secure information-systems. If others have access to the information (or type of information) that you try to hide in a private physical space, then there is less reason to maintain the physical isolation.

From this perspective, there is a common element in many recent changes in approach to physical place. The fusion of work and living spaces, the growth of coed dorms, the trend toward "open concept" offices, the experiments with conjugal visits for prisoners, the spread of the hospice movement (which encourages doctors and families to allow the terminally ill to die at home or in home-like settings), the liberalization of many hospitals' visiting policies, and the return to the pre-print "family bed" (where parents and children sleep together[9])—all these represent the merging of physical situations to match the merging of social information-systems.

Another potential manifestation of a new perception of physical places as a result of new information-systems is the law's increasing involvement in many institutions that once handled their own disputes and problems independently. Nursing homes, schools, prisons, mental institutions, and branches of the armed services have been sued recently by parties from within who were not satisfied with their treatment.[10]

Children were once frightened of distant abstract authority figures, and a threat to call "The Policeman" was sometimes used to control their behavior. In recent years, however, the tables have been turned. There have been a number of cases where children—now much more knowledgeable about police work and the law—have called police officers or lawyers to gain protection from their parents.

By giving everyone greater access to other places, electronic media also remove people socially and psychologically from their physical situations. The ease of "leaving" a place via electronic media has made it easier for children, employees, prisoners, government officials, and others to bypass the information channels and hierarchies of their physical environments. Anyone can use a telephone booth to make an anonymous call to alert authorities about some wrongdoing or problem. Because insiders no longer have to "go" somewhere to speak with an outsider, it is now much more common for information about private group interactions or problems to "leak" into the public forum. Members can "defect" without ever leaving the group's territory, and both amateur and professional investigators can "penetrate" the perimeter of an institution without ever going near it.

The flexibility and speed of "travel" through electronic media foster a trend toward flexibility and speed of access to physical places. Through radio, television, and telephone, messages move twenty-four hours a day, seven days a week. Confinement within, or exclusion from a place because of a "schedule" now seems more arbitrary and less acceptable. This may be one reason for the trend toward "flextime," which allows employees to choose their own work hours or work part-time on a permanent basis. Similarly, more stores are open on Sundays and all night. Even the process of moving goods has been transformed by the new sense of immediacy. One of the largest and most competitive businesses in the country is currently the "overnight delivery" service, which has been pushing the transportation of packages as close as possible toward the instantaneous movement of information afforded by electronic media.

The general sense of the openness of situations that has resulted from the widespread use of electronic media has given all closed social systems a bad name. Closed meetings are now suspicious, and membership in a club that excludes members on the basis of any social category—sex, race, or religion—can be the undoing of a political aspirant. In recent years, "sunshine" laws have opened government meetings to the public, women have been allowed into formerly all-male bars, and the male athlete's locker room has been opened to female reporters. Not only has the law begun to come into social situations that were once independent of it, but the law has also begun to eat away at the right of people to have a segregated sphere of interaction in the first place. Whether such changes are good or bad is open to question, but perhaps we should be more closely examining their causes and implications.

Because the new rules of access to places merge many additional formerly distinct social situations, many more old behavior patterns become untenable. The changing rules of physical access, lead to the development of additional "middle region" behaviors. These changes in access and behavior affect conceptions of "appropriate" behavior, and the changes in place access, behavior, and etiquette become the new subjects of media content—and so the spiral continues.

Ironically, however, these many changes also obscure the effects of electronic media on society. When speaking of the reasons for the development of new social behaviors, many observers point to the spontaneous "modernizations" of etiquette, to decisions made by media producers, editors, and authors, and to new laws and informal customs concerning access to physical places. Analysis of the roots of social change often focus directly on these variables rather than on the changes in media of communication that may affect all three of them.

PART IV
Three Dimensions of Social Change

Each of the next three "case study" chapters closely examines a specific example for each of the general types of roles that have been analyzed thus far. Chapter 12 examines recent changes in notions of masculinity and femininity (group identity), Chapter 13 explores shifting conceptions of childhood and adulthood (socialization), and Chapter 14 examines the changing performances of national political leaders (hierarchy).

I have chosen men and women as a case study for several reasons. First, male and female are the two largest human "groups," and the differences and similarities between them are therefore of concern to every person. Second, the feminist movement has replaced the issue of race as the dominant and most controversial "integration" movement. Most important, however, the roles of men and women have traditionally been thought of as being biologically rather than socially determined. If traditional distinctions in gender roles can be shown to be related to distinctions in social information-systems, and if the current merging of masculine and feminine behaviors can be related to merging information-systems, then there is even more evidence to support the argument that changes in situations have an effect on all other groups—groups that are more widely accepted as being shaped by social rather than biological factors (religion, class, race, nationality, profession, etc.).

I have selected child and adult roles as the focus of the case study on socialization because the socialization process from childhood to adulthood is one that is universally experienced. Further, of all socialization processes, the stages of childhood are most closely associated with "natural" stages of physiological and cognitive development. Similar to the analysis of masculinity and femininity, child socialization offers both the most difficult challenge to the theory presented here and the greatest promise of significant findings and implications for the study of other role transitions.

The roles of Presidents and presidential candidates were chosen for the case study of hierarchy because of the recent dramatic changes in the presidency: the unprecedented resignation of an American President, followed by the election of a political "outsider," followed by the election of a veteran actor. Among other things, the analysis will suggest that the credibility problems and the peculiar styles of recent Presidents are, in part, the result of the new information environments in which national leaders now perform their roles.

These three chapters may tackle broad and controversial issues, but they are not meant to be final statements on their topics. On the one hand, they serve to apply and to demonstrate further the plausibility of the broad theory of role change developed in the previous part of the book; on the other hand, they outline more specific questions for further analysis.

12

The Merging of
Masculinity and Femininity
A Case Study in Changing Group Identities

Today we are experiencing what may be the final feminist revolution. In the past, there have been fights for certain specific rights and freedoms for women—the right to own property, to vote, to practice birth control, to enter certain professions, and so forth. But now the movement is toward full equality with men, indeed, for a minimization or elimination of the dividing line between masculinity and femininity. In language, dress, education, and professions, women have demanded the simple status of "people," rather than that of a separate group—"females."

The battles against traditional sex stereotyping based on supposed differences in emotionality, stability, intelligence, rationality, and aggressiveness have been fought on many fronts.[1] Current arguments and research strongly suggest that while obvious biological differences exist, many of the traditional behavioral distinctions between men and women have been arbitrary and due more to socialization than to physiological determinants. What the arguments and research often obscure, however, is that the revolution concerning male and female roles is just that, a battle over social *roles*, not necessarily a movement toward the "natural."

Biology is never as neat as social conventions. There is no clear change in our physiology on the day of our eighteenth birthdays, though that day may signal the beginning of our "adult" lives. All men vary in height, weight, strength, agility, and natural intelligence, yet our Declaration of Independence declares that "all men are created equal." Social conventions often lead us to ignore and to enhance various similarities and differences among people. In this sense, the new drive toward the social equality of all men and women is just as arbitrary (and as plausible) as the old system of dividing all men from all women. Both are simple social conventions overlaid on complex realities.

Whether or not there are significant biological differences that "naturally" distinguish men from women is irrelevant to this discussion. If men and women are biologically different, then the current drive to merge their roles suggests the power of social forces to override biological differences. If men and women are biologically similar, then the traditional sharp distinctions in their behaviors suggest the ability of social conventions to protect themselves under the guise of natural reality. Either way, the social rules seem to dominate biology, and the social rules themselves, therefore, are worthy of close study.

While many of us may feel that the move toward the homogenization of gender roles is a correct and progressive trend, it is still legitimate for us to examine possible reasons for this development and to look for the forces that supported the old distinctions in gender behavior. This chapter briefly describes recent trends toward the merging of masculinity and femininity and suggests that the changes in conceptions of gender roles may have something to do with the merging of male and female information-systems through the widespread use of electronic media.

Gender Liberation

> *Their delicacy renders them unfit for practice and experience in the great businesses of life, and the hardy enterprises of war, as well as the arduous cares of state. Besides, their attention is so much engaged with the necessary nurture of their children, that nature has made them fittest for domestic cares.*—John Adams, 1776[2]

Not long ago, the role of housewife and mother was considered the only "normal" one for women. The indoctrination for traditional gender roles began early. Few people thought twice about dressing, speaking to, or handling male and female infants very differently. It was considered normal to give little boys trucks and blocks and guns to play with, while girls were given dolls and tea sets. And these distinctions in gender activity were reinforced by the reality of children's experiences with their own parents.*

By and large, the home was the women's world, the outside world was men's. It was understood that some women would work. But preferably this work was to be before marriage, perhaps in a job where they could "hook" a man. Those women who worked throughout their adult life, functioned almost exclusively in a sub-class of jobs, helpers to male professionals. They were nurses rather than doctors, secretaries rather than executives, grade school teachers rather than professors. A woman who did not long for husband and children as the prime goal of her life seemed odd and misguided. A woman's desire for a career removed her from the normal frame of life; it meant that she was trading potential

---

*Of course, many of these behaviors continue today, but they now generate much controversy and concern.[3]

maternal and connubial bliss for an unhappy existence as a "surrogate male." A 1948 cover story in *Life* magazine, for example, pictured the life of the "career girl" as lonely, desperate, and deviant. Among other things, the article informs us that she is unable to become close to the men she meets at work because they are "handicapped by the fact that they are in professional competition with her," and that "it requires only a letter from a happily married friend to make her pause—and wonder."[4]

Politics and business were the realms of men; cooking, cleaning, and raising children, the realms of women. Men went out to explore and conquer the cruel world and the business "jungle." Women stayed at home, keeping the hearth warm and waiting to salve the wounded bodies and egos of their men. Women were considered too weak, irrational, and emotionally unstable to do the work of men. By definition, therefore, those women who proved to be strong and competent could not be real women, and many were thought of as sexless amazons. Either way, women lost. And many women learned that to compete with men was usually the lonelier and more risky path. The lessons in many books and movies were that, in order to win a man, a woman had to give up competing with him.

The system was reinforced in virtually all literature, from children's books to scholarly monographs. School texts pictured girls in need of protection and boys as protectors, women as mothers and men as professionals.[5] Sociologists of the influential "functionalist" school implicitly supported the division of roles by describing how and why the system "worked." Among other things, they suggested that the division of roles functioned to promote solidarity in society and in the home. With women out of the marketplace, the husband-wife relationship could be more harmonious; the cruel competition of the business world could be offset by the communal comfort of home. And the isolated domestic sphere could serve as the necessary nurturant environment for the child.[6]

The view that women should give up their individual aspirations for the sake of the family and the society was also expressed in much popular nonfiction. In *Sixpence in Her Shoe*, for example, Phyllis McGinley, a Pulitzer Prize-winning writer, praised the "domestic profession."

> By and large . . . the world runs better when men and women keep to their own spheres. I do not say women are better off, but society in general is. And that is, after all, the mysterious honor and obligation of women—to keep this planet in orbit. We are the self-immolators, the sacrificers, the givers, not the eaters-up of life. . . . Few jobs are worth disrupting family life for unless the family profits by it rather than the housewife herself.[7]

The necessity for distinctions in male and female roles was based on the assumption of inherent differences in male and female personalities. "Femininity" and "Masculinity" were thought of in terms of two clearly distinct sets of psychological traits. Femininity was characterized by modesty, gentleness, humility, supportiveness, compassion, empathy, tenderness, nurturance, intuitiveness, sensitivity, and unselfishness. Masculinity, in contrast, was characterized by strength of will, courage, ambition, assertiveness, independence, aggressiveness, hardiness, emotional control, and "rationality"—the use of logical, abstract, and analytical thought.[8]

For centuries women and men have lived in the same societies but in different social, psychological, and legal worlds. As Joanna Bunker Rohrbaugh notes: "In many areas of life there is no truly human experience. There is only female experience and male experience."[9] Men and women have been measured by different standards and tested in terms of different demands.

Some people have insisted that women's traditional traits and experience have given them a *better* life than men's,[10] but there is much to suggest that this is not so. The Greeks were much more likely to murder female babies than male babies.[11] The Romans allowed men to do away with unwanted newborn daughters by exposing them on a hillside to die, and Roman husbands could condemn their wives to death.[12] In many societies, women were considered the property of their fathers and then of their husbands. In Biblical times, for example, rape was considered a crime against property, not an assault against a person. A "rapist" might have to pay damages even if the woman willingly engaged in the sex act.[13] To this day, orthodox Jewish males thank God every morning for not "making me a woman." (Women thank God for making them "according to Your will.") This blessing directly follows the one thanking God for "not making me a slave."

Under English common law, a woman became legally dead upon marriage. Like a prisoner, she could not sue, could not own property, could not even gain custody of her own children when widowed. Upon marriage, a husband and wife legally became "one person" and that person was the husband.[14]

There have been ups and downs in female rights in Western culture, but until recently the basic inequality of the sexes has remained. In 1872 the United States Supreme Court upheld a lower court's decision to bar women from practicing law. Another Supreme Court decision in 1894 allowed a state to interpret the word "person" to exclude women. In 1948, the Court upheld a state's right to exclude women from being bartenders unless they were wives and daughters of bartenders.[15]

The current feminist revolution began in the mid-1960s and blossomed in the early 1970s. Women in the civil rights and antiwar movements and in the New Left found that while their male colleagues were fighting to reorganize society, many of the men wanted some things to stay the same. They expected their women to cook, clean, and keep the kids out of their way. The division of labor among the sexes was taken for granted by so many men that when the women's liberation movement emerged from the general protest "Movement," it was looked on by many men as something of a joke. When young women discarded their bras the way young men had discarded their draft cards, even radical men seemed to respond the way rednecks had responded to antiwar protesters.[16] The war protesters were greeted with "America, Love It or Leave It!" The "women's libbers" (as they were derogatively called) were greeted with responses that said, in effect, "Love Men, or Leave Them!" Feminists were teased for their supposed ugliness, their lack of femininity, their assumed lesbianism. Just as draft dodgers could not be real Americans if they did not fight for their country, women could not be real women if they did not remove hair from their underarms, clean house, be receptive to sex on demand, have babies, and fill their husband's and children's stomachs with food. Ironically, many radical men were rejecting parts of the traditional masculine role of the soldier-knight who is duty-bound to honorable battle, but they were remarkably insensitive to the constraints of traditional conceptions of femininity. That women should see parallels to their own exclusion from society in the struggles for other groups' liberation seemed ridiculous—even to members of those oppressed groups. When Stokely Carmichael was asked about the position of women in the Black Power Movement, for example, his reply was "prone."[17]

Less than twenty years later, conceptions of appropriate behavior have changed dramatically. Although the change is incomplete, and there are many forces of resistance, there has been a striking disintegration of the barrier that once clearly divided male and female roles.

Women have now entered nearly every occupation from construction worker to Supreme Court judge. The 1970s and 1980s have seen a number of "firsts," including: first woman airline pilot, first women generals, first woman coal miner, first women's bank, first female senate pages, first woman firefighter, first female graduates from West Point, first woman governor elected in her own right, first woman corporation president, first female priests, ministers, and rabbis, first woman astronaut, and first female vice presidential candidate.[18]

But the most significant changes have been in the everyday lives of ordinary men and women. From 1970 to 1977, there was a 133% increase in women students between the ages of 22 and 34.[19] Women's athletics has grown beyond early dreams. Entrance to law school and medical school—once almost exclusively male domains—have now become much more evenly divided between males and females.* Police forces and the armed services have been sexually integrated. Between 1972 and 1982, five out of six new businesses were started by women.[21] "Ms.," only recently seen as an amusing "fake word," has now become the standard counterpart to "Mr.," and many women are keeping their birth names after marriage.

---

*In 1952, for example, the percentage of women students in ABA approved law schools was only 4%. A decade later, the percentage had actually decreased to 3.5%. By 1972, however, the percentage of women law students had more than tripled to 12%, and by 1982 it had more than tripled again to over 36%. The pattern in medical schools is very similar. In 1969, only 9% of U.S. medical school students were women. Within five years, the percentage doubled to 18%. In 1982, nearly 30% of medical students were women.[20]

The period since the late 1960s has been marked by dramatic changes in the rights of women. In 1968, the nondiscrimination and "affirmative action" policies for government contractors were extended to bar discrimination on the basis of sex, and in 1972, these policies were extended to all federally assisted education programs.[22] Many cities passed bills forbidding discrimination on the basis of sex in public accommodations, such as bars.[23] The Supreme Court ruled that companies could not turn down women job applicants because they have small children unless they also turn down men applicants who have small children.[24] The Boy Scouts admitted girls into their Explorer Scout division (15- to 20-year-olds).[25] Courts have outlawed voting regulations that require women to identify themselves as either "Mrs." or "Miss."[26] The Equal Credit Opportunity Act has prohibited discrimination in credit based on sex or marital status.[27] The census bureau has eliminated the "head of household" designation.[28]

As a result of thousands of large and small changes and developments, whole sets of once taken-for-granted behaviors surrounding courtship, marriage, child-rearing, and leisure activities have been exposed and rejected by millions as "sexist." Even the National Weather Bureau has had to change its procedures; storms—irrational forces of nature—are no longer named solely after women.[29] And a wide array of traditional joke themes and conversation topics have become taboo in many circles.

One has only to pick up almost any book written by either a man or woman before 1970 to see how different our sensibilities are today. The almost exclusive use of "he," "him," and "man" to refer to everyone, passing bits of humor about male and female characteristics, and the use of such phrases as "man and wife" betray these books as products of another age. Today, such sexist content and terminology are taboo. They are seen as evidence of the traditional "symbolic annihilation" of women. Professional journals in the social sciences, for example, will no longer publish articles using "male constructions."[30] In their place are joint phrases such as "he or she" or plurals. A whole list of nouns, once spoken without thought, are now "forbidden words" in many settings: mailman, policeman, spokesman, chairman, layman. They have been replaced by new terms such as mail carrier, police officer, chairperson, and lay person. One computer software firm has a program that not only checks for common spelling and grammatical errors but also for "sexist terminology."[31]

The move to liberate women is much more than a simple freeing of an "oppressed minority." The demands for changes in women's roles, rights, and responsibilities are also, of necessity, demands for changes in the roles, rights, and responsibilities of men. One part of the gender system cannot change without the whole system changing. Many men are resistant to the changes, but, nevertheless, the old division of labor in society, with men taking care of "instrumental" tasks and women taking care of "expressive" tasks, is being refashioned through feminist demands for more equal participation of men and women in wage earning, child care, and housekeeping. As a result, the boundary lines between private and public spheres, home and business, executive suite and nursery are becoming blurred.

As women have demanded more and more access to male rights and roles, men have begun to be freed from some of them. Just as women are now being told that it is acceptable for them to be aggressive in the office and home, men are being told that it is permissible for them to cry, to discuss publicly their private fears and other personal feelings, and to show their love for their children. As women have assumed identities other than "wife" and "mother," men have begun to be allowed to consider other means to "success" than career, wealth, and power.

The changes in masculinity are in many ways more difficult than the changes in femininity. For, as Margaret Mead argues, in every culture, men's work is valued over women's work—regardless of what that work is.[32] It is simpler for women to move into the more highly valued work of men than it is for men to take on the "lowly" work of women. Nevertheless, many men are discovering the joys of fatherhood and the emotional release of not having to be impassive and fearless.

The women's liberation movement, therefore, may be more properly called the "gender liberation movement." Male and female roles are merging. It is not simply that women are becoming more like men, but that members of both sexes are becoming more alike. Men are now much more likely to turn down overtime work, promotions, or job transfers that will enhance their careers for fear that they will disrupt their family lives.[33] A whole new liberation literature is emerging on the freeing of men from male roles and on the importance of "fatherhood" to both men and children.[34] New liberation groups such as "Fathers United for Equal Justice" have arisen to attempt to gain for men equal rights to custody of their children after divorce.[35] And the courts have begun to recognize the fact that fathers are becoming more involved in parenting. While many judges still give "automatic" preference to mothers, especially when young children are involved, change has been rapid and dramatic. In 1980, for example, it was estimated that fathers received custody in only one out of ten contested cases; by 1982 fathers obtained custody in 51% of the cases decided in appellate courts.[36] Within the last decade, divorcing couples have increasingly asked for joint custody of their children, and more than 30 states now have joint custody statutes.[37]

Many men now find themselves facing the same traditional sexist views that once outraged only feminist women. A man who stays home to raise children is seen as lazy and "unemployed." Those male executives who spend a great deal of time with their children during the evening and weekends, rather than bringing their work home with them, may be labeled "unprofessional" or "lacking a competitive edge." And fathers who feel involved with their children's lives have to tolerate comments such as those made by a Utah judge in 1974, who suggested that divorced men should not get equal rights to custody until they are able to lactate.[38]

Many men and women have discovered that the question may not be whether women "have the stuff" to be tough executives or officers in the formerly male domains of business and warfare, but whether the business and military worlds can be modified to recognize the existence of family, feelings, and fatherhood. If Betty Friedan's recent description of the questioning of male machismo at West Point is accurate, then these revolutions in consciousness among men as well as women are occurring even in places where they once seemed least likely.[39]

The assumption of the need for traditionally male-style "competition" in business and diplomacy has come under greater scrutiny in recent years. Traditionally female-style "cooperation" is now seen as a possible antidote to some of the uncomfortable and sometimes dangerous aspects of traditional corporate and international interactions. Peter Schwartz has described the differences between "alpha" (masculine) and "beta" (feminine) problem-solving styles and suggested that both are necessary for effective management.[40] A whole new field of study has emerged that transcends the research in sex roles: the area of cognitive or psychological androgyny. This type of androgyny has nothing to do with ambiguous genitalia or appearance. It is concerned, instead, with a blend of the cognitive styles traditionally associated with men and women. "An androgyne is a person who is able to be both rational and emotional, strong and nurturant, assertive and compassionate, depending on the demands of the situation."[41]

The changes in attitudes, laws, and behaviors have been so sudden, so widespread that they have been somewhat bewildering to everyone. Many forty- and fifty-year-olds are looking around them at the ashes of their marriages and dreams—indeed, at the demise of a whole belief system of "the way life is." Many young people are not certain of what roles to assume. Relationships have become more problematic because, while it is easy to spot a member of the opposite sex, it is much more difficult to spot a member of a complementary gender orientation.[42] Many once taken-for-granted aspects of male-female relationships now require frequent and explicit "negotiation." Even feminists themselves are very split over the definition of the changes. For example, there is intense disagreement as to whether the goal is simply to acquire for women the same power and positions once held exclusively by men, or whether women have special traits that will benefit both men and women as women "feminize" public spheres.[43]

Many older "ordinary" women feel threatened by the movement, which seems to redefine their once cherished and admired roles as mothers and wives into relatively useless, marginal, and subservient labor.[44] Many older men feel betrayed in that they always believed that they were sacrificing many facets of their lives in order to work and support their wives and families, and now these men are being told that what seemed to them like individual valor was actually organized oppression by a "male elite."

Even among the young, the changes are difficult. Many young men cling to the power offered to them by traditional roles. Many other young men endorse the liberation of women but flee from its complementary consequences for their own gender role. Perhaps more threatening to many men than the thought of women as their "equals" in business, sports, and other public spheres is the implicit demand of the women's liberation movement that men give up their own near-exclusive focus on success, money-making, achievement, and career in order to share in housework and childcare. Men can understand relatively easily why women might want to have a career, but it is more difficult to rethink their own roles and to balance the demands of an important business meeting with the need to nurse a sick child back to health.

Many young women want the benefits of the new consciousness, such as the right to work freely at equal pay or to be sexually active without stigma, yet the delays in achieving full equality also offer them a reason to cling to the old privileges of the "protected" feminine class when it seems necessary. (Why, for example, should women willingly embrace the right to get shot at in the army when they are still excluded from the inner core of government, military, and business power? And if women are discriminated against in hiring, why shouldn't a young unemployed woman shelter herself under the old belief that it is less of a stigma for a woman to be unemployed than it is for a man?) Further, even those who believe in liberation in the abstract may be unwittingly forced into traditional roles by logical, "individual" day-to-day decisions. (A woman who has been trained all her life to ignore or fear machines may find it simpler to have her husband tune-up the car while she cooks dinner.)

The lag in change, then, tends to lead to an even greater lag as all sides cling to the benefits of old roles before they receive the full benefits of new roles.

Given all the ambiguities and mixed feelings, it is no wonder that the change has not been complete. But contrary to the hopes of the Moral Majority and other reactionary groups, it seems quite unlikely that women will end up back in their old roles of "angels of the house," or even that the sexes will remain as divided as they still are today. Only 15% of American households now fit the "normal" mode of working father and full-time wife/mother. (In the 1950s, the figure was 70%).[45] And even women who reject the label of "feminist" now often take for granted those opportunities and options that were closed to women only a generation ago.[46] The direction of the change seems clear. Polls show increasingly strong support for "women's issues" among the majority of the population.*

---

*In 1982, for example, the Harris Survey found a clear majority of the public in favor of the passage of the Equal Rights Amendment to the Constitution. When read the wording of the amendment, 73% of those surveyed approved, 22% opposed, and 5% indicated they were not sure. Even when some of the controversy surrounding the ERA was introduced into the question, 63% of those surveyed approved of the ERA. Louis Harris observed that "rarely

To see how much most Americans' sensibilities have changed over the last two decades, we have only to look at some fixtures of our recent past that seem centuries away. It is hard to believe, for example, that in 1961 a NASA spokesperson was quoted as saying "talk of an American space-woman makes me sick to my stomach,"[48] that in 1967 an official of the then all-male Boston Marathon physically tried to remove a woman who was running in the race,[49] that, until a Supreme Court ruling in 1973, classified ads were segregated by sex,[50] and that before 1976 no married women were listed under their own names in the telephone book.[51] It is difficult now to believe that in the mid-1960s, a Southern Senator added the amendment to bar sex discrimination to the Civil Rights Act simply as a ploy to force others to vote against such a "ridiculous" bill.[52] There is no going back.

Feminist Continuities and Discontinuities

Proponents of any social movement must often take a paradoxical stance in relation to the changes for which they are fighting. On the one hand, they find it necessary to make broad claims for the goal of the movement in order to mobilize and energize followers. On the other hand, the movement must not be presented as too revolutionary, lest the average citizen become afraid that the ordinary aspects of social life will be completely abandoned for a strange and deviant future. Proponents of movements often resolve this dilemma by pushing for large-scale social change and yet framing the change as a movement *away* from the deviant and toward the normal. The women's movement is no exception. The old system of behavior and beliefs has been pictured as "restrictive," "repressive," and "sexist"; by implication, the movement's goal of full sexual equality must simply be "ordinary" and "normal."

The rhetorical ploy of framing sexual equality as "normal" may be a political necessity, but it also minimizes the significance of the extraordinary, if still incomplete, change in gender roles that has occurred in the United States over the past two decades. Further, because there is no need to study the occurrence of "normal" phenomena, the roots of the women's liberation movement have remained largely unexplored. Or, put dif-

---

has so controversial a measure met with such clear support." Other polls show striking changes in attitudes over the last twenty to forty years. In 1938, 75% of those surveyed disapproved of a married woman earning money if she had a husband who could support her; by 1978, that percentage had dropped to 26. In 1957, 80% of those surveyed believed that a woman must be "sick," "neurotic," or "immoral" to remain unmarried; by 1978, only about 25% held similar views. In 1937, only about 30% of those surveyed said they would vote for a qualified female candidate for President; in 1980, over 75% said they would vote for a woman presidential candidate. In the one decade between 1970 and 1980, the percentage of respondents who felt that both parents should have the responsibility to care for small children rose from 33% to 56%. Finally, in 1979, the idea of returning to the standards of the past concerning sexual mores and male/female division of labor was rejected by almost 80% of those surveyed.[47]

ferently, the "causes" of the movement are often identified simply by describing the restrictive nature of the old system.[53]

While much of the feminist literature suggests that people would have always found the old system deviant if only they had *noticed* its structure (i.e., had their consciousness raised), the truth is that the old social order was consciously observed, discussed, and usually praised. In a history of changing notions of "women's proper place" over the last century, for example, Sheila Rothman notes that the battles over role change in the 1960s and 1970s stand "in striking and significant contrast to the harmony that characterized attitudes and practices in earlier periods. . . . Our predecessors found interdependence just where we perceive competition and conflict."[54] Similarly, anthropological and historical evidence suggests that sex differentiation and inequality have probably been constant features of most, if not all, cultures. And studies of contemporary cultures suggest that "sexual asymmetry is presently a universal fact of human social life."[55]

The new conceptions of gender-appropriate behavior have not grown simply out of *greater* consciousness, but out of a *new* consciousness and a new set of values. And the real subject in studying the roots of the modern feminist movement should not be the absurdity of the old system but the new "lens" through which old phenomena are viewed in new ways.

To give the current women's movement a greater sense of continuity, many feminists have turned to history to look at the writings of those women of the past who wrote of sexual equality—Abigail Adams, Mary Wollstonecraft, Charlotte Perkins Gilman, and others. Also, the suffrage movement is presented as evidence of the continuity of the struggle.[56]

There are, however, a number of problems with viewing the current feminist movement merely as a continuation of earlier feminist thought. It is always possible to look back in history and find people who can be seen as precursors of almost any social movement (just as it is often possible to find "causes" in our childhood for almost any career we might choose). The expression in the past of what we now see as modern feminist sentiments, however, does not necessarily indicate the *continuity* of a feminist *movement*. The early feminist writers, for example, were extraordinary women, and as *extra*ordinary they did not project the feelings of the average women of their times, nor were they, in most cases, the leaders of any movements.

Even the women's suffrage movement had fewer similarities with the current feminist movement than is often thought. At no time were there more than a few thousand activists in the movement. "The great preponderance of women either had nothing to do with feminism, or actually scorned it as unnecessary and wrong-headed."[57]* Even among those who

*The current feminist movement, in contrast, is broad-based, with many distinct organizations and no central leadership. Just one of these organizations, NOW, boasts a dues-paying membership of 250,000 men and women.[58]

supported women's suffrage, many argued for the right to vote, not as a means of making women *equal* to men, but as a way of allowing women to bring their *special* standards as moral guardians to the larger "home" of society. For many, the vote was an extension of women's volunteer reform work outside the house. Similarly, others shunned the vote for fear that it would dissolve the boundary line between the domestic and public domains.

The movement to acquire the vote was a long, arduous one. Indeed, it took over seventy years—the longest battle for an expansion of the electorate in American history.[59] (Of the 250 women who met at Seneca Falls in 1848 to declare equal rights for women, only one—Charlotte Woodward—lived long enough to vote for a President of the United States.[60]) And even when the vote was achieved, it may have been more of a victory for ethnic, religious, and racial purity than for sexual equality. Suffrage was embraced by some men as a conservative measure to preserve the white, Anglo-Saxon politics that was being threatened by male immigrants and black men.[61] Finally, once given the vote, there was little that distinguished women's voting from men's. The "women's vote," it turned out, was basically an echo of that of the men in their lives. Indeed, one of the few major differences between men's and women's voting was that not until thirty-six years after being given the vote, did women, a majority of the population, vote in numbers equal to men.[62]*

The battle "won," the suffrage organizations were dismantled, yet women's suffrage was not followed by any major changes in male and female relations. There were still few women professionals, such as doctors and lawyers. And, for many years, relatively few women were educated beyond homemaking tasks. There was little that threatened the view that men and women were very different creatures with different skills and needs. As late as the mid-1960s, public schools still segregated boys and girls for some courses. One woman I know, for example, tells me that in 1968, her sixth grade school class in New York City was divided one afternoon a week—the boys did extra science projects, the girls sewed aprons.

Even women's increasing entry into the workforce through the first half of the twentieth century "neither revitalized nor sparked a feminist outlook among women."[63] With the exception of the tiny National Women's party, there was not a single feminist organization in the whole United States between the 1920s and mid-1960s, and "until the late 1960s . . . 'feminist' was a dirty word, redolent of old maids, 'blue stockings,' and man-haters."[64]

---

*Interestingly, this equalization of male and female voting rates in 1956 occurred during the first presidential election year to follow television's passing of the 50% mark in American households.

I am not suggesting that all women once lovingly embraced the role of mother and wife, but rather that most women did not actively reject their "special place" in a "man's world." In his comprehensive historical analysis of the roles of women in America, Carl Degler describes the women's movement of the 1970s as a continuation of the "enduring tension" between women and the family. Yet Degler is also surprised by the discontinuity between the present and the past. Changes in the family in the past occurred with "glacial slowness," yet the renewed feminist movement "fairly burst upon the nation in the 1960s. Few women or men had predicted it, or even thought it likely."[65] Similarly, Sheila Rothman notes that although there have been many struggles over definitions of womanhood, the new feminist ideal of women as "persons," who are in many ways similar to men and who do not possess special qualities or need special protection, shows "surprisingly little continuity with a feminist past."[66] Yet without this continuity and without any established political base, the current feminist movement, as Degler notes, "captured the . . . support of the mass media, the academic community, government, and even business" with "remarkable rapidity."[67]

If the current feminist movement is not simply a continuation of earlier battles, then the question remains: How could such a revolutionary change in social consciousness have taken place in such a short time? Why, after centuries of oppression and some sporadic protest, did the women's movement grow and flower within a single generation? Why, after many changes in the conception of the *type* of differences that existed between men and women, did people begin to question the existence of *any* significant differences? And why did the active move for change come from the traditionally "passive" members of the society? What altered the consciousness of women, and what has made the changes make sense—after a while—to so many men as well?

Many feminists argue that the current revolution is the result of individual brave women pushing out of the confines of the home, fighting against all odds, pressures, and traditions to establish a beachhead in the formerly all-male world. While this explanation of the feminist movement is both dynamic and appealing—the stuff of legend—it is insufficient. For although cultural attitudes constantly evolve, a sudden strong surge in feminist consciousness across a broad spectrum of people in a single generation suggests the influence of outside factors that may have given people a new perspective on gender-appropriate roles.

Any movement as complex and multi-faceted as the women's movement obviously cannot be attributed to a single cause. The changes in male and female roles have been fostered by many other changes: technological developments that reduce the significance of physical strength as a determinant of social status, improvements in health care that make childbirth a less momentous, life-threatening, and disruptive experience, the "automation" of many household tasks, and advances in birth control.* In recent years, economic conditions, increased education for women, and the high divorce rate have also encouraged women to be "on their own."

Without negating any of these factors, the theory developed in this book offers another possible significant reason for the blurring of male and female social roles: the merging of male and female situations, or "information-systems," through the widespread use of electronic media, especially television.

As suggested in earlier chapters, any "group" identity is supported by experience that is shared among members of the group and kept secret from those outside the group. A situational approach to analyzing changes in gender roles, therefore, suggests that traditional distinctions between men and women have been supported, at least in part, by distinctions in access to social situations and to the information available in them. The separation of male and female domains has allowed for socialization into distinct roles and for private backstage rehearsals for and relaxations from onstage gender behavior.

Indeed, unlike the different experiences and locations of most other groups, the separation of men's and women's worlds was, for many generations, an explicitly acknowledged and embraced doctrine: the "doctrine of two spheres."[69] The idea underlying this doctrine was that men's and women's natures were so different that they inhabited different psychological and emotional worlds and therefore had different natural responsibilities and rights and different appropriate places. Women's place was in the domestic sphere of family and home. Their responsibilities were to be nurturant caretakers, to raise children, to protect the home, and to ease the burdens of working husbands. Their rights were to define the moral code of the family, to shape children's character and behavior, and to direct their husbands' moral behavior. Men, on the other hand, were required to go out into the public sphere and earn a living to support their families. Their rights were to travel freely, to determine the residence of the family, and to direct all the public affairs of the household. The women were freed from the burdens of the marketplace, the men were freed from the burdens of childcare and housework.

The notion of separate spheres was supported by industrialization, which physically separated the workplace from the home and thereby

---

*Many people I have spoken to about changing male/female roles attribute the changes to such factors as the invention of "the pill" and the availability of infant formula. With these "technologies," it is argued, motherhood is no longer an inevitability for most sexually active women, and the child's survival after birth no longer depends on the mother's physical presence. Ironically, however, feminists have been most vocal in their attacks on the potential health hazards of the pill and the potential benefits of breast feeding. Both the pill and infant formula are sometimes framed as developments that allow males to continue to dominate female biology by making women more sexually accessible to men and by transforming women's breasts into pure sex objects without any natural function.[68] Feminism and many feminists thrive without either of these inventions.

made possible a greater division in male and female domains. Differences in access to physical locations fostered differences in perspective, perception, and sensibility. The post-industrial information age spurred by the use of electronic media, therefore, may be reintegrating many male and female situations. In spite of its sexist content, for example, television assaults the dividing line between the male and female worlds in several ways: It merges traditionally distinct gender information-systems, blurs the dividing line between the public and private behaviors of each sex, and undermines the significance of physical segregation as a determinant of sex segregation. If traditional distinctions between male and female roles were greatly supported by distinctions in social information-systems and by women's isolation in the home, then television may be a spur to the merging of gender behavior.

To understand the potential impact of electronic media on women's consciousness, however, we need to get a better sense of how important the segregation of men's and women's spheres was to the continuity of the traditional role structures. And since many feminists may be suspicious, at first, of this view of both the genesis of the modern feminist movement and of television's role in it, I include in the following discussion a situational reinterpretation of many themes in the feminist literature itself. The writings of Simone de Beauvoir, Betty Friedan, Germaine Greer, Shulamith Firestone, and others served to define the movement in its early stages. I hope to show that this literature and the analyses of a number of feminist scholars implicitly deal with the variable of "patterns of access to information" and thereby unwittingly describe the mechanism through which changes in media can lead to changes in gender roles.

Femininity and the Doctrine of Separate Spheres

The traditional image of women as delicate, fearful, emotional, unworldly, and in need of protection from men has much to do with women's traditional isolation from male information-systems. Men protected women from the world by excluding them from it. The social differences between men and women were reinforced not only through the simple *segregation* of spheres, which characterizes all group distinctions, but also by men having access to *more* of the world than women. Traditionally, men have been able to go most places women have been able to go, but women have not been able to go most places men have been able to go. The doctors who attended childbirth and the priests who gave last rites to women were men. But women were generally excluded from male rites of passage and from detailed information about the content of many social rituals. Women were also excluded from many all-male situations such as the workplace, battle, and sport. Yet men often had casual access to the kitchens and homes of their mothers, wives, and sisters. Women's private spaces were often violated by men.

Men's access to multiple social arenas allowed them to develop multiple social selves, to practice for and relax from one situation while in another situation, and to gain distance from and perspective on their roles. Men could also share this perspective with other men. Women's isolation in the domestic sphere, in contrast, gave them less perspective on society and on their own roles, and hence a more limited and ambiguous sense of self.

This situational analysis of gender differences is supported by many scholarly analyses of gender roles. Anthropologist Michelle Zimbalist Rosaldo, for example, suggests that the "opposition between domestic and public orientations . . . provides the necessary framework for an examination of male and female roles in any society."[70] She suggests that women's isolation from the public domain isolates them from public decision-making and makes their behind-the-scenes power seem mysterious, magical, and illegitimate.

The relationship between information isolation and "femininity" is also implicit in many of the popular feminist writings. In *The Female Eunuch*, for example, Germaine Greer describes the ways in which the powerlessness of the female is related to her traditional isolation.*

> Her recoil from external reality is reinforced by the punishments she gets for wandering off on her own. While little boys are forming groups and gangs to explore or terrorize the district, she is isolated at home, listening to tales of evil-minded strangers. Her comparative incarceration is justified in the name of protection. . . . She is taught to fear and distrust the world at large, for reasons which are never clearly stated.[71]

The training of men and women for different roles depends on separate environments of socialization. In *The Second Sex*, Simone de Beauvoir suggests that the distinctions in behavior begin when little boys are thrust or pulled into the outside world of men, and girls are left to cling to the home. Girls continue to be taken on their parents' knees or allowed into their parents' beds after their brothers are denied these rights.

> This is just where little girls first appear as privileged beings. . . . The boys especially are little by little denied the kisses and caresses they have been used to. As for the little girl, she continues to be cajoled, she is allowed to cling to her mother's skirts, her father takes her on his knee and strokes her hair.[72]

All children, suggests de Beauvoir, are afraid of growing up. Yet the "privilege" granted the girl—to remain a child—handicaps her in her future. She is condemned to stay at home while boys are drawn/pushed out of the women's world. "Maurras relates in his memoirs that he was jealous of a younger brother whom his mother and grandmother were

---

*I use the present tense in the rest of this section to match the tense used by the feminist writers. My argument, however, is that the isolation they describe is partially a thing of the past.

cajoling. His father took his hand and drew him from the room, saying to him: 'We are men, let us leave those women.'"[73]

Thus, regardless of whether the separation is pleasant or unpleasant for the boy, he is separated early from the world of women. As a result, he experiences a different and wider world. As Charlotte Perkins Gilman writes: "A thousand influences reach him that never come to her, formative influences, good and bad, that modify character. He has far less of tutelage, espionage, restraint; he has more freedom by daylight, and he alone has any freedom after dark."[74]

The outside world is the man's world, and, in relation to it, the woman is crippled by ignorance and fear, bred not by biology, but by isolation and mystery. Women's cowardice, suggests Gilman, is a "distinctly home product."

Keep a man from birth wrapped in much cloth, shut away from sky and sun, wind and rain, continually exhausting his nervous energy by incessant activity in monotonous little things, and never developing his muscular strength and skill by suitable exercise of a large and varied nature, and he would be weak. Savage women are not weak. Peasant women are not weak. . . . The home-bound woman is weak, as would be a home-bound man. Also she is ignorant. Not, at least not nowadays, ignorant necessarily of books, but ignorant of general life.[75]

Gilman sees the ways in which physical isolation leads to limited understanding. She sees women's plight as parallel to the experience of living on a small island with the resulting "insularity of mind."[76] Gilman also offers implicit examples of the relationship between physical restriction and informational isolation. She suggests, for example, that the child's isolation within the home is paralleled by tight clothing, and she notes the relationship between foot-binding and veiling of women,[77] both of which limit women's mobility and interactions.

As women languish for lack of meaningful engagement with life, the solution to their physical and mental "problems" is often seen as more rest. In the nineteenth century, for example, "the rest cure" was administered to many women—including Charlotte Perkins Gilman. As Barbara Ehrenreich and Deirdre English describe:

The rest cure depended on the now-familiar techniques of twentieth-century brainwashing—total isolation and sensory deprivation. For approximately six weeks the patient was to lie on her back in a dimly lit room. She was not permitted to read. If her case was particularly severe, she was not even permitted to rise to urinate. She was to have no visitors and to see no one but a nurse and the doctor.[78]

Because of her general isolation and restriction, the woman retains many of the characteristics of a child. She is dressed in frilly, delicate clothing. She is encouraged to be whimsical and withdrawn, emotional and irrational. Her husband cares for her as her father once did. The man can be the "master of the house" because he alone masters outside territory, which is unknown, dangerous, and forbidding to the woman. She depends on him to deal with all those things that involve the outside world. As an adult-child, she is called by diminutive names such as "baby," "chick," "my girl," or "my pet" even by men her own age. She is protected and nurtured like a favorite dog or cat; when she complains of her treatment, the man who makes "sacrifices" for her and cherishes her feels betrayed. How could she live without *him*?! And indeed, in this system, how *could* she live without him?

What has been discussed thus far suggests that women are "different" because they are not allowed to be like men and to have access to the male public domain. But this suggestion assumes that men's behaviors are "normal" and women's are "deficient." As anthropologist Nancy Chodorow argues, the difference between male and female socialization is not quite that simple. Because both boys and girls are raised by women, there is a basic asymmetry in their socialization. A girl is taught to grow up to be like Mommy, who is present in the home as a constant example and role model. But the boy is taught to grow up to be like Daddy, a distant figure who spends much time outside the home and away from his family.[79]

Because of the imbalance in child-rearing practices, boys come to reject all the "feminine" aspects of themselves just as girls are shielded from their potential "masculine" traits. Chodorow reasons that boys tend to develop their masculine traits in terms of abstract rights and duties because the masculine world is not one they are experiencing first-hand, but girls develop their feminine traits in terms of concrete and emotional day-to-day contact and relationships. Further, to be a man, the little boy must reject more than he must embrace because he has more experience with what he is *not* to be like than with what he is to become. So the little boy must go through a "second birth" into the male world and reject his mother, the home, and all deep emotional feelings and relationships. The boy's need to break away from the home to fulfill his gender destiny, suggests Chodorow, leads to his restlessness and disconnectedness. The girl, however, tends to emphasize human ties, feelings, and relationships throughout her life to the exclusion of male traits. In going through the traditional socialization process, therefore, both sexes lose parts of the spectrum of human thoughts, feelings, and action.

Commenting on Chodorow's thesis, Michelle Rosaldo notes that the girls' easy socialization is both "a liability and a privilege." It is a liability because girls may develop self-doubt and a low self-image from identifying with their mothers who are weak figures, devalued by the larger culture. "At the same time, they may enjoy a sense of ease, love, and acceptance in the process of becoming an adult."[80] Boys, in contrast, find that their status in life is much more difficult to achieve, that they must fight, compete, and struggle to "be a man."

The separation of men and women allows them to play complementary roles. They are mysteries to each other. "What does a woman want?"

asked Sigmund Freud, one of the most insightful men of his time.[81] It was a question that could still be understood well by teenage boys in the 1950s and 1960s. In the traditional sex-divided world, men and women cannot fully understand each other's experiences. Their meetings are explorations and adventures into the unknown. As Greer notes, "the acts of sex are themselves forms of inquiry, as the old euphemism 'carnal knowledge' makes clear."[82]

Mystery becomes the essence of the male/female encounter. While courtship rituals are the means to develop intimacy, they also often function to retain or enhance the mysteriousness of the other sex.

The separation of men and women from each other supports the development of distinct male and female ploys and strategies. Men discuss how to control and seduce women; women discuss how to avoid being seduced, how to marry the right man, or how to control certain aspects of their own and their family's lives without men fully realizing it. This distinction in social worlds allows for the development of all-male and all-female perspectives on the world; it allows for fascination with the "other" sex. Women, especially, remain a mystery, because unlike the male world, the female world is hidden from public view, hidden from education, and hidden from history.

Simone de Beauvoir suggests that the essence of the traditional female role in society is as "the other." A woman, at least a "real" woman, is a mystery to men. Those women who are familiar to men are, by definition, not real women. A woman exists in her strangeness and her apartness. Conversely, says de Beauvoir, the male world holds awe and mystification for her. Understandably, when she gets to know one man well through marriage, *he* loses his special aura, "but man nonetheless remains the truth of the universe, the supreme authority, the marvelous, master, eye, prey, pleasure, adventure, salvation; he still incarnates transcendence, he is the answer to every question."[83]

Similarly, Rosaldo suggests that men's ability to travel and to associate freely with other men allows them a great measure of control over their activities, emotions, and image. "Because men can be separate, they can be 'sacred'; and by avoiding certain sorts of intimacy and unmediated involvement, they can develop an image and mantle of integrity and worth."[84] A woman, in contrast, has little control over whom she associates with; she can gain neither privacy nor distance, and she therefore develops little personal value in her own eyes or in the eyes of society. "Whereas men achieve rank as a result of explicit achievement, differences among women are generally seen as the product of idiosyncratic characteristics, such as temperament, personality, and appearance." And, admits Rosaldo, the public/domestic split does indeed lead to real differences in male/female forms of thinking and reasoning. Because women work at repetitive intimate tasks which ignore their individual interests and goals, they develop "ways of seeing, feeling, and acting that seem to be 'intuitive' and unsystematic—with a sensitivity to other people that permits them to survive."[85] Men, on the other hand, value abstract, "rational" thinking that isolates one or two variables and is removed from the complexities and ambiguities of emotional and intimate life.

Man's freedom to roam the public realm allows him to define the culture's public values and then to succeed at those tasks so defined. Men work in activities that "transcend" biology, but women are engaged in childbirth, breastfeeding, cooking food, and cleaning dirt. This split in activities, suggests Sherry Ortner, is the reason that many cultures believe that "female is to male as nature is to culture."[86]

The domestic/public split, then, can be seen as underlying many of the traditional conceptions of femininity, including passivity, limited ability, "irrationality," intuitive thinking, closeness to nature, mysteriousness, and low evaluation of self.

The distinctions in experience for men and women create separate situations for each sex and, therefore, a certain distrust and envy on *both* parts. As Rosaldo and others note, men unconsciously envy women's rich emotional life and their secure existence at home; women envy men's freedom to roam, to engage the world, to make their own burdens and adventures. But the man has a distinct advantage. As Germaine Greer notes, he has a world of friendships and associations completely separate from her and from their home.

> She cannot play darts, drink beer, or kick a football about. Her distrust of these activities is not that her man will consort with other women in the company of his mates, but the knowledge that he enjoys these activities and is dependent upon them in a way that he does not enjoy or depend upon her.[87]

The man knows that he can always "come home" when the public world is too much for him. Indeed, the woman's "onstage" area of performance—the home—is, in effect, one of the man's "backstage" areas of rehearsal and relaxation.

> Every wife must live with the knowledge that she has nothing else but home and family, while her house is ideally a base which her tired warrior-hunter can withdraw to and express his worst manners, his least amusing conversation, while he licks his wounds and is prepared by laundry and toilet and lunchbox for another sortie.[88]

Because many women have access to one of the backstage areas of their men, however, the men's onstage behavior may lose much of its credibility in women's eyes. From their backstage perspective, women may find it amusing that men change their behavior as they step onstage. Shulamith Firestone notes, for example, that women are keenly aware of the ways in which men deny their private needs, such as the need for love. "Perhaps this explains the peculiar contempt women so universally feel for men ('men are so dumb'), for they can see their men are posturing in the outside world."[89]

Firestone's remark hints at another important distinction in male/female situations: Women's isolation in the home has rarely given them the opportunity or the need to play a number of vastly different social roles. Women have not had to or been able to "posture" as have men. The dividing line between women's backstage and onstage behaviors and spheres is much less clearly drawn than men's. Women's onstage arena—the home—is also their backstage arena. And women have a truly private backstage only when they are alone, away from men and children. Traditionally, women have not segmented themselves into multiple personal and public spheres.

These differences in role-staging contingencies for men and women can be seen in a between-the-lines reading of one of Germaine Greer's commentaries on sex roles.

> Men in our culture crippled themselves by setting up an impossible standard of integrity: women were not given the chance to fool themselves in this way. Women have been charged with deviousness and duplicity since the dawn of civilization so they have never been able to pretend that their masks were anything but masks.[90]

Men's chastisement of women for their public emotionality and women's chastisement of men for their frequently "distant" and "cold" demeanor may be related to these traditional differences in the clarity of the dividing lines between men's and women's public and private roles.

Although the special backstage perspective of women has given them some insight into men's behavior patterns, the isolation of women from the onstage world also makes them weak and fearful. And their weakness is doubly great because, unlike other "classes" and unlike males, women are isolated even from each other. A woman's insights into her experience, therefore, are often personal insights, rarely ones confirmed by her "group's" shared perspective. Women, notes de Beauvoir, have no history, no religion, and no common location to give them a sense of solidarity. "They live dispersed among the males, attached through residence, housework, economic condition, and social standing to certain men—fathers or husbands—more firmly than they are to other women."[91] Middle-class women, de Beauvoir suggests, tend to identify more with middle-class men than with lower-class women, white women identify more with white men than with black women.

Lacking frequent contact with other women, the woman often sees other members of her sex as competitors instead of comrades. Further, without access to many other women, she does not learn the details of her own biological and psychological life. Women may be a mystery to men as men are a mystery to women, but women are mysteries even to themselves. Greer observes that "women's sexual organs are shrouded in mystery" and that, unlike boys, little girls are not encouraged to explore their bodies or to learn about the physiological components of their sexuality. "I myself did not realize that the tissues of my vagina were quite normal until I saw a meticulously engraved dissection in an eighteenth-century anatomy textbook."[92]

Similarly, Adrienne Rich describes her and other women's experience—or lack of experience—in the birth of their children under general anesthesia. "None of us, I think, had much sense of being in any real command of the experience. Ignorant of our bodies, we were essentially nineteenth-century women as far as childbirth (and much else) was concerned."[93]

As a result of her lack of experience, a woman is supposed to be ignorant of certain topics and too innocent to speak certain words. Her innocence of the "real world" allows her the right to be placed on a pedestal above men, but not to speak to them from a public platform.* The woman's purity may allow her to attempt to safeguard her family's morals, but it also gives men the right to supervise and control all of women's interactions with "reality."

As an isolated member of the man's "backstage team," the woman is supposed to be supportive and passive and accepting of the greater knowledge and experience of her husband and sons. As Adrienne Rich notes, if a woman rejects this role and contradicts the opinions of a man, she risks being labeled "hostile," "ball-breaker," or "castrating bitch." "A plain fact cleanly spoken by a woman's tongue is not infrequently perceived as a cutting blade directed at a man's genitals."[96]

Charlotte Perkins Gilman decried the fact that a "man must pick and choose and adopt a different speech in talking to a woman." Gilman thought that, given women's "feminine" and "charming" "foolishness and ignorance," the man who is taught to say "he loves, he admires, he venerates" such a woman is "taught to worship ignoble things."[97]

Such distinctions in male and female language are based on different world views and perspectives. The woman is protected from the seamy side of the man's world. Firestone suggests that even if women have technically known about the topics and words of the all-male world, women's isolation from that world has not traditionally given them the "right" to speak such things. "A man is allowed to blaspheme the world because it belongs to him to damn—but the same curse out of the mouth of a woman or a minor, i.e., an incomplete 'man' to whom the world does not yet belong, is considered presumptuous, and thus an impropriety or worse."[98]

But what has happened? How is it that suddenly a large proportion of women have demanded the right to possess the "world" and to curse it? One answer, suggested by the theory outlined in this book, is that electronic media of communication, especially television, have been whittling

---

*Before women abolitionists demanded the right to speak against slavery in the mid-nineteenth century, virtually "no respectable woman . . . had appeared on a public platform."[94] Even then, a pastoral letter from the Congregational Church condemned the Grimke sisters for their "unnatural" behavior: "The appropriate duties and influence of women are clearly stated in the New Testament. Those duties and that influence are unobtrusive and private."[95]

away at the dividing lines between the male world and the female world and destroying the segregation of spheres that supported traditional notions of "femininity."

Television and the Raising of Feminist Consciousness

As numerous feminist writers have noted, before the current feminist movement, most women did not perceive themselves as a "group." They saw themselves as individuals or as members of families. Each woman felt aligned with "her" men. Each woman tended to perceive her problems as unique and related to her own individual situation. Her means to solving problems was to negotiate with the men she came in contact with. Those women who worked, observes Gloria Steinem, were "encouraged to believe that all progress was to be achieved by identifying upward, by attaching oneself to serving the most powerful men available."[99] Women, suggests Steinem, did not think of banding together with other women and other "out groups" to bring about political change. Instead they saw their individual chances for success in marrying the "right" men or being token women in a male-dominated business world.

In many ways, the notion of women as a "minority group" is a strange and new idea. As Sheila Rothman notes, there are few conceptual or political links between the "oppression" of white middle-class women and the oppression of blacks.[100] Similarly, Janet Zollinger Giele rejects Marxist interpretations of the women's struggle, because, unlike other classes, women live with their "oppressors" and therefore benefit from men's superior status.[101] Rothman notes that "during the nineteenth century and for most of the twentieth, it seemed logical and sensible to link the welfare of women directly to the welfare of their children, their family, and their society, and to assume that the best interests of women were at one with all these other interests."[102]

Steinem says that it took feminism to "reveal the politics of everyday life and the shared interests of women as a caste."[103] Steinem speaks, for example, of her own slow realization that the problems she faced as a journalist were shared by other women. There was, she says, an "odd echo of an experience that I had thought was idiosyncratic and mine alone." "Thousands of women," she continues, have "been strengthened and started on paths of lifelong change by hearing their experience as wives, mothers, and frustrated professionals accurately described."[104] Similarly, Betty Friedan notes that in the past, when women did not feel what they were supposed to feel, "each of us thought she was a freak."[105]

But Steinem and Friedan and other feminists are not very clear in describing what allowed feminism to conceptualize their relationships with men and women in new ways. How and why was this generation of women able to perceive their individual problems as shared? How is it that women who were physically interspersed among the males of the population were able to stop identifying with the individual men who walked through the door each night and start identifying with other women who were isolated in other men's homes? What new connection among women suddenly allowed them to perceive themselves as an "out group"? After all, even a clear sense of one's imprisonment requires an escape to an outside perspective.

An implicit theme in many descriptions of the rise of feminist consciousness is women's sudden new ability to "see" beyond their individual problems and concerns and to acquire an outside view, a shared understanding of *all* women's problems, and a sense of "connection" with other women despite physical barriers. Barbara Ehrenreich and Deirdre English, for example, describe the new perspective held by the feminists of the 1960s.

> Like the men of their generation, they had *seen* beyond the bucolic peacefulness of the suburbs to the war zone at the perimeter—the ghetto rebellions in the cities, the guerrilla struggles in the Third World. . . . Inevitably they drew the analogy between women and blacks, between women and all other "oppressed people."[106]

Similarly, Gloria Steinem describes the "breaking of boundaries between and among women"[107] and the creation of a "psychic turf"[108] that overcame the fact that women have no territory of their own. Elizabeth Janeway suggests that "what is happening to women involves a sudden enlargement of our world: the sky above us lifts, light pours in."[109]

Although many feminists use metaphorically the ideas of a new way of "seeing" and of the breaking down of barriers, their descriptions neatly coincide both with what women and others in the 1960s were literally seeing on television and with the new sets of experience that were available to people regardless of their physical location. Their descriptions sound very much like the analysis of the shift to electronic situations described earlier in this book.

Before, isolated from men and from each other, women had "no outside standards to reckon by." "For women at home . . . the loss of a direct tie to the outer world means a loss of cognitive knowledge of how things work and of real standards to test oneself against."[110] As an arena of news and entertainment shared by both sexes, television alters women's perspective. Television gives women access to "outside standards" and it provides knowledge of "how things work." The shared arena of television also invites public comparison of the males and females portrayed in it. And by the male standards offered by television, women are weak, isolated, and relatively useless. If a man were in the position of most female television characters, he would probably be considered a "failure."

In *The Feminine Mystique*, Friedan names those strange feelings that women were having about the conflict between how they were told to feel and act and their new feelings that something was missing in their lives. Friedan writes of a "schizophrenic split" between the ideal situation in which women were supposed to be enjoying their roles as wives and mothers isolated in the home and the actual feelings many women had of being trapped and unhappy.[111] Implicit in the idea of a "split" is the new perception of a wider world from which women were excluded.

A woman, says Friedan, was supposed to be a happy creature who had an "orgasm waxing the kitchen floor."[112] Yet women were not happy—perhaps because while this "instruction" was being given to them in women's magazines and books, other sources of information were tempting them with new possibilities.

Friedan writes that in 1960, women's magazines, such as *McCall's*, pictured the female as "young and frivolous, almost childlike; fluffy and feminine; passive; gaily content in a world of bedroom and kitchen, sex, babies, and home."[113] But in the same year, "the problem that has no name burst like a boil through the image of the happy American housewife."[114] What was the "problem"? Why did it burst forth? Friedan offers no explicit explanation, but her own description of the discrepancy between women's "proper" roles in 1960 and the scope of world events suggests the possible role of television.

Friedan writes that the frivolous magazine image of women was presented in the same year that "Castro led a revolution in Cuba and men were trained to travel into outer space; the year that the African continent brought forth new nations, and a plane whose speed is greater than the speed of sound broke up a Summit Conference."[115] Her list is long and her outrage strong over all those events that women were told were not their concern.

Interestingly, Friedan's list of events resembles a summary of the year's top stories on television news. Unlike *McCall's* magazine or the women's page of newspapers, television brought the same information and the same "outside world" to men and women. And by 1960, television had penetrated nearly 90% of American households. Suddenly, there was a split between women's role image and their informational worlds. There was a sharp discrepancy between the traditional image women were offered of their "special sphere" in women's magazines and the wider view of world events offered to them by television.

Television exposed women to many "male topics" that they might not have chosen to read about in print, and because television's information is in a "presentational" form, its content—regardless of discursive "subject"—was accessible to most women without any special prior training or knowledge. Further, men and women often watched television together, so that it became almost impossible for women and men to pretend that women were ignorant of certain worldly affairs. A woman who had watched many hours of news on television would be infuriated to hear a man tell her, "You know nothing about such things." In this sense, television liberated women informationally and thereby planted the seeds of discontent that would flower into other forms of revolt.

Isolated in the home, a woman's sense of "us" was once defined in terms of those in her physical environment: her husband, her children, her neighbors. Other men and women were "them." As television offers women direct access to the larger social environment (access that they know they share with millions of other women), their old sense of affiliation is blurred and overlapped by an identification with others who are equally excluded from full participation in the larger perceived environment.

As discussed in Chapter 3, notions of "equality" are often situationally determined; that is, we expect to be equal to those in "our environment," but we do not necessarily demand the same rights as people in other environments. If we were dining in a restaurant, for example, and were receiving the same quality of service and food as all the other people in the room, we would generally be content. But if we could see through a large plate glass window that there was another whole room of people who were dining much more elegantly than we, and if we were told that we—due to a biological characteristic—were not allowed to be served in that second room, we would be furious. Similarly, the perspective offered by television of a male world with male topics and male adventures and male opportunities, from which women are barred, may have a great deal to do with women's newfound ability to perceive themselves as a "minority," a group isolated from a world they can see but not enter. Television's constant exposure of the public male domain encourages women to demand sexual integration of all public spheres.

Sexist Content/Liberating Structure

In the last fifteen years, researchers have amassed extensive data on the stereotyped images of men and women in television entertainment and commercials.[116] Studies have shown that male characters far outnumber female characters in television programs. In some programs, the ratio is as high as five males to one female. In many popular adventure series, there have been no significant female characters at all. Male characters are often more exciting and interesting; they portray almost all the professionals, heroes, and criminals. Women characters, in contrast, tend to be dependent on men, less intelligent and competent than men, and more highly emotional. Women are also portrayed as more passive and less successful in achieving their goals. The sex bias of television content has been clear in adult entertainment, children's programming, and even news and documentaries. There have been some improvements in recent years, but the changes are still minimal, and some observers have argued that the presentation of women has actually worsened even as it has appeared to get better.[117]

Researchers have also concluded that the roles played by males and females in television are capable of influencing children's perceptions of appropriate gender roles. In one study, for example, children who saw women portrayed in traditionally male roles were more likely to claim that these roles were "appropriate" for women than were children who saw only men in these roles.[118] Such studies seem to suggest, therefore, that typical sexist television content not only reflects the current sex biases of the culture but also serves to maintain these biases by passing them on to the next generation. These data have been used as a serious indictment of television.

The conclusions of these studies are couched in terms of "hard scientific evidence" of the sexist influence of television, but the implications drawn from the data collected are based on many untested assumptions. The vast majority of these studies are simply "content analyses" that tally the number and type of male and female roles on television. In these studies, the *effect* of the content on behavior is not examined. It is logical, many researchers seem to suggest, that sexist content will reinforce sexist behavior among those who watch.[119]

The less common experimental studies do look for behavioral effects, but, for a number of ethical and practical reasons, most of them have examined only *immediate* reactions to television content, such as children's verbal response to what behaviors are "appropriate" for each sex or children's choice of "sex-typed" toys.[120] The findings for these studies are then extended to conclusions about the larger and long-term effects of television on gender behavior.

Unfortunately, the analysis of the impact of television on sex role socialization is often taken no further. Few studies consider other possible nonimitative effects of sexist content; almost no studies examine the long-term potential for a boomerang effect when these sexist images are portrayed publicly to both sexes on television. Indeed, it is ironic that many observers of the sexist content of television express horror over the power of television to impose "second-class citizenship" on young girls,[121] and yet they do not ask why it is that during the same period in which this powerful sexist medium spread through America women advanced in record numbers into the work force and then demanded equal rights and roles.

Although it is certainly offensive (and boring) to see strict stereotyping of any social group on television—whether women, Jews, blacks, hispanics, or American Indians—it is not at all clear that portrayal on television of apparently "appropriate" behaviors for different groups will lead to the long-term imitation of those behaviors on the part of those who are stereotyped.

The learning of how others view appropriate roles is, of course, a powerful contributant to behavior. The "mediated generalized other" adds to our sense of what aspects of our behavior will be viewed as normal or deviant. But the influence of television on attitudes and behavior is probably much more complex than a simple prod to imitate its content. Since we are all the heroes of our own adventures, we are likely to identify with the heroes of any adventure we see on television. In the long run, viewers may identify with those television characters who are successful and rewarded, rather than with those who are simply labeled similarly to them. Indian children who watch traditional cowboy films may be moved, over time, to think and act like cowboys, not like Indians—even as they learn that Indians are "not supposed to" behave that way. Similarly, stereotyped sex roles on television may lead women to begin to imitate male styles of behavior in real life, even though they may also learn that it is "inappropriate" for women to behave like men.

A key variable in determining long-term socialization patterns for any group may be the degree of access children in the group have to the experiences, adventures, rewards, and punishments of members of *other* groups. In order to consider an alternative view of the impact of television on gender behavior, we need to look beyond message content and short-term imitative responses and examine the ways in which television restructures the traditional "situational geography" of sex-role socialization.

As Nancy Chodorow's analysis of gender socialization suggests, it is not merely the *content* of sex-role "instructions" that causes differences in typical male and female characteristics. The traditional *structural* asymmetry inherent in a system where both boys and girls are raised by females also has a tremendous effect. The invisibility of the male world affects the attributes of both maleness and femaleness. The girl has no model to follow but the mother, the boy is told to imitate a father he rarely observes. If Chodorow is correct, television's introduction of an idealized form of the male world into the home would upset this traditional system in two ways: by giving the girl another "direct" role model, and by reducing the abstraction of the male world for the boy. Such exposure may structurally neutralize some of the old imbalances. For example, studies show that child viewers prefer and attend more to programs and scenes that focus on characters of their *own* sex, yet these studies also reveal that about a third of the programs and scenes attended to focus on the *other* sex.[122] Unlike most girls' books, such as *Little Women* or *Heidi*, where the central characters are female, television offers girls many male models for emulation.

Television content may actually function in two opposing directions at once. In the short run, the content may reinforce old stereotypes by providing children with more models for sexist behavior. In the long run, however, the fact that both boys and girls are exposed to male and female role models may weaken the traditional distinctions in socialization patterns.

Studies of imitative behavior in live interaction provide some support for this argument. They suggest that both male and female children imitate the behavior of models who are perceived as powerful or successful—regardless of the sex of the model.[123] Since television tends to reward men more often than women, it is quite possible that girls begin to imitate the male behavior they see rewarded on television.

Other studies of "modeling" behavior suggest a slightly more complex relationship between male models and girls' behavior, but they also support the contention that television may be teaching girls both female and male *behaviors*, even as it projects the cultural *attitude* that girls should act like girls. A study of imitation of filmed aggressive behavior, for example, has shown that boys imitate the behavior much more than girls do— that is, *until the girls are offered rewards for imitating the aggression.* When it is clear to girls that they will be rewarded rather than punished for "acting like boys," the imitation is relatively equal for both sexes.[124] What this finding suggests is that television teaches girls about male styles of interaction, which they may later imitate as soon as they come to believe that it is appropriate for them to do so.*

Because books aimed at young girls and books aimed at young boys tend to contain different content and themes, boys' and girls' distinct socialization patterns were once reinforced by what they were reading, by how different what they were reading was from what the other sex was reading, and by the lack of direct knowledge of what the other sex was reading. Because men have made most of the decisions concerning television programming thus far, the content has tended to be more similar to male literature, fantasies, and myths. Yet this male content may be having a new effect because it is now transmitted to girls as well as boys. The more information is *shared*, regardless of its specific content, the more difficult it is to maintain traditional distinctions in behavior and world view.

A theatrical or dramaturgical analogy helps to explain how the same sex-role instructions may be followed differently depending on how they are delivered. Imagine two young children—let us say a brother and sister—sitting in a "play house" in the middle of a stage. Both are young and afraid because they are in a new and strange environment. Both are crying sporadically. But then their parents come onstage, separate them, and take them each to opposite wings of the backstage area to teach them appropriate onstage gender behavior.

The boy is told by his father that he must be a man, be strong, bold, and protective of his weak sister. In the other wing, the mother instructs the girl that, as a woman, she should express her emotions freely and rely on her brother for comfort and support. After some rehearsal of their roles, they are each returned to the stage.

In all likelihood, the brother and sister will follow, to a large extent, the explicit instructions they have been given. The boy finds that, yes, he is stronger than his emotional sister, for she continues to cry and seems to need and appreciate his manliness. And the girl finds that, yes, women are weaker, for she is afraid, yet her brother shows no fears or tears and he comforts her. Not having heard the directions given to the other sex,

---

*To the extent that Betty Friedan's *The Feminine Mystique* is sometimes seen as a "cause" of the modern women's movement (Carl Degler calls it "social dynamite"), it might be tied to this issue. The seemingly explosive response to her work and the subsequent work of other feminist writers might have been a response to a message that said, in effect, that it *is* legitimate for women to imitate male role models, models that women had previously observed on television but had been told were taboo.

and not having observed the potential difficulties and rehearsals required to master them, both boy and girl see the behavior of the other as "real."

Further, if in the backstage area, the boy is shown by his father how to turn the heat and lights on and off and where and how to earn some money, and the girl is shown by her mother how to clean the house and cook the food, each sex will be even further in awe of the wondrous differences between themselves and "the other." The more removed each sex is from the backstage area of the other and the more the doubts, anxieties, rehearsals, and temporary rejections of a gender role are obscured from the other sex, the more the other will seem mysterious, unpredictable, and "different."

This scenario is similar, in its broad outlines, to the structure of gender socialization that existed before electronic media. Each sex received its set of sex-role instructions privately. There was, of course, some overlapping, especially among children with siblings of the opposite sex (indeed, that may be why opposite-sex siblings are apparently more psychologically androgynous than same-sex siblings[125]), but generally there was also a large area of private instruction—from elders, from peers, and through books. Each sex planned among its own members how to behave in front the other sex. Each individual may have doubted, at times, the validity of his or her own performance, but the behavior of members of the other sex seemed "real."

But what if the stage scenario is altered slightly? What if the parents come onstage and give each sex-typed set of instructions in front of *both* children? What if each sex observes the other question or protest the directions? What happens to the perception of the naturalness of each gender role when the other sex witnesses the rehearsal of it and then sees the performance? The children will, no doubt, continue to follow the "orders" of their parents for a while. They will also be aware of the fact that this is the way "things *should* be," but because both children now see and hear the same information, because both are exposed to the backstage training and instructions of the other (girls may see boys trying to fight back tears, for example), they are more likely, in the long run at least, to see the other's role as merely a role, something draped on a basically similar human being to make that person appear different.

Further, having heard the directions and instructions directed at the other sex, each sex now has some knowledge of the "secret" information of the other, and each child, therefore, has the new option of adopting some of the characteristics of the opposite gender role. Finally, because both children share the same information publicly, they even have the option of explicitly discussing the instructions among themselves. The boy might say, for example, "But sometimes I don't feel like being strong," and the girl might say, "Why can't *I* turn on the lights and go out and earn some money; I know how to do it too." Doubts and desires once expressed only among the members of one sex may now be expressed in front of members of the other sex. In the long run, the *sharing* of "sexist" instructions has the potential of undermining both sets of behaviors and of leading to more egalitarian roles.

In the same way, television has reduced the mystification of "the other." By including both boys and girls, men and women, in the same informational environment, it opens the behavior of both sexes to public scrutiny and analysis. Since television ends women's informational isolation in the "female sphere" of culture, its greatest impact is on women's conception of their role. When Friedan writes, for example, about the "schizophrenic split" felt by women in the 1960s, she may be describing the situation faced by the girl in the stage analogy described above who is told by her mother of her limited role but who also overhears her father tell her brother of *his* wider role, *his* adventures, *his* privileges. Ironically, the more "directive" and "instructional" television content is concerning the traditional division of roles, the more it may undermine those same role structures in everyday interaction. Because it is experienced publicly, very sexist television content may be sowing the seeds of its own destruction.[126]

In the past, each sex was exposed primarily to the onstage behavior of the other sex. The onstage roles of masculinity and of femininity were seen as the reality. But dozens of popular television programs, from "I Love Lucy" to "Dallas," give both sexes a "sidestage" view of each sex role. So do many television commercials. They show males moving from a backstage area of doubts and fears into an onstage area of fearless masculinity. They reveal women plotting among themselves to attract and control men and to enhance the aura of mysterious femininity.

In a sense, each sex is now able not only to eavesdrop on the backstage area of the other sex, but to do so with the knowledge of the other sex. Television's portrayal of traditional rituals of husband-wife interaction and of courtship may tell people that these are the expected norms of the culture, but the new type of exposure of traditional roles renders them somewhat ridiculous. Television's restructuring of the socialization environment and of the exposure to the other sex, therefore, may be much more significant than the specific content it transmits. The shared forum of television supports the liberation of men and women from old roles even when its messages are traditional or reactionary. The current trend toward an androgynous style of behavior can be seen as a move toward a "middle region" gender role that combines aspects of the traditional front and back region behaviors of both sexes.

Literacy and the Enhancement of Patriarchy

If electronic media have a great impact on male and female roles, then the invention of printing and the spread of literacy in Western Europe ought to have had an equally profound effect on male/female relations. As Elizabeth Eisenstein has detailed, the printing press and the spread of literacy swept away the cobwebs of tradition and ushered in an age of reformation and science.[127] But because scientific discoveries, religious reforms, and the histories that describe them have traditionally been conducted and recorded by *men*, there has been no full-scale study of the impact of the spread of literacy on the relative status of men and women. Nevertheless, there are many indications in various sources that the spreading of literacy during the sixteenth and seventeenth centuries may have widened the gap in male and female rights and enhanced the dominance of men over women.

Anne Oakley describes the century between 1540 and 1640 as the first major period of controversy over women's rights.[128] The fight by women, however, was not to gain new rights, but merely to retain those they already had. In the Middle Ages, according to Oakley, men and women shared many rights and responsibilities; by the sixteenth century, women's status was beginning to decline.

While strongly questioning the full implications of the decline in women's rights, historian David Hunt summarizes the facts in France as follows:

> They lost the right to participate in municipal affairs, to sit on certain courts or to testify before them, to substitute for husbands who were absent or who had become insane, to inherit the prerogatives of husbands who had died. Women were compelled to live with their spouses . . . and were forced to submit to their discipline, even when it involved physical punishment. By the sixteenth century, a woman's word (on a contract, for example) had no legal force unless it was countersigned by her husband or a judge. She was an *incapable*, a lowly subject in the "domestic monarchy" of her husband's household. [129]

Similarly, Lawrence Stone notes that despite the "monstrous regiment" of queens in England, the status and rights of women were on the decline in the sixteenth century. "Thomas More's *Utopia* is remarkable in that the subjection of wives to husbands is the one authoritarian feature in an otherwise egalitarian society. Some Elizabethans revived the Platonic doubts whether a woman could be considered as a reasoning creature; others questioned whether she had a soul."[130]

Stone also describes the sudden change that took place in both national and community life in the sixteenth and seventeenth centuries. The development of nation states with monarchs was paralleled on a lower level by the isolation of the nuclear family from the extended community of kin and neighbors. For a thousand years prior to this time, says Stone, the family structure was an "Open Lineage Family," marked by its "permeability by outside influences, and its members' sense of loyalty to ancestors and to living kin."[131] The boundary that marked "them" from "us" surrounded the community and kin, not the nuclear family. Relationships between husband and wife and parents and children were not necessarily any more intimate than relationships among neighbors. Indeed, by our standards, marital life was remarkably cool and distant. The home was "neither a castle nor a womb."[132] It lacked firm boundaries, its inhabitants had little sense of privacy or individualism. Advice, problem solving, and the settling of husband-wife disputes were community affairs.

Around 1530, however, another family type—what Stone calls the "Restricted Patriarchal Nuclear Family"—began to overlap the older form among certain classes. This family, observes Stone, was marked by more boundary-awareness, a greater sense of privacy, and more authoritarian control over the wife and children by the male head of the household. The growth of the patriarchal nuclear family was paralleled on the national scale by the growth of central monarchs who ruled as the "fathers" of their country.[133]

Stone notes that the "reasons for the . . . decline in the status and rights of wives in the sixteenth and early seventeenth centuries are not entirely clear,"[134] but his descriptions of "boundaries" and of the new conceptions of individualism, nationality, and hierarchy that accompanied the domestic transformation offer striking parallels to the claims of Marshall McLuhan and other medium theorists concerning the shift from orality to literacy.[135] Further, Stone's passing comments on the effects of literacy on women support the interpretation that literacy may have played a significant role in the shifting balance of male/female rights. Stone notes, for example, that the invention of the printing press and the new emphasis on reading as a source of wisdom and religious salvation "inevitably had the effect of widening the social and cultural gap between those who could read . . . and those who could not." He goes on to say that while there were some exceptional noblewomen who could read, the "new learning was monopolized by men, thus increasing their prestige and influence and reducing that of women."[136] Elsewhere he comments that with Bible reading as the post Reformation channel to salvation, women were placed at "a new and serious disadvantage."[137]

From the sixteenth century to the recent past, the gap between the education of men and women has been great. David Cressy's study of literacy in England suggests that by the seventeenth century, many men were at least minimally literate (the rate varied from 33% to 100% depending on occupation and location), yet "close to 90% of the women in seventeenth-century England could not even write their names."[138] Cressy adds that "in all sources and in all areas and periods, the literacy of women lagged behind that of men."[139] The domestic work of women, he notes, made it unnecessary for them to learn to read or write, and in many cases they did not have the time. Even when literacy was seen as the route to salvation, it was assumed that the husband—as head of household—would shoulder this responsibility.

The decline of women's rights in the sixteenth and seventeenth centuries at first led to harsh patriarchal discipline, but by the late seventeenth and early eighteenth centuries the marital relationship became more affectionate and caring. Women were still treated paternalistically, but they began to be cherished as innocent creatures rather than scorned as domestic slaves.[140] Nevertheless, the period from the sixteenth to the early twentieth century is set off from both the Middle Ages and our own time by the strong separation of male and female spheres.

Although the connection needs much more exploration, it is very likely that the increasing gap between the literacy of men and women helped make women seem childlike and incapable compared to men. The imbalance between the literacy of men and women must have grown out of an already existing imbalance—for women surely *could have* become as literate as men if given the opportunity. But the already more powerful men were apparently able to use literacy as a tool to divide further the worlds of men and women and to reinforce the patriarchal system. Just as southern plantation owners kept their slaves chained not only in irons but also in ignorance, so did many men from the sixteenth century onward restrict their women's access to the largely male domains of history, literature, philosophy, and science. Walter Ong has suggested, for example, that the continuing teaching of Latin to men long after it was no longer a "mothers' tongue" served as a male "puberty rite" from which women were almost completely excluded.[141] The spread of literacy allowed men to have "deeper" backstage areas to rehearse for more "forefront" stage performances. But women were left behind in a world of merged behavioral styles.* Further, as we will see in the next chapter, literacy may also have created a new awareness of a class of highly dependent beings—children. And when society considered who should assume the expanding responsibility for the care and molding of these "new" children, women—themselves viewed as partly children, partly adults—seemed the logical choice.

The gap in education between men and women continued until the mid-twentieth century. Some would say it still continues. Before the 1830s, no American college would admit a woman.[143] In England, Oxford University did not grant women and men similar degrees until 1920.[144] Not until 1978—well into the modern feminist movement—did more women than men enter American colleges.[145]

Even on lower levels, women's education was different from men's. Generally, the justification for educating women was not to make them equal to men, but to educate them only to the level necessary to make them tolerable companions to their husbands and fit mothers to their children. When the first women's college, Vassar, opened in 1865, its administrators were sternly warned by a host of doctors of the dangers associated with attempts to educate women as if they were men.[146] Since women's bodies were generally seen as a battleground between the uterus and the brain, one doctor concluded that educating women would lead to the atrophy of the uterus.[147]

---

*Of course, many of those women who were "educated like men" learned to "think like men" and "behave like men." Indeed, many of them began to reject the whole notion of a "separate sphere" for women. As one historian notes, "not every educated woman was a rebel, but nearly every rebel had been educated."[142]

Kate Millett sees the gap in male and female education as part of the process of "interior colonization" of women in our society. She suggests that the gap has not yet been closed. "A large factor in their subordinate position is the fairly systematic ignorance patriarchy imposes upon women."[148] Millett suggests that even today there is a subtle but significant gap in male and female education. Science, mathematics, and technology remain fields mostly male in character; women inhabit the lower prestige fields in the humanities and social sciences. (Indeed, even the labels "*hard* science" and "*soft* science" echo the labels of "masculinity" and "femininity.") The male fields are more valued by the culture; government and corporation grants go mostly to those areas dominated by men.

In a sense, many women are only partially socialized into literate culture. They learn the basic skills of reading and writing, but the extensions of "literate thought"—science and technology—remain male domains. Millett notes that, "in keeping with the inferior sphere of culture to which women in patriarchy have always been restricted, the present encouragement of their 'artistic' interests through study of the humanities is hardly more than an extension of the 'accomplishments' they once cultivated in preparation for the marriage market."[149]

Because women have advanced less into the culture, science, and philosophy that have been stimulated by literacy, it is tempting to consider the possibility that some of the traditional distinctions made in Western culture between male characteristics and female characteristics may parallel some of the observed differences between members of oral and literate societies. As we have seen, there are other sufficient explanations for different gender roles in the basic separation of social spheres, but literacy may have further enhanced these distinctions by leading to traditionally "masculine" styles of thought.

In his essay, "Culture, Psychiatry, and the Written Word," J.C. Carothers suggests that the "well-developed sense of spatiotemporal relations and of causal relationship on mechanistic lines" is highly dependent on the literate habit of "visual, as opposed to auditory, synthesis."[150] Oral cultures, he suggests, live in a magical mystery world of animistic powers, which passes away only when tribal cultures become literate and emphasize lineality, continuity, and rationality. Writing, he argues, leads to more introspection, to a greater sense of individuality, and to greater distance from neighbors and kin. Thus, many of the described differences between oral and literate peoples—irrational/rational; mysterious/open for inspection; emotional/distanced; concrete/abstract; tied to physical environment/freed from immediate environment—are invitingly similar to the traditional distinctions made between feminine and masculine traits. Women, like members of oral cultures, have been noted for their lack of a sense of individuality, their "irrationality," and for their strong bonds with other people and with things in their immediate physical environment. In contrast, men, like literate peoples, are noted for their heightened sense of individuality and remoteness, and for their abstract, rational, mathematical, and mechanistic thinking. Significantly, women are often said to excel at *verbal* ability, men at *spatial* tasks.[151] The link needs much more exploration and analysis, but it is tempting to consider the possibility that the "interior colonization" of women through restricted literacy may have given every "civilized" man his personal "savage in the kitchen."

Literate thinking emphasizes linear arguments, cause and effect relationships, abstractions, and categorizations. For highly literate societies, this is the only proper way to think. The intuitive, holistic, and "unsystematic" thinking of preliterate societies and of women has been ridiculed as "irrational." The returning importance of nonlinear forms of communication through the use of electronic media, however, may be blurring traditional stereotypical distinctions between men's and women's thinking and bringing about renewed interest in non-"rational" forms of thought.[152] Women have traditionally been accused of being so concerned with personal feelings that their judgments are always personal and emotional. As Elizabeth Janeway has written, women "are expected to take general remarks personally, to vote for candidates because they are handsome, to change their minds easily and to cry at the movies."[153] The merging of personal and political spheres through television, however, has begun to make these characteristics more typical of the population as a whole. As described in Chapter 6, the presentational, expressive, and analogic bias of television has tended to personalize politics for everyone; many people now vote for the candidates they "personally like" rather than for those whose stands on the issues they agree with. Similarly, in the 1960s, there was a strong new focus among both men and women on good and bad "vibes." And this interest continues to manifest itself in the current fascination with "beta" styles of problem solving and management. Interestingly, television is one of the only public arenas in which men routinely wear makeup and are judged primarily on their manner and appearance rather than on their "accomplishments." The widespread use of expressive forms of media may be supporting a rebirth of interest in the expressive skills traditionally held by women.

When a House Is Not a Home (and Not a Business)

This is the true nature of home—it is the place of peace. . . . In so far as it is not this, it is not home; so far as the anxieties of the outer life penetrate into it, and the inconsistently-minded, unknown, unloved, or hostile society of the outer world is allowed by either husband or wife to cross the threshold it ceases to be a home; it is then only a part of the outer world which you have roofed over and lighted fire in.—John Ruskin, 1865[154]

The power of television to reshape the traditional relations between men and women—which were supported by the literacy gap and industrialization—is suggested clearly by the romantic notion of the "home" as a separate domain apart from the "hostile society of the outer world." Television and other electronic media bring this world into the home and change both the public and domestic spheres.

With television, the four walls of the home no longer separate the woman's world from the man's world, the private sphere from the public sphere. Through television, the woman is suddenly "plugged in." On television, close-up views of the personal expressions and actions of others become public, and public and political issues become personal experiences in the home. Television may be the common denominator linking the "politicizing of the personal" and the "personalizing of the political," which have jointly characterized the women's movement.[155]

Even though many women continue to be physically isolated in the home, television has allowed them to "observe" and "experience" the larger world, including all-male interactions and behaviors. For the first time, boys and girls and men and women tend to share a great deal of similar information about themselves and about the "other." Television makes the private images of the other sex public and perusable. Through the television close-up, men and women see, in one month, many more members of the opposite sex at "intimate distance" than members of earlier generations saw in a lifetime. Further, unlike face-to-face interactions, in which the holding of a gaze may be construed as an invitation to further intimacy, the television image allows one to stare and carefully examine the face, body, and movements of the other sex. Television fosters a kind of easy and uninvolved intimacy.

Television's impact on gender orientations was neither immediate nor total. The greatest influence was on the "first television generation"—those children whose gender socialization processes were just beginning in the mid-1950s, and its effect was not seen, therefore, until the late 1960s. Further, the new consciousness supported by television's liberating situational structure has had to compete with many other sources of traditional socialization instructions and experiences, including television's explicitly sexist content.

If it is true that television has merged male and female perspectives on society, then earlier media such as the mass press, the telephone, movies, and radio must also have had significant effects. But television is the most potent merger of male and female spheres. Unlike the movies, television brings the world to women without taking women out of the home. And although newspapers and radio began to bring the man's world into the house, and although the telephone took parts of the house out into the world, that world remained literally "unexposed" to women.

Some scholars have suggested that war, sports, and politics are meant to be places of male comradeship and bonding, and are defined by the exclusion of women.[156] But television exposes these traditionally male domains to women, and it does so casually, without fanfare, without women having to choose to read an article or book on these topics, to leave the home to go see a particular event or movie, or even to stop doing traditional household chores. Unlike the abstractions of words such as "sportsmanlike" or "bravery" in books or on radio, television gives a down-to-earth, gritty, and demystified image of the male world. Indeed, television may even enhance the liberating potential of earlier media. Once television opens a crack in the door to the outside world, other media are used to open it more fully. Once television provides images of the types of people and locations that are heard on the radio and can be reached on the telephone, these media are used by women to create an informational territory, or "psychic turf," to be shared with other women. And books, essays, and articles by and for women become "places" in which to discuss and explore the newly widened consciousness of the world and women's role in it.

Because television breaks down the public/domestic division by bringing the outside world into the home, its first and strongest impact is on the perception that women have of the public male world and of the place, or lack of place, that they have in it. Television is an especially potent force for integrating women because television brings the public domain to women via women's traditionally emphasized concerns with personal expression, emotions, and feelings. Yet because television makes it more and more difficult for men as well as women to play old complementary roles, in the long run, television's shared environment has an impact on the behavioral style of both sexes.

Michelle Rosaldo and Louise Lamphere argue that the typical division of labor for men and women in all known societies is the result of women's ability to bear children and lactate.[157] Because involvement in many other tasks may be incompatible with pregnancy and nursing, many important activities are taken over exclusively by men. The more complex the society and the greater the domestic/public split, the more women become responsible for *all* domestic chores, even those that are beyond biological necessity. Child-*caring*, for example, is not as biologically determined as child-*bearing*, yet if women are already far removed from the public domain, they may inherit full responsibility for all those things that cannot possibly be done by men who work away from the home. Conversely, women lose responsibility for all non-homebound tasks.

In this sense, electronic media's invasion of the home not only liberates women from the home's informational confines but also tends to reintegrate the public and domestic spheres and to foster a "situational androgyny." Men are now able to "hunt" for information at home computers and women can breastfeed children while doing business on the telephone. And even when men and women remain physically separated in work and family spheres that are located in different places, electronic links create a greater sense of informational and experiential unity.

Electronic media undermine all previous societies' dependence on physical location as the prime determinant of access to and isolation from other people. Electronic media weaken the notion of men's spheres and women's spheres, of special huts or buildings, of places that are either sacred or profane. The new potential of electronic media to transform both work and home may finally remove the seeming necessity of the split in domestic and public domains and reintegrate men and women in a single social sphere of work and family. With the end of the place/situation link, a man and a woman can be physically separated yet socially together, or isolated together in the home yet connected to other social spheres. With telephone, radio, television, and computer, the home has, in many ways, become a part of the larger world which we have merely "roofed over and lighted fire in."

13

The Blurring of Childhood and Adulthood

A Case Study in Changing Role Transitions

In the last half century, psychologists have greatly enriched our knowledge of the physiological, cognitive, and linguistic stages through which children pass as they grow to adulthood. Arnold Gesell, Jean Piaget, Erik Erikson, Jerome Bruner, Jerome Kagan, and Lawrence Kohlberg are only a few of those who have worked at plotting the course of human growth and development. Much of this research has indicated that the differences between children and adults and between children of various ages are not simply ones of degree, but of clearly dissimilar capacities and perceptions of reality.

What these studies of children have generally ignored, however, is the current evolution in the social manifestations of "childhood." It is not unusual for social conventions to change along with the publication and popularization of research findings. What is peculiar in this case, however, is that the change is in direct opposition to the thrust of the research. The psychological studies suggest the need to treat children very differently from adults, and yet the present trend is to treat children more like "little adults" and to have people of different ages share much more similar roles, rights, and responsibilities than in the past.

We might call this recent trend the "end of childhood." But that would tell only half of the story. For without a clear sense of childhood, there can be no distinct notion of adulthood. What seems to be happening in our culture is an overall homogenization, or merging, of childhood and adulthood. This chapter briefly summarizes recent changes in the social roles of children and adults and then explores the possibility that these changes are related, at least in part, to changes in media of communication.

The Adultlike Child and the Childlike Adult

In the first half of the twentieth century, childhood was considered a time of innocence and isolation. The child was sheltered from the nasty realities of life. The child was dressed differently from adults. There were separate "languages" for children and adults; there were words and topics—such as birth, death, sex, and money—that were considered unfit for children's ears. And there was a strict age-grading system, supported by the structure of the school, that designated what a child of any given age should know and do.

In the last thirty years, however, there has been a remarkable change in the image and roles of children. Childhood as a protected and sheltered period of life has all but disappeared. Children today seem less "childlike." Children speak more like adults, dress more like adults, and behave more like adults than they used to. In fact, the reverse is also true. There are indications that many adults who have come of age within the last twenty years continue to speak, dress, and act much like overgrown children. Certainly, all children and adults do not and cannot behave exactly alike, but there are many more similarities in behavior than in the past. The traditional dividing lines are gone.

One of the clearest signs of differences in status in a culture is a difference in appearance and dress. The inferior status conferred on children once manifested itself in their clothing—whether knickers, or sailor suits, or cartoon character T-shirts. What was significant was not *what* children wore but the fact that children's clothing was different from adult's clothing.

Today, a walk on any city street or in any park suggests that the era of distinct clothing for different age-groups has passed. Just as children sometimes dress in three-piece suits or designer dresses, so do many adults dress like "big children": in jeans, Mickey-Mouse or Superman T-shirts, and sneakers. In addition to wearing each other's traditional clothing, new "uni-age" styles of dress have emerged. Designer jeans, for example, are worn by young and old alike. The phrase "designer jeans" would once have sounded like a contradiction in terms; now it represents a synthesis of the nonserious playclothes denim of children with the high-fashion clothing styles of adults. Some manufacturers have pushed the homogenization in dress to the limits by producing designer jean diaper covers.

The recent homogenization of age-related clothing may seem to be only a surface phenomenon—merely similar costumes covering very different social beings. Yet children and adults have also begun to behave more alike. Even casual observation suggests that posture, sitting positions, and gestures have become more homogenized. It is no longer unusual to see adults in public sitting cross-legged on the ground or engaging in "children's play." Indeed, the latest generation of playthings—video and computer games—are avidly played by both adults and children.

Differences in languages and vocabularies for different ages are also disappearing. Many slang words, phrases, obscenities, and grammatical constructions are shared across a broad spectrum of age-groups. Children are speaking more like adults, and adults are speaking more like children. Perhaps even more significant, they are speaking this way in each other's presence. The linguistic evidence of adults' authority in relation to children is also disappearing; increasingly, children are calling adults (in many cases, their parents) by first names.

There are fewer and fewer topics that society can agree are unfit for discussion with children. And in any case, children seem to know about once taboo topics before they are included in their formal education. Sex and drug education programs, for example, have had to chase the runaway increase in teenage pregnancy and drug abuse.* In recent years, alcoholism, abortion, and suicide have become "children's issues."[3]

For children, birth was once an issue clouded in the myths of storks and cabbage patches. Now, however, some psychologists and many popular books on childbirth suggest that children should be included in the birthing process of younger siblings, perhaps even to the point of being present at the delivery.[4]

Complementary changes have occurred for adults. Education, career choice, and developmental stages were once discussed primarily in relation to children, but an increasing number of adults are now enrolling in adult education programs, changing careers in mid-life, and becoming concerned with their "life stages."

Adult psychological temperament may also be changing. The much-discussed attitudes of the "me generation," for example, can be viewed as adult manifestations of the egocentrism traditionally associated with children. Indeed, surveys indicate that adults' sense of responsibility for children is shrinking. There is a drop in the willingness of parents to sacrifice for children, and a sharp decline in the numbers of parents whose thoughts about the future include concerns about their children's aspirations. Americans now rank cars above children as aspects of a "good life."[5]

---

*There was a rapid rise in teenage sexual activity in the 1970s. The most dramatic increase was among white females, 15 to 17 years old, whose rate of sexual activity doubled in just nine years. Overall, the proportion of sexually active unmarried female teenagers increased by two-thirds during the 1970s. By 1979, about 12 million of the 29 million teenagers in the country were sexually active. Nearly half of the 15- to 17-year-old boys and one third of the 15- to 17-year-old girls had had sexual intercourse, and close to a million 13- to 14-year-olds were also sexually active. More than one in ten teenagers gets pregnant each year.[1] There has been a similar sharp increase in drug use among teenagers. Between 1972 and 1979, for example, the proportion of 12- to 17-year-olds who used marijuana and cocaine more than doubled. In 1981, the National Institute on Drug Abuse reported that two-thirds of the high school seniors it studied admitted at least some illicit drug use. Indeed, more than half had used illegal drugs before finishing the 9th grade! A third of the drug users only smoked marijuana, but 66% had tried other drugs as well. The Institute regards these as "conservatively low" estimates.[2]

While many people continue to embrace the old conceptions of childhood and adulthood, the homogenization of status has been documented in recent changes in our entertainment and legal system.

The television and film roles played by children and adults have changed markedly over the last forty years. The Shirley Temple character of the past was merely a cute and outspoken child, but child stars of the 1970s and 1980s—such as Brooke Shields and Gary Coleman—have played the roles of adults imprisoned in children's bodies. Similarly, it is now difficult to find traditional adults in films or on television. In the age of the "anti-hero," adult characters—including many of those portrayed by Diane Keaton, Burt Reynolds, Chevy Chase, and Elliot Gould—often have the needs and emotions of overgrown children. Not only are adults often outsmarted by children in today's motion pictures, but children are sometimes portrayed as more mature, sensitive, and intelligent (as in the motion picture *E.T.*).

The relative legal status of children and adults has also been shifting in recent years. In 1967, for example, the Supreme Court gave children the right to counsel, declaring that "neither the Fourteenth Amendment nor the Bill of Rights is for adults alone";[6] subsequent decisions have provided children with many adult legal rights.[7] In the last few years there have been a number of cases in which minors have contacted lawyers on their own to fight parents or school authorities.[8]

With the great increase in the number of minors who run away from home and refuse to return,[9] the courts are often faced with deciding between the rights of the child and the rights of the parents. And the balance of rights is shifting toward the children. In more than twelve states, courts are now allowed to "emancipate" minors so that they can work and live apart from their parents. Connecticut, for example, allows sixteen-year-olds to "divorce" their parents and be treated legally as adults.[10] In California, freedom can be gained at age fourteen.[11]

The legal meaning of "child" has been further confused by the fact that children are increasingly committing "adult" crimes such as armed robbery, rape, and murder.* As a result, many states are moving away from special lenient treatment of juveniles. In 1978, for example, New York State passed a law that allows child murderers over the age of thirteen to

---

*The FBI's crime reports indicate that in 1951, children under 15 comprised only two-tenths of one percent of those arrested for murder, only four-tenths of one percent of those arrested for robbery, and only one-tenth of one percent of those arrested for rape. In 1981, however, children under 15 comprised one percent of those arrested for murder (a 500% increase), seven percent of those arrested for robbery (a 1750% increase), and four percent of those arrested for rape (a 4000% increase). These jumps would be less significant if those under 15 formed a higher proportion of the population in 1981 than they did in 1951, but the reverse is true: The proportion of the population that was under 15 dropped from 28% to 23% during the same three decades.[12] At least part of this apparent change in children's criminal activities may be attributable to a change in the *reporting* of crimes committed by children, but even such a trend would suggest a significant shift in conceptions of "childhood."

be tried as adults.[13] In 1979, the American Bar Association ratified a new set of standards for juvenile courts. Instead of being primarily concerned with the child's "best interests"—the original rationale for the juvenile court system—the ABA suggested that children should be punished in proportion to the severity of their crimes.[14]

Conceptions of adults' responsibility for their own actions have also become clouded in recent years. The increasing use and discussion of the pleas of "*temporary* insanity" or "diminished capacity" as adult excuses for committing a crime in a moment of anger, for example, suggest an attempt to legitimize temper tantrums for "big people."*

Even when the formal legal status of children and adults remains untouched, children have been receiving a new kind of respect from courts, medical institutions, and government agencies. Courts are now much more likely to consider a child's view in custody settlements, and children and adolescents are now often asked for consent before receiving medical or psychological assistance.[16] The new attitudes are reflected in New York City's decision to name two foster children—aged 13 and 16— as full-fledged members of a city panel to improve foster care.[17] Such moves represent a trend away from the traditionally paternalistic belief that adults always know what is in the best interests of a child.

In some circles, children have come to be seen as another disenfranchised "minority." Sociologist Elise Boulding argues that the Children's Rights Movement "should be included in the general process of consciousness raising about the human condition."[18] Marian Wright Edelman, director of the Children's Defense Fund, writes that, "After seven White House Conferences for children and countless reports and speeches on children's problems, they remain the poorest and most under-represented and under-served group in American society."[19]

Although some of the recent attention to children's rights focuses on the "right" not to starve or be beaten (children's *welfare*), other advocates of children's rights have pushed for full social, economic, and political participation of children in society (children's *liberation*). As a member of the latter camp, Richard Farson has argued passionately for basic "birthrights" for children to counter what he sees as systematic discrimination against them by adults.[20] Similarly, in *Escape From Childhood*, educator John Holt has outlined a "bill of rights" for children. He proposes that the "rights, privileges, duties, responsibilities of adult citizens be made *available* to any young person, of whatever age, who wants to make use of them."[21] The rights enumerated by Holt include the right to vote, to work, to have privacy, to own property, to sign contracts, to choose sexual partners, to travel, to have one's own home, and to choose one's own guardians.

---

*Some examples of "diminished capacity" include "Vietnam Stress Syndrome," "Premenstrual Syndrome," "Battered Woman Syndrome," "Occupational Stress," and even "General Life Situation" (such as poverty).[15]

If these proposed changes seem far-fetched, and perhaps even frightening, we must nevertheless recognize that they are an indication of a widespread shift in attitudes toward children. The "child-saving movement" of the nineteenth and early twentieth centuries was a segregationist movement designed to meet the "special needs" of children and guarantee them the "right to childhood," but the current trend is toward reintegration of children and adults.[22] Indeed, the relationships between parents and children have already changed dramatically. Kenneth Keniston, director of the Carnegie Council study on children, has noted that "a greater sense of parity between parents and children has certainly evolved. There is more democracy in families today, and parents are more likely to admit their flaws and inadequacies to their children. There is no longer the automatic 'parents always know best' attitude."[23]

Whether these changes in children and adults are good or bad is difficult to say. Whether children's "escape from childhood" should be viewed as liberation or aberration, or a little of both, is not clear. For better or worse, though, childhood and adulthood, as they were once defined, no longer exist.

The Myth of Age-Determinism

One of the reasons that the merging of childhood and adulthood has been difficult to observe, and once observed, difficult to accept, is that we have had few intellectual models that can account for it. Looking to developmental psychology for such a model is not as helpful as one might expect. Until recently, the dominant research and theory in developmental psychology has focused on describing the capabilities of individuals at different ages or stages of development. Most attention has been paid to studying those factors that contribute to or are associated with age- or stage-related changes. A variety of differences *between* age groups have been identified, and the typical characteristics of people *within* given age groups have been described. What is generally taken for granted, however, is the pre-existence of distinct life stages such as "infancy," "childhood," "adolescence," "adulthood," and "old age." For the most part, the research in developmental psychology is not geared toward studying those factors that might change the social character of different periods of life.

Most developmental psychologists have pressed the search for universal *differences* in behavior and thought over the life span; until recently, potential similarities in the behavior of people of all ages have generally been ignored.[24] The search for universal developmental stages has taught us a great deal, but such investigations are incomplete. Obviously, any description of *constants* in human development tends to overlook the many factors that would bring about widescale *change* in the definition of child and adult roles. Even a complete understanding of universal features of development would not necessarily tell us why age-related roles vary from culture to culture and within the same culture over time. To discover the processes through which changes in conceptions of childhood and adulthood take place, we must look beyond the sequence of *individual* development and examine larger *social* variables that influence the behavior and status of all people regardless of age or developmental stage.

Familiarity with mainstream developmental research—without equal knowledge of other perspectives both within and outside psychology— has made it possible for many Americans to overlook the possibility that cognitive and other levels of development may not be the only factors that have shaped the roles we traditionally assign to children and adults.

The findings of developmental studies are usually reported in terms of developmental stages matched to age-ranges. And while many psychologists have explained the limited implications of findings stated in terms of age-ranges,* these explanations are rarely stated in popularized summaries of developmental research. Many parents, teachers, and others have assumed, therefore, that developmental research demonstrates that age itself naturally "determines" a child's behavior and the appropriate style of interaction between children and adults. The notion of "age-determined" behavior has been reinforced and extended by popular and scholarly publications on adult "life cycles," "seasons," and "passages." These works describe such stages as the "age thirty transition" and the "age forty crucible."[28] In general, the idea of clear age-related "stages" of development appears to provide scientific support for our traditional distinctions in roles, rights, and responsibilities for people of different ages.

To a large extent, then, traditional developmental research has fostered a popular conception of human development that not only offers no explanation for the recent changes in childhood and adulthood but, as

---

*Psychologists Sheldon and Barbara White, for example, note that age is "a profoundly unbiological fact about a child" that merely represents the number of times the earth has circled the sun since the child was born. Descriptions of development in terms of age-ranges, then, are merely summaries and averages of developmental changes; children of the same age often have very different abilities. The Whites suggest that Piaget's age-related cognitive stages are the weakest part of his theory. "All the evidence shows that there are no sudden and total transformations in a child's thinking at any age."[25] Other psychologists have pointed out the problems in *any* studies that describe behavior as a function of age.[26] Unlike other presumed behavioral "causes," a person's age is not something that can be manipulated by a researcher, and therefore the effects of age cannot be tested experimentally. Further, for many practical reasons, most developmental studies cannot even follow the lives of subjects over many years. Instead, at a given time, people who are age X (4 years old, for example), are compared to those who are age Y (9 years old, for example). There is no direct evidence in such studies that in five years the 4-year-olds will respond the way the 9-year-olds do now, or that the 9-year-olds were similar to today's 4-year-olds five years ago. The developmental *process* must be inferred, and serious mistakes are possible. For many years, for example, people were taught that intelligence declined with age. But this belief was based on the results of intelligence tests given to people of different ages *at the same time*. The differences in scores were assumed to be related to age when they were probably due to economic and social change.[27]

interpreted by some, does not even allow for the view that such dramatic changes in age-related roles are possible.[29] While many people are aware of the fact that the treatment of children has varied tremendously from culture to culture and time period to time period, the faith in the superiority of our culture and science has permitted us to assume that only modern American and European societies have come to know and understand the "real" nature of the child, that only we have learned the "proper" adult/child roles.

During the nineteenth and early twentieth centuries, there was a symbiotic relationship between progressive social attitudes toward children and the "developmental approach" to thinking about and studying children's behavior. Many of the findings of developmental psychology supported the activities of the "child-savers," who were trying to create a completely separate social realm for children, and the social separability of children supported the findings of the developmental psychologists. The current merging of childhood and adulthood in our own time, however, demands some rethinking of the relationship between developmental research and behavioral conventions. And such rethinking has begun.

Noted Yale child psychologist William Kessen, for example, has recently warned his colleagues that their search for the "true nature" of the child may be futile. Kessen argues that the "child is essentially and eternally a cultural invention and that the variety of the child's definition is not the removable error of an incomplete science."[30]

Kessen does not detail any recent changes in childhood, but he attacks some of the basic assumptions that have dominated child psychology. While child psychology is noted for its diversity of methods, models, and approaches, Kessen suggests that child psychologists should look more closely at some of the beliefs they have tended to hold in common. Kessen argues that child psychology is itself a "peculiar cultural invention that moves with the tidal sweeps of the larger culture in ways that we understand at best dimly and often ignore."[31] Child psychology, he adds, has been influenced by the largely untested cultural assumptions and beliefs concerning the innocence of childhood, the centrality of home and mother, the importance of early experience, and the perfectibility of children and society. Child psychology has supported the cultural attitudes held at the time of the birth of the field, including the belief in the need to give the child special care, treatment, and protection.

Even child psychology's preferred "objective" laboratory method, argues Kessen, is based on an intersubjective cultural convention. The radical individualism of Americans has led American psychologists to see the individual child as the proper unit of analysis; the larger social context has been ignored. "Basically, we have observed those parts of development that the child could readily transport to our laboratories or to our testing sites." By isolating the child we have learned much, but with the "usual cost of uniform dogma" and "exaggerations and significant omissions."[32]

Looking at the other end of the age scale, gerontologist Bernice Neugarten has been speaking and writing about the concept of an "age-irrelevant society." After many years of studying the roles, behaviors, and needs of the elderly, Neugarten claims that "chronological age is becoming a poorer and poorer predictor of the way people live." She notes that the "whole internal clock I used to write about that kept us on time, the clock that tells us whether we're too young or too old to be marrying or going to school or getting a job or retiring, is no longer as powerful or as compelling as it used to be."[33]

After witnessing dramatic changes in age-related norms in her own lifetime, Neugarten has begun to study the ways in which societies "transform biological time into social time."[34] Neugarten's analysis suggests how the arbitrary age-distinctions in each society come to be seen as natural as they become intertwined with conventionalized rewards and punishments, divisions of labor, institutions, and other social systems.

It is interesting to note that at a time of rethinking of age-related roles, researchers have begun to find increasing evidence that infants and children possess certain skills earlier than was previously believed and that the elderly remain capable of certain behaviors longer than was once thought.[35] In reporting these findings, most researchers suggest that they are merely "correcting" previously "mistaken" findings. Some have argued, for example, that Jean Piaget may have underestimated children's cognitive abilities by using confusing instructions or by unintentionally testing linguistic rather than cognitive abilities.[36] It is also possible, however, that these studies are—at least to some extent—unwittingly measuring *historical* changes in age-related behavior and role conceptions.[37] That is, the newer studies may be documenting significant changes in the ways children and the elderly are encouraged and allowed to behave. The new research may be "historical" in another sense as well: For even if such studies reveal universal truths about the capabilities of children and the elderly, the findings may reflect new social attitudes among the *researchers*—who are now more open to looking for and seeing abilities where such abilities were once assumed to be absent.[38]

Recent changes in the social behavior of people of different ages and in some of the theoretical conceptions of development suggest that the degree to which we believe that age differences determine social conventions is itself a social convention. Just as many people now believe that past theories of the mental inferiority of blacks and women were shaped by social prejudices, so perhaps should we begin to question conceptions of traditional age-related roles.

We cannot, however, throw out the child with the bathwater of social conventions. For children's physiological and experiential reality is clearly different from adults'. A young child cannot be an adult no matter what "freedom" or liberties the child is given. In addition to physiological maturation, years of experience and social interaction are needed for development into a fully functioning member of society. Nevertheless, we need to distinguish between the biological existence of children and the social construction of "childhood." While children may always be children, conceptions of childhood are infinitely variable. The same is true of the distinctions between adults and "adulthood" and between the elderly and "old age." We can observe physiological development, and we can test the cognitive capabilities of people of different ages in specific places and times. It is much more difficult to discover the limits of individual differences in social development, the extent to which cultural factors can override or blur "actual" differences, or the degree to which observable psychological differences among people of different ages necessarily determine particular social roles. We can observe children and adults, but we do not know where the ultimate dividing lines within childhood and between childhood and adulthood lie. And it is unlikely that these mysteries will ever be solved. As the newly emerging discipline—the Sociology of Age—suggests, there is no "'pure' process of aging."

> The ways in which children enter kindergarten, or adolescents move into adulthood, or older people retire are not preordained. . . . The life course is not fixed, but widely flexible. It varies with social change—not only with the changing nature of the family, the school, the workplace, the community, but also with changing ideas, values, and beliefs. As each new generation (or cohort) enters the stream of history, the lives of its members are marked by the imprint of social change and in turn leave their own imprint.[39]

One significant aspect of social change is a shift in media environments. Many studies have examined the effects of media messages on people at different stages of socialization, yet very few have examined how changes in media may affect the structure of the socialization process itself. One way to do this is to look beyond specific messages and examine how different media may create different "situational geographies" for the worlds of childhood and adulthood.

Television and Child Integration

As described in earlier chapters, distinctions in social status are supported, in part, by separating people into different informational worlds. The movement from one social status to another generally involves learning the "secrets" of the new status and going to the places or situations where that information is available.

Each step in the socialization process from childhood to adulthood involves exposure to some new information and continued restriction from other social information. Traditionally, for example, we tell third graders things we keep hidden from second graders, and we continue to keep hidden to third graders things we will tell them when they become fourth graders. Children are walked up the ladder of adult information, but slowly and in stages. A child's cognitive development helps in the climb, but it is not the only factor that affects children's learning or social status. Another significant variable is the amount and type of information made available to children of different ages. If a society is able to divide what people of different ages know into many small steps, it will be able to establish many stages or levels of childhood. Conversely, if a society does not have sharp divisions in what people of different ages know, there will be fewer stages of socialization into adulthood. If we always taught second, third, and fourth graders in the same classroom, for example, we would have a very difficult time clearly dividing them into three different social statuses.

This perspective suggests that traditional notions of childhood "innocence" may have been related to children's exclusion from the social situations, or information-systems, of adults; and, conversely, that adults' seeming "omniscience" in the eyes of children may have been related to the extent to which adults were able to keep secrets from children and maintain a private "backstage" area to rehearse their "onstage" roles, hide their fears, doubts, anxieties, and childish behaviors, and "privately" discuss techniques for handling children. When the distinctions in information-systems for people of different ages become blurred, however, we would expect a blurring in the differences between child and adult behavior.

Implicit in many popular and scholarly analyses of television is the assumption that the effects of the medium on children are shaped primarily by the extent to which parents monitor their children's viewing and broadcasters regulate their programming. Those who perceive negative effects often see the blame resting with overly permissive parents who do not control what their children watch and with greedy broadcasters who are unwilling to provide quality children's programming.[40]

What this common perspective misses, however, is that television is not a passive conveyor of information, equivalent to, or interchangeable with earlier channels of communication, such as books. While explicit controls over content and access obviously have effects, they have different effects in different media. Other things being equal, print has a tendency to segregate children and adults while television has a tendency to reintegrate them.

By focusing below on the potential effects of a shift from "book situations" to "television situations," I do not mean to obliterate other explanations for recent changes in socialization or to dismiss the many factors that work to maintain traditional distinctions between childhood and adulthood. Certainly, the growing instability of marriages, economic issues, and many other variables contribute to recent changes; conversely, family traditions, religious beliefs, schooling, social class, and place of residence mute and channel many of the pressures toward merging age-related roles. I merely hope to show that changes in media may have much more to do with overall trends in conceptions of childhood and adulthood than might otherwise be assumed.

At Home in Television Land

What a young child knew about the world was once determined primarily by where the child lived and was allowed to go. Access to the larger society came slowly with increasing literacy and freedom to travel. Reading offered informational access to the world; travel offered complementary physical access.

The family home is often portrayed as a "protective" and "nurturing" environment. In modern urban societies, however, the home has also functioned as a de facto isolation chamber. For this reason, the early feminist writer, Charlotte Perkins Gilman, attacked the home as a prison that restricted both children and women from the outside world.[41]

Even those who support the traditional function of the home recognize its restrictive features. In *The Sociology of Childhood*, for example, Oscar Ritchie and Marvin Koller note that the home is the child's "small world" and that the "family serves as a screen to the culture of its society and selects only those portions that it deems worthy of attention."[42] The young child may make special trips outside the home—to visit grandma, for example—but the child's life is centered in home and family. Although the child is not completely isolated from information about the outside world, this information is generally filtered through parents and other adults who are allowed to leave the home freely.

Because of the child's limited knowledge and experience, Ritchie and Koller observe, visitors often become a center of interest and fascination. "As a person who lives outside the child's home, the guest functions as a transmitter, bringing into the world of the child new ideas and information, and new and different opportunities for vicarious participation in the outside world."[43]

The metaphor for a guest chosen by Ritchie and Koller is interesting and significant; in fact, it reveals a weakness in their own description of the role of the family and home in socialization. Writing in 1964, Ritchie and Koller should have realized that, in over 90% of American households, the restrictive environment they describe had already been transformed by a new and powerful "transmitter"—television.

Ritchie and Koller note that "largely because parents control the situation, the child-guest relationship is likely to be a positive aspect of socialization."[44] Yet while the traditional family guest is invited, remains under family control, and acts as an adult filter on child information, the guests who come through the television set are often uninvited visitors who broaden the child's informational world without parents' full approval or control.

The impact of television on the redefinition of "home" is all but lost in the dominant, message-oriented approach to the study of television. The focus on content rather than on situational structure has obscured the ways in which television bypasses the filters of adult authority and decreases the significance of the child's physical isolation in the home. In one sense, it makes little difference whether television programs reinforce the message that "adults always know best" or the message that "adults don't always know best," or whether a commercial tells children to buy a product themselves or to ask their parents to purchase it for them. For regardless of the specific messages in programs and advertising, the pattern of information flow into the home has changed.

Certainly, today's parents still control much of the atmosphere of the family home, yet home life is no longer the base of all a child's experiences. Children who have television sets now have outside perspectives from which to judge and evaluate family rituals, beliefs, and religious practices. Parents could once easily mold their young children's upbringing by speaking and reading to children only about those things they wished their children to be exposed to, but today's parents must battle with thousands of competing images and ideas over which they have little direct control. As a result, the power relationships within the family are partially rearranged. The influence of parents and family life continues to be seen: Children still differ markedly by class, religion, and ethnic background. But the family is no longer an all-powerful formative influence.

Unable to read, very young children were once limited to the few sources of information available to them within or around the home: paintings, illustrations, views from a window, and what adults said and read to them. Television, however, now escorts children across the globe even before they have permission to cross the street.

There's No Such Thing as "Children's Television"

The complexity of print's code excludes all young children from communication in print. In a sense, print creates "places" where adults can communicate among themselves without being overheard by children. Through books, adults can freely discuss things that they may wish to keep hidden from very young children. Further, because reading involves a complex skill that is learned in stages, adults can control the information given to older children by varying the complexity of the code in which books on various subjects are written. Because children must read simple children's books before reading complex adult books, print allows for the separation of children of different ages into different informational worlds.*

*There is, of course, nothing inherent in print that *demands* that adults use books to shield children from certain information. It is possible, for example, to revise children's books and substitute sentences such as "See Mrs. Smith feed the children milk and cookies" with "See Mrs. Smith go to bed with the milkman." Yet print *allows* adults to control what and how much children of different ages know about adult situations. General observation of social behavior suggests that when people *can* control access to private behaviors, they usually do

The varying complexity of the code in print not only serves to isolate children from adult situations, but it also works to isolate adults from children's situations. Children, for example, can be shielded from "adult" topics such as sex, crime, and death simply by encoding this information in long, difficult words and complexly written sentences. At the same time, however, the simplicity of most children's books makes them uninteresting for adults, and many adults would be embarrassed to be seen reading them. (Indeed, finding appropriate reading material is one of the major difficulties of teaching illiterate adults to read.) Children usually do not know what adults are reading, and adults (unless they are school teachers or parents who read books aloud to children) do not usually know what children are reading. With print, society tends to be divided into many different information-systems based on differences in the mastery of reading skills.

"Children's books" are special, then, for two significant reasons: They are the only type of books children can read, and generally only children read them. In this sense, children's literature is a kind of informational ghetto, both isolated and isolating.

There is no situational equivalent to a children's book on television. Television has no complex access code to exclude young viewers or to divide its audience into different ages groups. Adult programs may present children with information they do not fully understand, and children's programs may contain childish content, but the basic code in which all programs are presented is similar for every television show: pictures and sounds. Unlike print, television's symbolic form resembles the things it represents. Television pictures—like all pictures—look like real objects and people; television speaks in a human voice.

In contrast to books, television programs have few, if any, "prerequisites." There is no set order in which programs must be viewed because most programs require the same degree (or lack) of skill. One does not have to watch "Romper Room" before watching "Sesame Street"; one does not have to watch "The Muppet Show" before watching "Dallas." With television, there is no filter to shield children from exposure to adult programs, and there is no simplistic visual style to bore or embarrass adults when they watch children's programs. It is no surprise, therefore, that people of all ages tend to watch many of the same programs. While the world of children's books can be insulated to present children with an idealized view of life, television news and entertainment present young children with images of adults who lie, drink, cheat, and murder.

The nature of the medium, of course, is not the only determinant of what people learn from television. *Exposure* to information is not the same

---

so. If we know company is coming, we straighten up the house. If we have a family argument, we don't usually share it with the neighbors, unless they overhear it. If a political or personal scandal can be kept hidden, it usually is kept hidden. Thus, the situational characteristics of a new medium may interact with general rules of social behavior but also change the nature of social interaction.

as perception and integration of information. Attitudes and beliefs, experience, education, cultural and religious training, and intelligence all mediate an individual's perception of information. For a child, a very significant filter is the child's level of cognitive development. Jean Piaget's major contribution to the study of children has been to demonstrate that children's thinking is not simply "worse" than adults', but that it is structurally different. Piaget has identified a number of distinct stages and substages of cognitive development.

In exploring the relationship between cognitive stages and media comprehension, researchers have found that children of different ages generally perceive different things when they watch television. Very young children have difficulty following plots and distinguishing central events from peripheral ones. Young children also have difficulty sorting motives from consequences, causes from effects, and fantasy from reality.[45] Children, research suggests, must reach the age of eleven or twelve before their comprehension of television closely resembles the understanding of adults. In this sense, television's ability to integrate children into adult situations may be greatest after the age of eleven (still many years before they traditionally receive the status of "adults").

What the studies of children's comprehension of television have generally overlooked, however, is the net difference in the effects of *different media* on what children of all ages know about the social behavior of adults. Virtually no studies have been done comparing "oral cultures," "book cultures," and "television cultures" in terms of children's varying knowledge of adulthood or the resulting changes in conceptions of age-related roles. While children's television viewing may be most like adults' television viewing after the age of eleven, the net difference between access to information through books and through television may be greatest at earlier ages.*

Television may not be able to override the outside limits of a child's cognitive abilities, but unlike print, television does not superimpose another extremely difficult decoding task on top of the child's cognitive processing of information. Watching television and reading books are not equivalent cognitive tasks. (If we could find a seven-year-old child who

---

*A question that arises, for example, is whether full and immediate understanding is necessary for an experience to have a long-term effect on behavior and status. When a person first moves to a new place such as a large city, the first few trips to the downtown area may be remembered as a disconnected series of specific buildings, landmarks, or intersections. It may take several months, or even years, before the person can put all the elements in perspective, understand how some events are linked to others (number of police officers and time of day, for example), and distinguish peripheral events from central ones (a noon-time siren from an air-raid siren, for example). Yet would it therefore be meaningful to say that the first few downtown trips "had no effect" on the person because they did not "understand" what they saw? Clearly, the final comprehension is built on the previous experiences and partial understandings. In the same way, the long-term impact of children's exposure to a new and strange world via television may not be measurable through standard tests of comprehension.

had never watched television nor read a book, and if we exposed that child to both media for one month and then compared him or her to average seven-year-old book readers and television watchers, it is likely that he or she would be much more "normal" in television viewing skills than in reading skills.) Thus, while children under the age of eleven or twelve may not fully understand television in an adult sense, they still find television accessible and absorbing. Children between the ages of two and five spend very little time staring at words and sentences in a book, but over the last few years, they have spent an average of between 25 and 32 hours a week watching television.[46]

The study of cognitive stages and the study of media environments are two important, yet separate issues. Just as one can observe cognitive differences among children of different ages regardless of the environment, so can one observe the effects of different media environments regardless of the cognitive stages of the viewers. (Ideally, these two approaches will be integrated in the future.)

It is even possible that some of the apparent discrepancies between Piaget's original findings and many of the more recent discoveries of children's enhanced cognitive and social abilities are related in some way to television. Television, after all, provides children with a rich spectrum of novel stimuli and "social experience" and may thereby facilitate cognitive and social development.[47] Indeed, preschool children are now "smarter" by standardized measurements of intelligence than they were fifty years ago, and the differences have been attributed, in part, to television.[48] Yet even assuming that cognitive development is not affected at all by changing media environments, it is still meaningful to ask how children's social knowledge and status may be affected by their sudden exposure to a whole new set of information for them to process through their childlike perceptions.

While many child comprehension studies have highlighted what children do not fully understand, they have overlooked the significance of children grappling to understand issues that were once largely hidden from them. Three-year-old television viewers, for example, may not be able to explain why people in a program have been shot, and the child viewers may not be able to tell whether the action is real or fictional, but through television, three-year-olds are nevertheless exposed to people being shot and to other "adult" issues.*

---

*No studies that I know of suggest that children over the age of three cannot make *any* sense of the information they are exposed to on television. Indeed, some studies using nonverbal rather than linguistic tests suggest the possibility of surprisingly sophisticated understanding on the part of very young children. In one study, it was found that most preschoolers could correctly discriminate between program segments and commercials, even though they could not explain the difference verbally.[49] In another research project, 75% of the 2- to 3-year-olds studied passed a test that suggested that they understood the intent of commercials. (They identified a picture that showed someone selecting the product for purchase in a store.)[50]

What is revolutionary about television is not that it necessarily gives children "adult minds," but that it allows the very young child to be "present" at adult interactions. Television removes barriers that once divided people of different ages and reading abilities into different social situations. The widespread use of television is equivalent to a broad social decision to allow young children to be present at wars and funerals, court-ships and seductions, criminal plots and cocktail parties. Young children may not fully understand the issues of sex, death, crime, and money that are presented to them on television. Or, put differently, they may understand these issues only in childlike ways. Yet television nevertheless exposes them to many topics and behaviors that adults have spent several centuries trying to keep hidden from children. Television thrusts children into a complex adult world, and it provides the impetus for children to ask the meanings of actions and words they would not yet have heard or read about without television.

Not only are most children *able* to watch adult programs, but from the very beginning of the television era, children have *preferred* adult programming. As television began to invade the American home, teachers, parents, and researchers were surprised to note that children seemed to like opera and televised Broadway plays. Helen Parkhurst, educator and founder of the Dalton School, offered one possible explanation. "What they're really curious about is not the theatre but the grown-up world as seen in the theatre. . . . Actually, our children are among but not with adults. They want to be with, not among."[51]

A rigorous and detailed study in England in the 1950s revealed similar preferences among children for any program that exposed aspects of the adult world. Tallying children's preferences, Hilde Himmelweit and her colleagues observed that "three-quarters of the votes for the most favoured programme went to adult programmes. . . . Other types of pro-gramme—such as puppets, nature, and animal programmes, and how-to-make programmes—were not especially popular."[52] Himmelweit's anal-ysis of television's appeal to children echoes Parkhurst's analysis and sug-gests a reason for children's preference for "adult programs": Television provides children with the "satisfaction of being in the know, of going behind the scenes and of learning about the world and about people."[53]

More recent studies reveal exactly the same pattern. Children prefer programs aimed at adults to those aimed at children. According to one set of researchers, even the best available children's program cannot compete with adult programs for the child's interest.[54] Another recent study con-cludes that creating special "family viewing" times in the early evening would not work because most children stay up to watch the more "mature" programs shown later in the evening.[55] It has been estimated that five to six million children under twelve are watching television at 11 P.M., and that two million children are still watching television at midnight.[56]

It is evidence of the tenacity of wishful thinking, therefore, that many parents continue to demand more "children's programming" on television or look forward to the more age-specific programming of cable, direct satellite-to-home broadcasts, and video discs. Simply creating television programs that contain the *content* traditionally thought suitable for children will not create a separate information-system equivalent to the isolated world of children's literature. There may be children's books and adult books, yet there is no children's television and adult television. In terms of what people can and do watch, there is simply "television.".

From the Mouths of Babes

Electronic media not only give children more direct access to adult information, they also provide children with new opportunities to send messages and to see and hear other children. Because very few children are capable of writing books, books generally present an adult view of children. But the lack of skill required to send a message via telephone, radio, and television often allows children to speak for themselves.

Books on divorce, for example, often describe problems faced by the children of divorced couples. On television, however, children of divorced parents are often interviewed directly. And among those watching are many children. Although children cannot participate directly in the public printed discussion of divorce, television and radio permit children to speak to adults and other children about such issues.

In 1982, The American Psychiatric Association published a report on the psychosocial aspects of nuclear technology that included a study of children's fears of nuclear disaster,[57] While the study was *written* by and for adults, a "20/20" television program on the same issue (ABC, June 10, 1982) not only interviewed the two psychiatrists who conducted the study but also interviewed children on their feelings. In addition, the program included videotapes of all-children discussion groups on nuclear disaster (groups that were organized by the children themselves) and of young children reading poetry they had written on nuclear war. Unlike print, then, electronic media not only make children aware of pressing social issues, they also include children in the general social dialogue concerning those issues.

Similarly, most of the people reading this chapter are adults. In October 1982, however, I was interviewed on this same topic by Steve Hart on his National Public Radio call-in program, "Audio Jam Live." The program is designed for children, and all the people who called to ask me questions were between the ages of ten and twelve. With electronic media—as one ABC television program proclaims in its title—"Kids are People Too."

The vast difference between the coding variables of print and television are highlighted by the organizational structure of one of America's smaller television stations, Channel 4 in Sun Prairie, Wisconsin. The station has a staff of forty people who serve as camera operators, directors, and on-air personalities. A dozen people serve as a program committee to determine what is to be broadcast. So far, nothing sounds unusual about this station. But the forty staff members are all children, aged nine to fourteen, and they run the small cable television station with minimal adult input.[58] And many of their viewers are, of course, adults.

Electronic media affect not only today's children; they also reshape future generations' perceptions of childhood. Reflecting on the history of childhood, Mary McLaughlin notes that the "realities of early life must remain a largely hidden world, accessible to us only partially and indirectly, through the recollections, portrayals and fantasies of those who were no longer children."[59] Often adults failed to record anything about childhood at all. In his study of pre-industrial English society, Peter Laslett notes that the "crowds and crowds of little children are strangely absent from the written record." Laslett suggests that there is "something mysterious about the silence of all these multitudes of babes in arms, toddlers and adolescents in the statements men made at the time about their own experience," and he despairs of ever discovering the details of pre-industrial child nurture.[60] Similarly, historian James Ross notes that "no voices of children reach us directly." Instead, we "hear them, faintly and imperfectly to be sure, through the media of those who controlled their lives or observed their development."[61] Now, however, electronic media permit children to speak directly to the future.

It is no coincidence, perhaps, that the history of childhood has developed as a distinct field of inquiry only in the last few decades. Television's unique ability to project, record, and preserve the speech and behavior of children may have made us suddenly aware of the vacuum in our understanding of children in the past.

The Television Doorway

Many of the physical characteristics of books serve as filters for the information made accessible to children. Each book is a distinct object that a child must acquire individually. If the book is not given to the child by a parent, the child must leave the house and borrow or buy it—usually from an adult. Special library cards are given to children so that they cannot borrow adult books, and adult books are often placed on shelves beyond the child's reach. Additionally, children have little knowledge of what books are available or where to get them.

The fact that children rarely have direct access to, or choice over books was made painfully clear to Margaret Mead and Martha Wolfenstein in an ill-fated 1950s project to create a new type of literature for children. They planned to write a modern style of children's book that would fulfill children's psychological needs and perhaps offset problems such as sibling rivalry.

Mead and Wolfenstein found that the books that most satisfied children were completely unacceptable to their parents. Mothers objected, for example, "to any indication that pregnant women were ever tired and cross, and they wanted more emphasis on what the mother could do to get the child to prepare for the baby." After several attempts at revision, Mead and Wolfenstein found that they could not come up with stories that met the needs of both children and adults. "As we tried the story out at these various levels, it became increasingly clear that, after all, five-year-old children don't buy books and that the children's needs or preferences had to be mediated by layers of other people—mothers, fathers, grandmothers, aunts, librarians, publishers, bookstore buyers, experts."[62] The project failed.

As individual objects, books can be selectively chosen and selectively given to children. But television content is much more difficult to control. Once the child has access to *a* television, the child has direct access to everything that comes through it. The child does not have to go anywhere special to find a television program, or necessarily ask any adult to see it. While the reading code and physical characteristics of books provide "automatic" constraints that require minimal parental intervention, censorship of children's television viewing involves active and constant monitoring. With television, therefore, the important decision is whether to have a television or not have one, whether to expose children to almost *all* of television's offerings or *none* of them.

Further, because the child has not brought the specific program into the house, there is little guilt of association with a television program. For a child to buy a cheap novel or a "dirty" book and bring it into the house is to associate with its content; to watch a cheap or "dirty" television show is merely to view innocently what has been piped into the home (and what must be, from the child's perspective, implicitly sanctioned by the parents who provide the television set and by the larger society that presents itself through this medium).

A child's book is, in a sense, a "guest" in the house. It makes a "social entrance," that is, it comes through the door and remains under at least nominal parental authority. As a physical object it must be stored somewhere in the house and it can be discarded. The child's television set, in contrast, is like a new doorway to the home. Through it come many welcome and unwelcome visitors: schoolteachers, Presidents, salesmen, police officers, prostitutes, murderers, friends, and strangers.

Those parents who tackle the monumental task of censoring their children's television viewing are faced with at least two significant dilemmas. First, controlling television viewing involves a conflict of values: protecting children vs. allowing them to learn as much as they can. Parents once had to *encourage* children to read and learn. A good deal of the protection from adult information in books was taken care of automatically by the inherent features of print. Now parents find themselves in the uncomfortable position of actively *intervening* in the "learning process" of their youngsters. Parents must now try to evaluate the content of television and decide (often on the spot) whether their children can "handle it."

Second, it is difficult for parents to control their children's viewing of television without limiting their own viewing as well. While a child has very limited access to the content of the books and newspapers being read by adults in the same room, a television program being watched by adults is accessible to any child in the same space. Many children are exposed to adult news, for example, because their parents watch the news during dinner.* To control children's television viewing, therefore, parents must either limit their own viewing or physically divide the family. The situation is further complicated when there are several children of different ages in the household. The unique characteristics of books make it possible for adults to enforce the implicit rule, "Read what we want you to read about, not what we read about," but television offers little support for the admonition, "Watch what we want you to watch, not what we watch."

With book reading, a family can stay together in a single room and yet be divided into different informational worlds. In multiple-set television households, children and adults can be in different rooms and still be united into a single informational arena.

Exposing the "Secret of Secrecy"

In printed communication, it is common to have books for parents that discuss what books are suitable for children. This book-about-books is an adult-adult interaction in which young children cannot participate. Further, children do not usually even know about the existence of this type of book.

With the help of such private adult "discussions," children were once shielded from certain topics such as sex, money, death, crime, and drugs. Even more significant, however, children were shielded from the fact that they were being shielded. Print allowed for an "adult conspiracy." In terms of knowledge and awareness, the child was in a position of someone hypnotized to forget something and also hypnotized to forget the hypnosis.

The same thing does not apply to television. Television, it is true, often offers parents advice. Talk shows discuss children's television, and warnings are placed at the beginning of programs to let parents know that a program may contain material "unsuitable for pre-teenagers." Yet while the manifest content is similar to the content of parents' advice books, the structure of the communication situation is radically different. Television

---

*One study found that about 30% of kindergarten through fifth graders claimed they watched a national news program "almost every day."[63] A British study discovered that although many children expressed little explicit interest in television news and appeared not to be paying much attention to it, about half of the children studied were able to mention items on the news, including crises, fires, accidents, and bombings in Northern Ireland.[64]

discussions and warnings are as accessible to children as they are to adults. Ironically, such advice on television often cues children to which programs they are not supposed to see and increases children's interest in what follows. Even if such warnings are heard by parents, and even if parents act to censor the program, parental control is nevertheless weakened because the control becomes overt and therefore often unpalatable to both children and adults. For these reasons, perhaps, studies over several decades have found that parents exercise suprisingly little control over what children watch on television.[65]

Through books, adults could keep secrets from children, and they could also keep their secret-keeping secret. Television, in contrast, exposes many adult secrets to children and also reveals the "secret of secrecy." And while today's parental advice books remain private adult-adult interactions, the secrets they contain (and comprise) are exposed daily on television.

The importance of the "secret of secrecy" in adult-child interaction is implicit in many traditional advice books to parents. Parents were told, for example, to beware of the "secret smile" during a scolding that would reveal that they were, in part, amused by a child's misbehavior. Such a smile, parents were warned, would undermine the attempt to discipline the child.[66] Similarly, one nineteenth century minister warned:

> A nurse cannot be too guarded in what she says or does in the presence of children, nor must she fancy that they are always infants, or less alive than herself, to what passes before them. At the same time, the *precautions taken should be perceived as little as possible, for she will defeat her end, if she excite curiosity, by giving them the idea that there is something to be concealed.*[67]

In general, it is very difficult for most people to keep a secret once the existence of the secret is revealed. Claims that "I'm not supposed to tell you" or "It's a secret" generally lead to the demand for revelation. The knowledge that a secret exists is half of the secret. This principle was expressed by Norbert Wiener in relation to America's "mistake" concerning the atomic bomb. "It is perfectly fair to say that the one secret concerning the atomic bomb which might have been kept and which was given to the public and to all potential enemies without the least inhibition, was that of the possibility of its construction."[68] Wiener claims that once scientists in other countries knew that the atomic bomb was a possibility, they were already a long way to the solution themselves. In the same manner, once television provides children with the certain knowledge of the existence of adult secrets concerning children, complete and immediate comprehension of adult behavior is of secondary importance. It is not necessary for television to reveal all the secrets of adults; children already know a great deal about traditional adult roles just by knowing for certain that adults consciously conspire to hide things from children. Ironically, television may have its greatest effect on children's knowledge and behavior when adults use television forums (such as talk shows) to discuss how to control television's effects on children.

Contrary to many claims, therefore, children's access to adult information through television is not simply the result of a lapse in parental authority and responsibility. Print provides many filters and controls that television does not share. No matter what parents do in a television home, short of removing the television set altogether, the old information environment cannot be fully reinstated. (And even if the set is removed from one child's home, there remain many other sets in the homes of friends and relatives.)

Parents may be left somewhat helpless in the face of television, but surely regulation of what broadcasters are allowed to show on television will have a tremendous impact on what children know and learn. If, for example, only conservative programs such as "Little House on the Prairie" or "Leave It to Beaver" are permitted, and shows such as "One Day at a Time," "Different Strokes," and "Silver Spoons" are banned, won't children be provided only with the information traditionally given to them in books? Not necessarily.

Certainly, different programs have different effects. But the difference in impact is not as great or as simple as is generally assumed. Early television shows such as "Leave It to Beaver" are, in manifest content, much more conservative than more recent programs such as "One Day at a Time," but the two types of programs are, in one sense, very similar: They both reveal to children the existence of adult weaknesses and doubts.

As suggested in Chapter 9, even traditional, conservative programs reveal to children important secrets about the *structure* of adult roles. In "Father Knows Best" or "Leave It to Beaver," for example, parents are shown behaving one way in front of their children and another way when they are alone. The parents are shown as cool and rational with their children, but when they are by themselves, they display doubts and anxieties, and they agonize over "what to do with the kids."

Children's books of the past generally presented only an "onstage" image of adulthood, but even conservative television programs tend to reveal a backstage or "sidestage" view of adulthood. Child viewers see adults behaving one way when they are among adults and another way when they are with children. They see parents moving from the backstage to the onstage area. This view is very damaging to the traditional adult role.

In one episode of "Father Knows Best" ("Margaret Learns to Drive," NBC, November 20, 1957), for example, the three children keep quizzing their parents on their relationship. They wonder if their parents ever fight. After all, they have never seen any evidence of fighting. But when their mother, Margaret, asks their father, Jim, to teach her to drive a car, the wheels are set in motion for the revelation of a backstage argument to the children. Margaret and Jim have an argument on their first drive, but they are still composed enough to say "Let's look a bit happier before we face the kids," and they enter the house pretending that nothing unusual has happened. By the end of the program, however, the driving lessons have continued to go badly, and Jim and Margaret find themselves yelling at each other in the middle of the living room. Unknown to them, their three children have partially descended the staircase and are leaning against the banister (in size places, of course). The children witness the first argument between their parents they have ever seen. When Margaret and Jim turn and see the children, there is a moment of stunned silence. But the children begin to applaud, saying "great show," "good performance." The children declare (ask): "You were just pretending to fight for our benefit, right?" After a moment's hesitation, Jim and Margaret "admit" that, yes, they were just pretending to be fighting. Everyone laughs, and the show ends.

Thus, while the child *portrayed* on traditional television shows may be innocent and sheltered, the child *watching* the programs sees both the hidden behavior and the process of sheltering it from children. "Father Knows Best," for example, exposes child viewers to the ways in which a father and mother manipulate their behavior to make it appear to their children that they "know best." The behavior in the revealed adult backstage may be idealized, but from a social dynamics perspective, the particular *content* of the backstage behavior portrayed is less significant than the revelation of the *existence* of the backstage itself. If nothing else, children are shown through television programs that adults "play roles" for children. This is a dramatic discovery (in both senses). Children old enough to understand basic deception learn that the behavior adults exhibit before them is not necessarily their "real" or only behavior.

As a result of such views of adulthood, children may become suspicious of adults and more unwilling to accept all that adults do or say at face value. Conversely, adults may feel "exposed" by television and, in the long run, it may no longer seem to make as much sense to try to keep certain things hidden from children. Indeed, traditional "adulthood" was not something that simply developed as people grew older, it was a behavioral style that was supported, in part, by a large backstage area. Adults have always behaved in childlike ways in certain situations, for example, but rarely in front of children. As television blurs the dividing line between adults' backstage behaviors and their onstage roles, many childlike behaviors emerge into the new, public adult role. Television's exposure of the "staging of adulthood"—with its secret-keeping and the secret of secrecy—undermines both traditional childhood naiveté *and* the all-knowing, confident adult role and fosters the movement toward a "middle region," uni-age behavioral style.

Of course, by living with parents, children of a pre-television era must have witnessed many backstage adult behaviors. But before television, young children had a much narrower perspective from which to view, judge, and understand the behaviors they witnessed. As many autobiographies reveal, children often took their parents' behaviors for granted until some new experience with other grownups from outside the home gave them new insight into the world of adults. In a 1946 study of the role of the family guest as revealed in autobiographies, James Bossard and Eleanor Boll suggest that one of the key functions of the guest was to reveal to children inconsistencies in adult behaviors. "Children often have the opportunity to observe in the privacy of the family circle that parents do not always practice what they preach. But the social gathering together of adults can increase the opportunity for such observations, when those adults are being companionable or convivial, and forgetful of the penetrating scrutiny of the younger generation"[69]*

Other unusual circumstances might also lead to children being confronted for the first time with the backstage of adult life. Such a situation is recorded in Anne Frank's World War II diary. While hiding from the Nazis, Anne was thrust into a confined and not very private space with her parents, sister, and another family. The adults could no longer hide many of their backstage behaviors. One of Anne's greatest shocks concerned the poor behavior exhibited by the adults. She wrote: "Why do grownups quarrel so easily, so much, and over the most idiotic things? Up till now I thought that only children squabbled and that that wore off as you grew up."[70] Anne's image and awe of adults was shattered. Yet Anne had discovered only what the child viewer of "Margaret Learns to Drive" discovers: that parents argue and that they try to hide their stupidities and weaknesses from their children.

The praise of old television programs such as "Leave It to Beaver" is based on the simplistic assumption that children's primary response to television is to imitate the behaviors they see. What is generally overlooked is the possibility that television provides information that is used by children to help them understand and evaluate the social performances of adults. Thus, while the manifest content of some television programs may be conservative (parents are always right, crooks always get caught, and everything always ends happily), the latent revelation of the structure of adult roles may actually lead to the undermining of these same behaviors in real life. Even seemingly conservative programs may weaken traditional adult/child roles by revealing adult secrets and the secret of secrecy.

This analysis offers a new interpretation of the seemingly "radical" content of many of the television programs of the 1970s and 1980s. One major difference is that the parents portrayed in these programs often have no private backstage areas at all. The mother in "One Day at a

---

*As with Ritchie and Koller's description of the "transmitter" role of the guest, most of the guest's functions noted by Bossard and Boll have also been co-opted by television: an outside standard by which to judge parents' behaviors, a measure of the family's relative status, an increase in the child's awareness of social beliefs and customs, a source for learning rules of social behavior, a change in family activities that leads to special privileges for children, an intellectual stimulus for children, a source of family conflicts and tensions, and a source of anecdotes and "cue-words" that are integrated into the family's "heritage."

Time" and the father in "Silver Spoons," for example, are confused, angry, and anxious *in front* of their children. Although many people are upset by this portrayal of adults, the newer television images of adults give *real* children relatively little more access to adult secrets than the old images did. The major change is in the *fictional* child characters, who now appear less innocent. The new portrayal of adult-child interactions on television, though often condemned, may represent an adjustment in manifest content to match patterns of access to social information already established by earlier television programs.*

The Close-Up Medium: Beyond Movies and Radio

If television has an effect on child-adult interaction because it bypasses the filters of print, then the process must have begun with earlier media, such as the movies and radio. Yet, while film and radio no doubt had some preliminary homogenizing effects, neither medium has all of television's relevant characteristics.

Movies have an audio/visual code similar to television's, but they differ markedly from television in their physical characteristics and conditions of attendance. To view a movie, for example, a child has to *go* somewhere special. Children must ask an adult to allow them to go to the movies (or to take them) and adults serve as gatekeepers at movie theater entrances. These restrictions preclude frequent viewing by very young children, who are able to watch many hours of television each week. Even older children at the height of the motion picture era never attended the movies for as many hours a week as young children now watch television. In the 1930s, the Payne Fund's extensive study of movies found that most American children attended motion pictures "regularly," yet "regularly" meant an average of under two movies per month for five- to eight-year-olds and one movie per week for children nine to nineteen.[71]

With movies, a child must select, travel to, and pay for admission to an *individual* movie. This selection process is very different from the often random, flip-of-the-dial television viewing that provides children with information they have not sought. Further, in some ways, children at movie theaters are more subject to adult authority than children watching

---

*Of course, adults could choose to present on television only those programs that contain information available in traditional children's books. This analysis, therefore, may continue to appear to be a traditional discussion of television *content*, rather than information-system structure. Yet such a view overlooks the situational differences between television and books. The point here is that if one censors children's television, one also censors adults' television. Unlike a book, a television program cannot be directed only to a particular age group. Adults must either abandon television to their youngest children or share most of their programs with children of all ages. The decision of what to do with television, then, parallels the speech and behavioral decisions of a large family that lives in one room: To control what a child of one age experiences is also to control the experience of the other children and adults, and almost any information suitable for older children and adults exposes young children to "adult secrets."

television at home. As television critic Robert Lewis Shayon observed in the early 1950s, "At home, the figures of the usher, or the movie nurse, stern symbols of the adult, authoritarian world, do not loom above the TV screen."[72]

Because adults take their mobility for granted, they may be less aware of such differences between movies and television than children are. As one young girl told interviewers in an early study:

> If I had to choose one, it would be television because many times before I got it, I would say, "Mommy, can't we go to the movies today? And the answer usually was, "No, the weather's too bad." Or, "No, I have to go shopping." But now that we have television, on the rainiest of days, who wants to go to the movies, when I can watch a cowboy film? Another thing, at night I have an excuse for staying up late. "Just let me see the end of this film." Well, just this once," says my mother every night. If I didn't have television, do you think I could find something to do every night?[73]

Television is also more intimate than the movies. Its presence in the home brings it close to the hub of family activity. Often it is the hub. Many families gather around the television set as families of an earlier era gathered around the hearth. Most television viewers, including children, do other things while the television is on,[74] so television merges into everyday life in a manner quite distinct from the adventure of movie-going.

Television's content often matches its unique conditions of attendance. The serialization of fictional families' lives in sitcoms and soaps, for example, mimics the passing of real "family time." Television characters become part of a household's extended family as viewers follow their activities in episodes that parallel the weeks and "episodes" of real life.[75] And the same newscasters and talk and quiz show hosts join the family every day to tell tales and to entertain.

In addition, television's small screen and low quality image demand extensive use of close-ups in television programs. Television acting, therefore, is even more subdued than movie acting (for the same reasons that movie acting is more subdued than stage acting). Wide landscape shots, vistas, and panoramas are difficult to see clearly on television. The grand sweeping action of epics is more suited to the movies than to the tiny screen. Television's subject matter, therefore, tends to be more intimate, personal, and "ordinary"—in other words, more exposing of the cracks in the facade of the traditional image of adulthood.

Radio is also similar to television in some ways, but very different in others. Radio is similar to television in that it can be experienced without leaving the home. In this sense, radio, like television, is a new doorway to the house. Yet radio's code is wholly aural and verbal; it has no pictures. Young children are not as good at decoding aural information as they are at decoding visual information.[76] And even when children are old enough to understand the words on radio, radio does not necessarily provide children with the same information given to adults. Because radio has no pictures, the radio listener must create his or her own images based on *past experience*. This obviously puts the inexperienced child at a severe disadvantage. If a child has never seen a murder or a seduction, radio would not "fill in the picture" for the child. Children in a pre-television age who listened to radio dramas no doubt learned many adult secrets, but compared to television, radio had little power to fully "expose" the hidden aspects of adult life.

Radio permits much more shielding of the backstage area of adults than television does. Considering how intimate and personal radio messages feel, they convey surprisingly little backstage information. Radio can hide the fact that a speaker is reading from a prepared text. Radio hides the nervous twitch and the sweating brow. Radio can make a President seem like a warrior even though he may be sitting before the microphone in a wheelchair. Further, radio's dependence on language often takes the listener to the realm of high-level abstractions. One popular radio series was introduced by the mysterious "man in black." In some radio dramas, problems were solved by the "hand of God." Ironically, such "images" are more difficult to present effectively in the visual medium of television. Pictures of a specific man in a particular black outfit or of a particular large hand do not convey the same information as the corresponding "word-pictures." On radio, we were told to resist the "fear of fear," and wars could be fought for the "spirit of freedom." As discussed in Chapter 6, such abstractions are impossible to present visually, and even when such words are spoken on television, they tend to get lost amid the more concrete (and therefore less impressive and mystifying) images of everyday objects, gestures, and behaviors. Because of its "presentational" rather than "discursive" bias, television messages tend to avoid such high-level abstractions. Even the most ritualized performances—such as political speeches and religious sermons—often become less formal on television.

Thus, while radio is often said to be very "visual" because it demands listener creation of an image, radio's images and television's images are not the same. These media have different potentials for affecting children's conceptions of adult life. In comparison with television, radio is an "onstage medium." Television exposes more of the backstage aspects of people, actions, and events.

Mixed Grades for the School

Unlike the family, the school has no biological or natural foundation. To a large degree, the school is an "information-dispensing" institution, and any major change in the information-systems of the larger culture should, therefore, have a great impact on its function and structure.

In a print-dominated society, the school is a doubly powerful institution. Not only does the school teach children social knowledge, but it also teaches them the very skill required to gain access to further information:

reading. In a pre-electronic society, the school itself is the prime channel through which children break through the barriers surrounding the family sphere and gain access to information about the larger world.

When print was the prime means through which children learned about the adult world, schools could assume that what a child knew and could learn was determined largely by how well the child could read, and how well the child could read was roughly correlated with the child's age. It made a great deal of sense, therefore, to divide the school into many different grades based on chronological age. The graded structure of the school is closely related to the informational characteristics of print. Print allows for information segregation and gradation. Many distinct information-systems develop based on differences in reading skill. The required simplicity of texts for very young readers lends itself to ritualized statements, simplified ideas, and idealized versions of adult life.

The age-graded school not only gives children in each age group certain information, it also consciously holds back information. The school's lesson plans follow a set sequence of revelation and, by implication, a set pattern of secret-keeping. In early grades, basic cultural ideals and simplified conceptions of roles and social processes are presented as reality. In traditional schoolbooks aimed at young readers, the world is filled with cheerful parents who always do the right thing, with Presidents who never lie, and with social institutions that have admirable goals and always function smoothly. As children climb the ladder of literacy, more details are provided. Step by step, the myths are juxtaposed with "facts," and the inevitable flaws in people and in the system are revealed.

At each new stage of learning, the child is given the feeling of being "in the know." The first grader is taught things unknown to younger siblings at home; the second grader learns things kept secret from first graders. And so on. Each new level comments on earlier levels. Students may laugh when it is revealed to them that the story they were told a year or two earlier about George Washington chopping down the cherry tree was, after all, made up for the benefit of young children. And they may smile when, a few years later, they are taught that General Washington was a poor general, that Thomas Jefferson owned slaves, that the administration of President Grant was highly corrupt. At each new level of education, children are taught new secrets, secrets to be kept from younger children. In a sense, the age-graded school system gains the loyalty of its students by constantly confiding in them. Each year is a journey into a new realm that is closer to the core of adult life. Each grade offers a more grown-up perspective on what has already been learned. By the time students reach higher education, the process may be completely self-reflexive; the role of the school system and education itself may then be analyzed and criticized.

Although we have come to see this structure as a natural means of teaching children, the age-grading of students is a relatively recent innovation. In the sixteenth century, moralists began to complain about the mixed ages of children in schools, and by the end of the seventeenth century some European schools introduced age-grading and the age-graded curriculum.[77] The practice was far from universal, however, until the nineteenth century. In his study of American boarding schools, for example, James McLachlan notes that late in the eighteenth century, pupils of all ages still studied in the same room. In one school studied by MacLachlan, the age-range within one class was six years to thirty years![78] John Sommerville sees age-grading of students as part of the nineteenth century "standardization of childhood" that involved unrealistic stereotyping of children and a lack of attention to individual differences.[79]

Even sympathetic and approving observers of the school, such as Oscar Ritchie and Marvin Koller, note that the classroom is a "context for containment."[80] The child is confined to a room with a large number of others of the same age. There is minimal interaction with children who are even one year older or younger. The age-grading system demands consistency between chronological age and mental and social growth. The system does not foster "unusual" slowness or precocity. Children must follow strict rules; they must perform tasks required of all others in the same classroom. Movement and conversation are sharply restricted. In place of parents, the authority is in the hands of the teacher. The information flow—especially in the early grades—is linear and unidirectional: Information passes from teacher to students.

Television, however, bypasses this linear sequence. Unlike books, television does not divide its audience into people of separate ages, and television presents information to children in no particular order. With television, there is no clear, graded progression up the ladder of social knowledge.

The breakdown of the old sequence in which children received information about society leads to a new world view. Through electronic media, young children are witnesses to "facts" that contradict social myths and ideals even before they learn about the myths and ideals in school. Children see politicians disgraced, police officers and teachers on strike for higher pay, parents accused of battering their children. Through television news and entertainment, children learn too much about the nature of "real" life to believe the ideals their teachers try to teach them. The result is not only that they grow up fast, but that they grow up having an image of society and roles that differs markedly from that held by children of earlier generations.

In the traditional, print-based school system, children learned the myths and ideals before they learned about social reality. The "truth" about society did not necessarily obliterate the myths, but rather put them in perspective. The myths and facts were two separate but equal realities. One was the embodiment of social ideals, the other, the result of observations of social reality. They were complementary: the way we would like things to be and the way things often are as a result of human frailty.

The first was the invisible model for the second. Television largely destroys this bipolar reality.

As a result of television, the schoolteacher's control over information is far from absolute, and the school's step-by-step pattern of dispensing information to each age-group is bypassed. Teachers and school administrators can no longer expect children to view them as all-knowing authorities. Not only do school children now know about some things their teachers never heard of, but like all adults, educators' onstage behaviors have been undermined by the backstage disclosures of television. No matter what the school does, therefore, it can probably never regain the near monopoly over information it once held.

The child who has watched thousands of hours of television before coming to the first grade still needs to learn many things. Yet teachers can no longer assume that the child who cannot read does not know anything about "adult" topics. The child who comes to school today already has a broad mosaic image of the entire culture. The school still needs to fill in the details and correct misperceptions. But the school cannot assume that its function is to accompany the child in a slow climb up the steps of literacy from complete ignorance to social enlightenment. If children seem impatient with schools today, it may be because, in one sense, many schools do not teach children enough. And it is possible that children are grouped together according to a standard that is no longer as relevant as it once was to their social development. The current difficulty of maintaining school discipline and of teaching students reading and other subjects may lie more in the antiquated *structure* of the school than in a sudden change in children's basic abilities or willingness to learn.

Some teachers may welcome the increase in children's knowledge, but many others do not. I know of no surveys on this topic, but I have heard many informal comments from elementary school teachers who complain that their students "know too much." One teacher's lesson on the "greatness of Presidents" was interrupted by a student who protested that he knew from television that President Nixon was a crook. Another teacher complained to me about his students' wanting to discuss a recently televised boxing match in which a young Korean fighter was killed by a knockout punch—a topic he thought too "adult" for their young minds. And two friends of mine were chastised by a teacher because their daughter had fulfilled a third grade assignment to "write a story" by describing what it was like to watch Press Secretary James Brady get shot on television during the assassination attempt on Ronald Reagan. The traditional age-graded curricula cannot accommodate such "advanced" knowledge on the part of the students.

The two most common responses to the school's troubles are aimed at surface symptoms rather than root causes. When children fail to read and write at "grade-level," one response has been to go "back to basics" and attempt to restore children and the schools to their former statuses. When children who watch a great deal of television at home seem disinterested in the "live" performance of a teacher, some teachers have brought videotapes and movies into the classroom in order to maintain the students' interest. Neither of these represents an adjustment of the structure of the school to match the new information environment. The first ignores the change, the second abdicates to it.

It is obviously simpler to describe one source of the school system's problems than it is to suggest a clear solution. One possibility, however, is for the school to abandon the strict age-grading system that segregates children based on their age. The relationship between chronological age and social knowledge has already been weakened by television, and the increasingly widespread use of home computers and other electronic media will weaken it further.

Like all social customs that have lasted more than several generations, the age-grading structure now appears to bear the stamp of nature. A system of social rewards and punishments has been built around it. A parent is delighted when a child "skips" a grade and ashamed when a child is "left back." Yet the social information environment that led to this system and supported it has now been transformed by electronic media. There is no longer much justification for isolating a child from all children more than a few months older or younger. Further, even if it is found that children still need to be divided into relatively homogeneous age groups for some lessons (such as reading), there is no reason why students must always be divided into age groups for other lessons, such as discussions on politics, family life, or current events.

There are no simple answers. One thing is clear, however. If the school is to survive, it must maintain a "knowledge edge." The school must continue to give students the feeling that because of the school they are "in the know." The school must adapt to the new information environment. And it must do so by doing more than merely grudgingly accepting what children learn outside of school. The school must teach them *more* than they can learn elsewhere.

Reading remains the school's trump card. After all, even if reading is no longer the *only* means of gaining access to indirect experience, literacy is still the gateway to the worlds of philosophy, science, and poetry—and reading and writing offer a unique way of thinking and knowing. Further, if the computer continues to develop along its present path, reading and writing will be among the key skills needed to have access to electronically stored information. Yet children will have little incentive to read if the books and computer programs they are given tell them less about the world than they already know or can learn through other sources.

The other potential salvation of the school system is for it to recognize its role in fostering those skills and experiences that no communication technology from writing to computers can teach,[81] including systematic acquisition of knowledge, interpretation, criticism, and the "methodologies" of learning and thinking. Another key example of such a skill is the ability to interact with other people—to speak, listen, argue, and discuss.

Such a skill would be greatly enhanced by a class of mixed ages and backgrounds, where students could learn from, and teach others who have
different perspectives and views.

Literacy and the "Invention" of Childhood and Adulthood

If television can alter the social meaning of childhood and adulthood,
then it stands to reason that these life stages, as they have been defined
for many generations in our culture, are not natural or necessary states of
being. Indeed, implicit in all that I have argued thus far is the notion that
our old views of childhood and adulthood were dependent, at least in
part, on print and could not have existed in quite the same way in a primarily oral society.

The history of childhood is a relatively new field. Yet there is already
striking, if preliminary, support for the idea that our traditional notion of
childhood was related in great measure to printing. While the various
studies of childhood point to many fluctuations in attitudes toward children across time, country, class, and religion, one relatively consistent
theme that emerges is that of a major shift in attitudes toward children
beginning among some classes in the sixteenth century—the same century in which literacy and printing in the vernacular spread through Western Europe. Before that time, little special attention was paid to children.
From the sixteenth to the twentieth century, however, children were
increasingly isolated from adult society and perceived as a special group
requiring particular care, protection, and restriction.

The best known work on the history of childhood is Philippe Ariès'
Centuries of Childhood.[82] Ariès' most startling argument is that childhood
was "invented" in the sixteenth century. According to Ariès, the notion
of childhood as a separate time of life did not exist prior to that time. Or
more precisely, age did not define social status or role. Once past infancy,
children began to participate in adult activities, and they learned about
life through direct experience.

Children worked beside adults, drank in taverns with adults, gambled
with adults, went to war with adults, and shared beds with adults. Children and adults played the same games. There was no special dress for
adults or children; there were no topics or words or activities from which
children were supposed to be shielded. Even the art of the middle ages,
notes Ariès, often pictured children as "little adults," with clothes and
facial expressions similar to those of their parents.

What few formal schools existed (primarily to train clerics) were not
divided into separate classes. The medieval school, observes Ariès, was
characterized by the "lack of gradation in the curricula according to difficulty of the subject-matter, the simultaneity with which the subjects
were taught, the mixing of the ages, and the liberty of the pupils."[83]
Young students lived where they could find lodging, bore arms, drank,
and gambled.

Ariès' study is mostly of France, but his observations are echoed by historians of other European countries. Lawrence Stone, for example, notes that before the sixteenth century, English children were often neglected or ignored by their parents. The wealthy sent infants out to wet nurses until the children were about two, and all classes sent their children away from home when they were about seven or eight, usually to work in the home of another family. Stone observes little adult/child bonding and little separation of the child's world from the adult's. Children saw deaths and executions, witnessed sexual activities, and often engaged in sex play themselves.[84]

Thus, while children have always existed in the physiological sense, the pre-print oral society of Western Europe accorded them few special social roles or behaviors.

Beginning in the sixteenth century, however, a new concept of the child began to take hold. Ariès outlines the evolution of the image of the child from a relatively independent person into a weak and innocent being in need of special care, love, discipline, and protection from evil. Children, who in an earlier era were exposed to the same violent and vulgar folk tales as their parents, were now beginning to be considered too innocent to share fully in "adult" information. Clerics began to demand that children should read only expurgated versions of the classics. Etiquette books for children, along with special guides for their parents, were printed. The idea began to grow that children should not be left alone and that children should be restricted in their travels and activities and separated into homogeneous age groups. By the early twentieth century, there was "a striking differentiation between age groups which are really quite close together."[85] With the spread of the age-graded school, child precocity—once as valued as it was common—began to be seen as a dangerous disease.[86] The age of children became a strict guide to what they should know, where they could go, and what they could do.

Stone also notes the first evidence of a change in attitude toward children in the sixteenth century. In earlier years, parents did not mourn much over the death of young children, but in the late sixteenth century the images of long-dead children began to appear on the tombs of their parents.[87] Stone sees an evolution in attitudes beginning at that time and culminating in the nineteenth century view of children as a separate "class."

The new awareness of childhood did not necessarily lead to "better" care. In fact, early attention to children generally led to brutality and severe discipline. Stone notes that the "innocence" of children, first discussed by humanists in the Renaissance, was quickly "interpreted as liability to sin,"[88] and Ariès suggests that childish innocence led to "safeguarding it against pollution by life."[89] At first, there was a "fierce determination" among parents, especially Puritans, to "break the will of the child, and to enforce his utter subjection to the authority of his elders and superiors, and most especially of his parents."[90] As one seventeenth century minister put it, children "should not know, if it could be kept from them, that they have a will in their own."[91] Sixteenth century English children were expected to kneel before their parents, address their mother and father as "madam" and "sir," and never wear hats in their parents' presence.[92]

While children began to be protected from aspects of adult *life*, they were not, at first, isolated from *death*. For many years, fear of death and of eternal damnation was used to scare children into piety. Children were taken to see hangings and corpses and encouraged to "convert" to Christianity before it was too late.[93] (It was not uncommon for children to die at an early age, and this fact was impressed on young minds.) Indeed, during the seventeenth century, disobedience to parents in Massachusetts was punishable by death.[94]

Later, the new attention paid to children evolved in many places toward what Stone refers to as the more modern "maternal, child-oriented, affectionate and permissive mode."[95] The change occurred at different times in different countries, classes, and religions. By the nineteenth century, the belief in "infant depravity" and the need for young children to undergo "conversions" to Christ was generally abandoned in favor of views of children as at worst morally neutral, and at best angelic redeemers of adult sinfulness.[96]

Although the manifest treatment of children varied widely from the sixteenth through the early twentieth centuries, there was an underlying consistency that sets this entire period apart from earlier periods and from present trends. Whether children were seen as potentially depraved tools of the devil or as angels of grace who could save their elders, whether children were required to kneel before their parents or were indulged in their every whim, children were seen as a distinct category of people to be isolated from the adult world. In medieval society, children and adults mixed freely; the trend from the sixteenth century to the recent past was to segregate children in their own institutions and subculture. The questions arise, then, Why did the notion of a separate sphere for children develop in the sixteenth century, and why has it faded markedly in recent years?

Ariès is not certain of why "childhood" suddenly came into being. At first, he offers a demographic reason: Childhood could not exist until infant mortality rates declined, because parents could not become attached to children who were so likely to die. Then, however, Ariès admits that the decline in the numbers of infants who died did not take place until many years *after* the invention of childhood. "Statistically and objectively speaking," he notes, "this idea should have appeared much later."[97]

Stone argues that the new attention to children was promoted by the Puritans who, as a religious minority, needed to perpetuate their beliefs without relying on the larger community to socialize their children. Similarly, John Sommerville attributes the increased attention to children in the sixteenth century to the Reformation and to the rise of many "social movements." To promote change in society, many groups depended on winning the loyalty of their children.[98]

There are, no doubt, multiple reasons for so fundamental a shift in the social conception of childhood, but the analysis presented in this book suggests that the spread of printing and literacy may have been prime factors in the development of the "innocent" child. To share fully in a literate adult world, a child has to learn to read. Indeed, one thing Stone and Sommerville overlook in their descriptions of the spread of childhood among Puritans is how greatly the Puritan belief in Bible-reading as a means to salvation must have affected their views of children who could not yet read.

Many other features of the growth of childhood, as described by Ariès and other historians, support this analysis. Childhood as a separate time of life developed first among the middle and upper classes, as did literacy. Boys were considered children long before girls, perhaps because boys were sent off to school to learn to read and write, while their sisters stayed home and immediately took on the dress and the tasks of adult women.

As Ariès' history indicates, the spread of childhood closely paralleled the growth of schools and education.* Even as the schools began to redefine the notion of childhood, those children who remained outside of schools were still treated much like adults. In the seventeenth century, for example, young boys were isolated from adults in schools, but they mixed with old soldiers in the military. Some boys moved from the world of childhood—school—to the world of men—the military—at an early age. "Claude de Bonneval, born in 1675, entered a Jesuit college at the age of nine. He left at eleven . . . to sign on as a marine in the King's Navy. At the age of thirteen he was a sub-lieutenant."[102]

The growing influence of books led to changes in their form that highlighted the new belief in the distinctness of children. In the eighteenth century, children's literature began to shift away from pedantic moral instruction and joyless drill to books of entertainment and frivolous play. A whole subculture for children developed: children's fairy tales, toys, birthday celebrations, and nursery rhymes.[103] But these developments

---

*If literacy and childhood are correlated, then we might ask why the schools of the Middle Ages did not lead to a clear notion of childhood or to age-grading of students. Interestingly, medieval schools were generally more concerned with *memorization* than with writing and reading. Because of the high cost and rarity of manuscripts and writing materials, even teachers and clerics were greatly dependent on memory. In the age of manuscripts, to "know" continued to mean to know by heart. Ariès notes that "writing seemed a suspicious means of avoiding this effort."[99] Similarly, Elizabeth Eisenstein notes that "outside certain transitory special centers . . . the texture of scribal culture was so thin that heavy reliance was placed on oral transmission even by literate élites."[100] And H.L. Chaytor observes that the medieval monk was an exceptionally slow reader who "was in the stage of our muttering childhood learner";[101] he read aloud and haltingly. It was not until the spread of printed books that fluid reading and writing became central concerns, and only then did educators begin thinking of separating people based on their level of mastery of such skills.

occurred only in the literate middle and upper classes. In the lower classes, the new concepts of childhood did not take hold until much later. In the nineteenth century, many uneducated children continued to work in factories beside their parents. Sommerville notes the irony of the fact that the heights and depths of childhood were reached simultaneously in the nineteenth century. Children of the educated were glorified with their own subculture of special books and toys, yet children of the poor and illiterate often provided the labor to support this subculture. Publishers, for example, hired lower-class children to hand-tint the engravings in the growing number of books for middle-class children.[104]

As the ideal of universal education became a reality in the nineteenth century, childhood spread to the lower classes. Children were sent to school at an earlier age and remained there for a longer period of time. Age-grading of children and of lessons became stricter and stricter.

The historical literature contains so many implicit suggestions of the possible role of literacy in the increasing segregation of children and adults that it is odd that most historians have nothing explicit to say about it. Stone, for example, notes that new approaches to children developed first among the most literate groups, but he attributes this to the openness of literate peoples to "new ideas."[105] Further, although Stone suggests that the greater spread of literacy among men may have led to a decrease in the relative status of women,[106] he neglects to extend this argument to its obvious implications for the changing status of children and adults. Nevertheless, Stone does observe—without analysis—how a new concern over children's proper education led parents to "interfere" with children's freedoms in new ways.[107] And the general data presented by Stone and other historians suggest that the growth and spread of schooling was paralleled by a growing belief that certain things should be kept hidden from children.

Sommerville also provides some inadvertent clues to the role of literacy in the birth of childhood. He notes, in passing, that before the spread of literacy, people of all ages enjoyed listening to what we would today call "nursery tales." "What has changed since then is that adults have 'grown up' and have left these stories to children. Partly, this has been the result of literacy, which develops man's critical abilities but shrivels his imagination. . . . It may be that adults were more childlike in the early years of the modern era."[108]

Elsewhere, Sommerville notes that changes in community traditions occurred when "adults became too grownup and inhibited to take part in the songs, games, and dancing that had once bound the various age groups together."[109] Yet while Sommerville briefly suggests that literacy is responsible for making adults less childlike, he neglects to consider the other side of the coin: that literacy may have made children seem less adultlike.

To my knowledge, the only historian who has explicitly linked literacy with the invention of childhood is Elizabeth Eisenstein. And she does so, not in a history of childhood, but as one of many arguments in her massive study of the ways in which the printing press revolutionized social knowledge. Eisenstein suggests that the new views of childhood may have been related to the significant "shift from 'learning by doing' to 'learning by reading.'" The mechanical aspects of printing and the resulting potential for technical precision, she argues, caused a general fascination with system, method, and *sequence*. Further, the growth of the printing industry allowed for segregation of markets and audiences. Some books began to be aimed only at teachers or parents, and schoolbooks were newly structured to take students in a step-by-step sequence from elementary to advanced levels of a given subject. "As a consumer of printed materials geared to a sequence of learning stages, the growing child was subjected to a different developmental process than was the medieval apprentice, ploughboy, novice or page."[110]

Printing and spreading literacy, says Eisenstein, also created a new way of "adult thinking" based on "cumulative cognitive advance and incremental change," that, in effect, created childhood by default. "Indeed the more adult activities were governed by conscious deliberation or going by the book, the more striking the contrast offered by the spontaneous and impulsive behavior of young offspring, and the more strenuous the effort required to remold young "bodies and souls.""[111]

The potential link between literacy and childhood requires much additional historical research. We need to follow the thread of literacy to see if childhood trails behind. There are, however, many obstacles to such research. It is not clear, for example, how to define "literacy." As Eisenstein notes in a different context, there is a vast difference between basic literacy and habitual book reading. "Learning *to read* is different . . . from learning by reading."[112] It would make sense that the differences between children and adults would be most evident in the latter case. The more literate a parent, the more "childlike" children must have seemed. Yet it is extremely difficult to discover the degrees of literacy in the past. (Most studies must rely on the ratio of signatures to marks on parish and court records,[113] a measure that is probably not sensitive enough to relate to conceptions of childhood and adulthood.) Further, because the lower classes sometimes imitated the style of child-rearing in the middle and upper classes, some traces of childhood may have appeared in the lower classes before they were literate. To complicate things further, social reformers in the nineteenth century worked to "impose" childhood on the poor.[114] The best chance of studying the effects of literacy may seem to rest in currently oral societies in a stage of transition to literacy. Yet even in such "natural laboratories" of change, the effects are confounded by the concurrent spread of literacy and electronic media. To a large extent, therefore, we may have to rely on the plausibility of a link between literacy and childhood and on the general historical correlation between them.

The argument that literacy creates "childhood" may at first seem facile and mystical. Yet, it is logical to argue that similarity of social status is dependent on ability to participate relatively equally in social interaction, and that such participation depends on communication skills. In the primarily oral society of the Middle Ages, children may have been seen as less distinct from adults because, by the age of seven or eight, children generally master the basics of speech. Printing and literacy may have given a boost to the Renaissance, but they also created a new and lasting dark age for the young and illiterate.

The medium of print removed the child from the adult world in a manner and to a degree inconceivable in an oral culture.* To learn what adults knew, to be able to join adult interactions in print, now required many years of schooling and training. Printing allowed for all-adult interactions in which parents and teachers could "privately" discuss how to treat children, what to teach them, and what to keep from them. It is no surprise that the image of a weak and naive child should have developed alongside the growing impact of printing. Children began to be seen as very "innocent," not immediately in the moral sense (which developed much later), but in the sense of innocence of experience and knowledge. Conversely, adults gained in image and prestige as they were increasingly able to conceal their doubts, anxieties, and childish behaviors from children.

This analysis of the potential role of print in the rise of "childhood" and "adulthood" further supports the argument that television may be a prime factor in the evolution toward more homogenized adult/child roles. Once again, the form in which information is transmitted in our society conspires against controlling what children know about adulthood and adult roles. Children still pass through a sequence of cognitive and physiological phases, but the social stages of information exposure have been blurred. In contrast to print, there is no set sequence in the level or type of information accessible through television. Television undermines the hierarchy of information supported by stages of reading literacy and the age-specific grades of the school system. Indeed, the print-inspired

---

*Of course, it is not the existence of literacy in and of itself that leads to "childhood" and "adulthood," but rather the increased possibilities that literacy affords for the *separation of adult and child information-systems*. Because situation-separation is the key variable, we can see some evidence of distinctions between childhood and adulthood in various oral cultures where children are kept out of certain locations and discussions—but rarely do we see the division of childhood into thin, year-by-year slices until the spread of literacy and the age-graded school. Conversely, even in technically literate societies, certain social conditions may override the distinctions in information-systems that literacy makes possible. Thus, children continued to be seen as "little adults" in many early American colonial settlements because harsh and primitive conditions made it difficult to isolate children. Similarly, childhood was "delayed" among the lower classes, not only by the slow spread of literacy, but also by crowded conditions and the lack of adult privacy. Childhood was muted in many rural areas as well because children continued to work beside adults many hours a day and because the low density of the population often required the mixing of ages in a one-room school.[115]

fascination with linear "sequences" and "stages" (including stage theories of social development) seems to be disappearing from our culture.

Television makes it difficult for adults to create different informational and behavioral worlds for people of different ages. Just as we cannot clearly distinguish among the social statuses of students of different ages if we teach them all in the same classroom, neither can we make very clear status distinctions if we expose everyone to the same information through television. Fundamental developmental processes and the continuing importance of literacy in our culture place a limitation on the homogenization of childhood and adulthood. Yet the old sharp distinctions in behavior can no longer be supported.

Reflections in Black on White

Soon after the introduction of television, the new child/adult information-systems and some of the fears of adults concerning them began to be reflected in adult fiction. In a 1951 science fiction story, "The Veldt," for example, Ray Bradbury describes the "Happylife Home," a soundproofed house that automatically feeds, clothes, and bathes its occupants. The television analogue in the story is the nursery, which is a large room that can be transformed into any environment the children wish for. "Nothing's too good for our children," thinks the father.

The children in the Happylife Home, however, have not been using the nursery in a manner approved of by their parents. The children have been consistently turning the nursery into a hot, unpleasant African veldt complete with three-dimensional foliage and jungle beasts. The parents' concern over the children's use of the room grows, and they attempt to stop the children from entering it. But the children get angry with their parents, lie to them, attempt to appease them. In short, they do and say anything they must do and say to retain access to their nursery. When locked out of the room, they break into it.

A psychologist friend is summoned and he explains to the parents the obvious ways in which the room has changed their role in relation to their children. "You've let this room and this house replace you and your wife in your children's affections. This room is their mother and father, far more important in their lives than their real parents. And now you come along and want to shut it off. No wonder there's hatred here."[116]

Bradbury's children, fearing the "turning off" of the Happylife Home and their loss of access to the nursery, ultimately do away with their parents. They have them eaten by some of the veldt's inhabitants.

The message in "The Veldt" is twofold: Not only does the automatic nursery bypass the traditional function of the parents, but it also gives the children the means to control their own fate and to use their new-found power against their parents. Bradbury's description of the nursery broadly satirizes the effects of television on the family power structure.

Within twenty years after Bradbury's description of the Happylife Home, new conceptions of childhood, adulthood, and family interactions had entered children's literature as well. For as described in the "media content loop" section of Chapter 11, once children gain access to adult information on television, it becomes more and more difficult for them to accept the sanitized and idealized content of traditional children's literature.

In a guide to potential writers, Richard Balkin warns authors of the new rules for children's books. "If you haven't read any children's books since your own prepubescence, you are in for a surprise. There are scarcely any taboos left, and many books are candid and realistic about unmentionables as well as mentionables."[117] Many children's books—including some school texts—now discuss adult topics such as sex, homosexuality, drugs, and prostitution.*

Books now aimed at children, however, do much more than present once taboo topics; they also suggest the possibility that children have a sophisticated awareness of the *structure* of adult/child roles.

Judy Blume's children's book *Superfudge*, for example, features a five-year-old boy, Fudge, who is seen through the eyes of his older brother, Peter. At Christmas time, Fudge makes a big fuss over writing to Santa Claus. He makes every member of the family write, and insists that Peter write a letter for their baby sister and family dog. Peter privately complains to his mother and suggests that it is about time that they reveal the truth to Fudge. "After all, you told him where babies come from. How can a kid who knows where babies come from still believe in Santa?" But his mother rejects this argument and claims that one thing has nothing to do with the other and that, in any case, "He's so enthusiastic and the idea of Santa is so lovely that Daddy and I have decided it can't possibly hurt."[119] It is clear that the parents find Fudge's belief cute and see his innocence in this regard as refreshing.

After all the letters to Santa get written, and after Fudge receives the shiny red bicycle he requests from Santa, Fudge confides in his brother that he really knows there is no Santa, that he has always known there is no Santa. When asked why he pretends to believe in Santa, Fudge replies, "because Mommy and Daddy think I believe in him . . . so I pretend. . . . Aren't I a great pretender?"[120]

In *Superfudge* the traditional secret-keeping and secret of secrecy have been turned on their heads. The child puts on an act to make his parents

---

*The same changing sensibilities are evident in movies. It is now difficult to believe, for example, that in 1953, Otto Preminger's *The Moon is Blue* was denied movie association code approval because the film used the words "virgin" and "mistress."[118] Today, even movies rated G (General Audiences) are likely to include such words, and films rated PG (Parental Guidance Suggested) often contain some obscenities and nudity. Just a few years ago, these same movies would have been rated "R" (Restricted to Children under 17) or even "X" (Adults Only).

happy. The child is so aware of the structure of adult-child relations that he can pretend to be unaware. Fudge is able to keep others in ignorance of his access to information. In *Superfudge,* the literary representation of adult-child relationships has come full circle: It is the parents who are more innocent than the children.

14

Lowering the Political Hero to Our Level

A Case Study in Changing Authority

When the world was young and there were men like gods, no reporters were present . . . only poets.—Dixon Wector[1]

In *The Growth of Presidential Power*, William Goldsmith notes that: "After almost 200 years of dynamic if not always continuous growth and development, the American presidency is in real trouble, in a manner and to a degree never before approached in the span of its turbulent history."[2] Although Goldsmith wrote these words in the shadow of the Watergate scandal, our crisis in leadership began before Watergate and transcends it.

All our recent Presidents have been plagued with problems of "credibility." Lyndon Johnson abdicated his office; Richard Nixon left the presidency in disgrace; Gerald Ford's "appointment" to the presidency was later rejected by the electorate; Jimmy Carter suffered a landslide defeat after being strongly challenged within his own party; and even the comparatively popular Ronald Reagan has followed his predecessors in the now familiar roller coaster ride in the polls.[3]

We seem to be having difficulty finding leaders who have charisma and style and who are also competent and trustworthy. In the wish to keep at least one recent leader in high esteem, many people have chosen to forget that in his thousand days in office, John Kennedy faced many crises of credibility and accusations of "news management."[4]

During the 1980 campaign, *Newsweek* analyzed recent political polls and concluded that "perhaps the most telling political finding of all is the high degree of disenchantment voters feel about most of the major candidates."[5] Of course, every horse race has its winner, and no matter how uninspiring the field of candidates, people will always have their favorites. The obsession with poll percentage points and the concern over who wins and who loses, however, tend to obscure the more fundamental issue of the decline in the image of leaders in general.

There are at least two ways to study the image and rhetoric of the presidency. One is to examine the content and form of speeches and actions; in other words, to look at specific strategies, choices, and decisions. Another method is to examine the situations within which Presidents perform their roles. This second method requires a shift in focus away from the specific rhetorical strategies of individual politicians and toward the general environment that surrounds the presidency and is therefore shared by all who seek that office.

This chapter employs the latter method to reinterpret the causes of the political woes of some of our recent national politicians and to shed some light on our leadership problem in general. I suggest that the decline in presidential image may have surprisingly little to do with a simple lack of potentially great leaders, and much to do with a specific communication environment—a communication environment that undermines the politician's ability to behave like, and therefore be perceived as, the traditional "great leader."

The Merging of Political Arenas and Styles

Before the widespread use of electronic media, the towns and cities of the country served as backstage areas of rehearsal for national political figures. By the time William Jennings Bryan delivered his powerful "cross of gold" speech to win the nomination for President at the 1896 Democratic convention, for example, he had already practiced the speech many times in different parts of the country.[6]

The legendary oratory of Bryan and the treasured images of many of our other political heroes were made possible by their ability to practice and modify their public performances. Early mistakes could be limited to small forums, minor changes could be tested, and speeches and presentations could be honed to perfection. Politicians could thrill many different crowds on different days with a single well-turned phrase. Bryan, for example, was very fond of his closing line in the 1896 speech ("You shall not press down upon the brow of labor this crown of thorns, you shall not crucify mankind upon a cross of gold")—so fond, in fact, that he had used it many times in other speeches and debates. In his memoirs, Bryan noted his early realization of the line's "fitness for the conclusion of a climax," and after using it in smaller public arenas, he "laid it away for a proper occasion."[7]

Today, through radio and television, the national politician often faces a single audience. Wherever the politician speaks, he or she addresses people all over the country. Major speeches, therefore, cannot be tested in advance. Because they can be presented only once, they tend to be relatively coarse and undramatic. Inspiring lines either are consumed quickly or they become impotent clichés.*

---

*To meet the demands of frequent speaking engagements and campaigns, politicians still must rely on what is sometimes called their "basic speech." But today, this speech must be

Nineteenth century America provided multiple political arenas in which politicians could perfect the form and the substance of their main ideas. They could also buttress their central platforms with slightly different promises to different audiences. Today, because politicians address so many different types of people simultaneously, they have great difficulty speaking in specifics. And any slip of the tongue is amplified in significance because of the millions of people who have witnessed it. Those who analyze changing rhetorical styles without taking such situational changes into account overlook a major political variable.

Many Americans are still hoping for the emergence of an old-style, dynamic "great leader." Yet electronic media of communication are making it almost impossible to find one. There is no lack of potential leaders, but rather an overabundance of information about them. The great leader image depends on mystification and careful management of public impressions. Through television, we see too much of our politicians, and they are losing control over their images and performances. As a result, our political leaders are being stripped of their aura and are being brought closer to the level of the average person.

The impact of electronic media on the staging of politics can best be understood by analyzing it in relation to the staging requirements of *any* social role, as described in earlier chapters. Regardless of competence, regardless of desire, there is a limit to how long any person can play out an idealized conception of a social role. All people must eat, sleep, and go to the bathroom. All people need time to think about their social behavior, prepare for social encounters, and rest from them. Further, we all play different roles in different situations. One man, for example, may be a father, a son, a husband, an old college roommate, and a boss. He may also be President of the United States. He needs to emphasize different aspects of his personality in order to function in each of these roles. The performance of social roles, therefore, is in many ways like a multi-stage drama. The strength and clarity of a particular onstage, or "front region," performance depend on isolating the audience from the backstage, or "back region." Rehearsals, relaxations, and behaviors from other onstage roles must be kept out of the limelight. The need to shield backstage behaviors is especially acute in the performance of roles that rely heavily on mystification and on an aura of greatness—roles such as those performed by national political leaders.

Yet electronic media of communication have been eroding barriers between the politician's traditional back and front regions. The camera eye and the microphone ear have been probing many aspects of the

purposely low key so that all the elements are not picked up by the news media and "revealed" to every potential live audience in advance. Both politicians and journalists complain a great deal about the present situation. The reporters who covered candidate Carter, for example, complained that he kept repeating himself and rarely had anything new to say; Carter complained that his one-time, off-the-cuff remarks were more likely to be covered in the press than his oft-repeated basic ideas.[8]

national politician's behavior and transmitting this information to 225 million Americans. By revealing to its audience both traditionally onstage and traditionally backstage activities, television could be said to provide a "sidestage," or "middle region," view of public figures. We watch politicians move from backstage to onstage to backstage. We see politicians address crowds of well-wishers, then greet their families "in private." We join candidates as they speak with their advisors, and we sit behind them as they watch conventions on television. We see candidates address many different types of audiences in many different settings.

By definition, the "private" behaviors now exposed are no longer true back region activities precisely because they are exposed to the public. But neither are they merely traditional front region performances. The traditional balance between rehearsal and performance has been upset. Through electronic coverage, politicians' freedom to isolate themselves from their audiences is being limited. In the process, politicians are not only losing aspects of their privacy—a complaint we often hear—but, more important, they are simultaneously losing their ability to play many facets of the high and mighty roles of traditional leaders. For when actors lose parts of their rehearsal time, their performances naturally move toward the extemporaneous.

The sidestage perspective offered by television makes normal differences in behavior appear to be evidence of inconsistency or dishonesty. We all behave differently in different situations, depending on who is there and who is not. Yet when television news programs edit together videotape sequences that show a politician saying and doing different things in different places and before different audiences, the politician may appear, at best, indecisive and, at worst, dishonest.

The reconfiguration of the stage of politics demands a drive toward consistency in all exposed spheres. To be carried off smoothly, the new political performance requires a new "middle region" role: behavior that lacks the extreme formality of former front region behavior and also lacks the extreme informality of traditional back region behavior. Wise politicians make the most of the new situation. They try to expose selected, positive aspects of their back regions in order to ingratiate themselves with the public. Yet there is a difference between *coping* with the new situation and truly *controlling* it. Regardless of how well individual politicians adjust to the new exposure, the overall image of leaders changes in the process. The new political performance remains a performance, but its style is markedly changed.

Mystification and awe are supported by distance and limited access. Our new media reveal too much and too often for traditional notions of political leadership to prevail. The television camera invades politicians' personal spheres like a spy in back regions. It watches them sweat, sees them grimace at their own ill-phrased remarks. It coolly records them as they succumb to emotions. The camera minimizes the distance between audience and performer. The speaker's platform once raised a politician up and away from the people—both literally and symbolically. The camera now brings the politician close for the people's inspection. And in this sense, it lowers politicians to the level of their audience. The camera brings a rich range of expressive information to the audience; it highlights politicians' mortality and mutes abstract and conceptual rhetoric. While verbal rhetoric can transcend humanity and reach for the divine, intimate expressive information often exposes human frailty. No wonder old style politicians, who continue to assume the grand postures of another era, now seem like clowns or crooks. The personal close-up view forces many politicians to pretend to be less than they would like to be (and, thereby, in a social sense, they actually become less).

Some people were privy to a sort of "middle region" for politicians before television. Through consistent physical proximity, for example, many reporters would see politicians in a multiplicity of front region roles and a smattering of back region activities. Yet, the relationship between politicians and some journalists was itself a personal back region interaction that was distinguished from press accounts to the public. Before television, most of the news stories released were not records of this personal back region relationship or even of a "middle region." The politician could always distinguish for the press what was "on" the record, what was "off" the record, what should be paraphrased, and what must be attributed to "a high government official."[9] Thus, even when the journalists and the politicians were intimates, the news releases were usually impersonal social communications. Print media can "report on" what happens in one place and bring the report to another place. But the report is by no means a "presentation" of the actual place-bound experience. The print reporters who interviewed Theodore Roosevelt while he was being shaved, for example, did not have an experience "equivalent" to the resulting news reports. Because private interactions with reporters were once distinct from the public communications released in newspapers, much of a politician's "personality" was well hidden from the average citizen.

Private press-politician interactions continue to take place, but electronic media have created new political situations that change the overall "distance" between politician and voter. With electronic coverage, politicians lose a great deal of control over their messages and performances. When they ask that the television camera or tape recorder be turned off, the politicians appear to have something to hide. When the camera or microphone is on, politicians can no longer separate their interaction with the press from their interaction with the public. The camera unthinkingly records the flash of anger and the shiver in the cold; it determinedly shadows our leaders as they trip over words or down stairs. And, unlike the testimony of journalists or of other witnesses, words and actions recorded on electronic tape are impossible to deny. Thus, while politicians try hard to structure the *content* of the media coverage, the *form* of the coverage itself is changing the nature of political image. The revealing nature of television's presentational information cannot be fully counteracted by manipulation, practice, and high-paid consultants. Even a staged media event is often more personally revealing than a transcript of an informal speech or interview. When in 1977, President Carter allowed NBC cameras into the White House for a day, the result may not have been what he intended. As *The New York Times* reported:

> Mr. Carter is a master of controlled images, and he is obviously primed for the occasion. When he isn't flashing his warm smile, he is being soothingly cool under pressure. But the camera ferrets out that telltale tick, that comforting indication of ordinary humanity. It finds his fingers nervously caressing a paperclip or playing with a pen. It captures the almost imperceptible tightening of facial muscles when the President is given an unflattering newspaper story about one of his sons.[10]

Some politicians, of course, have better "media images" than others, but few can manipulate their images as easily as politicians could in a print era. The nature and the extent of this loss of control become even clearer when back and front regions are not viewed as mutually exclusive categories. Most actions encompass both types of behavior. In many situations, for example, an individual can play a front region role while simultaneously giving off covert back region cues to "teammates" (facial expressions, "code" remarks, fingers crossed behind the back, etc.). Further, as suggested in Chapter 6, because expressions are constant and personal, an individual's exuding of expressions is a type of on-going back region activity that was once accessible only to those in close physical proximity. Thus, the degree of control over access to back regions is not simply binary—access/no access—but infinitely variable. Any medium of communication can be analyzed in relation to those personal characteristics it transmits and those it restricts.

Print, for example, conveys words but no intonations or facial gestures; radio sends intonations along with the words but provides no visual information; television transmits the full audio/visual spectrum of verbal, vocal, and gestural. In this sense, the trend from print to radio to television represents a shrinking shield for back region activities and an increase in the energy required to manage impressions. Further, Albert Mehrabian's formula for relative message impact—7% verbal, 38% vocal, and 55% facial and postural[11]—suggests that the trend in media development not only leads to revealing more, but to revealing more of more. From the portrait to the photograph to the movie to the video close-up, media have been providing a closer, more replicative, more immediate, and, therefore, less idealized image of the leader. "Greatness" is an abstraction, and it fades as the image of distant leaders comes to resemble an encounter with an intimate acquaintance.

As cameras continue to get lighter and smaller, and as microphones and lenses become more sensitive, the distinctions between public and private contexts continue to erode. It is no longer necessary for politicians to stop what they are doing in order to pose for a picture or to step up to a microphone. As a result, it is increasingly difficult for politicians to distinguish between the ways in which they behave in "real situations" and the ways in which they present themselves for the media. The new public image of politicians, therefore, has many of the characteristics of the former backstage of political life, and many once informal interactions among politicians and their families, staff, reporters, and constituents have become more stiff and formal as they are exposed to national audiences.*

Most politicians, even Presidents, continue to maintain a truly private backstage area, but that area is being pushed further and further into the background, and it continues to shrink both spatially and temporally.

Writing and print not only hide general back region actions and behaviors, they also conceal the act of producing "images" and messages. Presidents once had the time to prepare speeches carefully. Even seemingly "spontaneous" messages were prepared in advance, often with the help of advisors, counselors, and family members. Delays, indecision, and the pondering of alternative solutions in response to problems were hidden in the invisible backstage area created by the inherent slowness of older media. Before the invention of the telegraph, for example, a President never needed to be awakened in the middle of the night to respond to a crisis. A few hours delay meant little.

Electronic media, however, leave little secret time for preparations and response. Because messages *can* be sent instantly across the nation and the world, any delay in hearing from a President is apparent. And in televised press conferences, even a few seconds of thought by a politician may be seen as a sign of indecisiveness, weakness, or senility. More and more, therefore, the public messages conveyed by officials are, in fact, spontaneous.

Politicians find it more difficult to hide their need for time and for advice in the preparation of public statements. They must either reveal the decision process (by turning to advisors or by saying that they need

---

*Although I concentrate here on how the new media environment shapes and limits the choices of politicians, there is also an important third variable: the choices of *news institutions*, which report on politics. As Michael Schudson has argued, the journalistic decision to highlight presidential politics at the expense of congressional politics is an important characteristic of modern political ritual, and this decision came many years before television.[12] Without discounting the importance of such news conventions, however, we can analyze how changes in media environments tend to shape journalistic choices as much as they influence the decisions of politicians. The speed and reach of the telegraph, for example, set the stage both for "national news" and for close "human interest" coverage of the chief executive. The telegraph enabled the whole country to monitor the minute changes in President Garfield's condition as he lingered for eleven weeks before dying from an assassin's bullet; it also made possible the "shocking and uncouth" completeness of the coverage of President Cleveland's wedding and honeymoon. Both of these events foreshadowed the close scrutiny of the President that began in earnest with Theodore Roosevelt's administration[13] and that was later enhanced by the possibilities of radio and television. Ideally, future analyses will consider the complex interaction of all three of these important variables: media environment, political decisions, journalistic decisions.

more time to study the issue) or they must present very informal, off-the-cuff comments that naturally lack the craftsmanship of prepared texts. The new media demand that the politician walk and talk steadily and unthinkingly along a performance tightrope. On either side is danger: A few seconds of silence or a slip of the tongue can lead to a fall in the polls.

The changing arenas of politics affect not only the perceptions of audiences but also the response of politicians to their own performances. In face-to-face behavior, we must get a sense of ourselves from the ongoing response of others. We can never see ourselves quite the way others see us. On videotape, however, politicians are able to see exactly the same image of themselves as is seen by the public. In live interactions, a speaker's nervousness and mistakes are usually politely ignored by audiences and therefore often soon forgotten by the speaker too. With television, politicians acquire permanent records of themselves sweating, stammering, or anxiously licking their lips. Television, therefore, has the power to increase a politician's self-doubt and lower self-esteem.

Highly replicative media are demystifying leaders not only for their own time, but for history as well. Few leaders are universally revered in their own lifetime. But less replicative media allowed, at least, for greater idealization of leaders after they died. Idiosyncrasies and physical flaws were interred with a President's bones, their good deeds and their accomplishments lived after them. Once a President died, all that remained were flattering painted portraits and the written texts of speeches. An unusual speaking style or an unattractive facial expression was soon forgotten.

If Lincoln had been passed down to us only through painted portraits, perhaps his homeliness would have faded further with time. The rest of the Lincoln legend, however, including Lincoln's image as a dynamic speaker, continues to be preserved by the *lack* of recordings of his unusually high, thin voice, which rose even higher when he was nervous. Similarly, Thomas Jefferson's slight speech impediment is rarely mentioned.[14] Through new media, however, the idiosyncrasies of Presidents are preserved and passed down to the next generation. Instead of inheriting only summaries and recollections, future generations will judge the styles of former Presidents for themselves. They will see Gerald Ford lose his balance, Carter sweating under pressure, and Reagan dozing during an audience with the Pope. Presidential mispronunciations, hesitations, perspiration, and physical and verbal clumsiness are now being preserved for all time.

Expressions are part of the shared repertoire of all people. When under control and exposed briefly, expressive messages show the "humanity" of the "great leader." But when they are flowing freely and constantly, expressive messages suggest that those we look up to may, after all, be no different from ourselves. The more intense our search for evidence of greatness, the more it eludes us.

There is a demand today for two things: fully open, accessible administrations and strong powerful leaders. Rarely do we consider that these two demands may, unfortunately, be incompatible. We want to spy on our leaders, yet we want them to inspire us. We cannot have both disclosure *and* the mystification necessary for an image of greatness. The post-Watergate fascination with uncovering cover-ups has not been accompanied by a sophisticated notion of what will inevitably be found in the closets of all leaders. The familiarity fostered by electronic media all too easily breeds contempt.

Political Ritual as Political Reality

Most social behavior has a ritualistic quality. Lawyers, doctors, judges, teachers, parents, students, and other social performers generally attempt to display symbolically appropriate behavior. To a large extent, the substance, or "reality," of individuals' *social* existence resides in their patterns of communication, their actions, and their expressions. When the means of communication and the forums of interaction change, so must the "characters" portrayed.

The new situations created by electronic media have a tremendous impact on politicians for two reasons: (1) political performers express their characters more directly and exclusively through the dominant forms of communication than do average citizens, and (2) political drama is even more highly ritualistic than everyday social behavior. A *single* inappropriate act can disqualify political performers from completing an ongoing ritual. Edmund Muskie's public shedding of tears, Thomas Eagleton's admission of mental difficulties, and Early Butz's racist joke-telling are a few examples of "contaminating" acts.

The changing image of political leaders, then, is much more than a surface change in style. Political reality and political ritual are closely interwoven. As Ferdinand Mount notes in *The Theatre of Politics*, "The idea that there is a *real* (efficient, useful) politics which is masked by an *unreal* (superficial) sham show is one of the most potent delusions of our time."[15]

W. Lance Bennett has argued that political campaigns serve two interrelated purposes. One is the politicians' short-term pragmatic desire to get elected. Politicians, therefore, do and say those things that are most likely to get them into office. But Bennett says that another, and perhaps more important, function of campaigns is social ritual: "the backdrop against which the public can work out its tensions and satisfy its needs for security, order, leadership, and control over the future." The election, says Bennett, acts "as a cultural drama on a grand scale—a drama so familiar, yet so profound, that even though most of us know the parts and the lines intimately, we still find it to be engrossing and worth attending."[16]

Bennett suggests that while it might seem simpler to analyze independently the pragmatic and the ritualistic elements of campaign discourse, it is unlikely that they can be separated. He argues that the pragmatic goal of being elected is supported by properly executed ritualistic acts, and the ritualistic function, in turn, is served by pragmatic appeals. There is, argues Bennett, a "cultural logic" that weds the two functions together. "It is this sort of logic that guides the participants in any well established cultural ritual to act in ways that both accomplish practical ends and that affirm important principles, values, and community identities."[17]

Politicians rarely discuss the ritual and performance aspects of politics. In fact, denying the ritualized nature of politics is itself part of the ritual. "Truth, not artifice" and "issues, not images," are themselves important chants and central themes in the political drama.

Even those who purport to report on politics often get caught in the web of performance and become part of the ritualized drama, just as sports commentators often become part of the ritual of sports. Both political and sports journalists speak of "frontrunners" and "dark horses," of good losers and humble winners. In such ways, reporters often help maintain the myths of social rituals rather than dispel or explain them.

While politicians and political journalists often speak of a difference between political realities and political images, any thoughtful examination of campaign discourse and political actions reveals that some artifice is required even to create the image of "honesty" and that often a "stand on the issues" is itself an image. Because politics is a dramatic ritual, it is ultimately impossible to separate the thread of reality from the thread of performance.

Two scholars of political communication, Dan Hahn and Ruth Gonchar note that despite the public's avowed rejection of images in favor of issues, survey findings reveal that over forty percent of voters are *most* influenced by the personal characteristics of candidates.[18] Similarly, Fred Greenstein notes that people's positive and negative views of Presidents are usually expressed in terms of the President's personal image rather than his policy positions.[19]

Hahn and Gonchar use Presidents Kennedy and Johnson as illustrations of the potency of image in politics. "The martyred Kennedy is revered; President Johnson is remembered, if at all, with enmity. No one would argue that the images of the two men differed. What people tend to forget is the remarkable similarity of their stands on issues."[20]

An even greater indication of the primacy of image over issues in politics is the often odd relationship between voters' first and second choices. Hahn and Gonchar suggest that in 1968 the "second choice of Robert Kennedy's white supporters was not the liberal McCarthy but the conservative Wallace, while the second choice of the Wallace supporters was Kennedy rather than conservative Governor Granigan." Similarly, in the 1972 primaries, Wallace and McGovern both attracted the same "lower-middle class alienated" voters. The order in which they finished in different primaries, argue Hahn and Gonchar, was "dictated more by the degree to which each was able to picture himself as anti-establishment than by the solutions each proposed for wresting power away from the establishment."[21]

Hahn and Gonchar suggest that those politicians who reject simplistic images and try to grapple with complex reality often suffer. Ironically, those who try to take a stand on the issues may *appear* not to have done so. Hahn and Gonchar note that before Muskie dropped out of the presidential campaign, even his advisors were complaining that he was not "talking the issues." But Hahn and Gonchar's analysis of Muskie's speeches indicates that Muskie's campaign may have been *too* issue-oriented. Instead of choosing a few issues and discussing them over and over again in simple terms, Muskie spoke in depth about many issues. Hahn and Gonchar conclude that, in part, Muskie lost "because he was not associated strongly with any single issue, i.e., because his *image* was blurred by lack of simplification and repetition."[22]

Political reality rests in political images. Ultimately, suggest Hahn and Gonchar, it can be no other way. "Real" issues, they note, do not usually function as the substance of a national political campaign because truly significant issues rarely arise at "appropriate" times (i.e., in time for elections), and such issues are often too complex to be briefly presented and quickly understood.

Similarly, Michael Novak suggests in *Choosing Our King* that there is only paradox and futility in attempting to ignore images in favor of "reality." George McGovern, he observes, "ran for office as a man of candor, a politician unlike other politicians, a person unconcerned about image. *That* was his image." Novak argues that it is impossible for a politician to avoid having an image. "A candidate has only limited exposure; he must reach over two hundred million citizens; no one can look into his soul." Further, notes Novak, there is naivety and hypocrisy in pretending not to depend on image. Public office is "liturgical" in nature. "An official does not act, should not act, is not expected to act solely in his or her private *persona*. He or she acts chiefly, and perhaps solely, as a public officer, representative of the people, in a role marked out by law and tradition."[23]

Political images, however, are not simply masks that cover the politicians' "true selves." Indeed, Hahn and Gonchar argue that political images are more tied to the individual than are abstract "stands on the issues." Images, they say, are at least based on actual personality traits (such as the rigidity and self-righteousness of both Wilson and Nixon). A stand on the issues, in contrast, is often an easily manipulated verbal pose.

Similarly, Michael Novak suggests that even though political roles are determined by "law and tradition," individual politicians must use their own unique personalities to bring the official roles to life. Further, "each holder of the office may draw out of it possibilities not before realized in it." While the leader role shapes and limits behavior, the role and the individual's personality need not be in conflict. Indeed, Novak sees the public political ritual as a unique forum that "channels, deepens, ordinarily fulfills personality, gives it outlet and scope."[24]

In politics, then, image and reality are two strands of a single cloth. The greatness of political leaders rests in how well they perform their ritual roles. Further, the *need* for "performance" is not what distinguishes the honest politician from the dishonest politician. We need to guard against unscrupulous politicians who have no true commitment to their own performances, yet we need to remember that *all* politicians must be concerned with style and image.

In discussing the impact of media on political performances, therefore, I am not suggesting that there is necessarily any change in the "reality coefficient" of politics. There is no clear trend from truth to artifice, or from artifice to truth. There is, however, a change in the style of the "real yet performed" political drama. There is a significant change in the types of images politicians can project. And this change in style is the result of the new staging contingencies created by electronic media.

Great Performances Require the Perfect Stage

Because political competence is closely tied to image, style, and performance, the characteristics of the "stage" of politics have a great effect on political ritual. Before the rise of electronic media, the President was a remote figure, accessible only to a tiny fraction of the population. Such inaccessibility allowed George Washington to escape wide criticism for his "painful speechmaking." And in order to rely more heavily on his "gifted quill" than on his "weak voice and diffident manner," Thomas Jefferson was not even very accessible to the Congress; he delivered messages to the lawmakers in writing to be read by a clerk.[25]

The nonelectronic communication environment favored people who looked powerful and forceful *at a distance*. The President's minute facial expressions and appearance mattered little. Even on campaigns and travels, Presidents were rarely seen long or closely enough to come under careful scrutiny. And reporters were not allowed into the White House on a regular basis until the twentieth century.[26]

In *Presidential Greatness*, Thomas Bailey gives an unusual account of what makes a president "great." It is unusual because in addition to the more traditional descriptions of presidential "accomplishments," Bailey describes such variables as religion, name, looks, size, age, marital status, speaking style, and even timing of death. Bailey acknowledges that many of these variables are seemingly "irrelevant, inconsequential and fortuitous," but his historical look at Presidents suggests that these features have had much to do with reputation and political success. Bailey analyzes the sources of political victory and fame in relation to the polls of historian Arthur Schlesinger, Sr.[27] Without using the metaphors, many of Bailey's observations implicitly deal with the "performances" and "stages" of presidential politics.

It is not surprising, for example, that Bailey discovers that all but one of the top six Presidents in the Schlesinger polls were tall and impressive men. Washington was six feet two inches tall; Linclon was six feet four inches in height. Bailey points out that "average" height was much lower in earlier generations and that a six foot tall individual in Washington's and Lincoln's days "towered over his fellows." Further, Washington and Lincoln, generally regarded as our greatest Presidents, were "almost certainly the two strongest. Washington could crack nuts between his fingers; the youthful Lincoln was the champion weight lifter of his community." Bailey notes that although shortness does not bar a politician from the presidency and does not absolutely restrict a short President from "greatness," shortness remains a definite handicap. Indeed, five of the six shortest Presidents rated no higher than "average" in the second of the Schlesinger polls.[28]

The height and strength of early Presidents made them imposing figures—but only at a distance. When placed on large white horses they must have looked like gods; at closer distances, there was greater evidence of mortality. Washington had deep pockmarks and poorly fitted false teeth. The freckled-faced Jefferson had been dubbed the homeliest student at William and Mary College. Lincoln was "stooped and shambling" and so ugly that he felt obliged to joke about his own appearance. Theodore Roosevelt had "squinty, myopic eyes" and "horsey teeth."[29] Because of their appearances, many of our former "great" Presidents would not be suited to television politics.

Taking the old nonelectronic stage as an unbiased standard, Bailey condemns the new television stage for eliminating potentially great leaders. "The horrifying conclusion emerges that three of the Greats could not hope to secure the nomination if they were here today and in their prime."[30] Yet, while it is true that some of our great Presidents would fare poorly today, it is no doubt just as true that many potentially great people were never considered for the presidency in the past because they did not possess the physical features suited to the *old* communication environment. A short, disabled, or extremely soft-spoken person would probably have been excluded from the early presidential hall of fame.

Interestingly, the first "great" President who was under six feet in height was Woodrow Wilson, who lived at the beginning of the film era. Real height is less important in film than in live encounters. Many leading men in film have also been under six feet tall. The film close-up makes appearance at a distance less significant, and the camera can be angled to give the viewer the feeling of "looking up" to people regardless of their real height.

What matters in terms of presidential style and dynamism is the specific medium through which the President is known to most of the public— or, put differently, the medium helps shape the definition of the situations in which the President "interacts" with the public. Film allowed a short Wilson to appear tall, just as radio permitted a disabled FDR to sound powerful, and television allowed a young Kennedy to look self-assured and experienced. In a sense, each medium is similar to a distinct type of room or theater that requires (and permits) its own "appropriate" type of performer and style of performance. Just as a small seminar room requires a teaching style different from what is appropriate in a large lecture hall, the style of politics must change with changes in media. Some politicians can make the transition from environment to environment (just as some teachers are skilled in both lectures and seminars), but many others cannot. A change in media usually leads to a shift in those politicians who can be viable candidates or successful Presidents.

FDR was a powerful radio speaker. He would have had far more difficulty projecting a powerful image on television, where his inability to walk on his own would have been much more apparent. Nixon was also a highly effective radio speaker, but he had many difficulties with television. On camera, he appeared uncomfortable and shifty. Indeed, those who *watched* the Nixon-Kennedy debates on television tended to agree that Kennedy had won, while many of those who *listened* to the debates on radio thought that Nixon had won.[31] The same political performance in different media, therefore, has different effects.

Kennedy's speaking style was well-matched to television, but it might not have worked so well in other political arenas. As Theodore Sorensen has written, "Kennedy's style was ideally suited to this medium. His unadorned manner of delivery, his lack of gestures and dramatic inflections, his slightly shy but earnest charm, may all have been handicaps on the hustings, but they were exactly right for the living room."[32] David Halberstam puts it more directly: "Television loved him, he and the camera were born for each other."[33] And Kennedy himself attributed his success to television.[34] Ironically, in 1980, John Kennedy's younger brother, Edward, used a campaign style more suited to large political rallies than to the television close-up. On television, his dramatic style often made him appear high strung, overzealous, and even fanatical.[35]

There are many parallels between the fate of actors and the fate of politicians. Some great stage actors seem overblown and silly on television; and many television actors cannot project well enough to act on the stage. Similarly, some silent movie stars were able to make the transition to sound movies, but many others faded from the scene because of the quality of their voices. Both "good" and "bad" actors and politicians are affected by changes in media.

Yet the impact of such changes often becomes invisible because those actors and politicians who are not minimally competent in the new environment soon disappear; people shift their attention to questions of who is best among those who remain. Thus, while we can discuss the relative quality of the media performances of currently prominent national politicians, in some ways the best examples of the effects of media are those potential leaders whom we never even consider. While the strategies and styles of individual politicians definitely have an important effect, a more general tone is established by the nature of the political communication environment.

This aspect of the impact of media on politics is often missed by many who study mass communication. Noted mass communication researcher Wilbur Schramm, for example, generally rejects McLuhan's notion that the medium has an effect apart from the particular messages sent through it. To support this view, he gives the example of people finding out that John Kennedy had been assassinated, and he suggests that people's response was generally the same regardless of whether they heard the bad news through television, radio, print, or word of mouth.[36] This is undeniably true. Yet by citing evidence of the effects of a *specific* message about a *particular* politician, Schramm focuses on a level of communication that cannot possibly reveal the larger impact of the medium on messages and politicians in general. What Schramm overlooks is the fact that it is unlikely that the young, Catholic Kennedy could have been elected to the presidency in the first place without television. Further, he overlooks the fact that the powerful, emotional response to Kennedy's death was closely tied to the "intimacy" that linked Kennedy and his family with people all around the world—an intimacy created by television.

The "stages" of politics are most visible when a candidate either violates their structures or exploits them to the fullest. Adlai Stevenson, for example, never quite conquered the stage of television. Governor Stevenson had difficulty keeping his speeches short enough to fit within the television time he had purchased. "Often after his time had run out, the Governor was cut off the air before he came to the punch lines and vote-seeking conclusions. Reporters grew all too accustomed to seeing Governor Stevenson still talking as the screen went black."[37] FDR, in contrast, was the master of his medium. Theodore White reports that

> friends still recall his glee at the out-foxing of Thomas E. Dewey one evening on radio in the campaign of 1944. Roosevelt reserved time for a quarter-hour radio address on the National Broadcasting Company network; his rival booked the following fifteen minutes to exploit Roosevelt's listening audience for his reply. But Roosevelt spoke to clock time for only fourteen minutes—then left one full minute of paid time in dead silence after his remarks. The listeners frantically twiddled their dials, searching for sounds on other wave lengths; and the millions, who found other stations as they twiddled, were simply not there when the Republican candidate, Dewey, came on the air to speak.[38]

Although the "staginess" of politics is most visible at such extremes, it is present in every presidential act and movement. Over the years, Presidents have routinely engaged in techniques to dramatize their actions: saving or "making" news to keep the flow constant and consistent; timing news releases to match correspondents' schedules and vacations; circling over airports to assure "prime-time" television landings, polling advisors on appropriate telephone calls to be made; and presenting dramatic ultimatums that have been preceded by successful secret negotiations.[39] "So important is the media to a president," writes Joseph Califano, "that he often spends at least as much time trying to anticipate and manipulate its reaction to various ways of enunciating policy as he does in formulating it."[40] Timing and style are features of *all* social performances. How could we expect a person to reach and to stay in high national office without a share of "technique"?

> President Eisenhower was considered by many to be naive about such matters, a political amateur, but he had a great deal more sophistication than came through. He knew exactly what he was doing when he went out to turn on the crowds. I remember being with him while he was waiting to go out into a town square in Latin America. Somebody came in and said, "Mr. President, the crowd is just about ready for you."
>
> He took a deep breath and said, lifting his arms into the familiar pose, "Okay, let's go give them VE-Day." Here was the gesture that everybody regarded as almost holy, yet Ike knew it for what it was—a very effective dramatic technique.[41]

It seems likely, therefore, that all of our Presidents have had to deal with the particular staging contingencies of their day. Contrary to the arguments of Thomas Bailey, the new electronic stages of politics do not simply eliminate potentially competent presidential contenders, they also permit a new set of political actors to compete for the starring political role. Yet Bailey's suggestion that things have changed is correct to the extent that there has been a significant change in the political communication environment and in the style of performance. The trend is away from abstract "communication" and toward personal image and "expression." Television does not foster the formal, front region behavior traditionally associated with the presidency. There is a change, therefore, not only in those who can become serious presidential contenders, but also in the overall image of the presidency itself. While we may not get objectively worse leaders, they are subjectively smaller. The new image of our leaders is clearly one of human beings, rather than of gods.

Media and Presidential Mortality

The new media not only change the information that Presidents can transmit, they also affect the information that Presidents can hide. Perhaps most damaging to the aura of greatness are revelations of the President's infirmities and illnesses. We know that even great leaders are mortal. But we prefer that our leaders die with their boots on, rather than linger in the hospital with tubes inserted in their noses and veins. We are uncomfortable seeing our leaders in any state that is between vigorous action and martyred death.

Our Presidents have never had a shortage of physical woes. George Washington, Thomas Jefferson, and Andrew Jackson all had recurrent malarial fever. In addition, Washington suffered severe toothaches; Jefferson had dysentery, rheumatism, migraine headaches, and terrible backaches; and Jackson suffered chronic dysentery and intestinal cramps, abscesses of the lung, and possibly tuberculosis and lead poisoning (from the "souvenirs" of his almost fatal duels).[42] Abraham Lincoln was "cursed with such overwhelming melancholia that at times his friends despaired of his sanity. He called these attacks 'the hypos'—from 'hypochondria.'"[43] Yet the communication environment surrounding the presidency allowed for these personal infirmities to remain hidden "backstage."

Grover Cleveland had serious medical operations while in the White House. The public was not informed. William Taft had an unusually slow metabolism. He weighed 350 pounds, and he often brought his wife, Nellie, along to official conferences so that she could jab him in the ribs when he began to fall asleep; he is said to have offended some people by snoring through a funeral.[44] But such actions were tolerated because of the communication environment that kept these incidents isolated from, and inaccessible to, the public. The selected appearances and performances of our leaders allowed them to choose a public image more to their liking and more fitting to the ritual of the presidency.

Woodrow Wilson suffered most of his life with various illnesses including neuritis, headaches, partial blindness, and nervous indigestion. "He entered the White House in 1913 with a stomach pump and a generous supply of headache pills."[45] But it was not until his *public* physical collapse that his image was affected.

Franklin Roosevelt was severely disabled, yet the public barely realized. In radio, FDR was only a voice; in film and news photos, his image was carefully structured and controlled.* White House correspondent Merriman Smith describes the contrast between Roosevelt's onstage and backstage image.

> He was virtually a hopeless cripple, but the public at large did not realize it until his death.

---

*White House Press Secretary Stephen Early asked reporters not to write about Roosevelt's paralysis and not to photograph him while he was in a wheelchair or on crutches. The honoring of this request is often attributed to completely different sensibilities among reporters in the past.[46] But what is rarely discussed is the different media environment of the time. In FDR's day, newspaper journalists, photographers, and sound engineers depended on a much more cooperative subject than is required today. Microphones and films were less sensitive to sound and light, respectively. There were no small, unobtrusive sound recorders (indeed, there were no commercially available *tape* recorders at all in the United States until after Roosevelt's death[47]). Until 1954, it was not even possible to film press conferences without the use of a number of very bright, hot lights. Under such conditions, the President and his staff could more easily dictate when and where pictures could be taken and statements made. Significantly, as soon as "fast" film was developed, Ike and his press secretary James Hagerty felt obliged to allow "live filming" for later broadcast on television.[48] With the current ability to capture every move, word, and grunt of a President—without asking him to stand in one spot, speak slowly for notetakers, look into the lights, and speak into the microphone—any requests similar to Stephen Early's would smack of serious censorship. In a sense, there is now a wider range of "available" personal backstage information to censor.

Not in his entire time in the White House could he stand unsupported. Yet, few people outside of Washington realized this. He always had to rely on heavy steel leg braces, canes, and, more often, the support of someone's arm. His legs were literally lifeless. He walked ... only by tremendous effort which often made perspiration pop from his forehead on a cold day.

But when appearing in public, he was the champion, the colorful leader with his chin arched upward and his big hand in the air. He knew he could thrill a crowded stadium by just this simple wave of a hand, or his brown felt hat. That was all it took to jerk a hundred thousand people to their feet in a screaming frenzy.[49]

Even Eisenhower, the first President to be watched closely on television, could linger near death in the hospital while the public saw a flurry of presidential activity through the news releases of Press Secretary Hagerty.[50] Kennedy, however, soon lost the ability to hide his back troubles and had to make a humorous symbol of his rocking chair. And by the time Lyndon Johnson had his gall bladder operation, he felt obliged to smile broadly and reveal his scars to the nation.

Today, the President's whereabouts and activities are subject to constant public scrutiny and concern. "The President doesn't make a move without us," boasts one network television news advertisement. Without recent developments in media, past Presidents were not, indeed could not be, monitored so closely.

The case of Grover Cleveland is especially illuminating because it reveals how greatly the range of control over image has changed in less than a century. Grover Cleveland is sometimes thought of as a President too honest for his own good. He admitted fathering an illegitimate child, and his willingness to tell the public "disagreeable truths" is said to have cost him his re-election.[51] Yet, at a crucial legislative juncture in 1893, Cleveland realized the importance of his image of physical strength.

On June 18, 1893, the White House physician identified a malignant growth in Cleveland's upper jaw. An operation was planned. Yet because of the legislative crisis, the operation "had to be kept a complete secret, for the knowledge that Cleveland's life was in danger would have precipitated a new and far greater panic."[52]

The communication environment of his time allowed Cleveland to pass through an arduous and lengthy physical ordeal with only minor and belated "leaks" to the public. An operation was performed secretly on board Commodore Benedict's yacht, *Oneida,* as it steamed slowly up the East River from New York to Buzzards Bay. Cleveland had arrived in New York the evening of June 30 and stayed on the yacht for five days. The operation involved the removal of the entire upper left jaw and part of the palate. But no external incision was made and this helped keep the operation secret. On July 17 a brief second operation was performed and Cleveland was later fitted with an artificial jaw made of vulcanized rubber.

The operations were kept so secret that for nearly sixty days "no outsider learned what had occurred."[53] And although the President's mouth was stuffed with bandages for almost a month, and his wounds did not heal until September, the public did not discover what had occurred for some time. Indeed, it took nearly twenty-five years for the main details of the operations to become public.[54]

By 1975, the delay time for such news had shrunk from years to minutes and had extended beyond the President to his family as well. A great change had taken place in the monitoring of presidential activities. Former President Ford writes:

> We never went anywhere, however, without a small pool of reporters close by. I understand the reason for this, too: if there had been an unpredictable incident, there had to be people present to report the news. Besides, I think that it's improper for a President to slip out the backdoor of the White House, figuratively speaking, without telling the press where he's going. I'm told that some Presidents have done that, but I don't think its right. . . .
> We told the press that Betty had cancer not 20 minutes after I had been given the news myself. And then we told them everything we knew.[55]

Of course, arguments about what Presidents could and can keep secret are hampered by the fact that part of the evidence is unavailable. That is, anything that has actually remained secret is not available for citation. To some extent, then, what is presented here is a circumstantial case. The suggestion is made that today's Presidents do not have the control that former Presidents have had. Presidents are now watched too closely and, more important, too consistently. It is highly unlikely that a President today could go through Cleveland's lengthy ordeal in secret.

An example from Lyndon Johnson, which at first seems to contradict this thesis, can actually be seen to illustrate it. Johnson did manage to "sneak in" a cancer operation without public notice. But this operation was only for skin cancer and was performed on his *ankle*. If the operation had been more serious or if his appearance had been affected, it is unlikely that the operation could have been kept secret. Further, the nature of the concern over the truth of the reports of the operation suggest that the issue was not the danger to the President so much as his having dared to have an operation—no matter how minor—without the benefit of press coverage. As *The New York Times* reported after the rumored operation was finally confirmed:

> The dispute over the skin cancer issue had attracted wide attention more because of the secrecy than for the seriousness of the ailment. Skin cancers are the most common form of cancer and are usually the most easily cured.
> But the medical matters of Presidents and other political leaders are regarded as public information, and the charge of secrecy has raised questions about the openness of the Johnson Administration.[56]

The strikingly different assumptions concerning presidential accessibility in Cleveland's era are suggested by the fact that the major historical account of Cleveland's life notes that he was on the secret operation yacht for five days following June 30, but no special mention is made of the fact that one of those days was July Fourth![57] The President was out of sight on Independence Day and no one noticed. Today, if the President's whereabouts are a mystery for even a day, reporters start clamoring, "Where is the President?"

It is little wonder, then, that Presidents now feel a need to be "candid" with the press. The speed and constancy of electronic coverage force Presidents to reveal more and to do so as soon as possible. Such candidness allows Presidents to appear to be in control of the flow of information. There is a parallel, therefore, between Jimmy Carter's revelation of his hemorrhoid condition and his 6 A.M. television announcement of the failure of the Iranian rescue mission. Both were attempts to be the first source of potentially discrediting information. Yet, while Presidents may maintain some control by revealing potentially damaging information before it is exposed by the press, there is also an overall decline in their image and prestige because of both the content of the disclosed information and the lack of time available to mold it for public distribution.

From "Private-Public" to "Public-Public"

Even those aspects of political behavior that always have been "public actions"—press conferences, congressional speeches, interviews, and political conventions—have been transformed by the presence of the television camera. Indeed, the dichotomy, public vs. private, is too simplistic to use in describing the impact of electronic media. For television takes already public events and makes them more public. Perhaps we should distinguish between "private-public" events and "public-public" events. By "private-public," I mean those events that involve public actions, but are still isolated in a particular time-space frame, and, therefore, are largely inaccessible to those not physically present. By "public-public," I mean those events that are carried beyond the time-space frame by electronic media, and therefore are accessible to almost anyone.

There is a vast difference between receiving second-hand "reports" on a politician's behavior at public events and seemingly experiencing these events directly through electronic media. This difference has a definite effect on political behavior. While press conferences, for example, have always involved onstage behavior for a politician, they were also once partly backstage interactions between Presidents and reporters. Merriman Smith, a veteran White House correspondent, notes that press conferences were quite different before they "were sanitized by the glare of television exposure."

Press conferences then were dueling matches where the President and reporters truly crossed swords. Exchanges could become angry, as when FDR told a reporter to "go stand in the corner" for asking a stupid question, and bizarre occurrences could happen, as when a haranguing woman, posing as a journalist, had to be bodily removed from one of the meetings in the President's office.[58]

Roosevelt's press secretary, Stephen Early, would sometimes interrupt the President during open press conferences if he thought Roosevelt was getting into trouble. "He would whisper in the President's ear, and then FDR would throw out his big arms in a gesture of hopelessness and say, 'Well, Steve tells me I'm wrong, that it didn't happen that way. I'll have to accept Steve's version. He says . . .'"[59] Yet such events generally remained hidden from the public.

Live television coverage of press conferences transforms the President-press interaction. Reporters bemoan the loss of tough questioning and detailed follow-ups and are dismayed by their role as extras in a presidential drama. But Presidents also lose much control. In an earlier era, Presidents Harding, Coolidge, and Hoover demanded that questions be submitted in advance, answered only those questions they chose to answer, and pressured the press not to mention unanswered questions in their newspaper reports.[60] Throughout his administration, FDR maintained the traditional ban against unauthorized direct quotation ("communication") of a President, and not until the middle of Eisenhower's first term was the press regularly permitted to film press conferences and thus capture and transmit the "expressions" of a President while he was being questioned.[61] John Kennedy took the final step and allowed for simultaneous, "live" television transmission of his press conferences.[62]

For the President, the live television press conference offers new possibilities and new problems. On the positive side, it allows the President to *appear* to be accessible to the press, while, in effect, bypassing them and speaking directly to the people. At the same time, however, the President is placed in a new position of danger. Like a stunt driver attempting a daring feat, the President may thrill the nation with a fine performance or take a series of hard falls. Misstatements, hesitations, evasive answers, mispronunciations, or signs of nervousness may all harm the image of the President.

Another private-public arena that has become public-public through television coverage is the House of Representatives. Interactions on the floor of the House were once fully accessible only to those physically present. The public *Congressional Record* carries no expressive information. A politician may read a statement while animated or exhausted, with a high-pitched voice or a low one, with a lisp or with the flair of a Shakespearean actor, yet the *Congressional Record* bears only the discursive verbal messages. Through printed words, politicians can speak with the "voice" (i.e., the language) of a king or a commoner, and they can easily choose their "tone" and "expression."

The presentational messages in television, however, are not so easily shaped, and once shaped and recorded, their nonlinear, holistic quality makes them essentially uneditable. The cameras in the House of Representatives are aimed only at the podium, so as to avoid capturing inappropriate behaviors or empty seats; even so, the congressional arena has been transformed. The television camera captures the intimate personal style of the politician. It captures a slip of the tongue, the nervous quiver in a voice, the weariness of slumped shoulders and rumpled clothing.

Because Congressional sessions were traditionally private-public events, members of Congress were once given great control over the content of the printed *Congressional Record*. Indeed, the *Congressional Record* has been a notoriously inaccurate account of actual House proceedings. Statements are known to have been enlarged, condensed, and substantially edited before they appeared in the *Record*. Because the actual proceedings "disappeared," however, the discrepancies between the proceedings and the written record were largely invisible. There was only one public version of the proceedings. Now that the actual proceedings are recorded and frozen on videotape (and are available for public purchase), moves are being taken to bring the two records of Congress—videotape and print—into synchrony. Representatives are being restricted in their power to "revise and extend" their statements for the *Congressional Record*.[63]

Political interviews are, by definition, public acts. But without electronic media, they also involve a personal and private interaction between politician and reporter. In interviews that are to be printed, politicians are able to separate their conversations with reporters from their "official" statements for publication. The television interview, however, merges the politician-reporter interaction into the politician-public interaction and demands a new behavioral style that is neither private conversation nor public proclamation.

The setting for television interviews is often an actual or mock living room. The "televised living room" is an appropriate symbol of the move from private-public to public-public. For the living room is an "onstage" area to those who visit a home, but a "backstage" area to those who are not invited into a house. Broadcasting the behavior that takes place in a living room brings the outside world into the "onstage" room of the home, but the television interview remains a public eavesdropping on a personal interaction. Even the knowledge of being overheard by millions does not change the fact that the words spoken and the behaviors exhibited are mostly intimate.

In television interviews, the interviewer and interviewee are often physically close. As anthropologist Edward Hall argues, conversational tone, facial expression, and choice of language are often determined by the distance between people.[64] It is as difficult to give a rabble-rousing speech when sitting three feet from an audience as it is to speak to a lover

about intimate affairs at a distance of twenty feet. The television interview, therefore, generally turns away from oratory and "ideas" and
moves toward the chatty and the personal.*

In 1973, the new Vice President, Gerald Ford, *and his family,* were interviewed *in their home* by Dick Cavett. From the questions asked, the American public found out a little of the family's personal life and something
about Gerald Ford's ignorance of rock groups. Even in the relatively formal Ford "farewell" interview with Barbara Walters, Mr. and Mrs. Ford
spoke of mastectomies and loneliness in the White House. And Ms. Walters heralded (and delivered) the premiere television view of the "First
Family's private quarters."

In her post-election interview with Mr. and Mrs. Carter in 1976, Barbara Walters asked intimate questions concerning marriage, love letters,
babies, mother-in-law problems, annoying habits, and single versus double beds in the White House. The Carters answered them all.

For many of us, watching these interviews is simultaneously pleasing
and disturbing. On the one hand, we feel a sense of awe. We appreciate
that we are getting closer to a "great leader." At first, the questions seem
oddly appropriate—what we might want to find out in a personal interaction with a public figure. On the other hand, there is something annoying about what we see and hear. Our leaders do not seem as great as we
would like them to be. The overall impression is: They are "ordinary people." William Jennings Bryan was called the "great commoner." In the
past we took pride in the greatness of the "common" American. Now we
often wince with shame at the commonness of our leaders.†

Televised political conventions offer a showcase of the effects of electronic media on politics. Conventions were once the party's private-public
celebrations and rituals of unity. Television coverage of conventions,
however, has turned them into middle region circuses which are neither
public nor private. They cease, therefore, to serve their old functions of
party unity, and they also fail to inspire the confidence of the voter.

---

*Programs such as "Meet the Press" and "Face the Nation" are often exceptions to this rule
of intimacy. Yet producers have apparently found that in order to create a formal atmosphere
in such shows, they must use tables or desks and establish increased distance among participants. Further, these programs are rarely considered "good television." They are often
designed to fulfill the "public service" requirements for a television broadcast license, and
they are usually aired during "dead times," when relatively small audiences are available to
sell to advertisers.

†In the early twentieth century, the Englishman Lord Bryce argued that, for a number of
reasons, Americans shy away from nominating and electing their most eminent statesmen
to the presidency. Americans, he said, opt for the "safer" candidates who have fewer admirers, but also fewer enemies, and who do not intimidate the average voter.[65] Bryce's analysis
is sometimes cited to suggest that our current "crisis of leadership" is merely a continuation
of a long trend. But arguing that "nothing has changed" misses the significant qualitative
shift in the image of the President. In the past, distance and mystification often allowed the
man who became President to transcend his "commonness" and to appear to be a "great
leader." Today, the longer we observe a President, the more common he seems.

Sig Mickelson, former president of CBS News, offers this description of the convention as it appears on television.

> The convention seems to be a chaotic and unmanageable circus that doesn't reflect the significance of the process. The public becomes cynical when it sees its presidential candidate selected in so disorderly a manner by a combination of apparent despots and over-aged adolescents parading in outlandish costumes with New Year's Eve noisemakers. The whole process on occasion looks like a parody.[66]

The new patterns of information flow created by media coverage of conventions serve as an analogy for the general undermining of hierarchy by electronic media. Douglass Cater gives the following example from the explosive 1968 Democratic Convention.

> At one moment, all hell broke loose in the area where the Wisconsin delegation was seated. Immediately, the TV cameras zoomed in and reporters rushed there with walkie-talkies. In an instant, the whole viewing nation knew the cause of the trouble, while Speaker Carl Albert, presiding over the convention, didn't know. Yet, Albert was the one who had to decide what to do about the problem. In microcosm, one witnessed how leadership can be hustled by such a formidable communication system.[67]

When electronic media attempt to reveal to their audience what is "really" going on, they often change what is going on. There is a parallel here to the changing role of the sports umpire with the advent of the "instant replay." A new direction of information flow undermines former authority and control.

The fact that conventions were originally designed to be private-public affairs is revealed by the fact that the presence of reporters often causes disturbances. Indeed, reporters are frequently greeted with hostility. In 1964, for example, John Chancellor was carried off the floor of the Republican convention. At the 1968 Democratic Convention, Mike Wallace was ejected from the convention floor, and Dan Rather was punched by a security officer while he was trying to obtain an interview. During the 1976 Republican convention, Gerald Ford surprised Ronald Reagan at the end of evening by asking him to come down to the rostrum. A reporter rushed to Reagan to ask his "feelings," but the moment was unrehearsed and there was no statement or sentiment at hand. The reporter was quickly pushed aside as Reagan's advisors gathered in a tight circle around their candidate in a desparate attempt to gain a back region.

In the private-public press conferences, legislative sessions, interviews, and political conventions of the past, politicians' mistakes, conferences with advisors, hesitations, and personal expressions tended to remain unexposed to the larger public. With television coverage that is both instant and relatively constant, political leaders no longer have the opportunity to hide their basic humanity or their need for decision time and advice.

Erving Goffman notes that behaviors that are necessary to the performance of a role must sometimes be sacrificed in order to give the *impression* that a role is being performed properly. He notes, for example, that
an umpire must often give up the moment of thought he needs to be certain of a decision in order to act instantly and thereby *appear* certain.[68] But
politicians play a game with higher personal and social stakes. Those politicians who now attempt to sound positive without taking the time to
speak to advisors often find that they have to make damaging statements
of correction. One middle region alternative is to emphasize the deliberation process and one's openness to the ideas of others, thereby attempting to make a virtue out of advice. But this stance is only a compromise;
it nevertheless weakens the image of a central authority figure.

In the new communication environment, many politicians lose either
way. If they attempt to play the old role of steady and certain leadership,
they are fouled by the glut of information. If they fully open themselves
to public view, they demystify their roles. The new nature of the political
arena, therefore, can be seen as the common thread linking the troubles
of the seemingly very different presidencies of Richard Nixon and Jimmy
Carter.

Watergate and "Cartergate"

For much of his political career, Richard Nixon was plagued by apparent
inconsistencies between his verbal message and his nonverbal style. He
was a good speaker and an excellent debater, and he was, therefore,
extremely effective in person and on radio. On television, however, he
often seemed uncomfortable and tense. His finely tuned verbal arguments
were often undermined by a clenched fist, shifty eyes, and a contemp-
tuous scowl.

Because of his style (as well as the content of some of his attacks on
political opponents), he was dubbed "Tricky Dicky," and taunted with
such queries as, "Would you buy a used car from this man?" Whether a
voter trusted Richard Nixon often seemed to depend on whether the voter
paid more attention to Nixon's verbal language or his body language.

After his image problems in the 1960 televised debates, Nixon became
more wary of television. Indeed, one factor that may have helped ease
Nixon into the White House in 1968 was his decision not to *appear* in
many of his campaign ads; only his voice was heard. In effect, these spots
presented Nixon's "radio voice" coupled with a picture show. Once in
office, however, the tension between Nixon's public pronouncements and
his personal style mounted.

President Nixon was the archetypal victim of the new middle region
politics. He attempted to be an old style "great leader" in blissful ignorance of the new communication environment surrounding the presidency. What ultimately undid Nixon were the blatant inconsistencies
between his onstage and backstage behaviors. Nixon was so certain of his

control over access to his back regions that he even taped his private conversations while making contradictory public statements on television. The tapes confirmed what many people had guessed about Nixon from observing his televised slips of the tongue and disturbing nonverbal style. Nixon had made public proclamations of his greatness and of his dedication to law and order; his backstage behavior revealed his pettiness and his use of the language of gangsters.

The shifting line between backstage and onstage behaviors is a theme that runs through the Watergate scandal, but it is rarely explicitly stated or discussed. Instead, the popular and scholarly discussions of Watergate have tended to focus on legal and moral issues. In a massive, 2,000 page documented history of the presidency, for example, William Goldsmith summarizes the implications of Watergate as follows:

> There have been presidential scandals and lackluster Chief Executives in the past, but the country has never experienced anything approaching the degradation of the White House which we have *witnessed* during the past few years. The American presidency has served the republic admirably, sometimes brilliantly, over the course of its almost 200 years of existence. There has been an ebb and flow of power just as there has been a rise and fall of particularly talented leadership. . . . But during this entire period, no President has so *clearly abused* the prerogatives of his office as Richard Milhous Nixon. It will not be easy to recover from this experience.[69]

The references to *witnessing* and *clear abuse* in this quote raise some uncomfortable questions: Were Nixon's behaviors really that unusual? Or was it the "clarity" of his acts, that is, their revelation to the public, that made them seem unusual and unacceptable?

Nixon claimed, of course, that his behaviors were not atypical. The meaning of this claim can be taken in two ways: (1) that many other Presidents were "corrupt" (which is a poor excuse), or (2) that all Presidents— good and bad—must behave privately in ways that seem to contradict their publicly proclaimed virtue and piety (which is a much more sophisticated argument).

There have been many theories put forward as to why Richard Nixon did not destroy the incriminating tapes: for reasons of history, for tax purposes, because of psychological imbalance.[70] One possibility that has generally been ignored is that Nixon did not immediately find anything damaging on the tapes. This may seem absurd, yet when asked by interviewer David Frost in 1977 why he did not destroy the tapes, Nixon indicated that when he had first listened to them in June 1973, he discovered nothing "detrimental to me."[71]

Nixon's seemingly ridiculous claim that he heard nothing damaging to him on the tapes makes some sense if we consider that Nixon may have listened to the tapes with "back region ears." That is, the tapes may have sounded "normal" to him because the general form of talk on them was not, after all, so unusual for backstage conversations among colleagues or friends.

Nixon's situation is analogous to that of a single-sex group of high school students who engage in a locker-room bull session. The conversation may be full of obscenities and fantasized sexual activities, discussions of the physical characteristics of teachers, administrators, and students of the other sex, and "plots" to undermine the legitimate and smooth functioning of the school. If the students taped their locker-room bull session and listened to it, they might still find their conversations quite humorous, and they might congratulate each other on cleverly turned phrases and devilishly obscene remarks. But if the same tape were played publicly for their teachers, parents, and friends of the opposite sex, it is likely that its reception would be quite different.

Nixon may even have mistakenly believed that his "natural" back region style would endear him to the public, show a more human Nixon (just as a high school boy might mistakenly believe that his girlfriend would be charmed by the style of an all-male discussion about women). Instead, Nixon found his back region conversations treated as if they were the shocking public statements of a psychotic.

Indeed, the horror felt by Republican editors when reading the transcripts of the "Watergate tapes" is very similar to the dismay sometimes felt by females upon overhearing an all-male conversation about women.

William Randolph Hearst, Jr., Editor-in-Chief of The Hearst Newspapers wrote:

> President Richard M. Nixon has made it impossible for me to continue believing what he claims about himself in the Watergate mess.
> . . .The point is that those shameful tapes reveal a man totally absorbed in the cheapest and sleaziest kind of conniving to preserve appearances, and almost totally unconcerned with ethics. . . .
> Over the years I have known quite a few Presidents and am very much aware of the often ruthless—even deplorable—actions made necessary by the pressures of their awesome power. But I have never heard anything as ruthless, deplorable, and ethically indefensible as the talk on those White House tapes. . . .
> To Lincoln, to Ike, and to most of our Presidents, the White House itself had to be just that—a house of pristine integrity, both in reality and appearance.[72]

Similarly, feminist writer Shulamith Firestone writes:

> To overhear a bull session is traumatic to a woman: So all this time she has been considered only "ass," "meat," "twat," or "stuff," to be gotten a "piece of," "that bitch," or "this broad" to be tricked out of money or sex or love! To understand finally that she is no better than other women but completely indistinguishable comes not just as a blow but as a total annihilation.[73]

It may seem astounding that a practiced politician such as Richard Nixon could not anticipate the shock waves that would be caused by the release of the tapes, but apparently he did not. *Newsweek* reported that "the sorry irony was that he had hastened [the crisis] by his own monumental miscalculation—the publication . . . of the transcripts of some of his secret Watergate tapes."[74] Astonishingly, the White House summary that accompanied the transcripts, proclaimed: "In all of the thousands of words spoken, even though they often are unclear and ambiguous, not once does it appear that the President of the United States was engaged in a criminal plot to obstruct justice."[75]

Apparently, Richard Nixon and his staff looked at the transcripts as "legal documents." They looked for *words* that revealed illegal actions. Perhaps they even saw in the "unclear and ambiguous" conversations the shadow of a doubt that often leans a jury toward a verdict of "not guilty." What they overlooked was the backstage behavioral *style* that seemed inappropriate for a President. With a focus on words, for example, Nixon's staff censored the content by deleting expletives, but that action did not dilute the shock to many people that there were expletives to be deleted. It is this shock over style that is visible in William Randolph Hearst's choice of the words "shameful," "cheapest," "sleaziest," and "conniving."

Nixon had portrayed himself in public as one type of person; the tapes revealed a different personality.

> To many transcript readers, he was trivial and indecisive, a Nixon completely at variance with the masterful hero of [his memoirs,] *Six Crises.*
>
> Transcript readers searched in vain for any discussion by the President of the welfare of the country or the constitutionality of his Watergate actions. Prior to the transcripts he had often been depicted as a tightly controlled, incisive man; but he was now shown letting control over events and persons slip from his grasp, spending hours avoiding any kind of decision.[76]

The "truth content" of back region behaviors, however, is questionable and elusive, and quick condemnation of them is not wise. *All* persons exhibit behaviors that are contradictory to their front region roles. Many good doctors, lawyers, priests, professors, and Presidents say and do things privately that might lead to their disgrace if they were treated as public statements and actions. Is there anyone, for example, who is not, at times, "trivial and indecisive"? Even the most honest and ethical professionals probably could not emerge unscathed from the publication of transcripts of private conversations. *The Chicago Tribune's* condemnation of the Nixon revealed in the transcripts, for example, would seem an apt description of many of the back region interactions of almost anyone: "He is vacillating. He is profane. He is willing to be led. He displays dismaying gaps in knowledge."[77]

Nixon is a very problematic example for the present analysis because it is so difficult to separate the situational and moral issues. Nixon remains such a contemptible figure to many people that it is not always easy to grasp that the type of scrutiny under which Nixon was placed would probably undermine the behaviors of any of our Presidents. This analysis is not meant to redeem Nixon's morally reprehensible behavior so much as it is designed to explain the dynamics of a credibility problem that is likely to harm the image of both moral and immoral performers.

Indeed, Nixon may even be fairly accurate in his claim that he did only what many other Presidents have done. There is ample evidence of many Presidents—including "good" ones—using profanity and lying to the people or to Congress.[78] In a sense, then, Nixon's political downfall resulted from his not gauging the new information environment. His "normal" private behavior became public. He was a bad performer, and to the extent that the presidency is based on style and performance, he was a "bad" President.

Is the public any wiser? The American people were shocked over Nixon's attempt to spy on the back regions of others, yet the public found out about these actions only through its own vicarious spying on Nixon's back region. And following the release of the White House transcripts, there were immediate demands for the release of the tapes themselves on long-playing records.[79]

The attitudes of journalists and many scholars may also be questioned. Was David Frost justified in using transcripts of Oval Office conversations to quiz Nixon on his presidential motives and intentions? In other words, should these back region comments have been analyzed and examined as if they were public statements? Could the reputation of any politician (or lawyer or doctor or teacher or, indeed, television interviewer) withstand such questions? And are many scholars and journalists correct in assuming that the problem with the presidency today is that Congress and the people do not have *enough* information about the President and the workings of the executive office?[80]

The current feelings of "right to know" and "honesty at all costs" have not been accompanied by a sophisticated notion of what is behind the public masks of all great leaders. As Goffman suggests in relation to hierarchical mystification: "The real secret behind the mystery is that there really is no mystery."[81]

Our newfound ability to peer into what was once the backstage of political life creates new dilemmas for us as a nation. At least some of our moral outrage at what we find in back regions is based on our naive assumptions concerning the underpinnings of authority. We obviously want to uncover gross incompetence and unmask ruthless dishonesty. But often what we take to be evidence of incompetence and dishonesty is simply the staging process needed for all social performances.

Difficult questions remain: When does disclosure equal social truth? Where is the dividing line between honest "performances" and dishonest ones? And most significant, Can we have both "great leaders" and "freedom of information"? The presidency of Jimmy Carter suggests a preliminary "No."

On November 2, 1976, Americans elected the first "middle region President." It is difficult to say whether Carter and his advisors were explicitly aware of the character of the new middle region politics, yet Carter's actions as a candidate and as a new President certainly seemed to be carefully tailored to the new political arena.

In maintaining the image and position of an "outsider," Carter gained a distinct advantage over other leading contenders for the presidency. As a political stranger, he was not associated with many of the front region/back region inconsistencies that had been whittling down the faith in the "old faithfuls" of both parties.

In his campaign, Carter projected himself as an ideological descendant of Harry Truman—the one recent President who is now perceived as having been consistent in front and back regions. Carter tried extremely hard to say nothing that would contradict himself. His message all over the country was nearly the same. Of necessity, it was not much of a message, but it was relatively consistent and persistent. Basically, he said, "Just trust me."* (Almost every time he got more specific he drew fire from one or another sector of the country.[83]) And this basic request for trust helped win him the Democratic nomination and later the presidency. As *Newsweek* observed:

> No candidate since Wendell Willkie in 1940 had won with a scantier public record; no Democrat since John W. Davis in 1924 had been nominated out of private life; no Deep Southerner since Zachary Taylor in 1848 had been proposed for the Presidency by either major party. And no modern political figure except Ike has offered a candidacy built so completely on personal trust and so little on programmatic detail. Carter *has* programs, but has blurred them to a point where one of his own staffers pleaded in mid-primary season for at least "the appearance of substance." What Carter has offered instead is his own person, displayed eighteen bone-wearying hours a day, and his carefully uncontoured promise of a government as good as the American people.[84]

Understanding the extent to which he would have to remain in the limelight, Carter chose an act which he himself could follow—again and again. Carter eschewed the traditional role of dynamic and forceful leader. He usually spoke quietly and slowly. His tone and manner were more suited to the sensitive microphone and the close-up lens than to the live audiences often addressed simultaneously. David Halberstam noted that Carter "more than any other candidate this year has sensed and adapted to modern communications and national mood. . . . Watching him again and again on television I was impressed by his sense of pacing, his sense of control, very low key, soft, a low decibel count, all this in sharp contrast to the other candidates."[85]

---

*Even in Carter's highly edited and selective book of speeches, *A Government as Good as Its People*—which includes fewer than 40 of his 2,100 presidential campaign speeches—the following statement (or its paraphrase) appears three times within a dozen pages: "There are a lot of things I would not do to be elected. I wouldn't tell a lie. I wouldn't make a misleading statement. I wouldn't betray a trust. I wouldn't avoid a controversial issue. If I do any of those things, don't support me, because I wouldn't deserve to lead this country."[82]

Carter made public statements filled with tentativeness. He said "we'll see" and "I think." He mentioned his own personal limitations. In a campaign speech before the Cleveland City Club in April 1976, for example, he said:

> I don't claim to know all the answers. I'm still searching for many answers.
> . . . I don't consider myself to be the best qualified person in this country. I'm
> sure there are many of you who are more intelligent, better trained, perhaps
> better managers than I would be as President. I want to express my personal
> thanks to all of you for not running this year.[86]

Carter emphasized his reliance on advisors and his cabinet and stated his determination to give an unprecedented role of importance to the Vice President, making him, in effect, "Assistant President."[87] He promised to open the executive branch of the government to the people's scrutiny. "Every time we have made a serious mistake in recent years, it has been because the American people have been excluded from the process through secrecy, through misleading statements, sometimes through outright lies."[88] He promised never to lie to the nation.

The imperial Richard Milhous Nixon had spoken about clean language in public and cursed in private; low-key Jimmy (not James Earl) Carter attempted to project a front that could not be undermined easily by anything the media could reveal.* He hoped, he said, "to build an intimate, personal relationship" with the American people.[89] Carter claimed for himself few uncommon virtues beyond a strong faith in God and a willingness to work hard. In his inaugural address, he told the people: "Your strength can compensate for my weakness, and your wisdom can help to minimize my mistakes."[90]

Many of Carter's early actions as President were symbolically appropriate to the new middle region politics:

- he held a "People's Inaugural" and invited the entire country to attend;
- he wore a regular business suit at his inauguration instead of the traditional morning coat and top hat, and he walked, rather than rode, down Pennsylvania Avenue;
- he wore jeans and workboots in public;

---

*While there was some stir over a campaign interview Carter gave to *Playboy*, in which he used some vulgarities, the publication never seemed to annoy Carter much, and it is even possible that it was part of his larger strategy. In retrospect, it is a model of consistency—the homogenization of back and front regions through the careful use of religion. Sure Carter has lust (doesn't everybody?), but he'd never fool around with Jesus watching! Perhaps most important, the interview suggested that Carter, though religious himself, would not impose puritanical standards on other Americans. This analysis may explain why, even after the election, Carter did not try to have the interview fade into history. Indeed, he reprinted a noncontroversial part of the interview in *A Government as Good as Its People* along with an introduction that refers to the uproar caused by his talk of "screwing," and "shacking up."

- he often stayed in private homes when he traveled around the country;
- he enrolled his daughter, Amy, in an integrated public school;
- he held a live call-in television show to answer questions from "the people";
- in his first televised presidential address, he wore a cardigan sweater and spoke "directly" from an easy chair without the increased formality and distance of an intervening table or desk;
- he emphasized (at first) the carrying of his own luggage;
- he eliminated door-to-door limousine service for most of the White House staff;
- he cut down on White House television sets, and eliminated the "court photographer" position; and
- he even banned, for a time, the playing of "Hail to the Chief."*

All of these "de-imperializing" actions seem to have been aimed at achieving consistency among all the bits of information that now make up our image of the President. Yet while Carter attempted to reshape presidential behavior to suit the high visibility of the office, he met problems from two sides. First, many people resented his "lowering" of the office and his lack of dynamism and power. At the same time, however, the amount of attention paid to the President seemed too great even for Carter's low-key style and "straightforward" approach. Immediately after the election, his designate for Attorney General was attacked for belonging to segregated clubs.[93] Then, the Bert Lance scandal undermined the credibility of the White House.[94] In 1978, a national men's magazine published a series of "exposés" titled "Cartergate," one installment of which was titled "The First Hundred Lies of Jimmy Carter."[95] (The illustration was a picture of Carter with an ax standing next to one hundred felled cherry trees.) Later in his term, Billy Carter's questionable associations

---

*There are some striking parallels between the 1970s' evolution of image at the White House and at the Vatican. Both the brief, 34-day reign of Pope John Paul I in 1978 and the current reign of John Paul II suggest a new, middle region style papacy. John Paul I is best remembered for his "ready smile, an irrepressible tendency to laugh and joke and an almost compulsive need to hug everyone he met." One of his first innovations was to use a new, intimate style in public appearances. He abandoned the impersonal papal "we" in favor of "I," refused to wear a papal crown, publicly confessed his ignorance of the workings of the Holy See, avoided prepared texts, and spoke in homely metaphors. (On one occasion, for example, he likened God to an automobile salesman and spoke of sinners as those who put champagne and jam in their engines and then complain that their car "ends up in a ditch.") And for his regular Wednesday audiences, he chose to *walk* humbly to his throne rather than be carried into the room in it.[91] The cardinals in Rome chose an unlikely, but equally gregarious successor—the first non-Italian Pope since 1523. John Paul II immediately continued and advanced the intimacy and humility of his predecessor. He broke tradition by directly addressing the crowds who came to greet him *before* delivering his first papal blessing. One of his first audiences was granted to journalists. Within days, "he set the style of a papacy less formal, more accessible to the people and the cameras, than any in the church's nearly 2000 years."[92]

with Libya and Jimmy Carter's handling of the affair were sharply criticized.

There are many indications, then, that Jimmy Carter made a serious attempt to adjust the style of his performance to match the requirements of the new political arena. Yet the close margin of his victory and the negative response to his "unpresidential" style point to the public's uneasiness over having only a "good man" as a leader.

By the time of his re-election bid, it looked as if Carter would lose no matter what he did. He was seriously challenged by other candidates even within his own party. Faced with his own widening "credibility gap," Carter began wavering in his style and approach to the presidency. He began to revert back to the techniques of more "imperial" Presidents. After many promises to keep an open administration, the Carter White House moved to stop the unauthorized flow of information and instituted a new security designation, one step above "top secret." Ironically, the administration that had pledged to deimperialize the presidency labeled the new secret status "Royal."[96]

With the apparent failure of his openness and accessibility, Carter seemed to seize on the Iranian hostage crisis as a reason to isolate himself from the public and the media. His "Rose Garden strategy" began to resemble the arrogant isolations of Johnson and Nixon.

When challenged by Edward Kennedy and Ronald Reagan, Carter became less soft-spoken and more aggressive. If Kennedy opposed him, he said, he would "whip his ass."[97] Carter then began frontal attacks on Ronald Reagan. He accused Reagan of racial prejudice and warmongering, and he suggested that "Reagan is not a good man to trust with the affairs of this nation." These attacks apparently delighted the Reagan camp because they made Carter appear "mean-spirited" and allowed Reagan to be humble, forgiving, and "statesmanlike." In a private memo to Carter, presidential advisor Hamilton Jordan warned that support for Carter as a "likable" and "well-intentioned" person had eroded badly. "This is the first time that 'personal qualities' are not a basic strength of ours."[98] A month before the election, an ABC-Louis Harris Poll indicated that twice as many people as a year before believed that "President Carter is not a man of high integrity."[99] With Carter's unintentional help, Reagan was able to out-Carter Carter; that is, he was able to present more of the soft, middle region style that had distinguished Carter from other candidates in 1976.

In a decisive battle of images—the Carter-Reagan debates—Carter played Nixon to Reagan's Kennedy. Carter was "tough," unrelenting, tense, and humorless. He spouted facts and figures. Reagan was calm, humble, and bubbling with anecdotes. He chuckled. In seeming good humor, he chided Carter for distorting the facts, "There you go again, Mr. President." The debates eased the public's fear that Reagan was a madman and would get the United States involved in a global war.[100]

If anything, Carter's change in style probably worked against him. The election ended in a landslide victory for Reagan.

The Presidency in the Eye of Television: Reagan and Beyond

Nixon, Carter, and Reagan are very different men with different personalities and programs, and different strengths and weaknesses. Their elections to the White House were dependent, in large measure, on their individual strategies and styles and on the particular desires and concerns of the American people. Yet all three of their presidencies share a common denominator: the new communication environment fostered by electronic media.

In navigating the ship of state, Nixon and Carter each ran aground in the same body of water, but on opposite shores. The task of subsequent Presidents is to negotiate the waters of the new communication environment without hitting either bank. This analysis is not about winners or losers, but about the ways in which the game of politics must now be played. The new rules may eliminate some contenders and allow others to compete, but the rules do not fully determine particular winners.

In the past, all those who ran for President were in the position of people who wished to speak in a large arena: They had to raise their voices and flail their arms in order to be seen and heard by people in the back row. But they also had the time and privacy to prepare carefully for their dramatic public performances. Today, all political contenders must act within the constraints and requirements of a new, "smaller" and more personal political environment. They are watched more closely and more consistently. Electronic media tend to create a new problem for all Presidents: the difficulty of being simultaneously "intimate" and "presidential," both "accessible" and "inspiring."

The extent to which television has reshaped the political arena, heightened the need for appropriate middle region style, and minimized other aspects of training and skill is suggested by the election of a professional actor with years of performance experience. If Nixon was thesis, and Carter antithesis, then Reagan is synthesis. He is a man who says he will "talk tough," but does so in a soft-spoken, folksy style. He seems comfortable in a full spectrum of costumes, from tuxedos to cowboy suits, and in a wide range of activities from ballroom dancing to gardening. He is part Nixon, part Carter, an "imperial" President who chops his own wood. Unlike Nixon, Reagan appears to be a sweet and likable person; unlike Carter, he offers a romantic notion of America's power and destiny.

Reagan's style is even purer "middle region" than Carter's. Reagan "takes a stand," but he does so with "aw shucks" humility and with speeches scattered with anecdotes and quotes from letters written by children and the common folk. Like Carter, he avoids traditional rhetorical flamboyance in favor of a simple, all-American-boy simplicity, but he and his wife have brought back a "high class" style that many saw as absent in the Carter White House. Reagan has tried to convey a personal style of accessibility and openness, but he has also moved to reverse the trend of opening the processes and files of government to the public. He has tried to stop leaks to the press through secrecy contracts, lie detector tests, and a tighter classification system for government documents.[101] Reagan has succeeded more than most recent Presidents in separating the reaction to his personality from the response to his political actions. As *The Boston Globe* observed, "Even Ronald Reagan's most ferocious partisan critics have prefaced nearly every denunciation with some qualifying allusion to the President's genial and amiable ways."[102]

Although Reagan's amiable style has made him more durable against attack than his two predecessors, the close media observation of the President has taken its toll on his credibility. Reports have highlighted his "detached managerial style," his many vacations (nearly 16 weeks during his first 20 months in office), his limited working hours, and his fondness for afternoon naps. Many of his televised press conferences have been disasters of misstatements, unintelligible replies, and parables that he cannot support with facts or evidence. Beyond the issue of credibility, Reagan has been charged with an "articulation gap" and difficulty in concentrating on reporters' questions or his responses to them. He has been dubbed by some people as an "amiable dunce."[103]

Reagan has pictured himself as reversing the trend of a declining presidency, yet he is nevertheless a part of it. Indeed, he has, in some ways, also consciously hastened it. For another peculiarity of Reagan's presidency is that he is a self-styled "strong leader" who is leading the people away from strong central leadership. His "new Federalism" is a move away from a powerful central government and a drive toward the decentralized authority so desired by the *Anti*-Federalists in the early days of the republic. Speaking to county officials in Baltimore in 1982, for example, Reagan spoke of "restoring" the 10th Amendment, which gives most powers to the states: "For the first time in too many years, the Federal Government will recognize a limit on what it should do, how fat it can grow and the power it can claim. With your help, we will reverse the flow of power, sending it back to the localities."[104] Paradoxically, Reagan has pictured himself as the central leader to support if one distrusts central leaders.

One of the reasons for our general loss of faith in powerful central leadership may be that the new communication environment coupled with our expectations of the office make impossible demands on a President. By revealing more, the new media demand more manipulation and control. And yet the new media reveal so much that they also make the President's *need* for control and advice more visible. As a result, people have become more cynical about the presidency as they begin to become more aware both of the manipulation of symbols and images and of the management of personal impressions. The new media create a dilemma for politicians: They demand the smooth performance of a professional actor, yet they also make such a performance appear to be a sham.

There is a certain irony in Reagan's reported public relations "successes." Reagan has been hailed as the "Great Communicator" because of his supposedly masterful manipulation of the media. Yet the public is not simply the audience to the onstage result of Reagan's public relations techniques. The accounts by journalists and even by Reagan's own advisors offer "sidestage" reports that emphasize the President's attempts to *create* certain onstage images and impressions. If Reagan visits a mostly black school, we learn that it is a symbolic visit to offset the impression of his lack of concern for the welfare of blacks. When Reagan visits the Olympic team's training center, we hear that the "media event" allows him to be photographed in athletic-looking clothing in order to highlight his health and vigor. His trips are discussed in terms of the "photo opportunities" they provide and his "picture book diplomacy" is described as an "advance man's dream." We are told about the First Actor's makeup, hair dye, and hearing aid. We learn about his techniques for avoiding answering reporters' questions. It is a mixed blessing for Reagan to be praised for being able to give a "flawless delivery" of a speech whose final script (written by someone else) was handed to him only seventeen minutes earlier.[105]

Once the techniques of establishing awe and mystification are opened to the public, the mystification is undermined. As George Reedy observes:

> The problem with all public relations techniques, motivational research and concepts of manipulating human behavior, is that as rapidly as the techniques become known, they become ineffective. . . . If they become a subject of common conversation, the people feel they are being sold a bill of goods. There was an excellent example of this process in the first few months after President Nixon took office. Day after day I saw story after story of his assistants congratulating themselves upon the excellence of President Nixon's public relations techniques. Well, the obvious answer is that when people start talking about a man's public relations techniques, he does not have any.[106]

The public's general acceptance of Reagan's style may be related to a new willingness among Americans to tolerate a sidestage view of the presidency. In the 1950s, there were rumblings of complaint when Dwight Eisenhower, a genuine war hero, felt the need to hire a Hollywood actor to give him advice on his television appearances. But Americans today accept that the President himself must be a skilled actor and that he must *perform* the role of President rather than simply *be* President. While Reagan's first term in office was filled with as many administration scandals, embarrassing moments, policy failures, and credibility problems as those of other recent Presidents, he has consistently *acted* as if nothing damaging has occurred—and the public has allowed him to do so. In the aftermath of several awful presidential performances, many Americans seem to have adopted a pragmatic acceptance of style as substance, at least until some better alternative arises.

Reagan's success in comparison with Nixon and Carter, therefore, should not be confused with a renaissance of the Presidency. Indeed, given the distinction between "communication" and "expression" discussed in Chapter 6, the label "Great *Communicator*" is misleading. Few people are cherishing Ronald Reagan's speeches or reading his books. But Reagan is a "Great *Expressor*." Even when dodging a reporter's question, he often humbly cocks his head, smiles, and waves. Even when he makes a terrible joke or speaks a sentence that has no beginning, middle, and end, he seems like a "nice person." Reagan's communications are often mundane, sometimes incomprehensible, but they are frequently salvaged by a voice that chokes with emotion or by eyes that fill with tears or by a playful grin—all perfectly timed and coordinated. Reagan's masterful expressions, apart from other questionable abilities, are the common ground underlying the positive perception of him as a good manipulator of the media and the negative view of him as an "amiable dunce." Reagan's many expressive successes and frequent communicative failures explain why polls suggest that a surprisingly large number of people who say they "like" Ronald Reagan also disagree with his policies, think that he is bringing the nation closer to war, and question his control over his own administration's activities. Thus far, a clear majority of those polled have rejected the idea that Reagan is a man of "exceptional abilities."[107] Ronald Reagan is not usually embarrassing to watch, but he is not an awe-inspiring leader reminiscent of great Presidents past.

Win or lose, today's Presidents and presidential hopefuls are judged by the same standards, those of "good television": are they lively and humorous; do they look friendly and alert; are their facial expressions pleasant to watch; can they offer off-the-cuff remarks without much thinking, pausing, or stumbling over words; and do they shape their words and expressions to the requirements of the camera and microphone rather than to those of the crowd?

Television has encouraged us to nominate candidates who, like Jimmy Carter, Ronald Reagan, and Walter Mondale avoid acting like "great leaders" and who have an easygoing sidestage, or "middle region," style that can bear a great deal of exposure. And although someone will obviously succeed in winning each upcoming presidential election, the presidency itself has lost much of its luster. We still hunger for something more.

PART V
Conclusion

15

Where Have We Been,
Where Are We Going?

No Sense of Place

For Americans, the second half of the twentieth century has been marked by an unusual amount and type of social change. The underprivileged have demanded equal rights, a significant portion of the visible political elite has weakened or fallen, and many of those in between have been maneuvering for new social position and identity.

Perhaps even more disturbing than the dimensions of the change has been its seeming inconsistency, even randomness. What is the common thread? We have recently witnessed peaceful civil rights demonstrations juxtaposed with violent looting and rioting. We have seen the persecution of the people by the agencies of government transformed into the virtual prosecution of a President by the people and press. And angry talk of social revolution has been transformed into the cool and determined pursuit of "affirmative action," community control, and a nuclear arms freeze.

Some social observers have comforted themselves by viewing the disruptions of the 1960s as an historical aberration and by pointing gleefully at former hippies who have clipped their locks and joined the materialistic middle class. Nothing has really changed, they seem to suggest. What they fail to see, however, are the male police and hardhats who now wear their hair long, the "redneck" farmers who let livestock loose in front of the Capitol (echoes of the Yippies?), the wheelchair sit-ins of the disabled, the court battles over returning land to the Indians, and hundreds of other small and large changes in behavior and attitudes. What does it all mean? Are we witnessing constant change and confusion? Or is there a central mechanism that has been swinging the social pendulum to and fro?

Social change is always too complex to attribute to a single cause and too diverse to reduce to a single process, but the theory offered here suggests that one common theme that connects many recent and seemingly diverse phenomena is a change in Americans' "sense of place." The phrase is an intricate—though very serious—pun. It is intricate because the word "sense" and the word "place" have two meanings each: "sense" referring to both perception and logic; "place" meaning both social position and physical location. The pun is serious because each of these four meanings represents a significant concept in the theory. Indeed, their interrelatedness forms the foundations of the two basic arguments presented here: (1) that social roles (i.e. social "place") can be understood only in terms of social situations, which, until recently, have been tied to physical place, and (2) that the logic of situational behaviors has much to do with patterns of information flow, that is, much to do with the human senses and their technological extensions. Evolution in media, I have suggested, has changed the logic of the social order by restructuring the relationship between physical place and social place and by altering the ways in which we transmit and receive social information.

I have argued that electronic media, especially television, have had a tremendous impact on Americans' sense of place. Electronic media have combined previously distinct social settings, moved the dividing line between private and public behavior toward the private, and weakened the relationship between social situations and physical places. The logic underlying situational patterns of behavior in a print-oriented society, therefore, has been radically subverted. Many Americans may no longer seem to "know their place" because the traditionally interlocking components of "place" have been split apart by electronic media. Wherever one is now—at home, at work, or in a car—one may be in touch and tuned-in.

The greatest impact has been on social groups that were once defined in terms of their physical isolation in specific locations—kitchens, playgrounds, prisons, convents, and so forth. But the changing relationship between physical and social place has affected almost every social role. Our world may suddenly seem senseless to many people because, for the first time in modern history, it is relatively placeless.

The intensity of the changes in the last thirty years, in particular, may be related to the unique power of television to break down the distinctions between here and there, live and mediated, and personal and public. More than any other electronic medium, television tends to involve us in issues we once thought were "not our business," to thrust us within a few inches of the faces of murderers and Presidents, and to make physical barriers and passageways relatively meaningless in terms of patterns of access to social information. Television has also enhanced the effects of earlier electronic media by providing us with a better image of the places experienced through radio and reached through the telephone.

The widespread social movements and disruptions since the late 1950s, this theory suggests, may be adjustments in behavior, attitudes, and laws to match new social settings. Many of the traditional distinctions among groups, among people at various stages of socialization, and among superiors and subordinates were based on the patterns of information flow that existed in a print society. The new and "strange" behavior of many individuals or of classes of people may be the result of the steady merging of formerly distinct social environments.

Television has helped change the deferential Negro into the proud Black, merged the Miss and Mrs. into a Ms., transformed the child into a "human being" with natural rights. Television has fostered the rise of hundreds of "minorities"—people, who in perceiving a wider world, begin to see themselves as unfairly isolated in some pocket of it. Television has empowered the disabled and the disenfranchised by giving them access to social information in spite of their physical isolation. Television has given women an outside view of their incarceration in the home. Television has weakened visible authorities by destroying the distance and mystery that once enhanced their aura and prestige. And television has been able to do this without requiring the disabled to leave their wheelchairs, without asking the housewife to stop cooking dinner, and without demanding that the average citizen leave his or her easy chair.

By merging discrete communities of discourse, television has made nearly every topic and issue a valid subject of interest and concern for virtually every member of the public. Further, many formerly private and isolated behaviors have been brought out into the large unitary public arena. As a result, behaviors that were dependent on great distance and isolation have been undermined; performances that relied on long and careful rehearsals have been banished from the social repertoire. The widened public sphere gives nearly everyone a new (and relatively shared) perspective from which to view others and gain a reflected sense of self. We, our doctors, our police officers, our Presidents, our secret agents, our parents, our children, and our friends are all performing roles in new theaters that demand new styles of drama.

Many formal reciprocal roles rely on lack of intimate knowledge of the "other." If the mystery and mystification disappear, so do the formal behaviors. Stylized courtship behaviors, for example, must quickly fade in the day-to-day intimacy of marriage. Similarly, the new access we gain to distant events and to the gestures and actions of the other sex, our elders, and authorities does not simply "educate" us; such access changes social reality. By revealing previously backstage areas to audiences, television has served as an instrument of demystification. It has led to a decline in the image and prestige of political leaders, it has demystified adults for children, and demystified men and women for each other. Given this analysis, it is not surprising that the widespread rejection of traditional child and adult, male and female, and leader and follower roles should have begun in the late 1960s among the first generation of Americans to have been exposed to television before learning to read. In the shared environment of television, women and men, children and adults, and followers and leaders know a great deal about each other's behavior and social knowledge—too much, in fact, for them to play the traditional complementary roles of innocence vs. omniscience.

A sub-theme running through this book has been a reinterpretation of the causes and significance of the widespread social upheavals of the 1960s. The discussion suggested a new explanation for what was unique about that decade: the clashing of formerly distinct social arenas, which led to moral reevaluation of social and political behavior. Given this analysis, recent social events have generally been a continuation, rather than a reversal of many trends that began in the 1960s. The manifest content of the rhetoric and actions of that era may be part of the past, but the latent structure of behavioral changes and merging situations continues.

"The Sixties" were at once less and more than has been claimed. Contrary to what many of those involved in the protests thought at the time, the sixties did not herald the birth of a world-wide utopia, with universal freedom, equality, and peace. But neither were they, as some now claim, simply a passing curiosity of "sound and fury signifying nothing." The social explosions of the 1960s marked the transition between two eras of social behavior; the lives of people and the character of a nation were permanently and profoundly changed. The behaviors that were considered odd and revolting (in both senses) have spread upward through older generations and outward throughout the American system. While the changes have not all been in accord with the manifest ideals and moral outrage of "The Movement," they have been adjustments to the same shift in social arenas that first led to widespread dissent and protest.

The opening of closed situations is a reversal of a trend several hundred years old. As Michel Foucault brilliantly argues in *Discipline and Punish*, the membranes around the prison, the hospital, the military barracks, the factory, and the school thickened over several centuries. Foucault describes how people were increasingly separated into distinct places in order to homogenize them into groups with single identities ("students," "workers," "prisoners," "mentally ill," etc.). The individuals in these groups were, in a sense, interchangeable parts. And even the distinct identities of the groups were subsumed under the larger social system of internally consistent, linearly connected, and hierarchically arranged units.[1] But Foucault does not observe the current counter-process. The old social order segregated people in their "special spheres" in order to homogenize individuals into elements of a larger social machine, but the current trend is toward the integration of all groups into a common sphere with a new recognition of the special needs and idiosyncrasies of individuals.

Nineteenth century life entailed many isolated situations and sustained many isolated behaviors and attitudes. The current merging of situations does not give us a sum of what we had before, but rather new, synthesized behaviors that are qualitatively different. If we celebrate our child's wedding in an isolated situation where it is the sole "experience" of the day, then our joy may be unbounded. But when, on our way to the wedding, we hear over the car radio of a devastating earthquake, or the death of a popular entertainer, or the assassination of a political figure, we not only lose our ability to rejoice fully, but also our ability to mourn deeply. The electronic combination of many different styles of interaction from distinct regions leads to new "middle region" behaviors that, while containing elements of formerly distinct roles, are themselves new behavior patterns with new expectations and emotions.

Gone, therefore, are many people's "special" behaviors, those that were associated with distinct and isolated interactions. Gone are the great eccentrics, the passionate overpowering loves, the massive unrelenting hates, the dramatic curses and flowery praises. Unbounded joy and unmitigated misery cannot coexist in the same place and time. As situations merge, the hot flush and the icy stare blend into a middle region "cool." The difference between the reality of behaviors in distinct situations versus the reality of behaviors in merged situations is as great as the difference between the nineteenth century conception that a man might have a virtuous wife and a raunchy mistress and the twentieth century notions of open marriages, "living together," and serial monogamy.

The Victorian era—the height of print culture—was a time of "secrets." People were fascinated with the multiple layers and depths of life: secret passageways, skeletons in the closet, masks upon masks upon masks. But the fascination with these layers did not drive the Victorians to destroy secrecy, but rather to enhance it as a natural condition of the social order. To a large degree, skeletons were meant to stay in the closet, sex was to remain behind closed doors (perhaps to be spied upon through keyholes), and scandalous acts were to be hidden from peering eyes. The rare exposures and discoveries were titillating, implicit hints of the vastness of undiscovered reality.[2]

Our own age, in contrast, is fascinated by exposure. Indeed, the *act* of exposure itself now seems to excite us more than the content of the secrets exposed. The steady stripping away of layers of social behavior has made the "scandal" and the revelation of the "deep dark secret" everyday occurrences. Ironically, what is pulled out of the closets that contain seemingly extraordinary secrets is, ultimately, the "ordinariness" of everyone. The unusual becomes the usual: famous stars who abuse their children, Presidents with hemorrhoids, Popes who get depressed, Congressmen who solicit sex from pages.

Still we hunger for heroes, and perhaps our search beneath social masks is filled with the hope of finding people whose private selves are as admirable as their public ones. But since most of the people who make enduring contributions to our culture remain under our scrutiny too long to remain pure in our eyes, we have also begun to focus on people who make one grand gesture or who complete a single courageous act that cannot be undermined by scrutiny. Our new heroes are men and women like Lenny Skutnik, who dove into the water—before television cameras—to save an airplane crash survivor, or Reginald Andrews, who saved a blind man's life by pulling him from beneath a New York subway car. Both men were saluted as heroes by the President of the United States.[3] We can admire such isolated heroic acts; the pasts and the futures of such heroes remain comfortably irrelevant and invisible.

While I have concentrated in this book on *change*, I realize that behind many obvious social changes much of our social order remains the same. There continue to be many distinctions in roles of group identity, different stages of socialization, and different ranks of hierarchy in spite of the homogenizing trend. (And after the dust of change from the current merging of roles settles, we are also likely to rediscover some of the many differences among us.) Further, while electronic media have merged many social situations, direct physical presence and mutual monitoring are still primary experiential modes. And regardless of media access, living in a ghetto, a prison cell, and a middle class suburb are certainly not "equivalent" social experiences. Nevertheless, roles and places have changed dramatically and an analysis of how and why they have changed helps to explain many social phenomena that are not otherwise easily understood. While the merging of spheres through electronic media has not given everyone the same knowledge and wisdom, the mystification surrounding other people and places has been pierced. Print still exists and holds many mysteries and secrets for those who master it, but many of the "secrets of secrecy" have been exposed.

The changing conceptions of secrecy and place, of gender distinctions, of childhood innocence, and of authority can all be seen in a single social event: the birth of a new human being. Not long ago, this scene was marked by highly isolated environments. Pregnant women were to stay out of public view. Husbands were distanced from the pregnancy and sheltered from the birth. During delivery, the father paced nervously in an isolated waiting room; the mother herself was "removed" from the birthing situation through drugs; young children were kept out of the hospital and were often further isolated through ignorance of the processes of pregnancy and birth. In charge of the birth were the all-powerful doctors, whose authority allowed them to defy gravity and nature and curiosity and mother-love as they wrenched the drugged infant from the womb in a cold stainless steel delivery room.

Today, the scene is vastly different. Pregnancy and birth are "family-centered"; fathers and children are often fully involved. A new phrase has entered the language: "*we* are pregnant," and it is now common practice for fathers and mothers to attend "childbirth classes" together and for fathers to be present at, and assist in, the birth.[4] Siblings as young as two may be involved in the process by attending special "prepared sibling" classes, taking tours of the hospital, and, in some cases, being present at the birth itself.[5]

Increasingly, many doctors and nurses are defining themselves more as "educators" than as "authorities";[6] the family is expected to make the final choices concerning the variables of delivery. In response to those hospitals and medical personnel who are not willing to allow families to choose their own "birthing options," some middle class families are opting for home deliveries with midwives. Others are giving birth in "alternative birthing centers," which are a cross between hospitals and motels. But the most significant trend is the move in regular hospitals to blur the differences between labor room and home. Many hospitals are building special "birthing rooms" that are designed to resemble home bedrooms. Some have double beds, flowery wallpaper, carpeting, and soft chairs. Equipment for delivery is present but kept out of sight until needed. A man and a woman may now give birth to their child while looking out a window or watching television.[7] The "specialness" of the place in which birth now takes place is further diluted by the increasingly popular trend toward photographing, filming, or videotaping the birth—so that the experience is "taken out" of the hospital and shared with friends, family, and, perhaps later, with the child itself.

Order, Not Chaos

The analysis here suggests that the new social order is indeed a new *order*, not a random or disorganized variation from the old social system. Certainly, the old structures have broken down, but an understanding of the relationship between situations and behavior suggests that there is both rhyme and reason in the change and in the new structures. Moreover, an analysis of the direction and type of change clearly indicates that the old conventions were not "natural" or God-given forms of social organization, but rather ones based on arbitrary distinctions among social situations—distinctions fostered, at least partially, by the characteristics of print. Indeed, many of the currently changing roles and institutions were first shaped or strengthened during the same period that saw the spreading of literacy and printing in the vernacular.

The relatively isolated nuclear family with a strong, dominant husband/father figure and an obedient and subservient wife first grew in England in the sixteenth and seventeenth centuries after a millennium of families built around community and kin. Similarly, the conception of the child as a weak creature in need of special attention and instruction first developed in the sixteenth century among the most literate classes and peaked in the nineteenth century along with the spread of literacy and schooling among the lower classes. Finally, the idea of a distant, powerful leader also developed in the sixteenth and seventeenth centuries. Before the sixteenth century, life was much more local and community-based.

The new relationships in each case were at first hostile: harsh, authoritarian patriarchal control over women, fierce desire to break the will of children, and divine monarchs' absolute control over subjects. Later, however, they all became more affectionate: marriages based on mutual attraction and respect, loving care and nurturing of children, and the decline of absolute monarchs in favor of more representative govern-

ments. But even this second stage was characterized by "separate and
unequal" statuses. In our time, we are seeing striking reversals of such
separatism in the merging rights and roles of husbands and wives and of
children and adults and in the renewed ideal of "community control."

Thus, while many of the changes in roles I have described are often
seen as causes of each other, this analysis suggests that they may all have
been influenced by similar forces. The isolation of women in the domestic
sphere is sometimes seen as a cause of the intense interest in the needs
and protection of the child; sometimes the new image of the child is seen
as the cause of the new views of feminine domesticity. Similarly, many
conservatives today blame the loss of childhood innocence on working
mothers and the feminist movement. But the analysis presented here suggests that both the rise and fall of childhood and the decline and rise in
women's rights and involvement in the public sphere may be closely
linked to major shifts in communication technology in the past and in our
own time. The spread of literacy, with its emphasis on hierarchy and
sequence, supported a linear chain of command, from God-the-father,
through a strong central national leader, to a father who was a god to his
wife and children. The increasingly dependent illiterate child was put in
the care of the minimally literate female.[8] As new means of communication blur hierarchy and sequence in our own time, we are experiencing a
reintegration of many splintered roles.

The proliferation of new information-systems that followed the spread
of literacy allowed for greater separation of backstage and onstage situations. Just as we are experiencing "sidestage," or "middle region," behaviors as situations merge, so did the period from the late Middle Ages to
the recent past allow for more "deep backstage" behaviors for many roles
and, therefore, for more idealized "forefront stage" behavior. The new
information-systems of literacy created distance between men and
women, between adults and children, and between leaders and the common person. Printing fostered the preparation of "training manuals" for
princes and priests (such as those written by Machiavelli and Gracian)
and led to the publication of many etiquette manuals aimed at people of
different ages and sex.

The sixteenth century also saw a striking change in the sense of place
and in the degree of "permeability" of the domestic sphere. Historians
have noted the new sense of "boundaries" dividing public and private,
domestic and political, family and community in the transition between
the pre-modern and modern age.[9] In our own time, we have found a dramatic reversal of this trend.

Just as in the late Middle Ages, a husband's power over his wife was
muted by the openness of the domestic sphere to public view, so now has
the idea of a man's home as his castle declined. For no matter how physically isolated the home is from other homes and people, the parental
stress hot line, the rape hotline, a lawyer, and the police are only a few
finger pulses away. As telephones, radios, televisions, and computers

increasingly link the home to the outside world, external behavioral norms begin to merge into internal ones. The living room, kitchen, and bedroom are being reintegrated into the larger public realm. The politicizing of the personal has redefined housecleaning as "unpaid labor" for which a wife may demand "back wages" in a divorce suit. Similarly, the notion of "marital rape" suggests a new blurring of public and private spheres. What was judged, for several centuries, to be a man's rightful "correction" of his wife and children in the privacy of his home is now being redefined as criminal abuse. And one recent criminological study of forgery, theft, and assault has examined the following types of "criminal acts": a child signing a parent's name on a report card, a child taking a dollar from his or her mother's pocketbook without permission, and a brother hitting a sister during a family argument.[10] These are among the many indications of a decreasing tendency to define actions and events in terms of the specific physical sphere in which they take place.

Hunters and Gatherers in an Information Age

To the extent that electronic media tend to reunite many formerly distinct spheres of interaction, we may be returning to a world even older than that of the late Middle Ages. Many of the features of our "information age" make us resemble the most primitive of social and political forms: the hunting and gathering society. As nomadic peoples, hunters and gatherers have no loyal relationship to territory. They, too, have little "sense of place"; specific activities and behaviors are not tightly fixed to specific physical settings.[11]

The lack of boundaries both in hunting and gathering and in electronic societies leads to many striking parallels. Of all known societal types before our own, hunting and gathering societies have tended to be the most egalitarian in terms of the roles of males and females, children and adults, and leaders and followers.[12] The difficulty of maintaining many "separate places," or distinct social spheres, tends to involve everyone in everyone else's business.

Although men and women in hunting and gathering societies usually have division of labor, it is not as sharp as it is in agricultural societies, and doing the work of the opposite sex is not usually considered demeaning. In many hunting and gathering societies, women play an active role in supporting the family, child-care is considered the responsibility of the whole community, and both men and women are expected to be gentle, mild-mannered, and noncompetitive.[13] Because of the inability of hunter and gatherer societies to separate domestic from public spheres, men cannot establish aura and distance, and women are involved in public decisions.[14] As in our own society, the lack of privacy in hunting and gathering societies often leads to community control over private arguments between husbands and wives.[15]

Because of the openness of life, hunter and gatherer children are not sharply segregated by age or sex, and they are not usually isolated from adult activities. Sex play among children and adolescents is common and sometimes includes sexual intercourse.[16] Like many of today's parents, hunters and gatherers stress self-reliance rather than obedience to adults, and they do not usually use physical punishment.[17]

In hunting and gathering societies, play and work often take place in the same sphere and involve similar activities. Children observe and play at hunting and gathering.[18] Similarly, work and play have begun to merge in our electronic age. Both children and adults now spend many hours a week staring at video monitors, whether video games or electronic spreadsheets. Further, as the young computer "hackers" have demonstrated, children's play now often takes place in the same public sphere as their parents' work—the jungle of national and international information networks.

Because leaders in hunting and gathering societies cannot get away from those they lead, leadership—to the extent that it exists—must be gained through persuasion rather than coercion. The leader cannot be easily "set apart"; leaders have to gain authority by setting "the best example by working the hardest and sharing the most."[19] For hunters and gatherers, as for us, exposed leadership is often more of a burden than a privilege. In both societies, even recognized leaders are not expected to make decisions by themselves or to impose their decisions on those who disagree.

There are many other similarities between the norms of hunters and gatherers and our newly developed behavior patterns. In both forms of social organization, marriages are often based on mutual attraction rather than kinship ties, marriages are easily arranged and terminated, and premarital sex and serial monogamy are common. Just as women today are increasingly keeping their birth names after marriage, hunters and gatherers often reckon kinship through the families of both mothers and fathers.[20] And compared to other forms of social organization, both we and hunters and gatherers have few large scale or long-term initiation rites.[21]*

One way to characterize ourselves, then, is as "hunters and gatherers of an information age." Our shared sphere of interaction is informational rather than physical, but it leads to a similar inability to distinguish clearly among gender, age, and hierarchical statuses. We bypass many previous generations' dependence on physical location as a prime determinant of access to people and information. Unlike tribes with special huts and

---

*Significantly, when the normally nomadic hunters and gatherers become sedentary and attach themselves to particular places, they lose most of the features that make them resemble our own new norms: women's autonomy, mobility, and influence decrease markedly; work becomes much more clearly sex-typed; the socialization experiences of boys and girls become much more dissimilar; men enter into extra-village politics; and there is increasing household segregation and privacy.[22]

sacred places, men's domains and women's domains, adult places and children's places, our culture is becoming essentially placeless.

Our advanced technological stage allows us to hunt and gather information rather than food. Like hunters and gatherers who take for granted the abundance of food "out there" and therefore only hunt and gather enough to consume immediately, we are increasingly becoming a "subsistence information society." Rather than engaging in long-term storage of knowledge in their memories or homes, many people are beginning to believe that information is available "out there" and that individuals do not need to stockpile it. Our children sing "we don't need no education,"[23] and even many scholars have begun to steer away from collecting and storing in their minds the long, linear arguments of literacy that linked new discoveries to old and that pointed to the future. Instead, the computer is increasingly used as an abundant jungle of bits and pieces of "data" (albeit, a jungle created and stocked by us). Some data are hunted, gathered, and analyzed when an appetite for correlations arises. The connections found are often consumed and digested immediately without being painstakingly linked to other knowledge and ideas.

The notion that we are "returning" to a primitive era or even to the pre-print period in Western Europe is, of course, much too simple for numerous reasons. Unlike pre-modern civilizations, we remain heavily dependent on literacy in both the way we store information and in the way we think. The electronic age has grown out of and retains many features of a "print culture."[24] Differences in literacy skills, therefore, continue to distinguish between children and adults and to divide people into separate social categories. Our less exclusive dependence on print and literacy, however, has muted the social distinctions among people of different stages of literacy. Thus, we are spiralling forward rather than circling backward. We regain some features of the pre-modern world as we advance into a new frontier.

Good or Bad?/Real or False?

Some people mistake any discussion of the "breaking down of boundaries among people" for a prophecy of a utopian society of harmony and bliss. Yet this has not been a theme in my analysis. I agree with Lewis Mumford's 1934 assessment that human beings "tend to be more socialized at a distance, than they are in their immediate, limited, and local selves: their intercourse sometimes proceeds best, like barter among savage peoples, when neither group is visible to the other."[25]

When people share the same environment, they often see more differences among themselves than when they are further apart. Family members who live together and share basically similar experiences, for example, often argue over minute differences in their behaviors and attitudes. Yet when a child moves away from home into a very different environment and adopts a life style that may, indeed, be at great variance with his or her parents' values and actions, the *distance* between the parents' home and the child's home often allows the family members to get along very well with each other.

In living together in the same environment, family members are more alike than when they live separately, yet *differences among people are often most visible when the differences are least present, and most present when they are least visible.* For the same reason, the new information environment that embraces the whole globe is not necessarily any more peaceful or harmonious than a bickering family—but like a large family, we are all in a more similar environment and our degree of interdependence is greater than it has ever been before.

While many corners of the earth remain informationally remote, and while political and economic factors exclude many accessible messages from our information channels, we are nevertheless exposed to an overwhelming range of information from around the globe. Unfortunately, observation of massacres, starvation, and oppression does not necessarily lead to active attempts to change things for the better. Why? Compared to the parochial past, perhaps, the *exposure* of horrors and scandals and massacres is itself symbolically powerful. We often get the sense that the mere reporting of a terrible event will somehow lead to its end. Surely *someone* will now do something about it![26] In many cases, an attitude shift has replaced action, and the publicized findings of opinion polls have partially replaced street demonstrations. Further, as our media lay bare more and more problems from around the world and push them into our consciousness, it has become impossible for an individual to assimilate or respond to all the issues raised. If a poor woman comes to your door while you are eating dinner, you may invite her in for a bite to eat; if a few minutes later, a stranded motorist comes to your house, you might allow him to use your phone to call for assistance. But if twenty or a hundred hungry, tired, or otherwise needy people are wandering in your street, you—*the same compassionate person*—may barricade the door.

I mentioned in an early chapter that it would be difficult for you to continue reading this book if there was someone in the same room with you asking for your help. But the greater the number of people in your space who need help and the longer they stay there, the more you might be able to ignore them. In the media-expanded environment of today, we may be like the prisoner in a crowded cell who hordes a bit of food and manages to ignore all but his or her defended corner of territory. We are increasingly aware of others' problems, yet fearful of their drain on our energies and resources. When the problems of all others become relatively equal in their seeming urgency, it is not surprising that many people turn to take care of "number one." In this sense, "meism" may, unfortunately, be the logical end result of the expanded consciousness of the world and its problems that first stirred the youth of the 1960s to moral indignation and political protest.

In describing our new situations and behaviors, I have tried to avoid making value judgments concerning the changes I describe. I have done this not only for the usually stated reason that analysis can be more thorough and objective before evaluative filters are lowered over one's eyes, but also because, as hinted at above, codes of morality and ethics are also affected by situational variables.

In an isolated situation, we might praise a person who stops to help a stray dog. But if, in another situation, there is both a hungry child and a hungry dog, we may be outraged at the person who overlooks the child to feed the dog. Yet we rarely consider condemning the person in the first situation for avoiding those streets and situations where hungry children might be found. Our evaluations of actions are shaped by the boundaries and definitions of situations. Most behaviors, even killing, are socially and religiously sanctioned if performed in the proper social context ("war" or "execution," for example). Procreation and pornography often involve similar *behaviors*, but different *situations*. The morality of many actions depends on where, when, and before whom they are performed. When media alter the boundaries of situations, value-systems are often affected as well.

Nevertheless, for those who would judge the new social order against the old, this book provides some general cautionary guidelines. By outlining a relationship among media, situations, and behavior, I have argued that we cannot have the old role structures and also have electronic media. Controlling the content of electronic media, for example, will not maintain old forms of social organization. Even conservative content may be revolutionary when disseminated in new ways.

Further, by outlining a single process that affects many different social phenomena, this theory indicates that we cannot have *some* of the forces for social change brought about by electronic media without having *all*, or most, of the forces. Because the effects are interrelated and widespread, we cannot easily pick and choose effects. We cannot select uses for new media that advance old goals without often altering the social systems out of which the goals developed. We cannot, for example, "buy the wife" a television set to ease her boredom with housework without changing her sense of place in the world. We cannot use television to "educate" our children without simultaneously altering the functions of reading and the structure of the family and the school. When we use "Sesame Street" to advance the speed of children's learning, we also heighten children's entrance into real streets, and for some, perhaps, into real street crime. We cannot have mediated intimacy with our political leaders, in the hope of getting closer to greatness, without losing a belief in heroes. And if we use media to teach many different groups about each other, we also change the lines of social association and the perimeters of group identities.

Any judgments about the new society relative to the old, therefore, must be made with great care. We can selectively condemn and praise, but to see parts of the new environment as disease and other parts as cure may be to misunderstand the unified dynamics involved in social change. Both the things we dislike and the things we like about the new environment may be parts of the same process. If, for example, we lose the extremes of many situation-specific behaviors of the nineteenth century, then we lose not only high manners and quiet "civilized" clubs, but also many of the extremes of debauchery, poverty, and neglect. If we are to measure accurately the new social order against the old, we must judge both systems as wholes and evaluate *all* the ways in which they differ from each other.

Just as the new environment is neither inherently better nor worse than the old, neither is it inherently more real nor false—though there have been claims in both directions.

Many people feel that they have stopped "playing roles," that they are now behaving "naturally" and just "being themselves." At the same time, many people have become more aware of the "staginess" of roles played by *others*, such as politicians, public relations executives, and advertisers. And so they have become more suspicious of what Daniel Boorstin has dubbed "pseudo events"—events that are created simply to be reported by media.[27]

Yet both of these views may miss the point. Social behavior continues to be based on projecting certain impressions and concealing others, behaving one way here, and another there. What has changed are the dividing lines between here and there; what is different is the number of distinct social settings. People's new "openness" may be based less on a new basic sense of "honesty" than on continuing attempts to avoid apparent discrepancies and inconsistencies. Many people are "revealing" aspects of themselves which were once concealed because it is now more difficult to keep such backstage information secret. For many of the most visible performers—Presidents and other "personalities"—however, the exposure is so great, the overview of many of their performances so accessible, that even the simplest rehearsed behavior or change in style from one place to another seems "contrived."

Contrary to Boorstin's analysis of "pseudo events," the significance of electronic media may be that the planning and staging of "media events" cannot be hidden as simply as the planning for face-to-face encounters. A politician, for example, cannot hide his campaign strategists as easily as the average business executive can hide the suggestions of a spouse or hair stylist. Electronic media may be exposing the general "pseudoness" of events rather than creating it. Boorstin and others may be responding more to the newness of the *visibility* of staging than to the newness of staging itself. We now have different performances rather than more or less performance; we have a different reality rather than a different measure of reality.

By thrusting the backstage area of life out into the public arena, electronic media have made it more difficult to play traditional formal roles.

The behaviors exhibited are still "roles," though newly patterned to match new staging contingencies. And though "etiquette" is thought to be passé in some circles, there is still an etiquette implicit in all our expectations of (and disappointments in) the actions of others. And part of the new etiquette is that we no longer should play certain traditional formal roles. As Richard Sennett describes in *The Fall of Public Man*, we have lost the sense of "distance" that once characterized much of social life. "The reigning belief today is that closeness between persons is a moral good."[28]

The "reciprocal informality" of our time has two sides. It could be said that people are now *allowed* to drop formal communication, or it could be said that we are now *forced* to drop it. In either case, the relationship between access to information and formality remains. In social relations, formality and intimacy seem to be mutually exclusive in any given time or place. Just as formality is a barrier to intimacy, so is intimacy a barrier to formality.

Whither "1984"?

We have now reached the era of George Orwell's gloomy prophecy. And there are many apparent similarities between Orwell's *1984* and our time. Our government sees the world as divided into two superpowers, Good vs. Evil. Our supposedly unavoidable conflict with The Enemy serves as a backdrop and rationale for many of our domestic and foreign policies. Language, too, has entered the battle. Our actions are always "defensive," theirs are always "aggressive." Our interventions are "rescue missions to preserve Freedom"; theirs are "invasions to crush the will of the people." Our economic assistance to underdeveloped countries is "humanitarian"; theirs is "propagandistic." Mind-boggling weapons of death are benignly labelled "peacekeepers," while many would-be peacekeepers are surrounded by hints of treason.

Many people jump from such observations to the assumption that developments in electronic media are hastening the arrival of an Orwellian nightmare. The evolution of sophisticated surveillance devices and the decline in privacy are seen as concrete manifestations of the type of totalitarianism described by Orwell. Yet these technological developments may actually be signs of a trend in the opposite direction.

Orwell offered a vision of society where Big Brother watched all, but was himself invisible. Orwell conceived of an "inner party" elite who observed but were unobservable. The Party demanded and received total loyalty and unquestioning obedience. Such a system is conceivable in an electronic age, but if the new technologies have any "inherent bias," it may be against such a sharply hierarchal system.

As described in Chapters 4 and 10, "authority" and "leadership" are unlike mere "power" in that they depend on performance and appeal. One cannot lead or be looked up to if one is not there to be seen. Yet one of the peculiar ironies of our age is that any person who steps forward into the media limelight and attempts to gain national visibility becomes too visible, too exposed, and is therefore demystified. Electronic media may be used by officials to spy on private citizens, but when an electronic medium such as television is used by leaders as a means of communicating with the people, the medium's expressive bias also often allows citizens to "spy" on officials.

Further, for a hierarchy to exist, there must be more followers than leaders. In an era of easy and relatively shared access to information about people, one leader may be able to keep a close watch on thousands of followers, but thousands of followers can keep an even closer watch on one leader. The simple mathematics of hierarchy suggests the stronger likelihood of an undermining of the pyramid of status in an electronic age.

Electronic media not only weaken authority by allowing those low on the ladder of hierarchy to gain access to much information, but also by allowing increased opportunities for the sharing of information horizontally. The telephone and computer, for example, allow people to communicate with each other without going "through channels." Such horizontal flow of information is another significant deterrent to totalitarian central leadership.

There is no doubt that new technologies—like old technologies—may be used by bad governments to bad ends. And once a totalitarian government exists, it can stop or control the flow of information. But the assumption that the new media or the "lack of privacy" they foster will, in and of themselves, support authoritarian hierarchies is based on a misunderstanding of the relationship between privacy and hierarchy. For it is privacy and distance that support strong central authorities. Our notions of privacy have a very short history in Western civilization, and as we know from studies of hunting and gathering societies and of pre-print Western Europe, the virtual lack of privacy tends to weaken rather than support great distinctions in status. It is the person who tries to stand apart or above, not the average citizen, who is most damaged by lack of privacy. We may be aesthetically uncomfortable with the thought of full and open access to information, but, all other things being equal, such access would tend to level hierarchies rather than erect them. Even the evidence we have been gathering recently about our leaders' "abuses of power" may, in this sense, testify more to our relatively increased ability to gather information on leaders than to an absolute increase in the abuse of power. The thing to fear is not the loss of privacy per se, but the *nonreciprocal* loss of privacy—that is, where we lose the ability to monitor those who monitor us.

As of now, electronic media may best support a "hierarchy of the people." For electronic media give a distinct advantage to the average person. Average people now have access to social information that once was not available to them. Further, they have information concerning the performers of high status roles. As a result, the distance, mystery, and mystification surrounding high status roles are minimized. There are still many "unusual" people with special knowledge and training, but the average person now knows more about what special individuals know and also more about high status people as "people." After seeing so much ordinariness in the close-up views of extraordinary people, we may continue to remain more ignorant and less powerful than they, but we are now more aware of the many things they do not know and cannot do. And even though much of this new information access is reciprocal, the common person has relatively less to lose from exposure and visibility. No one expects the common person to be anything but common. If Joe Smith finds out that the President cheats on his income tax, Joe is likely to be outraged—even he cheats on his own income tax. Great leaders are not supposed to suffer the frailties of greed, lust, or instability.

At this moment in history, we may be witnessing a political revolution of enormous proportions, a revolution that is masked by the conventions of our language and by the form of our traditional ideals. We are moving from a representative government of de facto elites to a government of direct participation with elected "administrators." The change is difficult to see, however, because we refer to both of these systems as "democracy" and because the new system involves the manifestation of many once unattainable ideals such as true "public servants" and "government by and for the people." Reality does not stay the same, however, when ideals become reality.

Electronic media offer the potential of government by direct referendum, and the growth of interactive television promises the mixed blessing of a political system modeled after the structure of the "Gong Show"—where performers can be removed from the stage in mid-performance. (A more pleasing metaphor for the same system is the Greek forum.) The new technology fosters the potential of the closest thing the earth has ever witnessed to participatory democracy on an enormous scale—with all the resulting problems and possibilities. Even if this comes to pass, however, we will need some rethinking of our conceptions of authority if we are to see the system for what it is. For whoever steps before us in the role of leader will seem to be a disappointment compared to our hazy, but glowing images of Washingtons, Jeffersons, and Lincolns, and any step taken without our knowledge, any move taken in opposition to a majority "vote" in a national poll, will be seen as the arrogance of power.

Although the political problems of our age may not be the obvious ones many people fear, there remain many reasons for caution. The decline in trust and faith in authorities is filled with paradox and some danger. The growth in weapons technology and the increase in speed in global communications have led to an enhancement of the raw power of national leaders even as our faith in governments and leaders has declined. Our recent Presidents have had the power to destroy the entire world, but not the authority to convince the majority of the population that they are doing a competent job. There is always the danger of leaders using their massive warmaking powers in attempts to rally the people behind them—or as an excuse for secrecy and information control.

Similarly, our increasingly complex technological and social world has made us rely more and more heavily on "expert information," but the general exposure of "experts" as fallible human beings has lessened our faith in them as people. The change in our image of leaders and experts leaves us with a distrust of power, but also with a seemingly powerless dependence on those in whom we have little trust.

Further, the vacuum in our visible political realm of authority may be giving undue power to *in*visible men and women who run large national and multi-national corporations. Unlike governments, corporations have no code of "openness." Indeed, competitive business is built on a tradition of secrecy. A business leader who refuses an interview is not viewed as suspiciously as a governor or a President who refuses to speak to the press. We do need to be wary, therefore, of the increasingly complex involvement of many corporations in university research, in government, and in all forms of national and international communication technologies—from book publishing to satellites.

There is also one visible class of "authorities" who, through their unique positions in our society, have been able to become exceptions to the decline in visible authority. These people have managed to maintain both controlled access to the people *and* controlled performances. They are the television newscasters whose daily performances are tightly controlled and scripted. In an implicit trade code, television news programs do not expose other news programs or news personalities. A few moments of prime time may be used to show a President fall down while skiing, collapse while jogging, or make a serious slip of the tongue, but there are few, if any, intentional television exposures of Tom Brokaw or Dan Rather falling down, cursing, or becoming irritable and tense. Such conventions maintain the fiction that the selectively revealed aspects of newscasters' personalities are representative of their whole selves. This situation may explain why Walter Cronkite has been described as "the most trusted man in America" and was considered to be a viable vice presidential candidate. Thus far, we have been lucky that the trade of electronic journalism has drawn men and women who do not seem to be abusing this "power"—Cronkite, for example, has often appeared to be concerned and embarrassed by it. But we need to be more aware of the staging contingencies that may be enhancing our trust in journalists just as they weaken our faith in the political process.

New Generations of Electronic Media

Many recent developments in media are likely both to enhance and to retard some of the trends I have described. There is a growing proliferation of sources of information, from personal mini-cassette players, which can create private spaces in the midst of crowded streets, to satellites that embrace the globe in a web of information channels. Such developments splinter the mass audience and largely transform the world of "broadcasting" we have come to take for granted. Yet, as I have argued in Chapter 5, the new divisions are not a return to the *same* group distinctions that were common in a print era, and the new divisions do not destroy the ability of a medium such as television to draw millions of people into a single event at a single point in time. Nevertheless, the current nightly attendance of nearly half the nation to three network sources will no doubt largely disappear.

The rising importance of the computer to our work and leisure activities is also bringing about many new changes. In some ways, the computer is a hybrid of the book and television. If the computer continues to rely heavily on "print," it may reinforce the levels of hierarchy associated with writing and reading. Further, computer programming is itself a new "code" to be mastered. In general, the demands of experience (and money) to gain access to the sophisticated and rapidly expanding capabilities of hardware and software are creating new distinct groupings, grades of socialization, and levels of expertness and authority.

But the effects of the computer on group identity, socialization, and hierarchy are not unidirectional. Although the computer now appears to be reestablishing many divisions in information-systems, its long-term effect may still be to increase the merging of various information-systems and experiences. As costs of hardware and software continue to decrease and as programs become increasingly "user friendly," the computer may further democratize information access. Just as the automobile involves more complex and expensive technology than the "technology" of the horse and buggy yet allows for increased mobility for many people who do not know anything about auto mechanics, the "user friendly" computer is based on sophisticated knowledge that gives the unsophisticated user increased informational mobility. Large corporations and governments may make much more extensive use of computers than the average person, and yet the size of the *gap* between the low and the mighty may nevertheless decrease. (And, of course, many "average people" work in corporations and have access to the computers used within them.) The teenage "hackers" who have recently used their inexpensive computers to "break into" multimillion dollar corporation and government defense information networks have shown that computers not only tend to consolidate power but also to dissipate it.[29]

On the surface, the complexity of computers may seem to separate children and adults further by giving children a new ladder to climb before they reach adulthood. Yet the speed with which many young children seem to master the workings of computers should lead us to question carefully their ultimate effects on adult-child interaction and on stages of learning. Even when the computer is used to store print information, children seem to develop a "feel" for the computer that surpasses their age (by which we usually mean "reading age").[30] Operation of a computer is much more difficult than watching television, but the sequence in which one learns to master the computer does not seem to be the same as the sequence through which one masters print. Further, as Seymour Papert has convincingly argued, even "programming" is not necessarily a complex adult skill, and young children can master it as well, and often better, than their elders.[31]

The fact that the computer involves a type of skill different from reading is most evident in the computer's nonlinguistic uses such as the complex video games that have swept the country (and world). Like television, the video game does not divide its "audience" into different ages. People of all ages play the games. Further, age and traditional education do not have any direct effect on level of skills. Indeed, many young children master games their parents cannot even fathom. Many video games involve multiple lines of action, increasing speed, and increasing rate of increasing speed. These aspects are all foreign to the one-thing-at-a-time, one-thing-after-another, and take-time-to-think world of reading.

Electronic media have been blamed by many critics for the recent decline in scores on Scholastic Aptitude Tests.[32] Less attention has been paid, however, to the possibility that electronic media may aid the development of other forms of "intelligence" that we do not yet even know how to name or measure. Traditionally, for example, we attempt to solve complex problems such as the causes of disease or crime by painstakingly *isolating* one set of variables after another and looking for simple, mechanistic cause-effect links. To many people this is the only possible way of "logically" analyzing phenomena. Such isolating techniques work well in playing chess, but they are of little use in playing video games. It is possible that video and computer games are introducing our children to a different way of thinking that involves the integration of multiple variables and overlapping lines of simultaneous actions. Although the best thing many critics have been able to suggest about video games is that they help the development of "hand-eye coordination," it is also conceivable that the video game wizards will grow up to find a complex cure for cancer.[33]

In a print society, the graded complexity of print data and the highly compartmentalized nature of print audiences leads to high esteem for "experts" (the "top" in a field) and "specialists" (people whose knowledge is focused in one tiny cluster of information about a particular subject). Indeed, the more highly trained and educated a person is in a print society, the more ensconced they usually become *in* a given body of literature, and, therefore, the more they are trained *out* of awareness of other fields of knowledge. Many of the traditional disciplines are, in this sense, not only bodies of structured knowledge, but also systems of organized ignorance. The specialist's skill is situationally defined. The key to being an "expert" is not to "learn everything," but to reduce the size of a "knowledge situation" until one is able to master all that is in it.

In an electronic society, however, messages from all bodies of knowledge are more equally accessible to all people. While such messages, especially as presented on radio and television, often offer more "awareness" than "understanding," the new communication pattern works to undermine the status of authorities whose knowledge and skills are based only on isolated communication networks. Experts and specialists continue to have much more specialized knowledge than the average person, but the new shared forum created by electronic media has affected our evaluation of such specialized knowledge. Because we are now more "aware" of the many areas that a given specialist knows nothing about, we are gaining a renewed appreciation of a kind of Renaissance generalism. On the one hand, no topic is expected to be so complex that it cannot be explained, at least in broad terms, to the common person; conversely, no authority or leader is fully respected unless he or she appears to have a sense of "general" social knowledge. Ironically, we are increasingly dependent on specialized knowledge, yet we also have less respect for such knowledge when it is presented in a vacuum.

In one sense, the new notion of "being smart" involves a dilution of knowledge so that it "plays well" on television and radio. But in another sense, electronic media offer potential enrichment of our culture's stock of knowledge and understanding. The means of storing and dispensing information through electronic media may, at first, seem disconnected and disorganized. But this perception is probably based on a print-oriented bias. By merging many formerly distinct knowledge situations, electronic media have been breaking down the boundaries among various disciplines, opening new dialogues, and fostering the development of cross-disciplinary areas of study.

Again, the impact of television and radio in this regard is small compared to the potential long-term effects of the computer. At this point, most people still use the computer to store, gain access to, and analyze data in their specialized fields of interest. But unlike books (where one must often go "bibliography-hopping" through a given field to find "relevant" sources), the computer gives potentially equal access to data from *all* fields. It may soon be possible for any person with a telephone and a portable terminal to have access to any book in the Library of Congress, any article in any journal, and any data that have been placed in a central research bank. Through a computer search, any mention of a topic (or a given combination of topics) could be located. With such an overwhelming amount of accessible data, a new "specialty" may develop: the ability to see patterns and interrelationships among various types of data, regardless of their "field" of origin. The resulting "specialist in generalism" would be someone who does not "know" everything about everything but who has a good idea of who knows what, where and how to find things, and how to link together similar questions in diverse fields. This person who would know "almost nothing about almost everything" could provide a balance for those specialists who, in our increasingly specialized world, know "almost everything about almost nothing."

Thus, although the computer may, on the surface, seem to establish a new hierarchy of access based on complex programming skills and on variations in the sophistication and cost of hardware and software, many features of the computer will enhance the merging of information-systems. Further, unless we stop using telephones, radios, and televisions, the spread of computers and other new media will probably not be able to reestablish the distance that once existed in a print culture.[34]

In addition, it is not at all clear that the computer will continue to rely as heavily as it has on abstract written symbols. The increasingly sophisticated use of interactive computer graphics and the drive toward computers that can understand and use human speech, both suggest that mastery of literacy may soon be as irrelevant to the basic operation of computers and computer-controlled machines as it is to the operation of television sets and automobiles. Whether we should applaud or condemn such a "demotion" of literacy is open to question, but it is clear that such an evolution would further integrate people of different ages and levels of education.

Regardless of which path dominates the evolution of the computer—discursive or presentational symbols—the computer and other new technologies certainly enhance the most significant difference between electronic and all previous modes of communication—the undermining of the relationship between social place and physical place. Anyone's personal computer can now be hooked into any other "mainframe" or personal computer through the massive telephone system. The computer is also stimulating the integration of various technologies—televisions, telephones, audio/video recorders, satellites, and printers—into one large information network. As more and more work and play in our society is becoming "informational" rather than "material," there is a further decline in the difference between here and there and an enhancement of our roles as new-age hunters and gatherers.

Controlling or Controlled?

On the surface, the theory presented in this book may appear to be part of a wholly "deterministic" philosophy. Some may wrongly interpret my analysis of the impact of media on human behavior as a suggestion that we are merely bit players in a drama whose script and scenes we do not control. But this is not my intention at all. I do believe, however, that we are each born into a physical and social world in which there are both freedoms and constraints. While we choose our friends, for example, we cannot choose our parents. Further, it is clear that we cannot meet people who are no longer living or not yet alive, and if we marry, we must choose one of the small fraction of living people we happen to meet. We cannot live without food, warmth, and sleep, though we are often free to choose what we eat and where we sleep. Because we cannot be physically in two places at the same time, even our choices of where we go and what we do are themselves limitations in disguise. And finally, regardless of any of the choices we make, we ultimately die (though sometimes we can decide how and when we do so). In studying the human condition, therefore, one can choose to focus on limits or on available options. Just as those who study human choices often take the constraints for granted, I have chosen to study one variable of social constraint while assuming obvious individual and group freedoms.

In many ways, my work parallels that of the anthropologists and psychologists who have studied the effects of interpersonal distances and architectural designs on the style and tone of social interactions.[35] Airport lounges with long rows of fiberglass chairs bolted to the floor obviously foster different types of interactions than do other lounges with soft armchairs loosely arranged in a circle. I argue, similarly, that once invented and used, media affect us by shaping the type of interactions that take place through them. We cannot play certain roles unless the stages for those roles exist.

Such analyses of the structure of interactional settings leave a large number of individual and group freedoms intact. *Individuals* behaving in physical or mediated environments still have a wide range of behavioral choices within the overall constraints. They may behave "appropriately" in many different personal styles; or they may choose to ignore the social cues and behave "inappropriately"—provided they are willing to take the social consequences. And finally, they may leave situations in which they feel uncomfortable or avoid them in the first place. On a *group* level, the situation is even less deterministic. For *we* design and use our rooms, buildings, media, rituals, and other social environments. We can redesign them, abandon them, or alter their use.

Ultimately, the most deterministic perspective may be unwittingly embraced by those who refuse to apply our greatest freedom—human reason and analysis—to the social factors that influence behavior. We do not retain free-choice simply because we refuse to see and study those things that constrain our actions. Indeed, we often give up the potential of additional freedom to control our lives by choosing not to see how the environments we shape can, in turn, work to reshape us.

APPENDIX:
DISCUSSION OF TERMS

A new theory is more than a set of new terms or new definitions for old terms; it is also a new set of relationships among concepts and ideas. Rather than present definitions for terms in alphabetical order, therefore, I have decided to discuss relevant terms in a sequence that highlights their interrelationships from the perspective of the theory developed in this book. In a sense, this discussion of terms also presents a summary of the book's approach and arguments. For those readers who want to read only about one or a few terms, they are in bold print in the following sequence: **media of communication, prediction, electronic media of communication, social situations, information-systems, information, behavior, social role, group identity, socialization, hierarchy, electronic society, print society, and media matrix.**

The term **media of communication** refers to all channels and means through which information is transmitted among people *except* direct, face-to-face modes of communicating. As I use the term, writing, photography, the telephone, and radio are examples of media; speech and nonverbal behavior are not. Media are many things at once: technologies, cultural artifacts, personal possessions, vessels for storing and retrieving cultural content and forms, and political and economic tools.

My primary interest with media, however, is to view them as certain types of social environments that include and exclude, unite or divide people in particular ways. Therefore, I examine how the widespread use of a medium may affect "who knows what," "who knows what about whom," and "who knows what compared to whom." I analyze how different patterns of access to social information have different effects on various social roles.

As Raymond Williams has argued convincingly in *Television: Technology and Cultural Form,* media do not develop and grow in a vacuum. The growth of certain technologies and the particular uses and configurations of those technologies are stimulated by various social, political, and economic forces. A political and economic system that is interested in the distribution of goods, for example, may foster the development of technologies such as radio and television that are capable of reaching into the homes of potential consumers and teaching them the joys and "necessity" of buying products. Other technologies (or similar technologies used differently—such as ham radio or community television) may receive much less support and encouragement.[1] Williams and others, therefore, focus on the political and economic structures and their interactions with communication technologies. I suggest, however, that regardless of the reasons for its development, the particular combination of a communication technology and a configuration for its use (a combination that might be called a "techno/use") often has many social consequences that are not directly related to the intentions of powerful political and economic forces. Indeed, new media may have profound effects on the economic and political structures that bore them. In order to look beyond the dominant research interest in media messages and to offer a new approach to the study of media as they have existed, I try to show how we can predict behavioral changes by examining how the use of a new communication technology affects the "situational geography" of social relations.

I use the term **prediction** in the sense of the description of the *conditions* under which certain social changes may take place.[2] "Conditional prediction" suggests that if variable(s) X change(s) in a certain way, variable(s) Y will probably respond in a predictable way. This form of prediction is distinct from what might be called "crystal ball prediction" or "prophecy," which is a description of future changes in variable(s) Y regardless of what happens to other variables in the interim. Conditional prediction is an explanatory device that can be used to describe how changes in behavior took place in the past (retrodiction), how they are taking place now, and how they may take place in the future. Unlike prophecy, conditional prediction often suggests the ways in which we can control and shape future changes. The "conditions" discussed here are changes in the structure of social situations as a result of the widespread use of new media—"all other things held constant" (see the introduction to Part III). While this situational approach can be used to study the effects of all changes in media—past, present, and future—the focus here is on the study of the changes fostered by the widespread use of electronic media of communication, particularly the effects that television has had over the last thirty years.

Electronic media of communication are a special type of media in which messages are encoded as electronic signals, transmitted, and then decoded. The telegraph, telephone, radio, and television are examples of electronic media. I argue that these media are worthy of special study, not only because they are recent innovations that are used almost universally, but also because they have unique physical characteristics that have significant sociological implications. The nature of the electronic signal allows it to be rapidly transmitted through wire or air, and the form of the message often resembles "real" face-to-face communication. As a result, communication can easily bypass many former physical barriers to information flow, and "interactions" can take place without regard to traditionally defined social situations.

Social situations are the social environments, or "contexts," in which certain types of behaviors are socially expected and exhibited. They are the complexly determined and often elusive settings in which we play out and witness social roles.

The meaning of a social situation is determined not only by what is *in* it but also by what is excluded from it. A wedding, for example, is distinguished from other events such as funerals not only by the presence of a bride and groom but also by the absence of a corpse. People consciously and unconsciously vary their behavior to match the definition of social situations and the "audience" for their performances.

Considering how often the terms "situation" and "context" are used with respect to communication and behavior, they have been, until very recently, surprisingly underdefined terms. Their meanings are usually left implicit, embedded in the assumptions about communication and social life. In both its implicit use and in the relatively few and recent instances of its explicit definition, the notion of "social situation" has generally been conceived of in terms of time/space coordinates: *where* one is, who else is *there*, the date and time, and the overall definition of the event taking place in that particular time/space frame ("party" vs. "meeting," for example).[3]

The theory presented here suggests that the relationship between situations and behavior provides one key to an analysis of the impact of new media of communication on social behavior. For when the boundaries of situations change to include or exclude participants in new ways, situational definitions and behavior must change as well. Yet the traditional linking of social situations to physical places has made the impact of media on social settings and behavior difficult to see. For changes in media do not visibly change the structure of places. I argue that electronic media create new types of social situations that transcend physically defined social settings and have their own rules and role expectations. To allow for the inclusion of media in the definition of social situations, situations are redefined here as "information-systems."

Information-systems are set patterns of access to information about others. **Information** is used in the sense of social information, that which we know about the behavior and actions of ourselves and others. My use of the term differs from the quantified "bits" of information used in "information theory,"[4] and also from the more popular and inclusive use of the term to refer to "facts" and "knowledge" in general. The meaning here is always tied to social performances and behavior.

As is suggested in Chapters 3 and 4, however, control over knowledge and facts often interacts with control over social information by affecting who is authorized to play particular roles and to have access to specific situations. In examining the situational nature of group differences, for example, we can see the relationship between social information-systems and access to "knowledge"—facts, data, and so forth. Members of different groups are often distinguished on the basis of what they know and what they know how to do. In the past, men and women were distinguished in relation to their possession of different knowledge (such as knowing how to fix a car versus knowing how to cook and sew). Such group distinctions begin with simple, low-level "data," but their cumulative effect is a different world view.

A focus on knowledge of facts and data alone, however, would miss the point because it matters less *what* one knows than who else knows it. To have a special personal or group identity, there must be others who do not know what you know. Control over knowledge, then, returns us to the issue of social information-systems—bounded situations to which only certain people have access. Because exclusive control over knowledge gives one the right and ability to exhibit certain social behaviors, the concern over access to knowledge ("who knows what") over-laps with the concern over social information flow ("who knows what about whom" and "who knows what compared to whom"). Access to group knowledge is intimately related to access to group situations from which members of other groups are separated.

It is possible, of course, for two or more people to be in the same location and still experience entirely different realities. In stereotyped conceptions of sex roles, for example, a man and woman can witness the same object—a car—and yet "see" different things: the woman, its color and the comfort of the seats, the man, its mechanical features. Access to location and access to information are not iden-tical. Similarly, as Clifford Geertz's elaborate description of the significance of Balinese cockfights suggests,[5] one can witness events without understanding the full situational definitions. In another example of the same principle, Christine Nystrom has noted that one of the ways girls have traditionally been discrimi-nated against in childhood is by being given physical access to some situations without being given full informational access. Girls may be allowed, for example, to participate in a softball game but without being told such important things as the set of relationships among all the players (they are told "just hit the ball and run.")[6] But such mismatchings between physical and informational access in a given setting are generally rooted in other important distinctions in access to sit-uations. The different perspectives on cars, cockfights, and softball games among those present at a *particular* time and place are made possible by distinctions in presence at *other* sets of situations. To be in the same group with others, you must have access to *all* or most of the group's situations, or what might be called the group's "meta-situation" or "meta-information-system."

Information-systems could also be thought of as "behavior-systems," but I chose the term *"information-*system" because I think "information" serves as a better common denominator to connect live encounters and mediated interac-tions. It is difficult initially to think of what we learn about an author through a book, for example, as access to "behavior," but it makes sense to consider it as access to a form of "information" about the author and about the characters, places, and events described in the book.

I suggest that a large measure of the social significance of an information-system lies in the patterns of access to others that it establishes. Situations (both mediated and live) include and exclude participants. Thus, while information is often defined in terms of its *content*, this study is more concerned with the *structure* of information-systems and with the extent to which different people have access to similar or different social information. I discuss how print media and electronic media tend to create different types of social information-systems because they generally differ in terms of complexity of "access code," physical characteristics, extent of "association" with content, "conditions of attendance," the degree to which an individual's access to information through the medium is public and explicit, the extent to which the form of information fosters personal or impersonal messages and responses, and the degree to which the medium strengthens or weakens the relationship between physical location and social experience (see Chapters 5, 6, and 7). I argue that because electronic media alter patterns of access to social information, they significantly reshape social behavior.

Behavior is used here in its broadest sense to include all that people do in conscious and unconscious expression and communication. This definition includes: speech, thought, vocalization, dress, facial expression, and gesture. The specific concern, however, is with the ways in which behavior is organized into socially meaningful and significant patterns—that is, into social roles.

A social role is a *selected* display of behaviors that, when taken as a whole, is perceived by members of the social community or group to be appropriate for an individual in a given social situation. As one sociologist notes, "Crying as such is behavior which cannot be described as a 'role'; crying at a funeral is behavior which can be so described—it is expected, appropriate, specific to that situation."[7] The performance of a social role is determined not only by the situation, but also by the relative status or position of those engaged in the situation. Thus the priest at a funeral is expected to enact a different set of behaviors from the widow. The sense of "appropriateness" is generally unconscious and becomes visible only when people behave "improperly."

Roles are, in a sense, arbitrary; they have no meaning apart from the larger social system. Yet human beings are inherently social animals, and a large measure of an individual's sense of self and identity is developed through the role behaviors he or she projects and through the responses received from others. Yet because roles are situationally defined, they can be greatly affected by a widespread restructuring of social situations caused by such factors as industrialization, war, disaster, migration, *or* changes in media of communication.

Most sociologists make a clear distinction between social "status" and social "role." "A *status* is simply a position in society or in a group. . . . A *role* is the dynamic or the behavioral aspect of status. Statuses are occupied, but roles are played."[8] While this distinction is important when the terms are being used to describe a static social order, it may actually obscure part of the dynamics of social change. Status and role have a symbiotic relationship. For a person to maintain a status requires that the appropriate role be played. If a priest or a President does not perform his role properly, he may lose possession of that status. Further, if social changes occur that affect the abilities of many holders of the same status to play their roles in traditional ways, then the definition of the status, in general, may change. There may be a difference between the status and role of "housewife," but in recent years, both have changed and probably for similar reasons. When I speak of types of roles and the informational dynamics that support them, therefore, I may cross over into what many sociologists prefer to call status. I try to demonstrate that both statuses and roles are dependent on the number and type of social information-systems, and that these, in turn, may be affected by changes in media of communication.

To study the effects of media on social roles, however, we must think of social roles in a new way. Social roles are generally studied in terms of observable behavior: What behaviors are associated with a given occupation? How do the activities of women in a society differ from the activities of men? How does the behavior of a teacher change in moving from interaction with students to interaction with parents or principal? How does the behavior of one individual change as he or she grows from childhood to adulthood to old age? Whether roles are examined in isolation or in relation to each other, the emphasis traditionally has been on describing what people *do* in given roles in a given society at a given time.[9]

Although the study of specific roles is grounded in concrete observation of speech, gesture, dress, and overall activity, the conception of "role," in general, is often so abstract as to be meaningless. "Role" is usually defined in terms of "proper," "expected," or "appropriate" behavior for a given status in a given situation, or in terms of the general "rights" and "obligations" associated with a particular social position.[10] Such conceptions of roles tell us little beyond the fact that people usually do what they usually do. As John Jackson notes, "one of the more surprising features of the intellectual history of contemporary sociology is the degree to which this elusive concept has been taken for granted by its users as a kind of theoretical haven."[11]

Between these two extremes—observed behavior and high-level abstraction— lie few theories of the social dynamics that lead to *variations* in the forms that roles take in different societies or in the same society over time. The poverty of the common conception of social roles, therefore, is most apparent in analyses of social change.[12] Why, for example, have the "rights" and "obligations" of women changed in recent years? Rather than answer this question directly, many observers simply outline the new role behaviors and contrast them with the old. For, as commonly conceived and used, the vague concept of "role" suggests no theory to account for *shifts* in "proper," "expected," and "appropriate" behavior. Sometimes a change in conceptions of appropriate roles is described as the cause of changing behavior. New gender roles, for example, are sometimes attributed, in part, to the women's liberation movement.[13] But such an argument is tautological—it suggests that the change is caused by itself.

Some theorists have argued that the notion of social role is so problematic that it should be abandoned altogether.[14] I suggest, however, that the concept of role can be strengthened by studying one key variable that affects the form of social roles: the structure of social situations and the patterns of access to the information available in them. By describing the relationship between roles and information-systems, the book extends the notion of role beyond a merely descriptive label of existing behavior and converts it into a concept that can be used to explain and predict widescale changes in social behavior.

To analyze a broad spectrum of social change, I have divided roles into three broad categories: roles of affiliation (group identity), roles of transition (socialization), and roles of authority (hierarchy).

I use the term **group identity** to refer to two complementary phenomena: (1) the individual's sense of association or identification with various groups or categories of people, and (2) the tendency of the members of a specific group to share a sense of what they have in common with each other and of what distinguishes them from other individuals or groups.

Any sense of group identity is both positive and negative. It includes and excludes. If I am a "typical male," then I am not a "typical female." If I act like a married man, then I am not a swinging bachelor. If I am an executive, then I am not a "hardhat." Of course, not all categories are mutually exclusive, and each individual generally develops a constellation of relatively complementary roles and associations (professor, spouse, son or daughter, parent, taxpayer, friend, etc.).

Many sociologists prefer to contrast "groups" with "social categories" and "aggregations."[15] In this three-part framework, true "groups" must be composed of members who actually interact in face-to-face situations ("the third floor typing pool" or "the board of trustees"); "social categories" merely share similar demographic characteristics (age, sex, or profession, for example); and "aggregations" are simply people who turn up at the same place at the same time (a theater audience or people waiting in a train station).

This common system of distinguishing types of association is helpful in describing a stable society, but it may be misleading in analyzing social change. An individual's sense of identity is often linked to all three types of "groups," and changes in any one will often affect that individual's social identity. One person, for example, may identify with a particular family (a primary group), with white collar workers (a category) and with people who attend football games (aggregations).

Further, all three types of association have a common characteristic: shared access to specific social information-systems. Although face-to-face group members share a very special type of "live" information, the social "sameness" that characterizes members of the same social category or aggregation can also be analyzed in terms of shared information and experience.

Finally, all three types of associations may be affected in similar ways by a single type of social change. The strength of the bond among members in a particular family (a primary group) will be very much affected by the changes television causes in the social experiences of most "children" (a social category), and the televising of concerts, sports events, and presidential debates will affect the special sense of sharedness felt by all the people present at the live events (aggregations). To encompass all these forms of change and to analyze the significance of information access to all affiliations, I use the term "group identity" in a broad sense to include what many others refer to as "social categories" and "aggregations." The potential impact of electronic media on group identity is examined by analyzing group identity in terms of access to "shared but special" information-systems and by looking at the changes in information-systems brought about by the widespread use of electronic media.

Socialization refers to the process through which individuals are incorporated into a group. While group identity refers to the individual's sense of self and "being," socialization refers to the individual's sense of "becoming," that is, the transition from status to status and the incorporation into some new group. In this study, as in many other analyses of socialization, the emphasis is on children's socialization into adulthood and the ways in which they learn about their society, institutions, and appropriate role behaviors. But the framework developed is also applied to adult socialization and to incorporation into any group (medical student to doctor, immigrant to citizen, husband to husband-father, John Smith to KKK member).

The common definition of the socialization process is so vague as to be almost mystical. The *Dictionary of Modern Sociology*, for example, states that, "In sociology and social psychology, [socialization] almost always denotes the process whereby individuals learn to behave willingly in accordance with the prevailing standards of their culture."[16] Metta Spencer puts it more succinctly: "Socialization is the process through which people come to *want* to do what they *must* do." [17] Elsewhere, socialization is defined simply as the learning of "appropriate" roles. What such definitions cannot account for, however, is a change in the notion of "appropriate" behavior. And because such definitions ignore the *dynamics* of the socialization process, they can offer no explanation for changes in the number, type, and significance of the distinct role stages through which children and others are required to pass as they are being socialized into new roles. The theory developed here, in contrast, examines socialization as staggered access to the group's "shared but special" situations, and thereby explains how shifts in social information-systems may affect the structure of socialization processes.

Hierarchy is used to refer to all social relationships where the participants are of unequal rank, authority, or status. I use the term to include face-to-face interaction (boss/worker) and larger social relationships among people who may never meet (President/"the people") and among social categories who never interact as whole groups (professionals/blue collar workers). An individual's hierarchal status often varies from interaction to interaction. As Hugh Dalziel Duncan notes, even a divine monarch changes status as he or she interacts with spouse, offspring, and god.[18]

As discussed in Chapter 4, authority is distinct from "power." Among other things, authority is more nebulous than power. The means to power—wealth, strength, weapons, and armies—can be *possessed*, but authority must be continuously *enacted*. Further, for very high status roles especially, the status may be one that seemingly needs no learning, rehearsing, managing, or "performing." (We are not surprised, for example, to see books on "how to be a potter" or "how to fix computers," but we might be a little disturbed to see a book for doctors on "how to gain the trust of your patients" and we would probably be shocked to see a book for priests on "how to become a Pope.") Many hierarchal roles, therefore, appear to rest on essence instead of action; that is, they seem to involve inherent superior qualities or traits that are derived from the natural (or supernatural) order rather than from the arbitrary structures of human interaction. More than in the other categories, the person and the role seem inseparable.

While many studies of authority and leadership focus on the unique capacities of individuals, this study examines the structure of the social performances and the control over social information that support different definitions of status in given situations. By looking at authority in terms of patterns of information flow, information control, and control over the need for information control, the theory analyzes the potential impact of new media on the social conceptions of different levels of status.

As discussed in Chapter 4, these three categories of roles are by no means mutually exclusive, but this "role triad" can be used to discuss almost every aspect of every social role. Further, the overlappings and similarities in the three role categories derive from a common reliance on information. Information access/restriction is the common denominator linking such familiar notions as "shared experience," "learning," and "all-knowing." Conversely, the distinctions in the three categories are related to different types of access to, or control over information: shared but special experience, gradual access to group information, mystery and mystification. I argue that the traditional forms (and the traditional overlapping pattern) of group identity, socialization, and hierarchy in this country were dependent on the patterns of information access that existed in a print society and are now being altered by our shift to an electronic society.

I speak of an **electronic society** in the same sense that one speaks of an "industrialized society." When we use such terms, we do not have to claim that literacy or agriculture have disappeared, only that some new technology is playing a major role in reshaping a society. Conversely, we can speak of a "print society" or an "agricultural society" to speak about the past without denying that print and agriculture continue to play important roles in electronic and industrialized societies, respectively.

To discuss the impact of electronic media on social situations, we need not argue that old media have disappeared or withered away. Electronic media have a great impact on social situations even though print media still survive and thrive. Radio and television did not destroy the newspaper or the book. Nevertheless, radio and television have affected the functions of print media and have changed the patterns of access to social information. If television removes restrictions to information flow, for example, it will clearly affect those situations and roles that were once defined in terms of isolation. The terms "print society" and "electronic society" are simply shorthand descriptions for a complex interaction among means of communication. A "print society" is actually an oral-writing-print society; an "electronic society" is actually an oral-writing-print-electronic society. The shortened labels merely emphasize the latest significant development to have caused shifts in the rest of the communication spectrum.

In many ways, it is a fiction to discuss any one medium or type of medium in isolation. Media interact with each other within what might be called the **media matrix**—the interlocking network of all coexistent media. Different types of media are often highly interdependent. Newspaper and radio reporters depend on the wire services, broadcasters use telephone lines to create "networks," many publishers use computers to set type, and most television programs are based on printed scripts. Nevertheless, we can talk about the ways in which the media matrix and its effects on social behavior change with the introduction of a particular new medium or of a new general type of medium. What is presented here is an introductory analysis of the shift in situational and role structures as electronic media have been added to the media matrix. The approach in this book is analogous to the study of the widespread changes in an ecological system when only one of many important factors change (a sharp change in amount of rainfall or a significant rise or drop in temperature, for example).

By examining a wide spectrum of media and behavior in a single study, I have been forced to bypass many subtle differences among different electronic media and among different print media. I have also not been able to examine the many similarities that both print media and electronic media have when contrasted with oral communication. I have focused, instead, on the most dramatic and striking changes in the media matrix as electronic media, particularly television, have been added to it.

I have tried to demonstrate that the addition of electronic media to the communication spectrum alters the relationship among earlier media and changes patterns of information flow. Electronic media bypass other modes of communicating the way superhighways bypass local towns and roads. Even those who greatly value face-to-face interaction, reading, and writing often turn to electronic media, just as many of those who value the texture of small-town life along back roads nevertheless use the highways for speed and convenience. Old and new forms of communication may coexist, yet the landscape of social life may be largely transformed.

NOTES*

Preface

[1]American Telephone and Telegraph, 1981, p. 87, reports that there are over 96 "main residence telephones" (as opposed to extensions) for every 100 households in the United States. The A.C. Nielsen Company, 1982, p. 3, indicates that 98% of American households own at least one television set. Ownership has been over 90% since 1962 (Nielsen, 1977, p. 5).

[2]Hiebert et al., 1982, p. 10.

[3]Martin Mayer, 1977, p. 238, reports that poor people share with others in the society a view of the telephone as an "extension of self" and therefore prefer a flat rate telephone service with no counting of telephone calls or call length, even if such a flat rate service costs them more than a rate based on usage. Philip Davis, Supervisor, Bureau of Program Compliance, New Hampshire Division of Welfare, personal communication, November 1983, notes that all states consider at least one inexpensive radio, television, and telephone as part of the basic necessities of life—along with items such as beds and food—and therefore do not include such media as "resources" when calculating benefits under programs such as Aid to Families with Dependent Children (AFDC). See note 4 in Chapter 7 for information on access to media in prisons.

[4]A. C. Nielsen, 1983, p. 6.

[5]President Johnson initiated the use of three side-by-side television receivers with remote controls so that he could monitor all three network news programs at once. The system was first set up in Johnson's bedroom and later duplicated in the Oval Office, the LBJ ranch, and, on one occasion at least, in Johnson's hospital room (Culbert, 1981, p. 218).

[6]A picture of Charles Manson watching television in his cell appeared in *Time* magazine in September 1982 ("Inside Looking Out," 1982, pp. 54–5).

[7]Meyrowitz, 1974. The theoretical portion of the study is extended in Meyrowitz, 1979.

Chapter 1

[1]Goffman, 1967, p. 3.

---

*These notes contain abbreviated citations of author and year. All published articles and books are listed in the bibliography.

Chapter 2

[1]See Comstock and Fisher, 1975, and Murray, 1980, for extensive bibliographies and reviews of television research and for indications of the near-exclusive concern with message content. My critique here applies mainly to the research conducted in the United States; the British and European approaches to media are more eclectic. See McAnany et al., 1981, and Slack and Allor, 1983.

[2]See DeFleur and Ball-Rokeach, 1982, pp. 143–198, for a summary of the evolution of mass communication research perspectives.

[3]See, for example, Gerbner and Gross, 1976. Unlike many other researchers, Gerbner and Gross do discuss a number of the unique features of television. But their discussion of these features serves more as a rationale for their focus on television's content than as the subject of their research, per se. Further, Gerbner and Gross do not see the unusual characteristics of television as having the potential to bring about widespread social change; indeed, they see television as working to subvert social change and to maintain "established power and authority."

[4]The study of gratifications began in the 1940s but was extended and popularized in the 1960s. For a brief overview of the history and assumptions of gratifications research, see Katz et al., 1974. For a critique of the perspective and the suggestion that uses and gratifications is a negative approach—growing more out of disenchantment with effects research than out of any positive theoretical contribution—see Elliott, 1974.

[5]See, for example, Barnouw, 1978; Epstein, 1973; Gans, 1979; and Gitlin, 1980 and 1983.

[6]For one way to categorize questions about media and for a discussion of the metaphors that underlie different types of questions, see Meyrowitz, 1980.

[7]My discussion of Innis is based on Innis, 1964 and 1972. For further discussion of Innis' work, see Melody et al., 1981, and Kuhns, 1971.

[8]My discussion of McLuhan's work is based primarily on his two best books on media: McLuhan, 1962 and 1964. Fittingly for a scholar who declared the renewed importance of oral forms of discourse, the various available interviews with McLuhan—especially the *Playboy* interview published in March 1969—provide the clearest and most logical presentation of his ideas. Although McLuhan expounded at length on the idea of media as "extensions," the notion of technological extensions was discussed by many others before McLuhan, including Samuel Butler, Ralph Waldo Emerson, Henri Bergson, Sigmund Freud, and Lewis Mumford. See Levinson, 1982, p. 172n, for a brief history of the concept.

[9]Carothers, 1959; Goody and Watt, 1963; Havelock, 1963; Luria, 1976; Ong, 1967, 1971, 1982. For a collection of case studies on the effects of literacy in traditional societies, see Goody, 1968.

[10]Chaytor, 1966; Eisenstein, 1979.

[11]Boorstin, 1973, pp. 307–410; Boorstin, 1978; Carpenter, 1973; Carpenter and Heyman, 1970; Ong, 1967, pp. 17–110, 259–262, 287–324; Ong, 1977, pp. 82–91, 305–341; Ong, 1982, pp. 79–81; 135–138; Schwartz, 1974.

[12]In *The Republic of Technology*, Boorstin offers a very positive view of technological change that stands in sharp contrast to the critical view he presents in his widely known earlier book, *The Image*. In the third part of his trilogy, *The Americans*, Boorstin offers his most neutral description of the role of media in "democratizing experience" (pp. 307–410). Perhaps Boorstin's most unusual contribution to medium theory is his analysis of the role of photocopying machines, such as Xerox, in the decline of secrets (1973, pp. 397–402).

[13]Ogburn, 1964, pp. 86–95.

[14]Havelock, 1963, p. 46.

[15]For an excellent discussion of the interplay of old and new media, see Ong, 1977, pp. 82–91.

[16]"Conversation with Marshall McLuhan," 1977, pp. 62–63.

[17]McLuhan, 1964, p. 3.

[18]McLuhan, 1964, pp. 4–5.

[19]McLuhan claims that his pronouncements on media are "probes" rather than completed analyses, explorations rather than expositions. He argues that he and Innis refuse to take and develop a fixed "point of view" because such a traditional, linear perspective mutes the potential for new insights. McLuhan says that he, Innis, and other explorers of media environments are like blind men tapping canes in the dark; if their canes were *connected* to any of the objects in their environment they could not feel their way around. Instead, they offer a "mosaic" or "interface" approach that juxtaposes seemingly disparate phenomena in an attempt to reveal new relationships among them. See, for example, McLuhan's introduction to Innis, 1964, and McLuhan and Nevitt, 1972, p. 8. (Also see Czitrom, 1982, p. 173, for the suggestion that in describing Innis' work, McLuhan merely projects his own approach onto Innis and neglects many salient features that distinguish Innis from McLuhan.) Ironically, both the strengths and weaknesses of McLuhan's "mosaic methodology" have worked against his reputation. McLuhan's form of exploration does lead many readers to insights and understanding. But many of those who gain such insight through McLuhan's lens, see the discoveries as their own and therefore feel no need to cite him. At the same time, many of those who are unable to make any sense of McLuhan have felt the need to "respond" to his well-known claims. As a result, it is usually books that disagree with him that have his name listed in the bibliography.

[20]For a collection of mostly angry critiques, see Raymond Rosenthal, 1968. The anger lingers twenty years after McLuhan penned *Understanding Media*. One scholar who was asked by a publisher to review a few sample chapters from the latter part of this book felt it necessary to comment that he was pleased to find that my work did not rely heavily on McLuhan's. He added, "McLuhan was one of those social artifacts of the late 1960s and early 1970s (much like earth shoes and lava lamps) that didn't have much substance. He is regarded by many of today's theorists as an interesting aberration. I am thankful the author is not resurrecting his ghost."

[21]A portion of the United Artists script is reproduced in "Conversation with Marshall McLuhan," 1977, p. 57.

[22]This idea is referred to in a number of Thomas' writings. See, for example, Thomas and Thomas, 1928, p. 572. The "Thomas theorum," as Robert K. Merton, 1968, pp. 19–20, has dubbed it, is one of the most frequently quoted statements in the situationist literature.

[23]Berger and Luckmann, 1966, p. 20. Berger and Luckmann's discussion of intersubjectivity and of the social construction of reality is an extension of the work of Alfred Schutz.

[24]See Thomas, 1925, pp. 41–69, for an early presentation of the concept of the "definition of the situation." For more recent treatments, see, Ball, 1972; Forgas, 1979; Goffman, 1959; and McHugh, 1968.

[25]Goffman, 1974.

[26]Shatz and Gelman, 1973.

[27]Goffman, 1971, pp. 335–390, suggests that lack of awareness of the importance of situational definitions often mistakenly leads us to think that we can examine and treat mental illness as if it is, like medical illness, a problem *within* the individual. Goffman suggests, instead, that mental illness is, in part, the "insanity of place."

[28]See Hall, 1959, for many excellent examples of mismatched situational definitions in cross-cultural encounters.

[29]Goffman, 1963, p. 7.

[30]Berger and Luckmann, 1966, pp. 50ff, describe how certain definitions of situations "thicken" and "harden" as they are passed down to a new generation. What the first generation sees as "the way we've *decided* to do things" becomes for subsequent gen-

erations "the way things are done." Berger and Luckmann call this the process of "institutionalization."

[31]See, for example, Rosenthal and Rosnow, 1969 and 1975.

[32]Rosnow, 1983, p. 333. See also, Rosnow, 1981.

[33]For relevant reviews of the literature, see Argyle et al., 1981; Forgas, 1979; Furnham and Argyle, 1981.

[34]Endler, Hunt, and Rosenstein, 1962; Mischel, 1968.

[35]Haney et al., 1973.

[36]See, for example, Giles and Powesland, 1975; Gregory and Carroll, 1978; and Hymes, 1967.

[37]For an overview of this literature, see Furnham and Argyle, 1981, pp. xli–xliii.

[38]See Furnham and Argyle, 1981, pp. xix-xx, for a review of the situationally related skills research.

[39]Garfinkel, 1967.

[40]Harré and Secord, 1973.

[41]Furnham and Argyle, 1981, p. xxiii. For a discussion of what should be the unit of psychological research, see Pervin's, 1978a, pp. 3–27, review of the person-situation debate. This debate has led many researchers to embrace an "interactional" compromise, but this often means different things to different researchers. Some view behavior as being shaped by two causal forces: personality and situation. In this view, personality and situation "interact" only to the extent that it can be statistically demonstrated that each accounts for aspects of behavior. Others view the interaction as a reciprocal relationship between situations and personality, where each is both a cause and an effect of the other. See Buss, 1981, for an excellent review of these two notions of "interaction."

[42]Goffman's dramaturgical model is presented in Goffman, 1959.

[43]Nigro and Neisser, 1983.

[44]Berger, 1963, p. 98.

[45]"Lost Identity," 1982.

[46]"Playboy Interview: Patricia Hearst," 1982, p. 92.

[47]For a critique of Goffman's work that sees it as a denial of self, see Sennett, 1977 pp. 35–36; for a view of Goffman's work as a celebration of the self, see Freidson, 1983.

[48]William James, 1890, and George Herbert Mead, 1934, for example, conceived of the self as divided into two parts: a social "me" and a personal, spontaneous "I" (roughly equivalent to Freud's superego and id, respectively). The dramaturgical approach, however, tends to emphasize the "me" and downplay the "I." Even those situationists who study individuals' idiosyncratic perceptions and responses to situations tend to take for granted the pre-existence of certain sets of situations. See, for example, Forgas, 1979, pp. 166–243.

[49]Forgas, 1979, p. 7.

[50]Forgas, 1979, p. 7. Forgas offers his own empirical analyses of social episodes as a potential solution to the problem.

[51]Furnham and Argyle, 1981, p. xxii, for example, note that in social psychology "there exist no theoretical models suggesting how situations function and what their components are." Part of the reason for the current lack of theory is the exploratory nature of much of the situational research at this time. In some cases, however, the research into situations has been intentionally atheoretical and existential in nature. See, for example, Rom Harré's introduction to Lyman and Scott, 1970. On the ambiguity of situationist terminology, see Forgas, 1979, pp. 10–12, and Pervin, 1978b.

[52]See Ditton, 1980, for a collection of essays on the significance of Goffman's work and for indications of the peculiarity of Goffman's style and the difficulty of drawing general principles from his writings.

[53]Goffman's emphasis on face-to-face rather than mediated interaction, for example, is clear throughout his work. He explicitly focuses on information received through the "naked senses," not through sensory augmenters (see, for example, 1963, pp. 14–15). Further, after defining situations in terms of "immediate physical presence," he divides the universe of social activity into two mutually exclusive categories: "By definition, an individual's activities must occur either in social situations or solitarily" (1967, p. 167). Even when Goffman mentions electronic and other media (often as literal footnotes to his work), he seems to view their effects as unusual or amusing and, in most cases, as peripheral to the core of social action he describes (see, for example, 1959, p. 119; 1963, p. 102n; 1971, p. 286; 1974, p. 169n). Perhaps the closest Goffman comes to studying a media environment is in the last book published before his death, *Forms of Talk*, in which he has an essay on "radio talk." But even here he does not study the ways in which radio *creates* new situations for the society; instead, he accepts the new situation as a given and narrowly focuses on the types of things radio announcers tend to say (1981, pp. 197–327).

Ironically, the development of electronic media has been cited by situationists as one possible cause of the recent interest in the study of situations. As Furnham and Argyle, 1981, pp. xxv–xxvi, note, video cameras and tape recorders have been among those developments that offer "new techniques and strategies to record, describe, and analyze social situations." Yet these media have generally been seen only as lenses to look through in order to examine face-to-face behaviors more closely. The study of the *transformation* of situations through new media (including the transformation that is inherent in a researcher's "removal" of events from their original situations by recording them on video or audio tape) has gone largely unexplored.

Chapter 3

[1]Goffman, 1959, p. 106, emphasis added.

[2]Barker, 1968, p. 11, emphasis added.

[3]Quoted in Furnham and Argyle, 1981, p. xvi., emphasis added. There are some situationists who are much more concerned with the individual's subjective psychological environment than with the objective setting. For a brief review of such work, see Forgas, 1979, pp. 12–15; for a collection of relevant readings, see Magnusson, 1981. But as Pervin, 1978b, suggests, a person-*place*-action conception of a situation is consistent with all the current strains of situationism.

[4]For discussions of the effects of different arrangements of furniture on behavior, see Hall, 1966, and Sommer, 1969.

[5]See, for example, Meyrowitz, 1974; Meyrowitz, 1979; Levinson, 1979.

[6]For a controversial discussion on "situation ethics" (though concerning a somewhat different conception of "situation"), see Fletcher, 1966; for evidence of the controversy surrounding Fletcher's plea for a nonuniversal standard of ethics, see Cox, 1968.

[7]For Goffman's primary concern with the maintenance of existing definitions, rather than with the creation of new ones, see Goffman, 1959, pp. 167–237. With some exceptions, this concern permeates Goffman's other works as well.

[8]McLuhan, 1964, p. 335.

[9]Stokely Carmichael's rhetorical strategies and dilemmas are described and analyzed by Brockriede and Scott, 1972.

[10]Read, 1974.

[11]Bronislaw Malinowski, 1931, pp. 629–630, for example, discounts biological explanations of the incest taboo and notes that the "sexual impulse, which is in general a very upsetting and socially disruptive force, cannot enter into a previously existing sentiment without producing a revolutionary change in it. . . . A society which allowed incest could not develop a stable family."

[12]For a description of Eisenhower's televised "cabinet meeting," see Mickelson, 1972, p. 42.

Chapter 4

[1]Greer, 1972, p. 243.

[2]de Beauvoir, 1961, p. xvii.

[3]There have been many accounts of moments of comradeship between enemy soldiers during the Civil War and World War I. For a moving fictionalized account of how the closeness of hand-to-hand combat can lead to identification with an enemy soldier, see Remarque, 1929, pp. 218–229.

[4]Cooley, 1964; Mead, 1934.

[5]See, for example, Hearst and Moscow, 1982, and "Playboy Interview: Patricia Hearst," 1982. See also Gelman, 1984, for a description of a case in which a kidnapped boy began to call his kidnapper "Dad." Even after he escaped several years later, the boy protected his kidnapper by telling the police that the kidnapper had been kind to him when, in fact, the boy had been sexually abused and psychologically terrorized.

[6]Goffman, 1959, pp. 77–105.

[7]Firestone, 1971, p. 103.

[8]I am using the phrase "reference group" here in the general sense of whatever group the individual is being socialized into. My use is somewhat different from, though closely related to "reference group theory," which, among other things, describes how people use standards of groups of which they are not (or not yet) members to evaluate and pattern their own behaviors. See, for example, Merton, 1968, pp. 279–440.

[9]van Gennep, 1960, p. 65.

[10]Montagu, 1981, p. 121. See also Chapter 13 of this book for a related discussion of the "myth of age-determinism."

[11]Montagu, 1981, pp. 123–124.

[12]Bossard, 1953, p. 273.

[13]Duncan, 1962, p. 255.

[14]Duncan, 1962.

[15]Edelman, 1964, p. 73.

[16]As Hannah Arendt, 1968, pp. 92–93, notes, "Since authority always demands obedience, it is commonly mistaken for some form of power or violence. Yet authority precludes the use of external means of coercion; where force is used, authority itself has failed." Arendt goes further and suggests that even the use of "persuasion" signifies lack of authority because it "presupposes equality" and depends on logical arguments. "Where arguments are used, authority is left in abeyance." Authority and power, however, are not as unrelated as these clear distinctions would suggest. For control over important social resources—money, land, munitions, etc.—may provide an individual with greater potential for controlling the staging of a high status role *and* with the potential for use of direct or indirect coercion, should "authority" alone be insufficient for reaching a desired goal.

[17]Steinberg, 1974, p. 261.

[18]Innis, 1972.

[19]Quoted in Duncan, 1962, p. 218.

[20]Machiavelli, 1952, p. 94.

[21]Duncan, 1962, p. 134.

[22]Mehrabian, 1971, pp. 5 and 31.

Part II

[1]Innis, 1964; Eisenstein, 1979.

[2]For some interesting hypotheses concerning the impact of electronic media on third world countries, see Carpenter, 1973, and Ong, 1967, pp. 256–258.

Chapter 5

[1]For discussions of the economic structure of broadcasting and its implications, see Barnouw, 1978; Gitlin, 1983; and Mankiewicz and Swerdlow, 1979. Because of the nature of the television business, some viewers' attention to a program is more valuable than other viewers' attention. Many advertisers are willing to pay more for women who are between the ages of 18 and 49—because these women, it is believed, do most of the purchasing of many products. A program may go off the air, therefore, even if it has high ratings, but is popular among the "wrong" people.

[2]My discussion of the different effects of different writing systems is drawn from Havelock, 1976.

[3]The difficulty and "unnaturalness" of reading were more apparent to people before literacy was taken for granted. On this subject, see Cressy, 1980, pp. 19–41. White and White, 1980, p. 73, note that in addition to cognitive skills, reading and writing require precise movements of eye and hand muscles, and this is why young children tend to produce very large letters and are given large print to decode.

[4]Eric Havelock, 1976, p. 46, describes how revolutionary the invention of the phonetic alphabet was and how much it differed from earlier writing systems in that "the script . . . came to resemble an electric current communicating a recollection of the sounds of the spoken word directly to the brain so that the meaning resounded as it were in the consciousness without reference to the properties of the letters used."

[5]Fields, 1982; Kozol, 1979; Wellborn, 1982.

[6]Nielsen, 1983, p. 9.

[7]For reviews of studies that suggest the arbitrariness of certain television and film conventions and therefore the degree of learning needed to master them, see Messaris and Sarett, 1981, and Noble, 1975. See also Chapter 13 of this book for a discussion of the relationship between children's developmental stages and perception of television and print.

[8]Meyrowitz, 1974 and 1979.

[9]See, for example, Dondis, 1973. Dondis begins his *A Primer of Visual Literacy* with the argument: "If the invention of movable type created a mandate for universal verbal literacy, surely the invention of the camera and all its collateral and continually developing forms makes the achievement of universal visual literacy an educational necessity long overdue." The analogy is flawed, however, because the first photographs were accessible to a greater proportion of the population than had mastered verbal literacy even after four and a half centuries of printing. I agree with Dondis' plea for the importance of *deeper* and more *conscious* understanding of the aesthetics of visual forms, but the parallels he and others draw between verbal and visual comprehension often obscure more than they reveal.

[10]Nielsen, 1981, pp. 14–15.

[11]Eisenstein, 1979, p. 432n.

[12]McLuhan, 1962. For more linear discussions of this point, see Carothers, 1959; Havelock, 1963; and Ong, 1967, 1977, and 1982.

[13]These figures are extrapolated from Gallup, 1972; Nielsen, 1983; and Roper, 1983.

[14]Mankiewicz and Swerdlow, 1979, pp. 88–89.

[15]Television Audience Assessment, 1983.

[16]Goodhart et al., 1975, pp. 15–17; 55–57; Barwise et al., 1982.

[17]Roszak, 1968, p. 261.

[18]"Falwell Says," 1981.

[19]Goodhart et al., 1975, pp. 130–131.

[20]Howitt, 1982, p. 146.

[21]Waters and Carter, 1978. Unfortunately, because of the way television audiences are measured, those who watched more than one segment of the series are counted more than once. Therefore, such figures are inflated. A more accurate measure of the ability of television to draw audiences from diverse groups into one experience can be gotten from the ratings for *single* television events, as discussed below.

[22]Daisy Maryles, Senior Editor, *Publishers Weekly*, personal communication, November, 1983.

[23]In a personal communication in March, 1984, Larry Hyams, Manager of Audience Analysis at the American Broadcasting Companies, offered the following examples: The top-rated programs, "A-Team" and "Dallas," draw 40 and 37 million viewers per episode, respectively; "Trapper John," which is number 30 in the ratings, has 23 million viewers per episode; the very low-rated show, "It's Not Easy," has "only" 15 million viewers per episode, and it is being canceled along with several programs with larger audiences. There is no magic number of viewers that must be reached by a program if it is not to be canceled (the decision is related to a number of factors, including the "competition" offered by the other networks and the potential of drawing a larger audience with a different program), but Hyams observed that any program with less than 15 million viewers per episode is a "good bet for cancellation." He added that even the lowest rated, soon-to-be-canceled prime-time show is likely to reach at least 10 million viewers.

[24]"Why 'Roots' Hit Home," 1977, p. 69, records the sales of *Gone with the Wind*; Christopher, 1976, gives NBC's estimate of the number of television viewers.

[25]Waters and Carter, 1978. As indicated in note 21, this figure may be inflated. However, the last episode of "Roots" alone drew an estimated 80 million viewers, or nearly 40 percent of the population of the country.

[26]Victoria Cherney, Editorial Department, Doubleday & Co., personal communication, November, 1983. *Roots* sold over two and one half million copies in hard cover and over two million copies in paperback—reaching only about 2 percent of the population.

[27]Gallup, 1972, pp. 900, 1286, 1293–1294.

[28]Forkan, 1983.

[29]Joanne Aidala, Cable Marketing Consultant, New York City, personal communication, September, 1983. The findings were based on interviews with 20,000 people nationwide.

[30]In some ways, this figure is less surprising than the figure concerning male viewers of "women's programs," not only because more women are available in the home, but also because as mentioned in note 1, female viewers are more valuable than male viewers to many advertisers, and programmers are often interested in shaping their programs to reach them.

[31]Handler, 1983.

[32]Handler, 1983.

[33]Roper, 1983.

[34]Murray, 1980, p. 25.

[35]Goodhart et al., 1975, p. 131, push this type of argument even further by claiming that people tend to watch only those television programs that are *not* about their special interests. "People with a real specialist interest do not generally feel a need to follow it *on television*. Artists do not feel they need to watch art programmes; knitters, knitting programmes; or businessmen, business programmes. . . . Specialists already know all that. Even religious people do not religiously watch all their programmes, but go to church instead."

[36]Mankiewicz and Swerdlow, 1979, p. 97.

[37]To my knowledge, studies of home video recording habits have not explored this question directly, but the data seem to suggest that many people will not bother to watch a "regular" program unless they can watch it while (or within a few days after) "everyone else" has watched it. Studies have found that movies, soap operas, and series are the most popular material for taping. Of those tapes of soaps or series that are ever watched, however, most are played back within three days. Many tapes are taped over without viewing. The tapes that people *save* to create "libraries" are much more likely to be movies rather than regular television programs (Arbitron, 1979; Levy, 1983; Paul Lindstrom, Research Manager, Nielsen HomeVideo Index, personal communication, November, 1983). Further, the "shared arena" phenomenon may even operate with pay television services, such as HBO. In personal communication, Paul Lindstrom of the Nielsen company informed me that viewers will try to watch a movie on pay TV the first time it "premieres" during prime time. The viewers behave as if this is an important public "event," Lindstrom observes, even though the film will be shown again many times during the coming weeks.

[38]Nielsen studies on cable households show that cable viewers do not stop watching network television. In fact, pay cable households watch more television than regular television households because they watch cable offerings *in addition* to watching about as much network television as other households ("Nielsen Gets," 1980, p. 27). Those households that pay a monthly fee for HBO and other pay services, still spend 62% of their prime time viewing hours watching "free" network television (Nielsen, 1983, p. 15). A recent study conducted for (and then disowned by) the National Association of Broadcasters made headlines because it found that people said they were largely dissatisfied with broadcast programming (Bedell, 1983). What was not highlighted in many reports, however, was that the one major exception to the negative view toward network television was the *greater* satisfaction with television news and information programs. In any case, objective measures show that people are watching more television than ever (Nielsen, 1983). Similarly, a pilot study of network vs. pay television viewing habits, conducted by one of my students, found that people did not want to give up "regular television" for specialized programming even when they liked the specialized programming better. Without network news and programs, responses suggested, people would feel disconnected. One woman interviewed said she watched every episode of "The Winds of War," even though she thought the program was terrible, just to see what everybody else was watching and to have something to talk about with her friends (Karen Reisch, unpublished paper, University of New Hampshire, 1983). Again, the odd thing about television is that people will watch it, indeed will sometimes feel they *have* to watch it, even when they do not like it.

Chapter 6

[1]Goffman, 1969.

[2]Langer, 1957.

[3]Watzlawick et al., 1967.

[4]Watzlawick et al., 1967, p. 65.

[5]Salomon, 1979, pp. 67–68.

[6]Gazzaniga, 1970.

[7]Reedy, 1977, p. 3.

[8]Alpern et al., 1981, p. 31.

[9]Mehrabian, 1971, p. 44.

[10]Steinzor, 1950.

[11]See, for example, photo in *Newsweek*, 27 Sept. 1976, p. 35.

[12]Cornwell, 1965, pp. 70–72.

[13]Gallup Organization, Report No. 199, April 1982, pp. 21 and 31.

[14]Clymer, 1982.

[15]Norback and Norback, 1980, p. 336.

[16]The transcript of the "CBS Evening News with Walter Cronkite" from October 25, 1972 was prepared by the Special Projects Department of CBS News. The newspaper stories quoted are Lewis, 1972, and De Onis, 1972.

[17]Ekman and Friesen, 1969, p. 52, note that while expressions can sometimes "lie," nonverbal behavior often "seems to escape efforts to deceive . . . providing either deception clues, *i.e.*, information that deception is in progress, or leakage, *i.e.*, the betrayal of the withheld information."

[18]Chambers, 1983.

[19]Roper, 1983.

[20]Watzlawick et al., 1967, p. 63.

[21]Ekman and Friesen, 1969, p. 50.

[22]Sancton, 1982, p. 16.

[23]For indications of this trend, see Cressy, 1980; Greven, 1970; Laslett, 1965; Shorter, 1975; and Stone, 1977. The phrase "the world we have lost" is taken from the title of Laslett, 1965.

[24]For some indication of how large a part television played in defining the situation surrounding the assassination attempt, see Waters et al., 1981. For evidence that television is also affecting the "rush to judgment" of newspapers, see Schardt et al., 1980.

[25]Waters et al., 1981, p. 104.

[26]Mathews, 1981, pp. 35–36.

[27]Waters et al., 1981, p. 105.

Chapter 7

[1]Genesis, Chapter 18, Verses 10–15.

[2]Settel, 1967, p. 17.

[3]One exception to this was the system of semaphore tower stations designed by Claude Chappe about fifty years before Morse's telegraph. The "arms" were set in different positions to signify different letters. The system was adopted by the French government. But the semaphore was only a crude forerunner of the telegraph. The transmission of semaphore messages still depended on "ordinary" sensory perception (the arms were large enough to be visible five miles away at the next relay station). No messages could be sent during bad weather or at night. And such a system must have been relatively difficult to construct and operate and impossible to duplicate in as many locations as the telegraph and other electronic media would later service. See Settel, 1967, p. 15 for a brief discussion of semaphores.

[4]Access to media in prisons varies from state to state and from prison to prison, and, apparently, there have been no comprehensive surveys of media access in correctional institutions. Available sources of information, however, indicate that there has been substantial access to media among most prisoners since the late 1960s. Charlotte A. Nesbitt, of the American Correctional Association notes that "in most jails and prisons, prisoners do have access to telephones, radios, and television" (personal correspondence, June 1983). A survey conducted in 1979 by the Criminal Justice Information Service (operated by the Contact orga-

nization) indicates that all states except Ohio allow prisoners to make telephone calls and that approximately fifty percent of the states allow inmates to receive calls ("Your Number, Please," 1979). The Director of the Federal Prison System, Norman A. Carlson, reports that federal prisons do not allow personal television sets, but that each housing unit within each prison generally has at least one television set and that a majority vote among prisoners determines program selection (personal correspondence, June 1983). Many state prisons do allow personal television sets, radios, tape players, and stereos in prisoners cells (Donna Hunzeker, Director, Information Services, Contact Inc., personal correspondence, June 1983).

[5]Hendrick, 1977, p. 5.

[6]Board of Institutional Ministry, 1978.

[7]Horton and Wohl, 1956, p. 215.

[8]Gross and Jeffries-Fox, 1978, p. 247.

[9]Horton and Wohl, 1956, p. 223.

[10]Levy, 1979.

[11]Candice Leonard, personal communication, December 1980.

[12]Mathews et al., 1980. Like Lennon, Chapman played the guitar and married a Japanese woman. Chapman had also taped Lennon's name over his own on his workplace identification tag.

[13]"Hinckley's Last Love Letter," 1981.

[14]Levinson, 1979.

[15]Cornwell, 1965, p. 18.

[16]"Playboy Interview: Barbra Streisand," 1977, p. 81.

[17]Goffman, 1959, p. 106.

[18]Television Audience Assessment, 1983, p. 1.

Part III

[1]Bogart, 1956, p. 10.

Chapter 8

[1]For an early article on "Women as a Minority Group," see Hacker, 1951.

[2]See, for example, Francke and Stadtman, 1975.

[3]The significant role played by television in the civil rights movement is an implicit theme throughout Sitkoff, 1981. See, in particular, pp. 86, 133, 136–140, 144, 164, 189–190, 195, and 207. The growth of television households is described in Nielsen, 1977, p. 5.

[4]In his study of Trobriand Islanders, Malinowski found that there was no organized response to deviant behavior unless there was a *public* revelation of the deviance. In a paper originally published in 1948, Lazarsfeld and Merton, 1971, p. 562, extend this principle to the possible effects of mass media. Ironically, however, they see this powerful shift in the dividing line between public and private behaviors and attitudes as leading simply to greater "enforcement of social norms," and their analysis of mass media leads to the conclusion that the "chief social effect of the mass media is no change" (Schramm and Roberts, 1971, p. 554).

[5]Viguerie, 1981, p. 132.

[6]Barnouw, 1970, p. 118. The Gallup Organization studied attitudes toward Khrushchev before and after his 1959 visit. After his visit, he was viewed as significantly more intelligent,

more cooperative, less unyielding, less domineering, and less ruthless. Only one factor tilted toward the negative: he was viewed as less trustworthy (Gallup, 1972, pp. 1631–1632).

[7]In a recent article in *Daedalus*, Michael Mandelbaum, 1982, argues that the common belief among politicians, journalists, and the public that the Vietnam War protests and the American defeat were somehow spurred by television coverage of the war is completely wrong. Mandelbaum argues that Americans have always been pacifists at heart and that opposition to the war in Vietnam—as measured by public opinion polls—was no greater than opposition to other wars, including Korea. While Mandelbaum makes some interesting points and presents a few convincing arguments, his analysis may miss the point because he essentially ignores the special nature of television. Mandelbaum searches for *messages* in the coverage that might have led to dissatisfaction with the war, and he finds none. With a focus on discursive language, he suggests that television is the most "timid" of the news media and that it provided less "information" about the war than newspapers. He rejects the idea that television images led to sympathy for the Vietnamese, and because he finds on television no "overt editorial content" against the war, he concludes that "it is just as plausible to suppose that television promoted *support* for the war as to assume that it generated opposition" (p. 161). But Mandelbaum underplays the significance of the shift in the *form* of war coverage, and he largely ignores the potential contribution of this shift to other social developments, many of which Mandelbaum himself sees as unique to the Vietnam era: a very vocal and active antiwar movement, a disruption and division of American life, a large "counterculture" movement, general dissatisfaction with the way our government was handling the war, and an intensity of feeling on all sides.

[8]Senator Edward Kennedy condemned the Shah and his regime (Newfield, 1979). Former Attorney General Ramsey Clark headed the American delegation, which also included three members of the clergy and a Noble Prize winner (Gwertzman, 1980).

[9]"Wanted: A Pen Pal," 1980.

[10]Bogart, 1956, p. 15.

[11]Crisis at Columbia, 1968, p. 4.

[12]Goffman, 1959, p. 128.

[13]Moore, 1978.

[14]Braestrup, 1977, p. 698–699.

[15]Rielly, 1979, p. 79.

[16]Yankelovich, 1981, p. 95.

[17]Yankelovich, 1981, pp. 94 and 96.

[18]Collins, 1983.

[19]Johnston et al., 1981, p. 13.

[20]Brecher et al., 1983, p. 52; Collins, 1983.

[21]Alan Guttmacher Institute, 1981, p. 9. Another sign of homogenization of sexual behaviors across groups is that the Methodist Church recently found that rates of premarital sexual activity among church-going teenagers are similar to those of teenagers overall (Alan Guttmacher Institute, 1981, p. 9).

[22]Keerdoja et al., 1983.

[23]Gallup, 1972, p. 1965.

[24]Carmody, 1983.

[25]Starr et al., 1982, p. 41. New York City officials estimated a crowd of 550,000 demonstrators; other estimates were as high as a million. Perhaps the most striking aspect of the demonstration was the broad representation of all ethnic groups and races, the mixture of young and old, and the punks and businessmen who walked side by side. See Montgomery, 1982.

[26]Kleiman, 1978.

[27]Williams et al., 1976; Williams et al., 1977.

[28]See, for example, Fraker et al., 1976.

[29]See, for example, Gwynne and Begley, 1978, and Walter Goodman, 1982.

[30]Meyrowitz, 1979, pp. 71–72. A more recent example of a "disturbing identification" for many Americans is the movie "Das Boot" in which the adventures of a World War II German U-Boat crew are chronicled. In direct contrast to virtually all *our* World War II movies, the Germans become "us" and the British and Americans become "them."

[31]See, for example, Popenoe, 1980, pp. 513–514.

[32]One indication of this was the role that cross-country travel could still play in radio dramas. The classic 1942 radio thriller with Orson Wells, "The Hitchhiker," for example, begins with the main character assuring his mother that her fears about his planned drive from New York to California are unfounded; the drama ends with his trip transformed into a journey from sanity to near-insanity, from normal life to a sort of purgatory. And, interestingly, his one hope for remaining sane is the telephone that will link him to the known world—his mother's house.

[33]Barnouw, 1970, p. 45.

[34]Boorstin, 1973, pp. 307–410.

[35]Nielsen, 1984, p. 10; Arbitron, 1982, p. 6.

[36]Since the "renewal movement" spurred by Vatican Council II in the 1960s, there has been a dramatic increase in access to electronic media among nuns and monastery brothers. Although media use varies from place to place, most nuns now have relatively free access to radio, telephone, and television (Father Francis L. Demers, Vicar for Religious, Diocese of Manchester, personal communication, May 1984). Communication among the Trappist monks was once highly restricted, brothers could not even speak to each other except in emergencies or with special permission from the Abbot. This changed in the late 1960s, however, and along with the increase in face-to-face communication has come an increase in access to electronic media. At the Abbey of the Genesee in Piffard, New York, for example, brothers now have access to a telephone (once the prerogative of the Abbot alone). The monks also use a computer for word processing and for running their bakery business, a video taping system is used to give "tours" of the facilities, and one brother is in charge of taping appropriate television programs off the air for later viewing by the monks. The Abbey also subscribes to weekly newspapers and news magazines. To maintain their goal of solitude," however, the monks avoid watching regular broadcast television or reading daily newspapers (Brother Anthony, Guestmaster, Abbey of the Genesee, personal communication, May 1984).

[37]U.S. Bureau of the Census, 1982, p. 44. In a recent study on single-member households, Hughes and Gove, 1981, are surprised to discover that, contrary to earlier findings, people who live alone are no longer associated with many pathological behaviors, including higher rates of suicide. They suggest that their findings undermine previous thinking concerning the importance of "social integration" and the detrimental effects of "social isolation." What they overlook, however, is the opportunity that electronic media have provided for "selective integration." In an electronic age, people who live alone *physically* are no longer necessarily isolated *informationally*.

[38]See, for example, Langway et al., 1983b.

Chapter 9

[1]Nielsen, 1981, pp. 14–15.

[2]See, for example, Anderson, 1978; Leboyer, 1975.

[3]See, for example, Kubler-Ross, 1969, and Woodward et al., 1978a.

[4]Gelman, 1982; Langway et al., 1983a.

[5]See, Goffman, 1961, pp. 85–152, for a discussion of "role distance" in which Goffman suggests that even while "in" a role, a performer may feel obliged to separate him or herself from it in some way.

[6]Glick and Spanier, 1980, document the dramatic rise in unmarried cohabitation in the 1960s and 1970s. In an update of that study, Spanier, 1983, describes the more than 300% rise in the number of unmarried couples living together between 1970 and 1981. From 1980 to 1981 alone, there was a 14% increase. Even when the overall growth in number of households is taken into account, the *proportion* of cohabitants has doubled in a span of only five years. While the percentage of couples who cohabit without marriage at *any given time* may remain relatively small (4% of couples who live together are unmarried), Spanier observes an important sociological and psychological transformation: "that unmarried couples are being drawn more fully into the mainstream of society, that society is more willing to ignore marital status in its evaluation and treatment of unmarried cohabiting individuals, and that those who are already in the mainstream of society are more willing to consider unmarried cohabitation as an acceptable (or tolerable) living arrangement" (p. 287). Spanier concludes that even if the rate of increase in cohabitation is to decline in the near future, social scientists must begin to view unmarried cohabitation "less as an alternative 'lifestyle' and more as a normative phenomenon" (p. 287).

[7]See, for example, Maeroff, 1977.

[8]Levinson et al., 1978; Sheehy, 1976.

[9]Furstenberg et al., 1981, p. 2. The researchers also note that nearly 60% of the births to females under 18 now take place out of wedlock. The rise in illegitimacy is even more striking considering the recent legalization in abortion. Further, in this and other areas of teenage sexuality, the most dramatic changes are occurring among whites; the once significant differences between whites and nonwhites are diminishing.

[10]Carmody, 1968.

Chapter 10

[1]Havelock, 1963, p. 126.

[2]Innis, 1972, p. 17.

[3]From "I'm Gonna Say It Now," by Phil Ochs, Barricade Music Co., 1965, emphasis added.

[4]Levine, 1980, p. 53.

[5]Levine, 1980, pp. 39–58.

[6]Levine, 1980, pp. 45–46.

[7]Levine, 1980, pp. 39–58.

[8]Grove, 1983, discusses Intel Corporation; Pauly and Joseph, 1983, describe union problems in high tech firms; Geoff Sackman, Manager, Personnel Policies and Procedures, Digital Equipment Corporation, discussed management styles at Digital in a personal communication, November, 1983.

[9]See, for example, Messaris and Sarett, 1981.

[10]For a brief history of the integration of commercial television into school curricula, see Goldsen, 1978, pp. 345–348. In a 1982 poll, 35% of parents of school-age children indicated that their children's teachers have assigned the watching of a television program as part of school homework (Roper, 1983, p. 19).

[11]See, for example, Herbers, 1978; Schlesinger, 1973, p. 209; and White, 1982.

[12]See, Nie et al., 1976, for a review of voter studies of the 1950s.

[13]See, for example, Nie et al., 1976. Their detailed and carefully reasoned book is based on a series of surveys conducted by the University of Michigan's Survey Research Center from 1952 to 1972.

[14]Nie et al., 1976, pp. 148–149. Nie et al., qualify their findings by suggesting that the 1950s may have been an unusual period of voter apathy and calm, but they suggest that if the 1950's were unusual in one direction, the period since 1960 has been unusual in the opposite direction.

[15]Shaver, 1980, p. 46.

[16]Binder, 1977.

[17]Morganthau, DeFrank, and Clift, 1983, p. 23.

[18]Lyons, 1977.

[19]Stuart, 1977.

[20]Ledbetter, 1977.

[21]For a discussion of the rise and fall of the authority of doctors in America, see Starr, 1982. For an indication of the feminist revolt against the traditionally male medical establishment, see The Boston Women's Health Book Collective, 1976. For a popular childbirth book that reflects the recent demystification of doctors, see Hotchner, 1979.

[22]Cornwell, 1965, p. 187. Halberstam, 1980, p. 21, gives a humorous example of FDR denying a blasphemous quote that appeared in *Time*.

[23]See, for example, Charlton, 1977.

[24]Alexander, 1974.

[25]Mankiewicz and Swerdlow, 1979, p. 108.

[26]Bradlee, 1975, pp. 106–107n.

[27]See, for example, the discussion among William Goldsmith, Arthur Schlesinger, Jr., and Leon Friedman, in Goldsmith, 1974, pp. 2127–2144; 2216–2226.

[28]See Barnouw, 1970, p. 119, for a discussion of some of the early concern over the change from traditional diplomacy to media appeals to public opinion.

Chapter 11

[1]Vanderbilt, 1970, pp. 28–29.

[2]Hearst/ABC's women-oriented "Daytime" cable programming, for example, has included the program, "Lucille's Car Care Clinic." Similarly, the show "Livewire," on "Nickelodeon" ("the first channel for kids"), has included children's discussions about drugs and the difficulties of talking to parents about sex.

[3]Rintels, 1976.

[4]See, for example, "Banter Before the End," 1982, for a partial transcript printed in *Newsweek* of Richard Nixon's "off-mike" comments before delivering his resignation speech.

[5]Goffman, 1971, p. 303n.

[6]Clemons et al., 1979, p. 51.

[7]Ariès, 1962, pp. 393-399; Stone, 1977, pp. 253–256.

[8]Ariès, 1962, p. 399.

[9]For a description of the use of the family bed several hundred years ago, see Stone, 1977, pp. 253-256. See Joblin, 1981, for a description of its return.

[10]See Footlick, 1977, and Lieberman, 1981, for descriptions of the trend.

Chapter 12

[1]See, for example, Rohrbaugh, 1979; Teitelbaum, 1976; and Weitz, 1977.

[2]From a letter from John Adams to James Sullivan in May, 1776, explaining why women, the unpropertied, and minors should be excluded from voting (quoted in Rossi, 1973, pp. 13–14). Although the statements about women form part of a hypothetical debate about women and voting, they seem to reflect both Adams' general opinion and the views of the times.

[3]For an attack on "sexist infancy," see Pogrebin, 1981, pp. 116–130.

[4]"The Private Life of Gwyned Filling," 1948, pp. 110 and 114.

[5]See, for example, Gersoni-Stavn, 1974.

[6]Talcott Parsons, 1954, p. 79, a prime figure in the functionalist school, noted that "absolute equality of opportunity is . . . incompatible with any positive solidarity of the family." See Friedan, 1977, pp. 117–128, for an attack on the "functionalist freeze."

[7]McGinley, 1964, p. 47. This passage is also quoted and discussed in Janeway, 1971, p. 40.

[8]These lists of traits were compiled by Mary Anne Warren and are discussed in Vetterling-Braggin, 1982, pp. 5–6.

[9]Rohrbaugh, 1979, p. 4.

[10]The head of the "Stop ERA" movement, Phyliss Schlafly, for example, notes that "the claim that American women are downtrodden and unfairly treated is the fraud of the century. The truth is that American women have never had it so good. Why should we lower ourselves to 'equal rights' when we already have the status of special privilege?" (Quoted in Levine and Lyons, 1980, p. 81.) Also see Gilder, 1975, for a more global claim that women have *always* been naturally superior to men and that the exclusively male activities that women now want to share in have merely been men's means of compensating for their inherent inferiority.

[11]Pogrebin, 1981, p. 85.

[12]Pogrebin, 1981, p. 85.

[13]Epstein, 1967, pp. 181–183.

[14]Stone, 1977, p. 195.

[15]Purcell, 1974, pp. 132–133.

[16]The idea of bra-*burning* was apparently an invention of the media—perhaps further evidence of an unconscious link with draft-card-burning rebels. At the feminist protest against the Miss America Pageant in 1968, however, bras—along with girdles, false eyelashes, and wigs—were thrown in the "Freedom Trash Can." Levine and Lyons, 1980, p. 27.

[17]Degler, 1980, p. 444.

[18]For a chronology of milestones in the "decade of women," see Levine and Lyons, 1980. See also, Lois Decker O'Neill, 1979. O'Neill set out to produce a book "celebrating women's world records and achievements in the late 19th and the 20th centuries." She discovered, unexpectedly, that there was no gradual growth in women's activities. She concluded that today's women "live in an epoch of firsts" in which "barriers to female participation have been falling at . . . a fairly astonishing rate" (p. ix).

[19]Levine and Lyons, 1980, p. 74.

[20]The information on law school enrollments was provided by Kathleen S. Grove, Assistant to the Consultant on Legal Education, American Bar Association, personal communication, October 1983. The information on medical school enrollments was compiled from Dubé, 1974; Thomae-Forgues and Tonesk, 1980; and from a data sheet on 1982–1983 enrollments sent to me in October 1983 by Dr. Robert Beran of the Association of American Medical Colleges.

[21]Kleiman, 1982.

[22]U.S. Dept. of Health, Education, & Welfare, 1972.

[23]Levine and Lyons, 1980, p. 6.

[24]Levine and Lyons, 1980, p. 8.

[25]Levine and Lyons, 1980, p. 8.

[26]Levine and Lyons, 1980, p. 16.

[27]Levine and Lyons, 1980, p. 14.

[28]Levine and Lyons, 1980, p. 24.

[29]Levine and Lyons, 1980, p. 24.

[30]In 1977, for example, the American Psychological Association prepared nonsexist guidelines for authors. In 1982, the APA Publications and Communications Board made the guidelines mandatory for submissions to all APA journals. See American Psychological Association, 1983, pp. 43–48.

[31]"Sexist-Grammatik" is produced by the Aspen Software Company.

[32]Mead, 1968, p. 168.

[33]Gelman et al., 1978, pp. 53–54.

[34]A look through the Cumulative Book Index reveals that more books on fathers were published in the five-year period, 1977–1981, than had been published in the previous two decades.

[35]There are currently more than 300 U.S. groups or programs concerned with fathers' issues, including many fathers' rights organizations. The vast majority of these groups and programs have developed within the last decade (James A. Levine, Director, The Fatherhood Project, Bank Street College of Education, personal communication, March 1984).

[36]Atkinson, 1984, pp. 8 and 11.

[37]Atkinson, 1984, p. 36.

[38]Foster and Freed, 1978, p. 20.

[39]Friedan, 1981, pp. 163–198.

[40]Peter Schwartz's work in this area is discussed in Friedan, 1981, pp. 244–249.

[41]Warren, 1982, p. 170.

[42]Candice Leonard, "Gender Orientation and Marital Quality: Some Theoretical Connections," unpublished manuscript, Department of Sociology and Anthropology, University of New Hampshire, August 1982.

[43]See, for example, Giele, 1978, p. ix.

[44]Rothman, 1978, pp. 260–261, describes this as a major tactical error of the current feminist movement, an error that could have been avoided.

[45]Yankelovich, 1981, p. xiv.

[46]For some excellent examples of this point, see Friedan, 1981.

[47]Harris, 1982; Yankelovich, 1981, pp. 93–96. Not everything has changed, however. As Yankelovich, 1981, p. 89, demonstrates, certain traditional attitudes remain strong, including the feeling that a woman should put her husband and children and her husband's career ahead of her own career.

[48]Quoted in Levine and Lyons, 1980, p. 35.

[49]Levine and Lyons, 1980, p. 68.

[50]Levine and Lyons, 1980, p. 12.

[51]Levine and Lyons, 1980, p. 18.

[52]Rothman, 1978, p. 232.

[53]This theme is implicit in much of the feminist literature, including Firestone, 1971; Friedan, 1977; and Greer, 1972.

[54]Rothman, 1978, pp. 3–4.

[55]Rosaldo and Lamphere, 1974, p. 3.

[56]See, for example, Rossi, 1973.

[57]Degler, 1980, p. 306.

[58]Lauretta Santelik, Assistant to the President, National Organization for Women, personal communication, July 1983.

[59]Degler, 1980, p. 360.

[60]Millet, 1978, p. 113.

[61]Grimes, 1967. Grimes' argument is summarized and critiqued in Degler, 1980, pp. 334–335.

[62]Degler, 1980, p. 356.

[63]Degler, 1980, p. 439. Talcott Parsons and Robert Bales, 1955, pp. 13-15, explained why women's entry into the work force did not upset the traditional division of labor: "The woman's job tends to be of a qualitatively different type and not of a status which seriously competes with that of her husband as the primary status-giver or income-earner." Even the "higher level" occupations for women—such as social worker, entertainer, nurse, private secretary, and teacher—were roles with a "prominent expressive component" that tended to be supportive of, rather than competitive with, men's "instrumental" occupations. Within the realm of work, noted Parsons and Bales, women's occupations were "analogous to the wife-mother role in the family." Even the few women in medicine, they observed, tended to be in pediatrics or psychiatry rather than surgery.

[64]Degler, 1980, p. 439. Degler notes that even Betty Friedan's *The Feminine Mystique* carefully avoided the traditional abstract arguments for equality of the sexes, and nowhere did Friedan refer to her cause as "feminist."

[65]Degler, 1980, pp. vii; 127; 436.

[66]Rothman, 1978, p. 231.

[67]Degler, 1980, p. 445. Degler attributes the widespread support for the movement to the "increasing participation of married women in the work force," the "general concern for equality which the Negro Rights Revolution sparked," and the "unprecedentedly high proportion of women between the ages of 20 and 24 who were single."

[68]See, for example, the Boston Women's Health Book Collective, 1976, pp. 181–196 and 337–361, for a strong attack on the male medical establishment's insensitivity to women and for a discussion of the potential dangers of medical technology and drugs, including "the pill." See pp. 311–312 of the same book for a supportive description of breast feeding and for the suggestion that many women feel ambivalent about using their breasts to nourish babies because men have made women feel that breasts are a woman's "sexiest parts."

[69]See, for example, Degler, 1980, pp. 26–29.

[70]Rosaldo, 1974, p. 24.

[71]Greer, 1972, p. 74.

[72]de Beauvoir, 1961, p. 252.

[73]de Beauvoir, 1961, p. 253.

[74]Gilman, 1972, pp. 253–254.

[75]Gilman, 1972, p. 169.

[76]Gilman, 1972, p. 274.

[77]Gilman, 1972, pp. 239–241; 34.

[78]Ehrenreich and English, 1978, p. 118.

[79]Chodorow, 1974.

[80]Rosaldo, 1974, pp. 25–26.

[81]From a letter to his friend, Marie Bonaparte, quoted in Jones, 1955, p. 421. A fuller excerpt is even more revealing: "The great question that has never been answered and which I have not yet been able to answer, despite my thirty years of research into the feminine soul, is 'What does a woman want'?" Similarly, Freud, 1965, p. 135, concluded his lecture on "Femininity" with: "If you want to know more about femininity, enquire from your own experiences of life, or turn to the poets, or wait until science can give you deeper and more coherent information."

[82]Greer, 1972, pp. 65–66.

[83]de Beauvoir, 1961, p. 515.

[84]Rosaldo, 1974, p. 27.

[85]Rosaldo, 1974, pp. 29–30.

[86]Ortner, 1974.

[87]Greer, 1972, p. 247.

[88]Greer, 1972, p. 247.

[89]Firestone, 1971, pp. 127–128.

[90]Greer, 1972, pp. 117–118.

[91]de Beauvoir, 1961, p. xix.

[92]Greer, 1972, p. 32.

[93]Rich, 1977, p. 172.

[94]Degler, 1980, p. 304.

[95]Quoted in Rich, 1977, p. 53.

[96]Rich, 1977, pp. 212–213. What Rich does not discuss, however, are the staging dynamics that may underlie different male and female conceptions of "disagreements." As a creature more trained in, and accustomed to, movement between "stages," the man may be much more sensitive to the difference between public and private contradictions or criticisms from a "teammate," while the woman may be more concerned with the simple "truth" and "falsity" of statements.

[97]Gilman, 1972, p. 276.

[98]Firestone, 1971, p. 88.

[99]Steinem, 1980, p. 11.

[100]Rothman, 1978, pp. 231–232.

[101]Giele, 1978, pp. 3–4.

[102]Rothman, 1978, pp. 3–4.

[103]Steinem, 1980, p. 11.

[104]Steinem, 1980, p. 11.

[105]Friedan, 1977, p. 1.

[106]Ehrenreich and English, 1978, pp. 283–284, emphasis added.

[107]Steinem, 1980, p. 19.

[108]Steinem, 1980, p. 25.

[109]Janeway, 1974, p. 12.

[110]Janeway, 1971, pp. 172–173.

[111]Friedan, 1977, p. 7.

[112]Friedan, 1977, p. 1.

[113]Friedan, 1977, p. 30.

[114]Friedan, 1977, p. 17.

[115]Friedan, 1977, p. 31.

[116]For reviews of the literature on the portrayal of the sexes on television, see U.S. Dept. of Health & Human Services, 1982; Pogrebin, 1981; and Tuchman et al., 1978.

[117]See, for example, Gerbner, 1978.

[118]For a review and discussion of some relevant studies, see Sprafkin and Liebert, 1978.

[119]See, for example, U.S. Dept. of Health & Human Services, 1982, p. 54, for some confusion between simple observation of content and presumed effects.

[120]See, for example, Çobb et al., 1982.

[121]See, for example, Dominick and Rauch, 1972, and Tuchman et al., 1978. The idea that TV (via its commercials) hands women "second-class citizenship" was expressed by Anne Tolstoi Foster and is quoted by Dominick and Rauch as part of the rationale for their study.

[122]Sprafkin and Liebert, 1978, pp. 235–237.

[123]Rohrbaugh, 1979, pp. 137 and 146.

[124]Bandura, 1965.

[125]Gersoni-Stavn, 1974, p. xvii.

[126]Shulamith Firestone, 1971, p. 154, observes that "one of the internal contradictions of this highly effective propaganda system is to expose to men as well as women the stereotyping process women undergo. Though the idea was to better acquaint women with their feminine role, men who turn on the TV are also treated to the latest in tummy-control, false eyelashes, and floor waxes. . . . Such a crosscurrent of sexual tease and exposé would be enough to make any man hate women, if he didn't already." But Firestone does not follow through on her own observation. What Firestone's example suggests is not simply that women are hated through this revelation, but that the traditional female role is undermined and demystified through disclosure of a traditionally private backstage area. While Firestone and many other feminists violently attack television as a "highly effective propaganda system," it may not be having the effects they assume.

[127]Eisenstein, 1979.

[128]Oakley, 1972, p. 9.

[129]Hunt, 1970, pp. 70–71. Hunt notes that "in its general outlines, the picture suggested by these facts is not inaccurate." But he suggests that women were "far from defenseless." Hunt's analysis is of the type that often infuriates feminists because he suggests that in spite of public ridicule and submission, women had an informal, behind-the-scenes power. The descriptions he offers of women's proper place are so strong, however, that they override his equivocations. He notes, for example, that "a model of humility, silence, and complete self-abnegation was held up for the wife. Like a child, she should be seen and not heard." In certain parts of France, he adds, women "were compelled to address their husbands in the third person, to serve them at table, and to stand while they ate." Yet Hunt suggests that such ideal role descriptions do not tell us about the status of women in actual family situations, and he suggests that historians "have been too quick to accept the extreme implications of this kind of evidence."

[130]Stone, 1977, p. 196.

[131]Stone, 1977, p. 4.

[132]Stone, 1977, p. 6.

[133]Stone, 1977, pp. 151–159. Shorter, 1975, gives a later date for the rise of the nuclear family in France. But his description of "domesticity" suggests the possibility that he is recording the *second* stage in the development of the nuclear family as described by Stone—the shift

from the "Restricted Patriarchal Nuclear Family" to the "Closed Domesticated Nuclear Family," the latter based on "Affective Individualism."

[134]Stone, 1977, p. 202.

[135]Stone, 1977, pp. 4–6; 151–159; 221–227. Stone, 1977, p. 661, lends further indirect support to the medium theorists' arguments concerning the effects of printing by arguing that many significant changes in social structure that are often attributed to the industrial revolution (such as the rise of the nuclear family) actually took place *before* industrialization.

[136]Stone, 1977, p. 158.

[137]Stone, 1977, p. 155.

[138]Cressy, 1980, p. 41. For estimated literacy rates of men of different times, locations, and occupations, see charts throughout Cressy, 1980.

[139]Cressy, 1980, p. 128.

[140]Stone, 1977, pp. 329ff. One indication of the warming of relationships between husband and wife, as described by Stone, was the abandonment of stiff and distant forms of address such as "Madam" and "Sir" and the use of first names and terms of endearment.

[141]Ong, 1971, p. 118.

[142]Quoted in Degler, 1980, p. 315.

[143]Degler, 1980, p. 309.

[144]Millett, 1978, p. 58n.

[145]Lyons and Levine, 1980, p. 22.

[146]Rothman, 1978, 26ff.

[147]Ehrenreich and English, 1978, p. 115.

[148]Millett, 1978, p. 58.

[149]Millett, 1978, p. 59.

[150]Carothers, 1959, p. 310.

[151]For a review of relevant studies of sex differences, see Weitz, 1977, pp. 93–111.

[152]Greer, 1972, pp. 110–111, suggests that new forms of media may legitimize "female intuition" and make us more aware of the fact that the traditional masculine style of analysis is only one way of knowing.

[153]Janeway, 1971, p. 172.

[154]Quoted in Millett, 1978, pp. 138–139.

[155]See McWilliams, 1974, for a discussion of these aspects of the women's movement.

[156]See, for example, Tiger, 1969.

[157]Rosaldo and Lamphere, 1974, p. 4.

Chapter 13

[1]Alan Guttmacher Institute, 1981, pp. 4, 7, 9.

[2]National Institute on Drug Abuse, 1980, p. 6; Johnston et al., 1981, pp. 13–14. Johnston et al., 1981, pp. 11–14, note that after a rapid rise over two decades, the use of many illicit drugs is declining from peaks hit in the 1970s. Nevertheless, the current United States levels "are still probably the highest levels of illicit drug use among young people to be found in any industrialized nation in the world'" (p. 14).

[3]Recently, the National Institute on Drug Abuse (Johnston et al., 1981, p. 283) found that 93% of high school seniors had tried alcohol, and 87% had used it during the last year. Over 40% of the students had consumed five or more alcoholic drinks on at least one occasion

within the previous two weeks; 6% reported heavy drinking on six or more occasions. The Alan Guttmacher Institute, 1981, pp. 17 and 57, notes that in 1978, 434,000 teenagers had abortions; another 160,000 wanted abortions but were unable to obtain them. The suicide rate among adolescents has risen 300% over the past two decades ("Adults Are Failing," 1984).

[4]See, for example, Hotchner, 1979, pp. 269-272, for suggestions on how to decide whether a sibling should be present during the birth. See also Rivard, 1980, for an interesting Associated Press story on one 10-year-old youngster who attended the birth of his baby sister.

[5]Watts, 1981.

[6]Stier, 1978, p. 48.

[7]Kihss, 1978; Stier, 1978.

[8]See, for example, Footlick et al., 1977.

[9]By conservative estimates, more than a million children between the ages of 10 and 17 now run away from home each year, though about 90% return home within forty-eight hours (Langway et al., 1982).

[10]Langway et al., 1982.

[11]Blackburn, 1980.

[12]These statistics were compiled from Federal Bureau of Investigation, 1951 and 1981, and from U.S. Bureau of the Census, 1951 and 1982.

[13]Castillo, 1981; Greenhouse, 1979.

[14]Greenhouse, 1979.

[15]For a discussion of the general issues of criminal responsibility and "irresistible impulse," see Gaylin, 1982, pp. 245-271, and the chapter on "Criminal Intent and Responsibility" in Monahan and Walker, forthcoming. Gaylin, 1982, p. 247, observes that, "by the eighteenth century, the insanity defense was increasingly common, but until very recent times one had to be really and totally insane to be even considered for freedom from responsibility on the basis of insanity."

[16]Stier, 1978, p. 49.

[17]Kihss, 1979.

[18]Boulding, 1977, p. 39.

[19]Edelman, 1978, p. 16.

[20]Farson, 1974, p. 1.

[21]Holt, 1974, p. 18.

[22]See Takanishi, 1978, for a brief history of "child advocacy."

[23]From an interview, "More Rights for Children," 1977.

[24]One recent example of a researcher who searches for *similarities* in the thinking and behavior of people of different ages is Marilyn Shatz. Shatz, 1977, suggests that the idea of structurally different stages of thinking for people of different ages is too simple because the same child seems to vary in mastery of a cognitive or communicative skill depending on the nature of the situation. She suggests that a structural constant that unites the thinking and communication skills of people of all ages is the notion of "cognitive workload." While children have less sophisticated "processors" than adults, both children and adults make similar *types* of mistakes when presented with too many stimuli for them to integrate simultaneously. Indeed, argues Shatz, adults can be made to "look like children" when the cognitive workload is increased.

[25]White and White, 1980, p. 53. According to the Whites, Piaget's stages are much discussed as the essence of his theory because they are easy to talk about, but the most important part of his work is actually the idea that children are active "theorists" who constantly reconstruct their "structure of thought" in order to make sense of the world. "The stages are nonetheless useful rough descriptions of qualitative changes that do tend to take place."

[26]See, for example, Wohlwill, 1970.

[27]See Rosnow, 1981, pp. 90–91.

[28]See, for example, Levinson et al., 1978; Sheehy, 1976. It is ironic that just as the "stage theories" of adult development have captured popular interest, they are being abandoned by a number of psychologists. Proponents of the new "life span development" approach, for example, are strongly opposed to the notion of "stages," which they suggest wrongly conceive of development as "uni-directional, hierarchical, sequenced in time, cumulative, and irreversible." They argue, instead, that development is much more individualistic than was previously thought and that it is difficult to find general patterns (Brim and Kagan, 1980, p. 13).

[29]To my knowledge, I was the first to discuss and analyze the current merging of childhood and adulthood, and when I began speaking and writing about these changes as part of my doctoral research in the mid-1970s, my observations and analyses were often greeted with hostility and ridicule. I was frequently lectured on the "naturalness" of childhood as "proven" in developmental research or told that the changes I described were merely "superficial" because they did not deal with "real" developmental processes. In the last few years, the changes in childhood have become more numerous and explicit, and a number of others have written about them. David Elkind, 1981, has described "the hurried child," Marie Winn, 1983, has written of "children without childhood," and one of the faculty sponsors of my doctoral dissertation, Neil Postman, 1982, has described the "disappearance of childhood." But even these writers tend to view the current changes as negative distortions of "proper" child-adult roles.

[30]Kessen, 1979, p. 815.

[31]Kessen, 1979, p. 815.

[32]Kessen, 1979, p. 819.

[33]From interview by Hall, 1980, p. 66.

[34]Neugarten, 1981, p. 813.

[35]For descriptions of recent research that overturns previous beliefs about the intellectual and sexual limitations of the elderly, see Goleman, 1984, and Starr and Weiner, 1981. For descriptions of some of the recent research that suggests that children have much greater skills than was previously believed, see Shatz, 1977, Shatz and Gelman, 1973, and Siegel and Brainerd, 1978. For a review of recent work suggesting that even newborn infants are capable of complex perceptual discriminations and of imitating adults, see Friedrich, 1983.

[36]See, for example, Siegel, 1978. Siegel and Brainerd, 1978, p. xi, have suggested that the inconsistencies between new findings and Piaget's original theories are so great that "a comprehensive reassessment and revision of the theory is in order." Developmental psychologist Carolyn Mebert, personal communication, October 1983, argues that one source of the current refutation of many early studies of children may be, ironically, the "success" of the earlier research itself. "Because the knowledge we have gathered of the characteristics of infants and children has been widely and popularly disseminated, it is quite likely contributing to further advances in the competencies of children by altering the ways in which they are perceived and treated by the adults who care for and teach them."

[37]For an excellent discussion of the unintentionally "historical" nature of most behavioral science research, see Gergen, 1982.

[38]Developmental psychologist Rochel Gelman, 1981, p. 161, for example, explains that she and her colleagues were blind, for many years, to much evidence of preschoolers' cognitive and social abilities because they were unwilling to "recognize facts that contradict existing theories." Similarly, infant specialist, Dr. T. Berry Brazelton describes how the same interactions between parents and children are now perceived differently: "We used to see the parents shaping the child, but now we see the child also helping to shape the parents" (quoted in Friedrich, 1983, p. 57).

[39]Riley, 1978, p. 39.

[40]See, for example, Leifer et al., 1974; and Tannenbaum and Gibson, 1980.

[41]Gilman, 1972, p. 75.

[42]Ritchie and Koller, 1964, pp. 86 and 109.

[43]Ritchie and Koller, 1964, p. 103.

[44]Ritchie and Koller, 1964, p. 105.

[45]See Murray, 1980; Noble, 1975; Wackman and Wartella, 1977; Wartella, 1979; and Winick and Winick, 1979, for reviews of relevant research.

[46]See, Nielsen, 1980, 1981, 1982, and 1983.

[47]For arguments and research concerning television's enhancement of cognitive development, see Salomon, 1979.

[48]Terman and Merrill, 1973, p. 360.

[49]Butter et al., 1981.

[50]Donohue et al., 1980.

[51]Quoted in Shayon, 1951, p. 27.

[52]Himmelweit et al., 1958, p. 13.

[53]Himmelweit et al., 1958, p. 15.

[54]Webster and Coscarelli, 1979.

[55]Mohr, 1979a.

[56]Mankiewicz and Swerdlow, 1979, p. 87.

[57]Beardslee and Mack, 1982.

[58]Pick, 1981.

[59]McLaughlin, 1974, p. 101.

[60]Laslett, 1965, p. 104.

[61]Ross, 1974, p. 183.

[62]Mead, 1955, pp. 454–455.

[63]Atkin, 1978.

[64]Howitt, 1982, pp. 43–44.

[65]See, for example, Himmelweit et al., 1958, p. 378; Leifer et al., 1974, p. 237; Mohr, 1979b; and Tannenbaum and Gibson, 1980, p. 203. Further, even though many cities require cable operators to make "channel locks" available to subscribers, they are rarely asked for or used (Townley, 1982). After all, the channel locks (which permit adults to lock a certain channel so that children cannot watch it) also do not recreate the information-systems of print. They demand constant adult research as to what is on many different channels at many different times. And the devices are—like a locked panel covering a window in a child's room—visible and uncomfortable evidence of adult "censorship."

[66]Wolfenstein, 1955, p. 148.

[67]Quoted in Sunley, 1955, pp. 158–159, emphasis added. The Reverend Thomas Searle's book was originally published in 1834.

[68]Wiener, 1967, p. 170.

[69]Bossard and Boll, 1947, p. 196.

[70]Frank, 1953, p. 29.

[71]Dale, 1935, p. 33. Dale found that 22% of the 5- to 8-year-olds never attended the movies at all. No data were collected for children under the age of five.

[72]Shayon, 1951, p. 29.

[73]Quoted in Shayon, 1951, pp. 29–30.

[74]Allen, 1965; Bechtel et al., 1972.

[75]As a number of people have noted, including Noble, 1975, p. 38, many viewers tend to think of television characters as real people, while movie characters are seen merely as masks for famous actors. Television actors such as Carroll O'Connor ("Archie Bunker") are often addressed on the streets as if they were the characters they portray, yet relatively few people confuse Robert Redford (or even Sean Connery, who is associated with a single character) with their screen roles. One reflection of this dual response was the caption on a recent picture of two actors on the cover of a gossip magazine. The caption read: "Lou Grant and Shirley MacLaine." Himmelweit et al., 1958, p. 15, make a similar observation concerning the distinction, in children's eyes, between television and movie characters: "Television also offers the appeal of personalities, presented more intimately and in more everyday terms than the stars of the cinema. The personalities of television seemed to be liked by the children in particular for their warmth and friendliness."

[76]Studies of children's attention to television have shown that young children pay less attention to the audio portion and concentrate mostly on the visual. Hayes and Birnbaum, 1980, for example, found that very young children often do not notice when cartoons are shown with the wrong audio track. These findings point to another limitation to young children's full comprehension of television, but they also suggest that children have at least partial access to television's information long before they have any meaningful access to radio's information.

[77]Sommerville, 1982, p. 190.

[78]McLachlan, 1970, p. 42.

[79]Sommerville, 1982, pp. 189–208.

[80]Ritchie and Koller, 1964, p. 113.

[81]McLuhan, 1964, p. 305, suggests that education should "become recognized as civil defense against media fallout." McLuhan's notion of education as a "thermostatic" counterbalance to the technological environment has been insightfully expanded by Neil Postman, 1979.

[82]Ariès, 1962.

[83]Ariès, 1962, p. 115.

[84]Stone, 1977.

[85]Ariès, 1962, p. 177.

[86]Ariès, 1962, pp. 238–239. On the evolution of the notion of "early ripe, early rot," see also Kett, 1978, and Wishy, 1968, p. 71.

[87]Stone, 1977, pp. 408–409. Another indication, mentioned by Stone, of a new view toward children is the increasing tendency among parents to give children *individual* names, rather than giving two or more children the same name or naming children after the head of the household or after an older sibling who had died.

[88]Stone, 1977, pp. 14, 174.

[89]Ariès, 1962, p. 119.

[90]Stone, 1977, p. 162.

[91]Quoted in Stone, 1977, p. 162.

[92]Stone, 1977, p. 171.

[93]Stone, 1977, pp. 170, 207, 453; Wishy, 1968, pp. 18ff.

[94]Stone, 1977, p. 175. The law was an enactment of Calvin's decree that disobedient children should be put to death. Stone assures us that "only a handful" of children were executed under this law. However, I should think that one execution (or even a rumor of one) would suffice to instill obedience in the hearts of most children.

[95]Stone, 1977, p. 405.

[96]Wishy, 1968, pp. 85, 108.

[97]Ariès, 1962, p. 39. Some scholars have suggested that the decline in infant mortality could not be a logical stimulus for parental affection since it was the lack of parental affection and loving care itself that was a prime cause of high infant mortality. The change in attitudes, therefore, would have to come first. See, for example, Shorter, 1975, p. 203.

[98]Stone, 1977, p. 176; Sommerville, 1982, pp. 108–119.

[99]Ariès, 1962, p. 292.

[100]Eisenstein, 1979, pp. 10–11.

[101]Chaytor, 1966, p. 10.

[102]Ariès, 1962, p. 193.

[103]Kiefer, 1948; Sommerville, 1982, pp. 136–147; Stone, 1977, pp. 410–411.

[104]Sommerville, 1982, pp. 145 and 160.

[105]Stone, 1977, p. 449.

[106]Stone, 1977, p. 158.

[107]Stone, 1977, p. 216.

[108]Sommerville, 1982, p. 136.

[109]Sommerville, 1982, p. 182.

[110]Eisenstein, 1979, p. 432.

[111]Eisenstein, 1979, pp. 432–433.

[112]Eisenstein, 1979, p. 65.

[113]See, for example, Cressy, 1980, and Schofield, 1968.

[114]Sommerville, 1982, p. 189.

[115]See, for example, Demos, 1970, and Kett, 1971.

[116]Bradbury, 1951, p. 27.

[117]Balkin, 1977, pp. 20–21.

[118]Mast, 1981, pp. 268–269. This was the beginning of the "war" against the movie code. The current movie "rating" system was established after the code was abandoned in 1968.

[119]Blume, 1980, p. 129.

[120]Blume, 1980, p. 136.

Chapter 14

[1]Wector, 1972, p. 4.

[2]Goldsmith, 1974, p. 2055.

[3]Reagan began his presidency with a 51% job approval rating which rose to 68% in May 1981. Then approval sank to 49% in January 1982, to 44% in June 1982, and to 35% in January 1983. His approval rating rose during the rest of 1983 to a high of 54% by December (Gallup Organization, Report No. 219, December 1983, p. 18). In an article originally published in 1965, Greenstein, 1969, p. 290, argues that "most of the time a clear majority of the electorate . . . approve" of the way the President is handling his job. When Greenstein wrote that article only one President since the 1930's (when Gallup began the presidential approval survey) had ever experienced frequent approval ratings below 50%. Similarly, the re-election of a President was once the most likely scenario. Bailey, 1966, p. 208 notes that "in the century since Lincoln . . . only three incumbents have been defeated for re-election."

And one of those, Cleveland, was later re-elected to a second term. He concludes that sitting Presidents are "virtually unbeatable." But much has changed in the last two decades.

[4]Califano, 1975, p. 112; Small, 1972, p. 104.

[5]Alpern, 1980, p. 29.

[6]Bryan and Bryan, 1971, p. 110; Werner, 1929, p. 56.

[7]Bryan and Bryan, 1971, p. 103.

[8]See, for example, Carter, 1977, p. 8.

[9]See Cornwell, 1965, for an account of how various Presidents have manipulated and controlled news flow.

[10]O'Connor, 1977.

[11]Mehrabian, 1971, p. 43.

[12]Schudson, 1982.

[13]Cornwell, 1965, p. 13.

[14]Barton, 1930, p. 80, describes Lincoln's unusual voice; Bailey, 1966, p. 162, notes Jefferson's speech impediment.

[15]Mount, 1973, p. 8.

[16]Bennett, 1977, pp. 219–220.

[17]Bennett, 1977, p. 220.

[18]Hahn and Gonchar, 1972, cite a study of the 1968 campaign conducted by the American Institute for Political Communication. Only 25% of the voters said that an issue or a set of issues most influenced their vote.

[19]Greenstein, 1969, p. 291, notes that when asked about their likes/dislikes concerning a President, people "most commonly refer to aspects of his personal image—for example, his sincerity and integrity, his conscientiousness, his warmth or coldness, his physical vigor."

[20]Hahn and Gonchar, 1972, p. 57.

[21]Hahn and Gonchar, 1972, p. 57.

[22]Hahn and Gonchar, 1972, p. 58, emphasis added.

[23]Novak, 1974, pp. 48–51.

[24]Novak, 1974, p. 51.

[25]Bailey, 1966, pp. 198 and 202.

[26]As Cornwell, 1965, p. 17, notes the first President to provide space for reporters in the White House was Theodore Roosevelt. Roosevelt's term began in 1901.

[27]The distinguished Harvard professor solicited the views of historians, political scientists, and other experts in 1948 and in 1962. The first poll involved 55 people, the second, 75. The experts were to rate each President as Great, Near Great, Average, Below Average, and Failure. Bailey, 1966, pp. 23–34, discusses the strengths and weaknesses of the Schlesinger surveys.

[28]Bailey, 1966, pp. 68–69.

[29]Bailey, 1966, pp. 69–70.

[30]Bailey, 1966, p. 206.

[31]This point has been mentioned by many writers, including Mickelson, 1972, p. 207.

[32]Sorenson, 1965, p. 195.

[33]Halberstam, 1980, p. 444.

[34]Bailey, 1966, p. 205.

[35]Kennedy's frantic style led *The Boston Globe* to ask on its front page, "Why is that man on the television always shouting?" (Oliphant, 1980).

[36]Schramm, 1973, p. 128.

[37]Mickelson, 1972, p. 105.

[38]White, 1973, p. 250.

[39]See, for example, Bailey, 1966, p. 140; Califano, 1975, pp. 112–121; Cornwell, 1965, p. 76.

[40]Califano, 1975, p. 102.

[41]Smith, 1972, p. 30.

[42]Bailey, 1966, pp. 70–71.

[43]Bailey, 1966, p. 71.

[44]Bailey, 1966, p. 341, notes Taft's weight; Cormier, 1966, p. 29, reports the funeral incident.

[45]Bailey, 1966, p. 71.

[46]See, for example, Halberstam, 1980, p. 21.

[47]Hiebert et al., 1982, p. 388.

[48]Cornwell, 1965, p. 188.

[49]Smith, 1972, p. 30.

[50]Cornwell, 1965, pp. 218–220; Small, 1972, pp. 93ff.

[51]Bailey, 1966, pp. 50; 155–156. For an interesting account of Cleveland's admission during his presidential campaign that the illegitimate son of Maria Halpin might be his, see Nevins, 1932, pp. 162–169.

[52]Nevins, 1932, p. 529.

[53]Nevins, 1932, p. 532.

[54]Nevins, 1932, p. 533. A circumstantial account of the operation was leaked to the press at the end of August 1893, but it was quickly and vehemently denied by Cleveland's staff and friends.

[55]Ford, 1978, p. 4.

[56]Altman, 1977.

[57]The major work on Cleveland is the Pulitzer Prize winning biography by Nevins, 1932.

[58]Smith, 1972, p. 61.

[59]Smith, 1972, p. 96.

[60]Cornwell, 1965, pp. 61–114.

[61]Cornwell, 1965, pp. 147; 187.

[62]Cornwell, 1965, pp. 187–188.

[63]Garay, 1981.

[64]Hall, 1966.

[65]Bryce, 1906, pp. 78–85.

[66]Mickelson, 1972, p. 235.

[67]Cater, 1975, p. 4.

[68]Goffman, 1959, p. 30.

[69]Goldsmith, 1974, pp. 2055–2056, emphasis added.

[70]See, for example, Lukas, 1976, pp. 374, 385; and Rothenberg, 1975.

[71]"Excerpts from Interview," 1977.

[72]Quoted in "Thunder from the Heartland," 1974, p. 25.

[73]Firestone, 1971, p. 150.

[74]"Will Nixon Resign," 1974, p. 22.

[75]Quoted in Johnson, 1974, p. xvii.

[76]Whitman, 1974, pp. 10–11.

[77]Quoted in "Thunder from the Heartland," 1974, p. 24.

[78]See, for example, Bailey, 1966; Cornwell, 1965; Evans and Myers, 1974; Heath, 1975; and Schlesinger, 1973.

[79]Oelsner, 1977.

[80]See, for example, the discussion among law professor Leon Friedman and historians Arthur Schlesinger, Jr. and William Goldsmith, in Goldsmith, 1974, pp. 2126–2144; 2216–2226.

[81]Goffman, 1959, p. 70.

[82]Carter, 1977, pp. 56, 63, and 67.

[83]See, for example, Carter, 1977, p. 78.

[84]Goldman, 1976, p. 22.

[85]Halberstam, 1976.

[86]McMorrow, 1976, n.p.

[87]Mathews and Doyle, 1977, p. 16.

[88]McMorrow, 1976, n.p.

[89]Carter, 1977, p. 9.

[90]Carter, 1977, p. 260.

[91]The quotes are from Woodward, Sciolino, and Matthews, 1978. I have also drawn examples from Watson et al., 1978.

[92]The quote is from Quint, 1979, p. 5. Woodward et al., 1978b, also report on John Paul II's immediate breaks with tradition.

[93]Alpern, 1977.

[94]Steele et al., 1977.

[95]Karpel, 1978.

[96]Burt, 1980.

[97]"I'll Whip His Ass," 1979.

[98]Jordan, 1982, pp. 306–309. Also see Jordan, 1982, pp. 347–351, and White, 1982, pp. 388–390, for comments on the Carter "meanness" issue.

[99]Jordan, 1982, p. 351.

[100]White, 1982, pp. 404–405.

[101]See, for example, Strasser et al., 1983.

[102]"Who is Ronald Reagan," 1984. See Clymer, 1982, for a report on a survey that showed that 30% of those polled disagreed with Ronald Reagan's policies, but liked him "personally." See also note 107, below.

[103]For sample negative characterizations of Reagan's abilities and performance, see Beck and Clift, 1981; Lerner et al., 1983; McGrath et al., 1981; McGrath et al., 1982; and Wilkie, 1982.

[104]"Excerpts from Reagan Address," 1982.

[105]For sample "sidestage" descriptions of Reagan's behavior, see Morganthau et al., 1984; Shapiro et al., 1983; and Strasser et al., 1984.

[106]Reedy, 1973, p. 45.

[107]In August 1983, for example, the Gallup Organization found that only 35% of those polled felt that Reagan was "a person of exceptional abilities" (the same percentage as in 1980), only 33% thought he was "a man you can believe in," only 23% thought "he sides with the average citizen," and only 21% saw him as "sympathetic to the problems of the poor." Yet 50% saw him as a "likable person" (Gallup Organization, Report No. 217, October 1983). In December 1983, Reagan had reached his highest overall approval rating in two years

(54%), yet only 46% approved of his handling of foreign policy, only 48% approved of his handling of the economy, only about 35% approved of his handling of problems in Lebanon and Central America, and only 28% felt that his policies were bringing us closer to peace (Gallup Organization, Report No. 219, December 1983).

Chapter 15

[1]Foucault, 1977.

[2]For a discussion of the fascination of the Victorians with secrecy, disguise, and masks, see Reed, 1975.

[3]Goldman et al., 1982; Fritz, 1983.

[4]Ninety percent of U.S. hospitals now allow fathers to be present at deliveries, and 80% of fathers participate in births. The participation rate of fathers has doubled over the last ten years and has risen from virtually zero twenty-five years ago (James A. Levine, Director, The Fatherhood Project, Bank Street College of Education, personal communication, March, 1984). Many hospital visiting practices have also changed dramatically. Babies were once secluded in the hospital's nursery, to be brought out for brief visits with the mother. The father was often not allowed to touch the baby until the mother and child left the hospital. Siblings would not meet the baby until it was brought home. Today, however, many hospitals allow babies to "room in" with their mothers and permit fathers to visit and handle the baby 24 hours a day. The baby's siblings are also often encouraged to visit. Some hospitals even offer special "introductions" to the new baby, where the baby is undressed and displayed to its brothers and sisters. See, for example, Nancy Goodman, 1982. There have been a number of articles in health care publications that suggest a significant shift in attitude toward children's visits to hospitals and children's abilities to cope with the events that take place there. See, for example, Gremillion, 1980. For a popular article on the trend to allow children in maternity wards, see Marks, 1978.

[5]Nancy Goodman, 1982; Hotchner, 1979.

[6]In a personal communication in March, 1984, Dr. William McNary, Associate Dean of Boston University Medical School, confirmed the existence of such a trend and suggested that it began in the late 1960s as an extension of the civil rights movement and the general redefinition of authority in our society. The new attitude, he noted, is now "built into the medical education system." See also the sources listed in note 7.

[7]For discussions of the changing relationships between health care personnel and patients as well as the blurring of distinctions between hospital and home, see Gorvine, 1982; Hotchner, 1979; Pillitteri, 1981; and Van Dyke, 1980.

[8]As Kuhn, 1947, notes in her study of New England childhood education, the recognition of the child as a special being in need of special care preceded the recognition of the importance of women and motherhood. Further, the first widespread call for female literacy and education (in the mid-eighteenth century) had as its purpose the education of women sufficiently to be good mothers (for they needed to be able to read the growing literature on child care). There was little initial drive to educate women for their own sake or to teach them beyond the level necessary for "scientific mothering."

[9]Shorter, 1975, pp. 5 and 22; Stone, 1977, pp. 4–6.

[10]Lincoln and Straus, forthcoming.

[11]Hunting and gathering societies have differed in form over time and in different locations. I am discussing them here as a Weberian "ideal type." I am generalizing about the ways in which nomadic hunting and gathering societies have differed, in broad terms, from other forms of social organization. If a "return" to a hunting and gathering society seems aberrant, it may be comforting to realize that, according to Lee and Devore, 1968, p. 3, for 99% of the estimated two million years that Cultural Humans have existed, they have lived as hunters

and gatherers, and more than half of the people who have ever lived on earth have been hunters and gatherers.

[12]O'Kelly, 1980, pp. 74–106.

[13]O'Kelly, 1980, pp. 82–100. See also Draper, 1975, pp. 77–94; Goodale, 1971, pp. 151–153 and 332–338; Marshall, 1976, pp. 175–176; and Turnbull, 1961, p. 154. Friedl, 1975, pp. 18–19 suggests that there are four major forms of division of labor among hunters and gatherers: both men and women gather, men hunt; communal hunting and gathering by both men and women; men hunt, women gather; men hunt, women process the meat and skins. O'Kelly, 1980, p. 91, suggests a fifth pattern: women hunt and gather, men hunt and fish. As Friedl, 1975, notes, the degree of overlapping subsistence responsibilities is directly correlated with the degree of sexual equality. Thus, those hunters and gatherers who hunt communally are the most egalitarian, while those in which women only process the men's catch exhibit more sexual asymmetry, including higher incidence of rape and violence against women. The relevance of hunting and gathering societies to changes in male and female roles in our own time was pointed out to me by Candice Leonard. Leonard deals with similar themes in her unpublished paper, "Sexual Equality in the Post-Industrial Society," University of New Hampshire, 1983.

[14]Rosaldo, 1974, p. 39.

[15]O'Kelly, 1980, p. 96. See also Marshall, 1976, p. 177, and Turnbull, 1961, p. 124.

[16]O'Kelly, 1980, pp. 97–101.

[17]O'Kelly, 1980, p. 98.

[18]See, for example, Goodale, 1971, pp. 151–153; Marshall, 1976, pp. 96, 130, 314, and 318; and Turnbull, 1961, pp. 128–129.

[19]O'Kelly, 1980, pp. 77–78. See also Friedl, 1975, p. 31, and Turnbull, 1961, pp. 124–125.

[20]O'Kelly, 1980, pp. 78–102. See also, Friedl, 1975, p. 23; Draper, 1975, p. 92; Goodale, 1971, p. 335; Marshall, 1976, p. 261; and Turnbull, 1961, pp. 127–128.

[21]Friedl, 1975, p. 30.

[22]Draper, 1975.

[23]From "Another Brick in the Wall (Part II)," lyrics by Roger Waters, Pink Floyd Music Publishers, 1979. This song was number one for four weeks during 1980 and was the fifth most popular song for the year.

[24]The continuing significance of print and the literate mind-set to the structure and functioning of our electronic age is a theme that runs through much of the writing of Walter Ong. See, for example, Ong, 1977, pp. 82–91.

[25]Mumford, 1963, p. 240.

[26]The inactivity that often results from the exposure of real-life horrors on television may be related to the findings of the "bystander" studies. This area of social psychological research suggests that the greater the number of bystanders who witness an event that seems to demand intervention—such as a crime or accident—the *less* likely it is that someone will step forward and help. The smaller the number of people present, the *more* likely that someone will help. See Hilgard et al., 1979, pp. 520–523, for a brief review of this research.

[27]Boorstin, 1962.

[28]Sennett, 1977, p. 259.

[29]Marbach et al., 1983.

[30]See, for example, Papert, 1980, and Golden, 1982.

[31]Papert, 1980. Papert worked for a time with Piaget. Although Papert builds on many of Piaget's ideas about children "learning without being taught," Papert argues that the cross-cultural evidence that seems to support the invariance of cognitive stages of growth may not really indicate the universality of such stages. Papert argues that all the cultures studied have

been, in a sense, one type of culture: "pre-computer" cultures. He suggests that what have up till now been "formal," or abstract, operations may be "concretized" by the availability of computers (see, for example, pp. 7–28, 174–176).

At least part of the edge that young children now have with computers is likely to disappear with the next generation whose parents may already be experts at computing. What we are witnessing now may be only a transitional phase similar to the period following the introduction of literacy into a society. Initially, literacy among the young, who are first to learn it, undermines the authority of elders, but in the long run literacy strengthens adult authority and causes greater distance between adults and children. The same long-term trend may be true of "computer literacy." It is not yet clear, however, how much differentiation in age-related skills the computer will foster compared to literacy. Further, if the rate of change in computer hardware and software remains as high as it is today, the younger generation may always have at least a partial advantage over the older generation (in the same sense that the children of immigrant families often learn the language of the new country better than their parents do). For an excellent discussion of how the increasing rate of social change enhances the status of the younger generation, see Mead, 1970.

[32]See, for example, Mankiewicz and Swerdlow, 1979, pp. 211–217.

[33]The potential of the computer to allow for the consideration of multiple variables is already evident in the computer's fostering of the development of "multivariate analysis," which allows researchers to analyze the interaction of many variables in a manner and with a speed that would be virtually impossible without computers.

[34]One of the reasons that the continuing existence of books does not override the existence of television, while the continuing existence of television may override the "literate" character of computers, is that the distance between two roles is only as great as the shortest informational channel between them. Or, put differently, when they coexist, intimacy overrides distance, but distance cannot override intimacy. Moving in with someone whom you once knew only through business correspondence, for example, overrides the distance fostered by the written medium of letters, but writing letters to the person you share your bed with does not reestablish much distance. In the same way, new "distancing" forms of interaction, such as discursive text sent by computer, are unlikely to reverse the presentational "closeness" of the telephone, radio, and television—unless we abandon the older technologies.

[35]See, for example, Sommer, 1969, and Hall, 1966.

Appendix

[1]Williams, 1975.

[2]See Popper, 1957, for his distinction between "prediction" and "prophecy."

[3]See Chapters 2 and 3.

[4]For an introduction to "information theory," see Broadhurst and Darnell, 1970.

[5]Geertz, 1973, pp. 412–453.

[6]Nystrom, personal communication, March 1976.

[7]Sennett, 1977, p. 33.

[8]Bierstedt, 1974, p. 255.

[9]For reviews of the concept of "role," see Banton, 1965; Biddle and Thomas, 1966; and Biddle, 1979.

[10]For a discussion of a number of different definitions of roles, see Biddle, 1979, pp. 55ff.

[11]Jackson, 1972, p. 1. Others have expressed similar dissatisfaction with the concept. Three decades ago, for example, Neiman and Hughes, 1951, surveyed about eighty sources in which the concept "role" was used and concluded that the "concept role is at present still

rather vague, nebulous, and non-definitive" (p. 149). And even Biddle, 1979, who defends the concept of role, quotes Neiman and Hughes and then adds, "One wonders to what extent two (sic) succeeding decades have served to reduce this confusion" (p. 56).

[12]See Biddle, 1979, p. 346, for a very brief discussion of the weakness of role theory in dealing with social change. Biddle's comments on the lack of consideration of social change are unintentionally reinforced by the fact that in his detailed review, analysis, and original contribution to the study of roles, he leaves less than one page to discuss the issue of social change. Biddle's work is meant to rescue role theory from confusion and ambiguity, but Biddle follows most other role theorists in presenting more of a system for describing and categorizing existing role behavior than a true "theory" of roles with propositions that can be tested or used to predict and understand role change. See Moore, 1974, for a discussion of the traditional lack of attention to the study of social change in sociology in general, a situation that has been remedied only recently and, as yet, only partially.

[13]See, for example, Popenoe, 1980, p. 179.

[14]See, for example, Jackson, 1972, and Coulson, 1972.

[15]For overviews of conceptions of different types of "groups," see Babbie, 1977, pp. 131ff, and Bierstedt, 1974, pp. 280ff.

[16]Hoult, 1969, p. 299.

[17]Spencer, 1979, p. 86.

[18]Duncan, 1962, pp. 205–206.

BIBLIOGRAPHY

"Adults Are Failing, Not the Children." *USA Today*, 27 Feb., 1984.

Alexander, Shana. "I'd Wondered What Became of Sally." *Newsweek*, 21 Jan. 1974, p. 32.

Allen, Charles L. "Photographing the TV Audience." *Journal of Advertising Research*, 5, No. 1 (1965), 2–8.

Alpern, David M. "Clubs: The Ins and Outs." *Newsweek*, 10 Jan. 1977, pp. 18–19.

Alpern, David M. "A Newsweek Poll on the Issues." *Newsweek*, 3 March 1980, pp. 27–29.

Alpern, David M. et al. "The President's Men." *Newsweek*, 20 April 1981, pp. 27–32.

Altman, Lawrence K. "Navy Confirms Johnson Had Surgery for Skin Cancer." *The New York Times*, 29 June 1977.

American Psychological Association. *Publication Manual of the American Psychological Association*. 3rd ed. Washington, D.C.: American Psychological Association, 1983.

American Telephone and Telegraph. *The World's Telephones*. Morris Plains, NJ: AT&T Long Lines, 1981.

Anderson, Susan Heller. "A Plea for Gentleness to the Newborn." *The New York Times*, 21 Jan. 1978.

The Arbitron Company. *Home Video Cassette Recorders: Ownership/Usage, 1978*. New York: The Arbitron Co., 1979.

Arbitron Ratings Company. *Radio Today*. New York: Arbitron Ratings Co., 1982.

Arendt, Hannah. *Between Past and Future: Eight Exercises in Political Thought*. Rev. ed. New York: Viking, 1968.

Argyle, Michael, Adrian Furnham, and Jean Ann Graham. *Social Situations*. Cambridge: Cambridge Univ. Press, 1981.

Ariès, Philippe. *Centuries of Childhood: A Social History of Family Life*. Trans. Robert Baldick. New York: Vintage, 1962. (French edition, 1960)

Atkin, Charles. "Broadcast News Programming and the Child Audience." *Journal of Broadcasting*, 22 (1978), 47–61.

Atkinson, Jeff. "Criteria for Deciding Child Custody in the Trial and Appellate Courts." *Family Law Quarterly*, 18 (1984), 1–42.

Babbie, Earl R. *Society by Agreement: An Introduction to Sociology*. Belmont, CA: Wadsworth, 1977.

Bailey, Thomas, A. *Presidential Greatness: The Image and the Man from George Washington to the Present*. New York: Appleton–Century, 1966.

Balkin, Richard. *A Writer's Guide to Book Publishing*. New York: Hawthorn, 1977.

Ball, Donald W. "'The Definition of Situation': Some Theoretical and Methodological Consequences of Taking W.I. Thomas Seriously." *Journal for the Theory of Social Behaviour*, 2 (1972), 61–82.

Bandura, Albert. "Influence of Model's Reinforcement Contingencies on the Acquisition of Imitative Responses" *Journal of Personality and Social Psychology*, 1 (1965), 589–595.

"Banter Before the End." *Newsweek*, 14 June 1982, p. 27.

Banton, Michael. *Roles: An Introduction to the Study of Social Relations*. New York: Basic Books, 1965.

Barker, Roger G. *Ecological Psychology: Concepts and Methods for Studying the Environment of Human Behavior*. Stanford, CA: Stanford Univ. Press, 1968.

Barnouw, Erik. *The Image Empire: A History of Broadcasting in the United States, Vol. 3--From 1953*. New York: Oxford Univ. Press, 1970.

Barnouw, Erik. *The Sponsor: Notes on a Modern Potentate*. New York: Oxford Univ. Press, 1978.

Barton, William E. *Lincoln at Gettysburg*. Indianapolis: Bobbs–Merrill, 1930.

Barwise, T.P., A.S.C. Ehrenberg, and G.J. Goodhart. "Glued to the Box?: Patterns of TV Repeat-Viewing." *Journal of Communication*, 32, No. 4 (1982), 22–29.

Beardslee, William, and John Mack. "The Impact on Children and Adolescents of Nuclear Developments," In *Psychosocial Aspects of Nuclear Developments*. Task Force Report No. 20. Washington, D.C.: American Psychiatric Association, 1982, pp. 64–93.

Bechtel, Robert B., Clark Achelpohl, and Roger Akers. "Correlates Between Observed Behavior and Questionnaire Responses on Television Viewing." In *Television and Social Behavior, Vol. 4., Television in Day-to-Day Life: Patterns of Use*. Ed. Eli A. Rubinstein, George A. Comstock, and John P. Murray. Washington, D.C.: National Institute of Mental Health, 1972, pp. 274–344.

Beck, Melinda, and Eleanor Clift. "Reagan's Articulation Gap." *Newsweek*, 29 June 1981, p. 20.

Bedell, Sally. "Study for TV Industry Says Viewers Are Watching Less." *The New York Times*, 18 April 1983.

Bennett, W. Lance. "The Ritualistic and Pragmatic Bases of Political Campaign Discourse." *The Quarterly Journal of Speech*, 63 (1977), 219–238.

Berger, Peter, L. *Invitation to Sociology: A Humanistic Perspective*. New York: Anchor, 1963.

Berger, Peter L., and Thomas Luckmann. *The Social Construction of Reality: A Treatise in the Sociology of Knowledge*. New York: Doubleday, 1966.

Biddle, Bruce J. *Role Theory: Expectations, Identities, and Behaviors*. New York: Academic, 1979.

Biddle, Bruce J., and Edwin J. Thomas, eds. *Role Theory: Concepts and Research*. New York: Wiley, 1966.

Bierstedt, Robert. *The Social Order*. 4rth Ed. New York: McGraw-Hill, 1974.

Binder, David. "Guide Tells Citizens How to Gain Access to U.S. Data." *The New York Times*, 4 Nov. 1977.

Blackburn, Mark. "Teen-Agers Leave Home—Legally." *The New York Times*, 20 Feb. 1980.

Blume, Judy. *Superfudge*. New York: Dutton, 1980.

Board of Institutional Ministry. *The Prisoner's Yellow Pages*. 2nd ed. Los Angeles: Universal Press, 1978.

Bogart, Leo. *The Age of Television*. New York: Frederick Ungar, 1956.

Boorstin, Daniel J. *The Image: Or What Happened to the American Dream*. New York: Atheneum, 1962.

Boorstin, Daniel J. *The Americans: The Democratic Experience*. New York: Random House, 1973.

Boorstin, Daniel J. *The Republic of Technology: Reflections on Our Future Community*. New York: Harper & Row, 1978.

Bossard, James H. S. *Parent and Child: Studies in Family Behavior*. Philadelphia: Univ. of Pennsylvania Press, 1953.

Bossard, James H.S., and Eleanor S. Boll. "The Role of the Guest: A Study in Child Development." *American Sociological Review*, 12 (1947), 192–201.

The Boston Women's Health Book Collective. *Our Bodies, Ourselves: A Book By and For Women*. 2nd ed. New York: Simon & Schuster, 1976.

Boulding, Elise. "Children's Rights." *Society*, Nov./Dec. 1977, pp. 39–43.

Bradbury, Ray. *The Illustrated Man*. New York: Doubleday, 1951.

Bradlee, Benjamin C. *Conversations with Kennedy*. New York: Norton, 1975.

Braestrup, Peter. *Big Story: How the American Press and Television Reported and Interpreted the Crisis of Tet 1968 in Vietnam and Washington, Vol. 1*. Boulder, CO: Westview, 1977.

Brecher, John, et al. "Taking Drugs on the Job." *Newsweek*, 22 Aug. 1983, pp. 52–55; 57–60.

Brim, Orville G., Jr., and Jerome Kagan, eds. *Constancy and Change in Human Development*. Cambridge: Harvard Univ. Press, 1980.

Broadhurst, Allan R., and Donald K. Darnell. "An Introduction to Cybernetics and Information Theory." In *Foundations of Communication Theory*. Ed. Kenneth K. Sereno and C. David Mortensen. New York: Harper & Row, 1970, pp. 59–72.

Brockriede, Wayne, and Robert L. Scott. "Stokely Carmichael: Two Speeches on Black Power." In *Language, Communication, and Rhetoric in Black America*. Ed. Arthur L. Smith. New York: Harper & Row, 1972, pp. 176–194.

Bryan, William Jennings, and Mary Baird Bryan. *The Memoirs of William Jennings Bryan,Vol. I*. Rpt. of 1925 edition. Port Washington, NY: Kennikat, 1971.

Bryce, James. *The American Commonwealth*. New York: Macmillan, 1906.

Burt, Richard. "Administration Tightening System of Keeping National Secrets Secret." *The New York Times*, 7 Sept. 1980.

Buss, Allan R. "The Trait-Situation Controversy and the Concept of Interaction." In *The Psychology of Social Situations: Selected Readings*. Ed. Adrian Furnham and Michael Argyle. Oxford: Pergamon, 1981, pp. 227–234.

Butter, Eliot J., et al. "Discrimination of Television Programs and Commercials by Preschool Children." *Journal of Advertising Research*, 21, No. 2 (1981), 53–56.

Califano, Joseph A., Jr. *A Presidential Nation*. New York: Norton, 1975.

Carmody, Deirdre. "Head of Barnard Asks Parents of Defiant Girl for their Views." *The New York Times*, 19 April 1968.

Carmody, Deirdre. "City's Police Dept. Getting 'New Breed' of Young Officers." *The New York Times*, 8 May 1983.

Carothers, J.C. "Culture, Psychiatry, and the Written Word." *Psychiatry*, 22 (1959), 307–320.

Carpenter, Edmund. *Oh, What a Blow That Phantom Gave Me!* New York: Holt, Rinehart & Winston, 1973.

Carpenter, Edmund, and Ken Heyman. *They Became What They Beheld*. New York: Outerbridge & Dienstfrey/Ballantine, 1970.

Carter, Jimmy. *A Government as Good as Its People*. New York: Simon & Schuster, 1977.

Castillo, Angel. "Juvenile Offenders in Court: The Debate Over Treatment." *The New York Times*, 24 July 1981.

Cater, Douglass. "Introduction: Television and Thinking People." In *Television as a Social Force: New Approaches to TV Criticism*. Ed. Douglass Cater and Richard Adler. New York: Praeger, 1975, pp. 1–7.

Chambers, Marcia. "Videotaped Confessions Raising Conviction Rate." *The New York Times*, 5 June 1983.

Charlton, Linda. "Stern Plan to Guard Privacy Is Expected." *The New York Times*, 15 May 1977.

Chaytor, H. J. *From Script to Print: An Introduction to Medieval Vernacular Literature*. Rpt. of 1945 edition. London: Sidgwick & Jackson, 1966.

Chodorow, Nancy. "Family Structure and Feminine Personality." In *Woman, Culture, and Society*. Ed. Michelle Zimbalist Rosaldo and Louise Lamphere. Stanford, CA: Stanford Univ. Press, 1974, pp. 43–66.

Christopher, Maurine. "Jimmy & Rhett Help NBC Top Nielsen Ratings." *Advertising Age*, 15 Nov. 1976, p. 2.

Clemons, Walter, Martin Kasindorf, and Maggie Malone. "Telling All." *Newsweek*, 15 Jan. 1979, pp. 50–56.

Clymer, Adam. "Poll Finds Reagan Popularity Rating Misleading." *The New York Times*, 31 Jan., 1982.

Cobb, Nancy J., Judith Stevens-Long, and Steven Goldstein. "The Influence of Televised Models on Toy Preference in Children." *Sex Roles*, 8 (1982), 1075–1080.

Collins, Glenn. "U.S. Social Tolerance of Drugs Found on Rise." *The New York Times*, 21 March 1983.

Comstock, George, and Marilyn Fisher. *Television and Human Behavior: A Guide to the Pertinent Scientific Literature*. Santa Monica, CA: Rand, 1975.

"Conversation with Marshall McLuhan." *Videography*, October 1977, pp. 30; 57; 59–60; 62–67.

Cooley, Charles Horton. *Human Nature and the Social Order*. Rev. ed. New York: Schocken, 1964. (originally published in 1922)

Cormier, Frank. *Presidents Are People Too*. Washington, D.C.: Public Affairs Press, 1966.

Cornwell, Elmer E. Jr. *Presidential Leadership of Public Opinion*. Bloomington: Indiana Univ. Press, 1965.

Coulson, Margaret A. "Role: A Redundant Concept in Sociology? Some Educational Considerations." In *Role*. Ed. J. A. Jackson. Cambridge: Cambridge Univ. Press, 1972, pp. 107–128.

Cox, Harvey, ed. *The Situation Ethics Debate*. Philadelphia: Westminster, 1968.

Cressy, David. *Literacy and the Social Order: Reading and Writing in Tudor and Stuart England*. Cambridge: Cambridge Univ. Press, 1980.

Crisis at Columbia: Report of the Fact-Finding Commission Appointed to Investigate the Disturbances at Columbia University in April and May 1968. New York: Vintage, 1968.

Culbert, David. "Johnson and the Media." In *Exploring the Johnson Years*. Ed. Robert A. Divine. Austin, TX: Univ. of Texas Press, 1981, pp. 214–250.

Czitrom, Daniel J. *Media and the American Mind: From Morse to McLuhan*. Chapel Hill: Univ. of North Carolina Press, 1982.

Dale, Edgar. *Children's Attendance at Motion Pictures*. New York: Macmillan, 1935.

de Beauvoir, Simone. *The Second Sex*. Trans. H.M. Parshley. New York: Bantam, 1961. (French edition, 1949)

DeFleur, Melvin L., and Sandra Ball-Rokeach. *Theories of Mass Communication*. 4th ed. New York: Longman, 1982.

Degler, Carl N. *At Odds: Women and the Family in America from the Revolution to the Present*. New York: Oxford Univ. Press, 1980.

Demos, John. *A Little Commonwealth: Family Life in Plymouth Colony*. London: Oxford Univ. Press, 1970.

de Onis, Juan. "Letter-Bombs Injure Arabs." *The New York Times*, 26 Oct. 1972.

Ditton, Jason, ed. *The View from Goffman*. New York: St. Martin's, 1980.

Dominick, Joseph R. and Gail Rauch. "The Image of Women in Network TV Commercials." *Journal of Broadcasting*, 16 (1972), 259–265.

Dondis, Donis A. *A Primer of Visual Literacy*. Cambridge, MA: The MIT Press, 1973.

Donohue, Thomas R., Lucy L. Henke, and William A. Donohue. "Do Kids Know What TV Commercials Intend?" *Journal of Advertising Research*, 20, No. 5 (1980), 51–57.

Draper, Patricia. "!Kung Women: Contrasts in Sexual Egalitarianism in Foraging and Sedentary Contexts." In *Toward an Anthropology of Women*. Ed. Rayna R. Reiter. New York: Monthly Review Press, 1975, pp. 77–109.

Dubé, W. F. "U.S. Medical School Enrollment, 1969–70 Through 1973–74." *Journal of Medical Education*. 49 (1974), 302–307.

Duncan, Hugh Dalziel. *Communication and Social Order*. New York: Bedminster, 1962.

Edelman, Marian Wright. "In Defense of Children's Rights." *Current*, April 1978, pp. 16–20.

Edelman, Murray. *The Symbolic Uses of Politics*. Urbana, IL: Univ. of Illinois Press, 1964.

Ehrenreich, Barbara, and Deirdre English. *For Her Own Good: 150 Years of the Experts' Advice to Women*. New York: Anchor, 1978.

Eisenstein, Elizabeth L. *The Printing Press as an Agent of Change: Communications and Cultural Transformations in Early Modern Europe.* 2 Vols. New York: Cambridge Univ. Press, 1979.

Ekman, Paul, and Wallace V. Friesen. "The Repertoire of Nonverbal Behavior: Categories, Origins, Usage, and Coding." *Semiotica,* 1, No. 1 (1969), 49–98.

Elkind, David. *The Hurried Child: Growing Up Too Fast Too Soon.* Reading, MA: Addison-Wesley, 1981.

Elliott, Philip. "Uses and Gratifications Research: A Critique and a Sociological Alternative." In *The Uses of Mass Communications: Current Perspectives on Gratifications Research.* Ed. Jay G. Blumler and Elihu Katz. Beverly Hills, CA: Sage, 1974, pp. 58–67.

Endler, Norman S., J. McV. Hunt, and Alvin J. Rosenstein. "An S-R Inventory of Anxiousness." *Psychological Monographs,* 76, No. 17 (1962), 1–33.

Epstein, Edward Jay. *News from Nowhere.* New York: Random House, 1973.

Epstein, Louis M. *Sex Laws and Customs in Judaism.* New York: Ktav, 1967. (originally published in 1948)

Evans, Les, and Allen Myers. *Watergate and the Myth of American Democracy.* New York: Pathfinder, 1974.

"Excerpts from Interview with Nixon About Watergate Tapes and Other Issues." *The New York Times,* 4 Sept. 1977.

"Excerpts from Reagan Address to County Officials' Meeting." *The New York Times,* 14 July 1982.

"Falwell Says He Will Press $10 Million Penthouse Suit." *The New York Times,* 5 Feb. 1981.

Farson, Richard. *Birthrights.* New York: Macmillan, 1974.

Federal Bureau of Investigation. *Uniform Crime Reports for the United States and Its Possessions.* Washington, D.C.: Department of Justice, 1951.

Federal Bureau of Investigation. *Uniform Crime Reports for the United States.* Washington, D.C.: Department of Justice, 1981.

Fields, Howard. "U.S. Agency to Coordinate Attack on Illiteracy." *Publishers Weekly,* 22 Oct. 1982, pp. 14 and 16.

Firestone, Shulamith. *The Dialectic of Sex: The Case for Feminist Revolution.* Rev. ed. New York: Bantam, 1971.

Fletcher, Joseph. *Situation Ethics: The New Morality.* Philadelphia: Westminster, 1966.

Footlick, Jerrold K. "Too Much Law?" *Newsweek,* 10 Jan. 1977, pp. 42–47.

Footlick, Jerrold K., Susan Agrest, and Janet Huck. "Kids in Mental Hospitals." *Newsweek,* 12 Dec. 1977, pp. 116–117.

Ford, Gerald R. "Every Mistake a Headline." *TV Guide,* 29 April 1978, pp. 2–4; 7.

Forgas, Joseph, P., *Social Episodes: The Study of Interaction Routines.* London: Academic, 1979.

Forkan, James P. "CBS Regains Some Wind." *Advertising Age,* 7 March 1983, p. 2

Foster, Henry H., Jr., and Doris Jonas Freed. *Current Developments in Child Custody.* New York: Law Journal Seminars-Press, 1978.

Foucault, Michel. *Discipline and Punish: The Birth of the Prison.* Trans. Alan Sheridan. New York: Pantheon, 1977. (French edition, 1975)

Fraker, Susan, et al. "The Marines Face Life." *Newsweek,* 10 May 1976, p. 46.

Francke, Linda Bird, and Nancy Stadtman. "Adoptees Unite." *Newsweek,* 28 April 1975, p. 86.

Frank, Anne. *Anne Frank: The Diary of a Young Girl.* New York: Pocket Books, 1953. (Dutch edition, 1947)

Freidson, Eliot. "Celebrating Erving Goffman." *Contemporary Sociology,* 12 (1983), 359–362.

Freud, Sigmund. *New Introductory Lectures on Psychoanalysis.* Trans. and Ed. James Strachey. New York: Norton, 1965. (German edition, 1933)

Friedan, Betty. *The Feminine Mystique.* Rpt. of 1963 edition with new introduction and epilogue. New York: Dell, 1977.

Friedan, Betty. *The Second Stage.* New York: Summit, 1981.

Friedl, Ernestine. *Women and Men: An Anthropologist's View*. New York: Holt, Rinehart & Winston, 1975.

Friedrich, Otto. "What Do Babies Know?" *Time*, 15 Aug. 1983, pp. 52–59.

Fritz, Sara. "Hello, This Is Ronald Reagan--Yes, Really." *U.S. News & World Report*. 21 March 1983, p. 48.

Furnham, Adrian, and Michael Argyle, eds. *The Psychology of Social Situations: Selected Readings*. Oxford: Pergamon, 1981.

Furstenberg, Frank F., Jr., Richard Lincoln, and Jane Menken, eds. *Teenage Sexuality, Pregnancy, and Childbearing*. Philadelphia: Univ. of Pennsylvania Press, 1981.

Gallup, George H. *The Gallup Poll: Public Opinion 1935–1971*. New York: Random House, 1972.

Gallup Organization. *The Gallup Report*. Princeton, NJ: The Gallup Poll. (Published monthly since 1965.)

Gans, Herbert. *Deciding What's News*. New York: Pantheon, 1979.

Garay, Ronald. "Congressional Television vs. the *Congressional Record*: What Congress Says and What Congress Means." *The Quarterly Journal of Speech*, 67 (1981), 193–198.

Garfinkel, Harold. *Studies in Ethnomethodology*. Englewood Cliffs, NJ: Prentice-Hall, 1967.

Gaylin, Willard. *The Killing of Bonnie Garland: A Question of Justice*. New York: Simon & Schuster, 1982.

Gazzaniga, Michael S. *The Bisected Brain*. New York: Appleton–Century-Crofts, 1970.

Geertz, Clifford. *The Interpretation of Cultures*. New York: Basic Books, 1973.

Gelman, David. "Growing Old, Feeling Young." *Newsweek*, 1 Nov. 1982, pp. 56–60.

Gelman, David. "A Stranger Comes Home." *Newsweek*, 19 March 1984, p. 82.

Gelman, David, et al. "How Men Are Changing." *Newsweek*, 16 Jan. 1978, pp. 52–56; 59–61.

Gelman, David, et al. "The Games Teen-Agers Play." *Newsweek*, 1 Sept. 1980, pp. 48–53.

Gelman, Rochel. "Preschool Thought." In *Contemporary Readings in Child Psychology*. Ed. E. Mavis Hetherington and Ross D. Parke. New York: McGraw-Hill, 1981, pp. 159–165.

Gerbner, George. "The Dynamics of Cultural Resistance." In *Hearth and Home: Images of Women in the Mass Media*. Ed. Gaye Tuchman, Arlene Kaplan Daniels, and James Benét. New York: Oxford Univ. Press, 1978, pp. 46–50.

Gerbner, George, and Larry Gross. "Living with Television: The Violence Profile." *Journal of Communication*, 26, No. 2 (1976), 173–199.

Gergen, Kenneth J. *Toward Transformation in Social Knowledge*. New York: Springer-Verlag, 1982.

Gersoni-Stavn, Diane, ed. *Sexism and Youth*. New York: Bowker, 1974.

Giele, Janet Zollinger. *Women and the Future: Changing Sex Roles in Modern America*. New York: Free Press, 1978.

Gilder, George F. *Sexual Suicide*. Rev. ed. New York: Bantam, 1975.

Giles, Howard, and Peter F. Powesland. *Speech Style and Social Evaluation*. London: Academic, 1975.

Gilman, Charlotte Perkins. *The Home: Its Work and Influence*. Rpt. of 1903 edition. Urbana, IL: Univ. of Illinois Press, 1972.

Gitlin, Todd. *The Whole World Is Watching: Mass Media in the Making and Unmaking of the New Left*. Berkeley: Univ. of California Press, 1980.

Gitlin, Todd. *Inside Prime Time*. New York: Pantheon, 1983.

Glick, Paul C., and Graham B. Spanier. "Married and Unmarried Cohabitation in the United States." *Journal of Marriage and the Family*, 42 (1980), 19–30.

Goffman, Erving. *The Presentation of Self in Everyday Life*. New York: Anchor, 1959.

Goffman, Erving. *Encounters: Two Studies in the Sociology of Interaction*. Indianapolis: Bobbs-Merrill, 1961.

Goffman, Erving. *Behavior in Public Places: Notes on the Social Organization of Gatherings*. New York: Free Press, 1963.

Goffman, Erving. *Interaction Ritual*. New York: Anchor, 1967.

Goffman, Erving. *Strategic Interaction*. Philadelphia: Univ. of Pennsylvania Press, 1969.

Goffman, Erving. *Relations in Public: Microstudies of the Public Order.* New York: Basic Books, 1971.

Goffman, Erving. *Frame Analysis: An Essay on the Organization of Experience.* New York: Harper & Row, 1974.

Goffman, Erving. *Forms of Talk.* Philadelphia: Univ. of Pennsylvania Press, 1981.

Golden, Frederick. "Here Come the Microkids." *Time,* 3 May 1982, pp. 50–56.

Goldman, Peter. "Sizing Up Carter." *Newsweek,* 13 Sept. 1976, pp. 22–27; 29; 30; 33–34; 36; 41; 44; 49–50; 52; 57; 59; 60; 63–65.

Goldman, Peter, et al. "The Reagan Gamble." *Newsweek,* 8 Feb. 1982, pp. 24–27.

Goldsen, Rose K. *The Show and Tell Machine: How Television Works and Works You Over.* New York: Dell, 1978.

Goldsmith, William M. *The Growth of Presidential Power: A Documented History.* 3 Vols. New York: Chelsea House, 1974.

Goleman, Daniel. "The Aging Mind Proves Capable of Lifelong Growth." *The New York Times,* 21 Feb. 1984.

Goodale, Jane C. *Tiwi Wives: A Study of the Women of Melville Island, North Australia.* Seattle: Univ. of Washington Press, 1971.

Goodhart, G.J., A. S. C. Ehrenberg, and M. A. Collins. *The Television Audience: Patterns of Viewing.* Farnborough, England: Saxon House, 1975.

Goodman, Nancy T. "Children Are Family, Too!" *Nursing Management,* June 1982, pp. 52–54.

Goodman, Walter. "Of Mice, Monkeys and Men." *Newsweek,* 9 Aug. 1982, p. 61.

Goody, Jack, ed. *Literacy in Traditional Societies.* Cambridge: Cambridge Univ. Press, 1968.

Goody, Jack, and Ian Watt, "The Consequences of Literacy." *Comparative Studies in Society and History,* 5 (1963), 304–345.

Gorvine, Beverly, et al. *Health Care of Women: Labor and Delivery.* Belmont, CA: Wadsworth, 1982.

Greenhouse, Linda. "Pragmatism Brings Changes in the Juvenile Justice System." *The New York Times,* 18 Feb. 1979.

Greenstein, Fred. "Popular Images of the President." In *The Presidency.* Ed. Aaron Wildavsky. Boston: Little, Brown & Co., 1969, pp. 287–296.

Greer, Germaine. *The Female Eunuch.* New York: Bantam, 1972.

Gregory, Michael, and Susanne Carroll. *Language and Situation: Language Varieties and Their Social Contexts.* London: Routledge & Kegan Paul, 1978.

Gremillion, David H. "The Child Visitor: A Hospital Hazard?" *Forum on Medicine,* Sept. 1980, pp. 566–567.

Greven, Philip J., Jr. *Four Generations: Population, Land, and Family in Colonial Andover, Massachusetts.* Ithaca, NY: Cornell Univ. Press, 1970.

Grimes, Alan P. *The Puritan Ethic and Woman Suffrage.* New York: Oxford Univ. Press, 1967.

Gross, Larry, and Suzanne Jeffries-Fox. "'What Do You Want to Be When You Grow Up, Little Girl?'" In *Hearth and Home: Images of Women in the Mass Media.* Ed. Gaye Tuchman, Arlene Kaplan Daniels, and James Benét. New York: Oxford Univ. Press, 1978, pp. 240–265.

Grove, Andrew S. "Breaking the Chains of Command." *Newsweek,* 3 Oct. 1983, p. 23.

The Alan Guttmacher Institute. *Teenage Pregnancy: The Problem That Hasn't Gone Away.* New York: Alan Guttmacher Institute, 1981.

Gwertzman, Bernard. "Ramsey Clark Mission Tests Law." *The New York Times,* 3 June 1980.

Gwynne, Peter, and Sharon Begley. "Animals in the Lab." *Newsweek,* 27 March 1978, pp. 84–85.

Hacker, Helen M. "Women as a Minority Group." *Social Forces,* 30 (1951), 60–69.

Hahn, Dan F., and Ruth M. Gonchar. "Political Myth: The Image and the Issue." *Today's Speech,* 20, No. 3 (1972), 57–65.

Halberstam, David. "The Coming of Carter." *Newsweek,* 19 July 1976, p. 11.

Halberstam, David. *The Powers That Be.* New York: Dell, 1980.

Hall, Edward. *The Silent Language.* New York: Doubleday, 1959.

Hall, Edward. *The Hidden Dimension*. New York: Doubleday, 1966.

Hall, Elizabeth. "Acting One's Age: New Rules for Old—Bernice Neugarten Interviewed." *Psychology Today*, April 1980, pp. 66; 68; 70; 72; 74; 77–78; 80.

Handler, David. "Now the Playmates Move—But will America Pay to Watch?" *TV Guide*, 25 June 1983, pp. 45–48.

Haney, Craig, Curtis Banks, and Philip Zimbardo. "Interpersonal Dynamics in a Simulated Prison." *International Journal of Criminology and Penology*, 69 (1973), 69–97.

Harré, Rom, and Paul F. Secord. *The Explanation of Social Behaviour*. Totowa, NJ: Littlefield, Adams & Co., 1973.

Harris, Louis. "Public Support for ERA Soars as Ratification Deadline Nears." *The Harris Survey*, 6 May 1982.

Havelock, Eric A. *Preface to Plato*. Cambridge, Harvard Univ. Press, 1963.

Havelock, Eric A. *Origins of Western Literacy*. Toronto: Ontario Institute for Studies in Education, 1976.

Hayes, Donald S., and Dana W. Birnbaum. "Preschoolers' Retention of Televised Events: Is a Picture Worth a Thousand Words." *Developmental Psychology*, 16 (1980), 410–416.

Hearst, Patricia Campbell, with Alvin Moscow. *Every Secret Thing*. New York: Doubleday, 1982.

Heath, Jim F. *Decade of Disillusionment: The Kennedy-Johnson Years*. Bloomington: Indiana Univ. Press, 1975.

Hendrick, Grant H. "When Television is a School for Criminals." *TV Guide*, 29 Jan. 1977, pp. 4–10.

Herbers, John. "Interest Groups Gaining Influence at the Expense of National Parties." *The New York Times*, 26 March 1978.

Hiebert, Ray E., Donald F. Ungurait, and Thomas W. Bohn. *Mass Media III: An Introduction to Modern Communication*. New York: Longman, 1982.

Hilgard, Ernest R., Rita L. Atkinson, and Richard C. Atkinson. *Introduction to Psychology*. 7th ed. New York: Harcourt Brace Jovanovich, 1979.

Himmelweit, Hilde T., A.N. Oppenheim, and Pamela Vince. *Television and the Child: An Empirical Study of the Effect of Television on the Young*. London: Oxford Univ. Press, 1958.

"Hinckley's Last Love Letter," *Newsweek*, 13 April 1981, p. 35.

Holt, John. *Escape from Childhood*. New York: Dutton, 1974.

Horton, Donald, and R. Richard Wohl. "Mass Communication and Para-Social Interaction. Observations on Intimacy at a Distance." *Psychiatry*, 19 (1956), 215–229.

Hotchner, Tracy. *Pregnancy and Childbirth: A Complete Guide to a New Life*. New York: Avon, 1979.

Hoult, Thomas Ford, ed. *Dictionary of Modern Sociology*. Totowa, NJ: Littlefield, Adams & Co., 1969

Howitt, Dennis. *The Mass Media and Social Problems*. Oxford: Pergamon, 1982.

Hughes, Michael, and Walter R. Gove. "Living Alone, Social Integration, and Mental Health." *American Journal of Sociology*, 87, No. 1 (1981), 48–74.

Hunt, David. *Parents and Children in History: The Psychology of Family Life in Early Modern France*. New York: Basic Books, 1970.

Hymes, Dell. "Models of the Interaction of Language and Social Setting." *Journal of Social Issues*, 23, No. 2 (1967), 8–28.

"I'll Whip His Ass." *Newsweek*, 25 June 1979, p. 40.

Innis, Harold A. *The Bias of Communication*. Rpt. of 1951 edition with new introduction by Marshall McLuhan. Toronto: Univ. of Toronto Press, 1964.

Innis, Harold A. *Empire and Communication*. Rev. ed. Toronto: Univ. of Toronto Press, 1972.

"Inside Looking Out." *Time*. 13 Sept. 1982, pp. 42–55.

Jackson, J. A., ed. *Role*. Cambridge: Cambridge Univ. Press, 1972.

James, William. *The Principles of Psychology, Vol. 1*. New York: Henry Holt, 1890.

Janeway, Elizabeth. *Man's World, Woman's Place: A Study in Social Mythology*. New York: Dell, 1971.

Janeway, Elizabeth. *Between Myth and Morning: Women Awakening.* New York: Morrow, 1974.

Joblin, Judith. "The Family Bed." *Parents,* March 1981, pp. 57–61.

Johnson, Haynes. "Initial Reaction on Hill Divided Along Party Lines." In *The Presidential Transcripts: With Commentary by the Staff of* The Washington Post. New York: Dell, 1974, pp. xvii–xix

Johnston, Lloyd D., Jerald G. Bachman, and Patrick M. O'Malley. *Student Drug Use in America, 1975–1981.* Rockville, MD: Department of Health and Human Services, 1981.

Jones, Ernest. *The Life and Work of Sigmund Freud, Vol 2.: Years of Maturity, 1901–1919.* New York: Basic Books, 1955.

Jordan, Hamilton. *Crisis: The Last Year of the Carter Presidency.* New York: Putnam's, 1982.

Karpel, Craig S. "Cartergate V: The First Hundred Lies of Jimmy Carter." *Penthouse,* April 1978, pp. 52–58; 164–170; 174–181.

Katz, Elihu, Jay G. Blumler, and Michael Gurevitch. "Utilization of Mass Communication by the Individual." In *The Uses of Mass Communications: Current Perspectives on Gratifications Research.* Ed. Jay G. Blumler and Elihu Katz. Beverly Hills, CA: Sage, 1974, pp. 19–32.

Keerdoja, Eileen, Ron Moreau, and Jerry Buckley. "David Dellinger's Life of Protest." *Newsweek,* 11 July 1983, p. 9.

Kessen, William. "The American Child and Other Cultural Inventions." *American Psychologist,* Oct. 1979, pp. 815–820.

Kett, Joseph F. "Growing Up in Rural New England, 1800–1840." In *Anonymous Americans: Explorations in Nineteenth-Century Social History.* Ed. Tamara K. Hareven. Englewood Cliffs, NJ: Prentice-Hall, 1971, pp. 1–16.

Kett, Joseph F. "Curing the Disease of Precocity." In *Turning Points: Historical and Sociological Essays on the Family.* (Supplement to Vol. 84 of the *American Journal of Sociology.*) Ed. John Demos and Sarane Spence Boocock. Chicago: Univ. of Chicago Press, 1978, pp. S183-S211.

Kiefer, Monica. *American Children Through Their Books: 1700–1835.* Philadelphia: Univ. of Pennsylvania Press, 1948.

Kihss, Peter. "A Manual Warns Social Workers of Extension of Children's Rights." *The New York Times,* 2 July 1978.

Kihss, Peter. "2 Children in Foster Care Named to City Panel to Improve System." *The New York Times,* 11 June 1979.

Kleiman, Carol. "Our Fortune 200." *Ms.* Aug. 1982, p. 45.

Kleiman, Dena. "Reopening of 'People's Firehouse' Is Celebrated." *The New York Times,* 18 June 1978.

Kozol, Jonathan. "Operation Illiteracy." *The New York Times,* 5 March, 1979.

Kubler-Ross, Elisabeth. *On Death and Dying.* New York: Macmillan, 1969.

Kuhn, Anne L. *The Mother's Role in Childhood Education: New England Concepts, 1830–1860.* New Haven, CT: Yale Univ. Press, 1947.

Kuhns, William. *The Post-Industrial Prophets: Interpretations of Technology.* New York: Harper & Row, 1971.

Langer, Susanne K. *Philosophy in a New Key: A Study in the Symbolism of Reason, Rite, and Art.* 3rd ed. Cambridge: Harvard Univ. Press, 1957.

Langway, Lynn, et al. "A Nation of Runaway Kids." *Newsweek,* 18 Oct. 1982, pp. 97–98.

Langway, Lynn, et al. "Bringing Up Superbaby." *Newsweek,* 28 March 1983, pp. 62–68. (a)

Langway, Lynn, et al. "Showdown on Smoking." *Newsweek,* 6 June 1983, pp. 60–63; 67. (b)

Laslett, Peter. *The World We Have Lost.* New York: Scribner's, 1965.

Lazarsfeld, Paul F., and Robert K. Merton. "Mass Communication, Popular Taste, and Organized Social Action." In *The Process and Effects of Mass Communication.* Rev ed. Ed. Wilbur Schramm and Donald F. Roberts. Urbana: Univ. of Illinois Press, 1971, pp. 554–578.

Leboyer, Frederick. *Birth Without Violence.* New York: Knopf, 1975. (French edition, 1974)

Ledbetter, Les. "More and More, Voters Write Law." *The New York Times,* 30 Oct. 1977.

Lee, Richard B., and Irven DeVore, eds. *Man the Hunter.* Chicago: Aldine, 1968.

Leifer, Aimee Dorr, Neal J. Gordon, and Sherryl Browne Graves. "Children's Television: More Than Mere Entertainment." *Harvard Educational Review,* 44 (1974), 213–245.

Lerner, Michael A., Eleanor Clift, and Thomas M. DeFrank. "Presidential Fatigue?" *Newsweek,* 16 May 1983, p. 30.

Levine, Arthur. *When Dreams and Heroes Died: A Portrait of Today's College Student.* San Francisco: Jossey-Bass, 1980.

Levine, Suzanne and Harriet Lyons, eds. *The Decade of Women: A Ms. History of the Seventies in Words and Pictures.* New York: Paragon, 1980.

Levinson, Daniel J., et al. *The Seasons of a Man's Life.* New York: Knopf, 1978.

Levinson, Paul. "Human Replay: A Theory of the Evolution of Media." Diss. New York Univ. 1979.

Levinson, Paul. "What Technology Can Teach Philosophy: Ruminations Along Kantian/ Popperian Lines." In *In Pursuit of Truth: Essays on the Philosophy of Karl Popper.* Ed. Paul Levinson. Atlantic Highlands, NJ: Humanities, 1982, pp. 157–175.

Levy, Mark R. "Watching TV News as Para-Social Interaction." *Journal of Broadcasting,* 23 (1979), 69–80.

Levy, Mark R. "The Time-Shifting Use of Home Video Recorders." *Journal of Broadcasting,* 27 (1983), 263–268,

Lewis, Flora. "U.S. Is Said to Agree with Hanoi on Framework of a Cease-Fire; North Vietnam Discloses Plan." *The New York Times,* 26 Oct. 1972.

Lieberman, Jethro K. *The Litigious Society.* New York: Basic Books, 1981.

Lincoln, Alan, and Murray A. Straus. *Crime and the Family.* Springfield, IL: Charles C. Thomas, forthcoming.

"Lost Identity." *Time,* 26 April 1982, p. 24.

Lukas, J. Anthony. *Nightmare: The Underside of the Nixon Years.* New York: Viking, 1976.

Luria, A.R. *Cognitive Development: Its Cultural and Social Foundations.* Trans. Martin Lopez-Morillas and Lynn Solotaroff. Ed. Michael Cole. Cambridge: Harvard University Press, 1976. (Russian edition, 1974)

Lyman, Stanford M., and Marvin B. Scott. *A Sociology of the Absurd.* New York: Appleton-Century-Crofts, 1970.

Lyons, Richard D. "Refusal of Many to Heed Government Health Advice Is Linked to Growing Distrust of Authority." *The New York Times,* 12 June 1977.

McAnany, Emile G., Jorge Schnitman, and Noreene Janus, eds. *Communication and Social Structure: Critical Studies in Mass Media Research.* New York: Praeger, 1981.

McGinley, Phyllis. *Sixpence in Her Shoe.* New York: Macmillan, 1964.

McGrath, Peter, Thomas M. DeFrank, and Eleanor Clift. "A Disengaged Presidency." *Newsweek,* 7 Sept. 1981, pp. 21–23,

McGrath, Peter, Eleanor Clift, and Thomas M. DeFrank. "20 Months, 12 Vacations." *Newsweek,* 6 Sept. 1982, p. 18.

Machiavelli, Niccolò. *The Prince.* Trans. Luigi Ricci. Rev. E. R. P. Vincent. New York: New American Library, 1952. (Italian edition, 1532)

McHugh, Peter. *Defining the Situation: The Organization of Meaning in Social Interaction.* Indianapolis: Bobbs–Merrill, 1968.

McLachlan, James. *American Boarding Schools: A Historical Study.* New York: Scribner's, 1970.

McLaughlin, Mary Martin. "Survivors and Surrogates: Children and Parents from the Ninth to the Thirteenth Centuries." In *The History of Childhood.* Ed. Lloyd deMause. New York: Psychohistory Press, 1974, pp. 101–181.

McLuhan, Marshall. *The Gutenberg Galaxy: The Making of Typographic Man.* Toronto: Univ. of Toronto Press, 1962.

McLuhan, Marshall. *Understanding Media: The Extensions of Man.* New York: McGraw-Hill, 1964.

McLuhan, Marshall, and Barrington Nevitt. *Take Today: The Executive as Dropout.* New York: Harcourt Brace Jovanovich, 1972.

McMorrow, Fred. *Jimmy: The Candidacy of Carter.* New York: Whirlwind, 1976.

McWilliams, Nancy. "Contemporary Feminism, Consciousness-Raising, and Changing Views of the Political." In *Women in Politics.* Ed. Jane L. Jaquette. New York: Wiley, 1974, pp. 157–170.

Maeroff, Gene I. "Diplomas May Be Earned By Excellence at Real Life." *The New York Times,* 13 March 1977.

Magnusson, David, ed. *Toward a Psychology of Situations: An Interactional Perspective.* Hillsdale, NJ: Erlbaum, 1981.

Malinowski, Bronislaw. "Culture." *Encyclopaedia of the Social Sciences,* Vol. 4 (1931), 621–646.

Mandelbaum, Michael. "Vietnam: The Television War." *Daedalus,* 111, No. 4 (1982), 157–169.

Mankiewicz, Frank, and Joel Swerdlow. *Remote Control: Television and the Manipulation of American Life.* New York: Ballantine, 1979.

Marbach, William, et al. "Beware: Hackers at Play." *Newsweek,* 5 Sept. 1983, pp. 42–46; 48.

Marks, Jane. "Welcome Mat in the Maternity Ward." *McCall's,* Aug. 1978, p. 68.

Marshall, Lorna. *The !Kung of Nyae Nyae.* Cambridge: Harvard Univ. Press, 1976.

Mast, Gerald. *A Short History of the Movies.* 3rd ed. Indianapolis: Bobbs-Merrill, 1981.

Mathews, Tom. "Reagan's Close Call." *Newsweek,* 13 April 1981, pp. 31–38.

Mathews, Tom, and James Doyle. "Fritz and Company." *Newsweek,* 10 Jan. 1977, pp. 16–17

Mathews, Tom, et al. "Lennon's Alter Ego." *Newsweek,* 22 Dec. 1980, pp. 34–35.

Mayer, Martin. "The Telephone and the Uses of Time." In *The Social Impact of the Telephone.* Ed. Ithiel de Sola Pool. Cambridge, MA: MIT Press, 1977, pp. 225–245.

Mead, George Herbert. *Mind, Self, and Society: From the Standpoint of a Social Behaviorist.* Ed. Charles W. Morris. Chicago: Univ. of Chicago Press, 1934.

Mead, Margaret. "Implications of Insight-II." In *Childhood in Contemporary Cultures.* Eds. Margaret Mead and Martha Wolfenstein. Chicago: Univ. of Chicago Press, 1955, pp. 449–461.

Mead, Margaret. *Male and Female: A Study of the Sexes in a Changing World.* New York: Dell, 1968. (originally published in 1949)

Mead, Margaret. *Culture and Commitment: A Study of the Generation Gap.* Garden City, NY: Doubleday, 1970.

Mehrabian, Albert. *Silent Messages.* Belmont, CA: Wadsworth, 1971.

Melody, William H., Liora Salter, and Paul Heyer, eds. *Culture, Communication, and Dependency: The Tradition of H. A. Innis.* Norwood, NJ: Ablex, 1981.

Merton, Robert K. *Social Theory and Social Structure.* Rev. ed. New York: Free Press, 1968.

Messaris, Paul, and Carla Sarett. "On the Consequences of Television-Related Parent-Child Interaction." *Human Communication Research,* 7 (1981), 226–244.

Meyrowitz, Joshua. "The Relationship of Interpersonal Distances to Television Shot Selection." Masters Thesis, Queens College 1974. (ERIC: ED 210 734)

Meyrowitz, Joshua. "Television and Interpersonal Behavior: Codes of Perception and Response." In *Inter/Media: Interpersonal Communication in a Media World.* Ed. Gary Gumpert and Robert Cathcart. New York: Oxford Univ. Press, 1979, pp. 56–76.

Meyrowitz, Joshua. "Analyzing Media: Metaphors as Methodologies." Paper presented at the New England Conference on Teaching Students to Think, Amherst, MA, November 1980. (ERIC: ED 206 030)

Mickelson, Sig. *The Electric Mirror: Politics in an Age of Television.* New York: Dodd, Mead & Co., 1972.

Millett, Kate. *Sexual Politics.* New York: Ballantine, 1978. (originally published in 1970)

Mischel, Walter. *Personality and Assessment.* New York: Wiley, 1968.

Mohr, Phillip J. "Efficacy of the Family Viewing Concept: A Test of Assumptions." *Central States Speech Journal,* 30 (1979), 342–351. (a)

Mohr, Phillip J. "Parental Guidance of Children's Viewing of Evening Television Programs." *Journal of Broadcasting,* 23 (1979), 213–228. (b)

Monahan, John, and Laurens Walker. *Social Science in Law: Cases, Materials and Problems.* Mineola, NY: Foundation, forthcoming.

Montagu, Ashley. *Growing Young.* New York: McGraw-Hill, 1981.

Montgomery, Paul L. "Throngs Fill Manhattan in Arms Protest." *The New York Times,* 13 June 1982.

Moore, Gary. "What America is Really Like." *Newsweek,* 10 April 1978, p. 23.

Moore, Wilbert E. *Social Change.* 2nd ed. Englewood Cliffs, NJ: Prentice-Hall, 1974.

"More Rights for Children: What an Expert Says." *U.S. News & World Report,* 31 Oct. 1977, p. 33.

Morganthau, Tom, Eleanor Clift, and Thomas M. DeFrank. "Master of the Media." *Newsweek,* 18 June 1984, p. 25.

Morganthau, Tom, Thomas M. DeFrank, and Eleanor Clift. "The Leaks at the White House." *Newsweek,* 4 April 1983, pp. 23; 27.

Mount, Ferdinand. *The Theatre of Politics.* New York: Schocken, 1973.

Mumford, Lewis. *Technics and Civilization.* New York: Harcourt, Brace & World, 1963. (originally published in 1934)

Murray, John P. *Television and Youth: 25 Years of Research and Controversy.* Boys Town, NB: Boys Town Center for the Study of Youth Development, 1980.

National Institute on Drug Abuse. *Excerpts from the National Survey on Drug Abuse: 1979.* Rockville, MD: Department of Health and Human Services, 1980.

Neiman, Lionel J., and James W. Hughes. "The Problem of the Concept of Role: A Re-Survey of the Literature." *Social Forces,* 30 (1951), 141–149.

Neugarten, Bernice L. "Age Distinctions and Their Social Functions." *Chicago Kent Law Review,* 57 (1981), 809–825.

Nevins, Allan. *Grover Cleveland: A Study in Courage.* New York: Dodd, Mead & Co., 1932.

Newfield, Jack. "The Media: Kennedy Obsession and Carter Protection." *The Village Voice,* 31 Dec. 1979, pp. 15–17.

Nie, Norman H., Sidney Verba, and John R. Petrocik. *The Changing American Voter.* Cambridge: Harvard Univ. Press, 1976.

A.C. Nielsen, *Nielsen Report on Television.* Northbrook, IL: A.C. Nielsen Co. (An edition of this booklet is published every year.)

"Nielsen Gets First Good Grip on Cable and Viewing Levels." *Broadcasting Age.* 4 Aug. 1980, pp. 27–28.

Nigro, Georgia, and Ulric Neisser. "Point of View in Personal Memories." *Cognitive Psychology,* 15 (1983), 467–482.

Noble, Grant. *Children in Front of the Small Screen.* Beverly Hills, CA: Sage, 1975.

Norback, Craig T., and Peter G. Norback, eds. *TV Guide Almanac.* New York: Ballantine, 1980.

Novak, Michael. *Choosing Our King: Powerful Symbols in Presidential Politics.* New York: Macmillan, 1974.

Oakley, Ann. *Sex, Gender and Society.* New York: Harper & Row, 1972.

O'Connor, John J. "TV: A Full Day at the White House." *The New York Times,* 14 April 1977.

Oelsner, Lesley. "High Court Upholds U.S. Control Over Papers and Tapes of Nixon." *The New York Times,* 29 June 1977.

Ogburn, William F. *On Culture and Social Change: Selected Papers.* Ed. Otis Dudley Duncan. Chicago: Univ. of Chicago Press, 1964.

O'Kelly, Charlotte G. *Women and Men in Society.* New York: Van Nostrand, 1980.

Oliphant, Thomas. "Why Is That Man on the Television Always Shouting?" *The Boston Globe,* 2 May 1980.

O'Neill, Lois Decker, ed. *The Women's Book of World Records and Achievements.* New York: Anchor, 1979.

Ong, Walter J. *The Presence of the Word: Some Prolegomena for Cultural and Religious History.* New Haven, CT: Yale Univ. Press, 1967.

Ong, Walter J. *Rhetoric, Romance, and Technology: Studies in the Interaction of Expression and Culture.* Ithaca, NY: 1971.

Ong, Walter, J. *Interfaces of the Word: Studies in the Evolution of Consciousness and Culture.* Ithaca, NY: Cornell Univ. Press, 1977.

Ong, Walter J. *Orality and Literacy: The Technologizing of the Word.* New York: Methuen, 1982.

Ortner, Sherry B. "Is Female to Male as Nature is to Culture?" In *Woman, Culture, and Society.* Ed. Michelle Zimbalist Rosaldo and Louise Lamphere. Stanford, CA: Stanford Univ. Press, 1974, pp. 67–87.

Papert, Seymour. *Mindstorms: Children, Computers, and Powerful Ideas.* New York: Basic Books, 1980.

Parsons, Talcott. *Essays in Sociological Theory.* Rev. ed. New York: Free Press, 1954.

Parsons, Talcott, and Robert F. Bales. *Family, Socialization and Interaction Process.* Glencoe, IL: Free Press, 1955.

Pauly, David, and Nadine Joseph. "High Tech's Challenge." *Newsweek,* 5 Sept. 1983, p. 53.

Pervin, Lawrence A. *Current Controversies and Issues in Personality.* New York: Wiley, 1978. (a)

Pervin, Lawrence A. "Definitions, Measurements, and Classifications of Stimuli, Situations, and Environments." *Human Ecology,* 6 (1978), 71–105. (b)

Pick, Grant. "The Anchorboy Falls Off His Chair, the Anchorgirl Shoots Spitballs." *TV Guide,* 14 Nov. 1981, pp. 45–46.

Pillitteri, Adele. *Maternal-Newborn Nursing: Care of the Growing Family.* 2nd ed. Boston: Little, Brown & Co., 1981.

"Playboy Interview: Barbra Streisand." *Playboy,* October 1977, pp. 79–82; 87–92; 95–98; 100; 102; 104; 106–107; 193–194, 197–200.

"Playboy Interview: Marshall McLuhan." *Playboy,* March 1969, 53–54; 56; 59–62; 64–66; 68; 70; 72; 74; 158.

"Playboy Interview: Patricia Hearst." *Playboy,* March 1982, 69–70; 74; 76, 84; 86; 88–89; 91–93; 96; 98; 100.

Pogrebin, Letty Cottin. *Growing Up Free: Raising Your Child in the 1980s.* New York: Bantam, 1981.

Popenoe, David. *Sociology.* 4rth ed. Englewood Cliffs, NJ: Prentice-Hall, 1980.

Popper, Karl. *The Poverty of Historicism.* Beacon, 1957.

Postman, Neil. *Teaching as a Conserving Activity.* New York: Delacorte, 1979.

Postman, Neil. *The Disappearance of Childhood.* New York: Delacorte, 1982.

"The Private Life of Gwyned Filling." *Life,* 3 May 1948, pp. 103–114.

Purcell, Susan Kaufman. "Ideology and the Law: Sexism and Supreme Court Decisions." In *Women in Politics.* Ed. Jane L. Jaquette. New York: Wiley, 1974, pp. 131–154.

Quint, Bert. "Television and the Pope—A Perfect Match." *TV Guide,* 29 Sept. 1979, pp. 4–6; 8.

Read, Piers Paul. *Alive: The Story of the Andes Survivors.* Philadelphia: J.B. Lippincott, 1974.

Reed, John R. *Victorian Conventions.* Athens, OH: Ohio Univ. Press, 1975.

Reedy, George E. *The Presidency in Flux.* New York: Columbia Univ. Press, 1973.

Reedy, George E. "A Symbol is Worth More Than a Thousand Words." *TV Guide,* 31 Dec. 1977, pp. 2–5.

Remarque, Erich Maria. *All Quiet on the Western Front.* Trans. A. W. Wheen. Boston: Little, Brown, & Co., 1929. (German edition, 1928)

Rich, Adrienne. *Of Woman Born: Motherhood as Experience and Institution.* New York: Bantam, 1977.

Rielly, John E. "The American Mood: A Foreign Policy of Self–Interest." *Foreign Policy,* 34 (1979), 74–86.

Riley, Matilda White. "Aging, Social Change, and the Power of Ideas." *Daedalus,* 107, No. 4 (1978), 39–52.

Rintels, David W. "Why We Fought the Family Viewing Hour." *The New York Times,* 21 Nov. 1976.

Ritchie, Oscar W., and Marvin R. Koller. *Sociology of Childhood.* New York: Appleton-Century-Crofts, 1964.

Rivard, Kathy. "One Way to Head Off Sibling Rivalry: Involve Brothers and Sisters in Birth." (Associated Press) *Fosters Daily Democrat*, 11 Aug. 1980.

Rohrbaugh, Joanna Bunker. *Women: Psychology's Puzzle*. New York: Basic Books, 1979.

Roper Organization. *Trends in Attitudes Toward Television and Other Media: A Twenty-Four Year Review*. New York: Television Information Office, 1983.

Rosaldo, Michelle Zimbalist. "Woman, Culture, and Society: A Theoretical Overview." In *Woman, Culture, and Society*. Ed. Michelle Zimbalist Rosaldo and Louise Lamphere. Stanford, CA: Stanford Univ. Press, 1974, pp. 17–42.

Rosaldo, Michelle Zimbalist, and Louise Lamphere, eds. *Woman, Culture, and Society*. Stanford, CA: Stanford Univ. Press, 1974.

Rosenthal, Raymond, ed. *McLuhan: Pro and Con*. New York: Funk & Wagnalls, 1968.

Rosenthal, Robert, and Ralph L. Rosnow, eds. *Artifact in Behavioral Research*. New York: Academic, 1969.

Rosenthal, Robert, and Ralph L. Rosnow, eds. *The Volunteer Subject*. New York: Wiley-Interscience, 1975.

Rosnow, Ralph L. *Paradigms in Transition: The Methodology of Social Inquiry*. New York: Oxford Univ. Press, 1981.

Rosnow, Ralph L. "Von Osten's Horse, Hamlet's Question, and the Mechanistic View of Causality: Implications for a Post–Crisis Social Psychology." *The Journal of Mind and Behavior*, 4 (1983), 319–337.

Ross, James Bruce. "The Middle Class Child in Urban Italy, Fourteenth to Early Sixteenth Century." In *The History of Childhood*. Ed. Lloyd deMause. New York: Psychohistory Press, 1974, pp. 183–228.

Rossi, Alice S., ed. *The Feminist Papers: From Adams to de Beauvoir*. New York: Columbia Univ. Press, 1973.

Roszak, Theodore. "The Summa Popologica of Marshall McLuhan." In *McLuhan: Pro and Con*. Ed. Raymond Rosenthal. New York: Funk & Wagnalls, 1968, pp. 257–269.

Rothenberg, Alan B. "Why Nixon Taped Himself: Infantile Fantasies Behind Watergate." *The Psychoanalytic Review*, 62, No. 2 (1975), 201–223.

Rothman, Sheila M. *Woman's Proper Place: A History of Changing Ideals and Practices, 1870 to the Present*. New York: Basic Books, 1978.

Salomon, Gavriel. *Interaction of Media, Cognition, and Learning: An Exploration of How Symbolic Forms Cultivate Mental Skills and Affect Knowledge Acquisition*. San Francisco: Jossey-Bass, 1979.

Sancton, Thomas A. "He Dared to Hope." *Time*, 4 Jan. 1982, pp. 13–20; 22–26.

Schardt, Arlie, et al. "TV's Rush to Judgment." *Newsweek*, 28 July 1980, pp. 72; 75.

Schlesinger, Arthur M., Jr. *The Imperial Presidency*. Boston: Houghton-Mifflin, 1973.

Schofield, R. S. "The Measurement of Literacy in Pre-Industrial England." In *Literacy in Traditional Societies*. Ed. Jack Goody. Cambridge: Cambridge Univ. Press, 1968, pp. 311–325.

Schramm, Wilbur. *Men, Messages, and Media: A Look at Human Communication*. New York: Harper & Row, 1973.

Schramm, Wilbur, and Donald F. Roberts, eds. *The Process and Effects of Mass Communication*. Rev. ed. Urbana: Univ. of Illinois Press, 1971.

Schudson, Michael. "The Politics of Narrative Form: The Emergence of News Conventions in Print and Television." *Daedalus*, 111, No. 4 (1982), 97–112.

Schwartz, Tony. *The Responsive Chord*. Garden City, NY: Anchor, 1974.

Sennett, Richard. *The Fall of Public Man*. New York: Knopf, 1977.

Settel, Irving. *A Pictorial History of Radio*. New York: Grosset & Dunlap, 1967.

Shapiro, Walter, et al. "Testing Time: 'Reagan Was Reagan.'" *Newsweek*, 7 Nov. 1983, pp. 80 and 82.

Shatz, Marilyn. "The Relationship between Cognitive Processes and the Development of Communication Skills." In *Nebraska Symposium on Motivation, 1977: Social Cognitive Development*. Ed. Charles Blake Keasey. Lincoln: Univ. of Nebraska Press, 1977, pp. 1–42.

Shatz, Marilyn, and Rochel Gelman. "The Development of Communication Skills: Modifications in the Speech of Young Children as a Function of Listener." *Monographs of the Society for Research in Child Development*, Serial No. 152, Vol. 38, No 5 (October 1973).

Shaver, Phillip. "The Public Distrust." *Psychology Today*, Oct. 1980, pp. 44; 46; 48–49; 102.

Shayon, Robert Lewis. *Television and Our Children*. New York: Longmans, Green, & Co., 1951.

Sheehy, Gail. *Passages: Predictable Crises of Adult Life*. New York: Dutton, 1976.

Shorter, Edward. *The Making of the Modern Family*. New York: Basic Books, 1975.

Siegel, Linda S. "The Relationship of Language and Thought in the Preoperational Child: A Reconsideration of Nonverbal Alternatives to Piagetian Tasks." In *Alternatives to Piaget: Critical Essays on the Theory*. Ed. Linda S. Siegel and Charles J. Brainerd. New York: Academic, 1978, pp. 43–68.

Siegel, Linda S., and Charles J. Brainerd, eds. *Alternatives to Piaget: Critical Essays on the Theory*. New York: Academic, 1978.

Sitkoff, Harvard. *The Struggle for Black Equality: 1954–1980*. New York: Hill & Wang, 1981.

Slack, Jennifer Daryl, and Martin Allor. "On the Political and Epistemological Constituents of Critical Communication Research." *Journal of Communication*, 33, No. 3 (1983), 208–218.

Small, William J. *Political Power and the Press*. New York: Norton, 1972.

Smith, Timothy G., ed. *Merriman Smith's Book of Presidents: A White House Memoir*. New York: Norton, 1972.

Sommer, Robert. *Personal Space: The Behavioral Basis of Design*. Englewood Cliffs, NJ: Prentice-Hall, 1969.

Sommerville, C. John. *The Rise and Fall of Childhood*. Beverly Hills, CA: Sage, 1982.

Sorensen, Theodore C. *Kennedy*. New York: Harper & Row, 1965.

Spanier, Graham B. "Married and Unmarried Cohabitation in the United States: 1980." *Journal of Marriage and the Family*, 45 (1983), 277–288.

Spencer, Metta. *Foundations of Modern Sociology*. 2nd ed. Englewood Cliffs, NJ: Prentice-Hall, 1979.

Sprafkin, Joyce N., and Robert M. Liebert. "Sex-Typing and Children's Television Preferences." In *Hearth and Home: Images of Women in the Mass Media*. Ed. Gaye Tuchman, Arlene Kaplan Daniels, and James Benét. New York: Oxford Univ. Press, 1978, pp. 228–239.

Starr, Bernard D., and Marcella Bakur Weiner. *The Starr-Weiner Report on Sex and Sexuality in the Mature Years*. New York: McGraw-Hill, 1981.

Starr, Mark, John Carey, and Madlyn Resener. "Give Peace a Chance." *Newsweek*, 21 June 1982, pp. 40–41.

Starr, Paul. *The Social Transformation of American Medicine*. New York: Basic Books, 1982.

Steele, Richard, et al. "What Damage to Carter." *Newsweek*, 19 Sept., 1977, pp. 24–27; 29–30; 35.

Steinberg, S. H. *Five Hundred Years of Printing*. 3rd ed. Rev. James Moran. Middlesex, England: Penguin, 1974.

Steinem, Gloria. "Introduction." In *Decade of Women: A Ms. History of the Seventies in Words and Pictures*. Ed. Suzanne Levine and Harriet Lyons. New York: Paragon, 1980, pp. 7; 9; 11; 13; 15; 17; 19; 21; 23; 25.

Steinzor, Bernard. "The Spatial Factor in Face to Face Discussion Groups." *Journal of Abnormal and Social Psychology*, 45 (1950), 552–555.

Stier, Serena. "Children's Rights and Society's Duties." *Journal of Social Issues*, 34, No. 2 (1978), 46–58.

Stone, Lawrence. *The Family, Sex, and Marriage in England 1500–1800*. New York: Harper & Row, 1977.

Strasser, Steven, et al. "Reagan's Secrecy Campaign." *Newsweek*, 26 Sept. 1983, p. 38.

Strasser, Steven, John Walcott, and Thomas M. DeFrank. "Reagan and China: Afterglow." *Newsweek*, 14 May 1984, pp. 22–23.

Stuart, Reginald. "Cleveland to Use Questionnaires to Determine Obscenity Standard." *The New York Times*, 13 June 1977.

Sunley, Robert. "Early Nineteenth-Century American Literature on Child Rearing " In *Childhood in Contemporary Cultures*. Ed. Margaret Mead and Martha Wolfenstein. Chicago: Univ. of Chicago Press, 1955, pp. 150–167.

Takanishi, Ruby. "Childhood as a Social Issue: Historical Roots of Contemporary Child Advocacy Movements." *Journal of Social Issues*, 34, No. 2 (1978), 8–28.

Tannenbaum, Percy H., and Wendy A. Gibson. "The Political Environment for Change." In *Children and the Faces of Television: Teaching, Violence, Selling*. Ed. Edward L. Palmer, and Aimée Dorr. New York: Academic, 1980, pp. 201–218.

Teitelbaum, Michael S., ed. *Sex Differences: Social and Biological Perspectives*. New York: Anchor, 1976.

Television Audience Assessment, Inc. *Executive Summary: The Audience Rates Television*. Cambridge, MA: Television Audience Assessment, 1983.

Terman, Lewis M., and Maud A. Merrill. *Stanford-Binet Intelligence Scale: Manual for Third Revision, Form L-M*. Boston: Houghton Mifflin, 1973.

Thomae-Forgues, Maria E., and Xenia Tonesk. "Datagram: 1979–80 Enrollment in U.S. Medical Schools." *Journal of Medical Education*, 55 (1980), 1042–1044.

Thomas, William I. *The Unadjusted Girl: With Cases and Standpoint for Behavior Analysis*. Boston: Little, Brown, & Co., 1925.

Thomas, William I., and Dorothy Swaine Thomas. *The Child In America: Behavior Problems and Programs*. New York: Knopf, 1928.

"Thunder from the Heartland." *Newsweek*, 20 May 1974, pp. 24–25.

Tiger, Lionel. *Men in Groups*. New York: Random House, 1969.

Townley, Rod. "The Mystery of the Unloved Channel Lock." *TV Guide*, 27 Nov. 1982, pp. 33–34.

Tuchman, Gaye, Arlene Kaplan Daniels, and James Benét, eds. *Hearth and Home: Images of Women in the Mass Media*. New York: Oxford Univ. Press, 1978.

Turnbull, Colin M. *The Forest People*. New York: Simon & Schuster, 1961.

U.S. Bureau of the Census. *Statistical Abstract of the United States: 1951*. 72nd Ed. Washington, D.C.: U.S. Government Printing Office, 1951.

U.S. Bureau of the Census. *Statistical Abstract of the United States: 1982–83*. 103rd Ed. Washington, D.C.: U.S. Government Printing Office, 1982.

U.S. Department of Health and Human Services. *Television and Behavior: Ten Years of Scientific Progress and Implications for the Eighties*. Rockville, MD: National Institute of Mental Health, 1982.

U.S. Department of Health, Education, and Welfare. *Higher Education Guidelines, Executive Order 11246*. Washington, D.C.: Department of Health, Education, and Welfare, 1972.

Vanderbilt, Amy. *Amy Vanderbilt's Everyday Etiquette*. 2nd rev. ed. New York: Bantam, 1970.

Van Dyke, Charlotte. "Family-Centered Health Care Recognizes Needs of Patients, Families, Employees." *Hospital Progress*, Aug. 1980, pp. 54–57; 68.

van Gennep, Arnold. *The Rites of Passage*. Trans. Monika B. Vizedom and Gabrielle L. Caffee. Chicago: Univ. of Chicago Press, 1960. (French edition, 1909)

Vetterling-Braggin, Mary, ed. *"Femininity," "Masculinity," and "Androgyny": A Modern Philosophical Discussion*. Totowa, NJ: Littlefield, Adams & Co., 1982.

Viguerie, Richard A. *The New Right: We're Ready to Lead*. Rev. ed. Falls Church, VA: 1981.

Wackman, Daniel B., and Ellen Wartella. "A Review of Cognitive Development Theory and Research and the Implication for Research on Children's Responses to Television." *Communication Research*, 4, No. 2 (1977), 203–224.

"Wanted: A Pen Pal for the Ayatollah." *Newsweek*, 15 Sept. 1980, pp. 97 and 99.

Warren, Mary Anne. "Is Androgyny the Answer to Sexual Stereotyping?" In *"Femininity," "Masculinity," and "Androgyny": A Modern Philosophical Discussion*. Ed. Mary Vetterling-Braggin. Totowa, NJ: Littlefield, Adams & Co., 1982, pp. 170–186.

Wartella, Ellen, ed. *Children Communicating: Media and Development of Thought, Speech, Understanding*. Beverly Hills, CA: Sage, 1979.

Waters, Harry F., and Betsy Carter. "'Holocaust' Fallout." *Newsweek*, 1 May 1978, p. 72.

Waters, Harry F., et al. "TV News Under the Gun." *Newsweek*, 13 April 1981, pp. 104; 107.

Watson, Russell, et al. "A Death in Rome." *Newsweek*, 9 Oct. 1978, pp. 70; 74–76.

Watts, William. "The Future Can Fend for Itself." *Psychology Today*, Sept. 1981, pp. 36–48.

Watzlawick, Paul, Janet Helmick Beavin, and Don D. Jackson. *Pragmatics of Human Communication: A Study of Interactional Patterns, Pathologies, and Paradoxes*. New York: Norton, 1967.

Webster, James G., and William C. Coscarelli. "The Relative Appeal to Children of Adult vs. Children's Television Programming." *Journal of Broadcasting*, 23 (1979), 437–451.

Wector, Dixon. *The Hero in America: A Chronicle of Hero-Worship*. New York: Scribner's, 1972. (originally published in 1941)

Weitz, Shirley. *Sex Roles: Biological, Psychological, and Social Foundations*. New York: Oxford Univ. Press, 1977.

Wellborn, Stanley N. "Ahead: A Nation of Illiterates?" *U.S. News & World Report*, 17 May 1982, pp. 53–56.

Werner, Morris R. *Bryan*. New York: Harcourt, Brace & Co., 1929.

White, Sheldon, and Barbara Notkin White. *Childhood: Pathways of Discovery*. London: Harper & Row, 1980.

White, Theodore H. *The Making of the President 1972*. New York: Atheneum, 1973.

White, Theodore H. *America in Search of Itself: The Making of the President 1965–1980*. New York: Harper & Row, 1982.

Whitman, Alden. "Who and What is Richard Nixon?" In *The End of a Presidency*. Ed. staff of *The New York Times*. New York: Holt, Rinehart & Winston, 1974, pp. 9–21.

"Who Is Ronald Reagan?" *The Boston Globe*, 11 April 1984.

"Why 'Roots' Hit Home." *Time*, 14 Feb. 1977, pp. 69–71.

Wiener, Norbert. *The Human Use of Human Beings: Cybernetics and Society*. New York: Avon, 1967. (originally published in 1950)

Wilkie, Curtis. "Reagan in Control, Advisers Emphasize." *The Boston Globe*, 27 March 1982.

Williams, Dennis A., Eleanor Clift, and William Schmidt, "The Klan Also Rises." *Newsweek*, 12 Jan. 1976, pp. 33–34.

Williams, Dennis A., Lea Donosky, and Martin Kasindorf. "The Great White Hope." *Newsweek*, 14 Nov. 1977, p. 45.

Williams, Raymond. *Television: Technology and Cultural Form*. New York: Schocken, 1975.

"Will Nixon Resign." *Newsweek*, 20 May 1974, pp. 22–28; 31; 34; 38; 43.

Winick, Mariann Pezzella, and Charles Winick. *The Television Experience: What Children See*. Beverly Hills, CA: Sage, 1979.

Winn, Marie. *Children Without Childhood*. New York: Pantheon, 1983.

Wishy, Bernard. *The Child and the Republic: The Dawn of Modern American Child Nurture*. Philadelphia: Univ. of Pennsylvania Press, 1968.

Wohlwill, Joachim F. "The Age Variable in Psychological Research." *Psychological Review*, 77 (1970), 49–64.

Wolfenstein, Martha. "Introduction to Part Three." In *Childhood in Contemporary Cultures*. Ed. Margaret Mead and Martha Wolfenstein. Chicago: Univ. of Chicago Press, 1955, pp. 145–149.

Woodward, Kenneth L., Elaine Sciolino, and Christopher Matthews. "The 34 Days of John Paul I." *Newsweek*, 9 Oct. 1978, pp. 72–73.

Woodward, Kenneth L., et al. "Living With Dying." *Newsweek*, 1 May 1978, pp. 52–56; 61. (a)

Woodward, Kenneth L., et al. "A Pope From Poland." *Newsweek*, 30 Oct. 1978, pp. 78–82. (b)

Yankelovich, Daniel. *New Rules: Searching for Self-Fulfillment in a World Turned Upside Down*. New York: Random House, 1981.

"Your Number, Please." *Corrections Compendium*, 3, No. 9 (April 1979), 1–3.

Index

"Alice," 145n
Allen, Woody, 22
"All in the Family," 176, 177
Allor, Martin, 342n.1
"American Bandstand," 178
American Bar Association, 191n, 230
American Indians (*see* Native Americans)
Amnesty International, 144
Andrews, Reginald, 311–12
Androgyny, 194
Animal rights, 143
Annie Hall, 22
Arendt, Hannah, 346n.16
Argyle, Michael, 28, 344nn.33,37,38,51; 345n.53
Ariès, Philippe, 258, 259, 260, 261, 261n
"A-Team," 348n.23
Audiences:
    behavior shaped for, 1–2, 25, 44–51, 320
    combination of, 4–5, 43, 47–9, 176, 269, 271
    division of, 47–9
    effect on social performance, 4–7, 28
    expectations of, 30–31
    rearranged by media, ix, 7, 149
Audio cassettes (*see also* Radio), 81, 90n
"Audio Jam Live," 243
Audio tape (*see also* Radio):
    and history, 109, 113
Augustine, St., 99
Authority (*see also* Hierarchy), 7–8, 52, 53
    and control over information, 62–7, 160, 162
        and isolation of information-systems, 63
    declining faith in, 3, 141, 149, 160–72, 323–4, 327
    and media, 17, 18, 86, 114, 160–72, 327
    and mystification, 62, 65, 65n, 67
    and performance, 62–7
    and place, 66–7
    vs. power, 62, 321, 338, 346n.16
    and "vanishing truth" paradox, 168

Backstage (back region) behavior (*see also* Regions, behavioral):
    of adults, 154–5, 236, 248–51, 253
    back region bias of some media, 109–14
    and censorship, 284n
    deep backstage (back region) behavior, 7, 46–9, 50, 51, 66, 143, 156, 220, 314

exposure of, by media, 8, 127, 136, 138, 143, 154–5, 156, 175, 248–51, 253, 256, 289, 309–10, 320
    and decline of authority, 167–9, 170–71
    effects on childhood, 248–9
    effects on performance, 46–9, 177–8
    and group identity, 135–43, 137n
    and group cohesion, 55–6
    as news, 112
    in 1960s, 138–40, 140n
    of politicians, 168–9, 272–4
    of Presidents, 3, 274, 284, 287, 292–6, 297, 304
    and regression, 139–40
    and rehearsal, 46–7, 64, 113
    secrecy about, and hierarchal roles, 64–6
    and sex roles, 206–7, 215–17, 220
    socialization as access to, 60, 70
    and truth, 30, 295
Bailey, Thomas, 279–80, 283, 366n.3
Baker, James, 100
Bales, Robert, 358n.63
Balkin, Richard, 266
Ball, Donald W., 343n.24
Ball-Rokeach, Sandra, 342n.2
Banton, Michael, 372n.9
Barker, Roger, 35
"Barney Miller," 177
Barnouw, Erik, 136, 342n.5, 347n.1, 355n.28
Barriers:
    as defining situations, 35, 36
    media access codes as, 77–8, 79
    media as bypassing, 170, 308
    physical characteristics of media as, 81–2
Beavin, Janet, 97
Begin, Menachem, 171
Behavior (*see also* Backstage behavior, Onstage behavior, Regions, Roles)
    "appropriate," ix, 127, 173–5, 271, 276, 329, 336
    defined, 335
    and furniture arrangement, 36n, 354n.4
    and information-systems, 333
        as behavior systems, 334
    and personality vs. situation, 344n.41
    "reciprocal informality," 321
    and role categories, 7–8
    as situationally determined, 1–2, 23–33, 40–51, 143, 310, 311, 332–3
    effects of merging situations, 44–6
Bennett, W. Lance, 276–7
Berger, Peter L., 31, 342n.23, 343n.30